W9-CFQ-733

1. *The A to Z of Buddhism* by Charles S. Prebish, 2001. *Out of Print. See No. 124.*
2. *The A to Z of Catholicism* by William J. Collinge, 2001.
3. *The A to Z of Hinduism* by Bruce M. Sullivan, 2001.
4. *The A to Z of Islam* by Ludwig W. Adamec, 2002. *Out of Print. See No. 123.*
5. *The A to Z of Slavery and Abolition* by Martin A. Klein, 2002.
6. *Terrorism: Assassins to Zealots* by Sean Kendall Anderson and Stephen Sloan, 2003.
7. *The A to Z of the Korean War* by Paul M. Edwards, 2005.
8. *The A to Z of the Cold War* by Joseph Smith and Simon Davis, 2005.
9. *The A to Z of the Vietnam War* by Edwin E. Moise, 2005.
10. *The A to Z of Science Fiction Literature* by Brian Stableford, 2005.
11. *The A to Z of the Holocaust* by Jack R. Fischel, 2005.
12. *The A to Z of Washington, D.C.* by Robert Benedetto, Jane Donovan, and Kathleen DuVall, 2005.
13. *The A to Z of Taoism* by Julian F. Pas, 2006.
14. *The A to Z of the Renaissance* by Charles G. Nauert, 2006.
15. *The A to Z of Shinto* by Stuart D. B. Picken, 2006.
16. *The A to Z of Byzantium* by John H. Rosser, 2006.
17. *The A to Z of the Civil War* by Terry L. Jones, 2006.
18. *The A to Z of the Friends (Quakers)* by Margery Post Abbott, Mary Ellen Chijioke, Pink Dandelion, and John William Oliver Jr., 2006.
19. *The A to Z of Feminism* by Janet K. Boles and Diane Long Hoeveler, 2006.
20. *The A to Z of New Religious Movements* by George D. Chryssides, 2006.
21. *The A to Z of Multinational Peacekeeping* by Terry M. Mays, 2006.
22. *The A to Z of Lutheranism* by Günther Gassmann with Duane H. Larson and Mark W. Oldenburg, 2007.
23. *The A to Z of the French Revolution* by Paul R. Hanson, 2007.
24. *The A to Z of the Persian Gulf War 1990–1991* by Clayton R. Newell, 2007.
25. *The A to Z of Revolutionary America* by Terry M. Mays, 2007.
26. *The A to Z of the Olympic Movement* by Bill Mallon with Ian Buchanan, 2007.
27. *The A to Z of the Discovery and Exploration of Australia* by Alan Day, 2009.
28. *The A to Z of the United Nations* by Jacques Fomerand, 2009.
29. *The A to Z of the "Dirty Wars"* by David Kohut, Olga Vilella, and Beatrice Julian, 2009.
30. *The A to Z of the Vikings* by Katherine Holman, 2009.
31. *The A to Z from the Great War to the Great Depression* by Neil A. Wynn, 2009.
32. *The A to Z of the Crusades* by Corliss K. Slack, 2009.
33. *The A to Z of New Age Movements* by Michael York, 2009.
34. *The A to Z of Unitarian Universalism* by Mark W. Harris, 2009.
35. *The A to Z of the Kurds* by Michael M. Gunter, 2009.
36. *The A to Z of Utopianism* by James M. Morris and Andrea L. Kross, 2009.
37. *The A to Z of the Civil War and Reconstruction* by William L. Richter, 2009.
38. *The A to Z of Jainism* by Kristi L. Wiley, 2009.
39. *The A to Z of the Inuit* by Pamela K. Stern, 2009.
40. *The A to Z of Early North America* by Cameron B. Wesson, 2009.

83. *The A to Z of the Chinese Cultural Revolution* by Guo Jian, Yongyi Song, and Yuan Zhou, 2009.
84. *The A to Z of African American Cinema* by S. Torriano Berry and Venise T. Berry, 2009.
85. *The A to Z of Japanese Business* by Stuart D. B. Picken, 2009.
86. *The A to Z of the Reagan–Bush Era* by Richard S. Conley, 2009.
87. *The A to Z of Human Rights and Humanitarian Organizations* by Robert F. Gorman and Edward S. Mihalkanin, 2009.
88. *The A to Z of French Cinema* by Dayna Oscherwitz and MaryEllen Higgins, 2009.
89. *The A to Z of the Puritans* by Charles Pastoor and Galen K. Johnson, 2009.
90. *The A to Z of Nuclear, Biological and Chemical Warfare* by Benjamin C. Garrett and John Hart, 2009.
91. *The A to Z of the Green Movement* by Miranda Schreurs and Elim Papadakis, 2009.
92. *The A to Z of the Kennedy–Johnson Era* by Richard Dean Burns and Joseph M. Siracusa, 2009.
93. *The A to Z of Renaissance Art* by Lilian H. Zirpolo, 2009.
94. *The A to Z of the Broadway Musical* by William A. Everett and Paul R. Laird, 2009.
95. *The A to Z of the Northern Ireland Conflict* by Gordon Gillespie, 2009.
96. *The A to Z of the Fashion Industry* by Francesca Sterlacci and Joanne Arbuckle, 2009.
97. *The A to Z of American Theater: Modernism* by James Fisher and Felicia Hardison Londré, 2009.
98. *The A to Z of Civil Wars in Africa* by Guy Arnold, 2009.
99. *The A to Z of the Nixon–Ford Era* by Mitchell K. Hall, 2009.
100. *The A to Z of Horror Cinema* by Peter Hutchings, 2009.
101. *The A to Z of Westerns in Cinema* by Paul Varner, 2009.
102. *The A to Z of Zionism* by Rafael Medoff and Chaim I. Waxman, 2009.
103. *The A to Z of the Roosevelt–Truman Era* by Neil A. Wynn, 2009.
104. *The A to Z of Jehovah's Witnesses* by George D. Chryssides, 2009.
105. *The A to Z of Native American Movements* by Todd Leahy and Raymond Wilson, 2009.
106. *The A to Z of the Shakers* by Stephen J. Paterwic, 2009.
107. *The A to Z of the Coptic Church* by Gawdat Gabra, 2009.
108. *The A to Z of Architecture* by Allison Lee Palmer, 2009.
109. *The A to Z of Italian Cinema* by Gino Moliterno, 2009.
110. *The A to Z of Mormonism* by Davis Bitton and Thomas G. Alexander, 2009.
111. *The A to Z of African American Theater* by Anthony D. Hill with Douglas Q. Barnett, 2009.
112. *The A to Z of NATO and Other International Security Organizations* by Marco Rimanelli, 2009.
113. *The A to Z of the Eisenhower Era* by Burton I. Kaufman and Diane Kaufman, 2009.
114. *The A to Z of Sexspionage* by Nigel West, 2009.
115. *The A to Z of Environmentalism* by Peter Dauvergne, 2009.
116. *The A to Z of the Petroleum Industry* by M. S. Vassiliou, 2009.
117. *The A to Z of Journalism* by Ross Eaman, 2009.
118. *The A to Z of the Gilded Age* by T. Adams Upchurch, 2009.
119. *The A to Z of the Progressive Era* by Catherine Cocks, Peter C. Holloran, and Alan Lessoff, 2009.

The A to Z of
Organized Labor

James C. Docherty

The A to Z Guide Series, No. 174

THE SCARECROW PRESS, INC.
Lanham • Toronto • Plymouth, UK
2010

Published by Scarecrow Press, Inc.
A wholly owned subsidary of
The Rowman & Littlefield Publishing Group, Inc.
4501 Forbes Boulevard, Suite 200, Lanham, Maryland 20706
http://www.scarecrowpress.com

Estover Road, Plymouth PL6 7PY, United Kingdom

British Library Cataloguing in Publication Information Available

Library of Congress Cataloging-in-Publication Data

The hardback version of this book was cataloged by the Library of Congress as
follows:

Docherty, J. C.
   Historical dictionary of organized labor / James C. Docherty.—2nd ed.
      p. cm. — (Historical dictionaries of religions, philosophies, and movements
; no. 50)
   1. Labor movement—History—Encyclopedias. 2. Labor unions—History—
Encyclopedias. I. Title. II. Series.
HD4839.D58 2004
331.88'03—dc22   2003021283

ISBN 978-0-8108-7601-9 (pbk. : alk. paper)

To the evergreen memory of my father
Thomas Hill Docherty.
Born: St. Andrews, Scotland, September 12, 1914
Died: Niagara Park, New South Wales, August 25, 2003
And to the mother he never knew,
Jessie Docherty (née Hill).
Born: Forfar, Scotland, September 29, 1874
Died: St. Andrews, Scotland, November 20, 1918
Domestic servant and victim of tuberculosis.

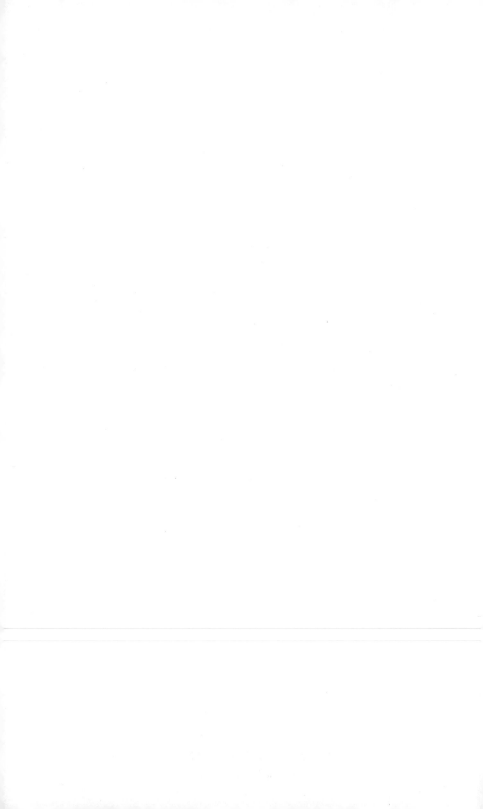

CONTENTS

EDITOR'S FOREWORD

These are still trying times for organized labor. Many old-established labor unions are losing members, while young ones in the Third World are having trouble striking root. The old threat of Communism on the left has receded, but the growing penchant for untrammeled free enterprise around the world entails other perils. Worse in certain ways, while labor or socialist parties remain in office in many countries, the policies they espouse appeal less and less to workers. And the tide of globalization keeps mounting. This has resulted in what some regard as a "crisis" in organized labor, but it is not the first nor will it be the last. And part of the problem derives from past successes as some of what the unions have achieved over recent decades is challenged while the rank-and-file occasionally feels it has little more to gain and is not yet afraid of what may be lost.

To know how much has been achieved by organized labor in the advanced countries, it is sufficient to consider the not-too-distant past, which is amply portrayed in this book. Meanwhile, the situation in many developing countries remains harsh and worrisome. There is still much to be done, and, of the bodies committed to progress there, the unions are among the most important. What the tasks are is also described herein. The many entries on significant persons, places, and events, those on specific unions and countries, and others of a more general nature give us an excellent view of the past and present and an inkling of the future. Additional background is provided in the introduction and chronology, and even an experienced reader could get lost without the list of acronyms. The statistical appendixes give us a more concrete feel for the growth of unionism. Further information on all these aspects can be found in the bibliography.

The author of the *Historical Dictionary of Organized Labor*, *Second Edition*, James C. Docherty, knows the field well from both the academic and practical viewpoints. He carried out the first scholarly investigation of the early years of organized labor in the railroads of southeastern Australia for his master's thesis and examined the social and urban impact of heavy industry on Newcastle for his doctoral thesis at the Australian National University. Professionally, he has worked for the Australian Bureau of Statistics and the Department of Industrial Relations, and the Department of Immigration, Multicultural, and Indigenous Affairs, and was an Honorary Research Associate with the National Centre for Australian Studies at Monash University. Dr. Docherty has written on statistics and labor more generally as well as producing two other historical dictionaries, those on Australia and Socialism. This new, updated, and expanded edition will contribute even more to our knowledge of a topic that has been with us for a long time and will be around for an even longer time to come.

Jon Woronoff
Series Editor

ORGANIZED LABOR: WORLD MEMBERSHIP, 1870-2001

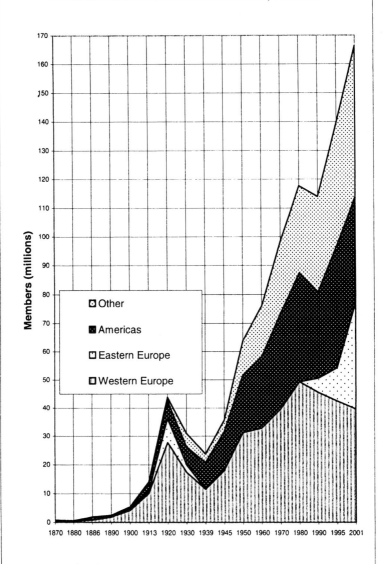

Members (millions)

Legend:
- ◙ Other
- ◼ Americas
- ◘ Eastern Europe
- ◘ Western Europe

1870 1880 1886 1890 1900 1913 1920 1930 1939 1945 1950 1960 1970 1980 1990 1995 2001

Source: Table 1, Statistical Appendix.   Copyright: James C. Docherty

PREFACE

The second edition of this dictionary, like the first, is an introduction and invitation to the historical study of organized labor. It is about what organized labor has done or tried to do rather than what it ought to have been. It is about a mass movement with many enemies. Some see organized labor as a barrier to the operation of a free-market economy and therefore harmful to economic growth; others consider it to be the vanguard of radical economic and social change. Too few consider organized labor in its own terms. Moreover, for all the research of the last 40 years, there is still a tendency to treat organized labor as a marginal topic in the general and economic histories of most countries.

This work is not an encyclopedia, but a work of first resort for the subject. It is designed as a research tool and to complement my *Historical Dictionary of Socialism* (1997), also published by Scarecrow Press. It provides 400 entries covering most countries, international as well as national labor organizations, major labor unions, leaders, and other aspects of organized labor such as changes in the composition of its membership. References to ideas and political parties have been kept to a minimum because they are addressed in my companion work, *Historical Dictionary of Socialism.* There are appendixes containing a short, annotated guide to relevant Internet websites, a glossary of terms, lists of leaders of international labor organizations, and union membership statistics.

The entries are biased towards institutions because they tend to survive and so provide a framework for the interplay of individuals and ideas. They are also a useful way of capturing the unsuccessful as well as the successful part of the historical process. The entries are my selection from what is available and make no claim to cover everything or to be necessarily representative. The entries are primarily concerned with the 20th century and reflect my judgments about what is important in a work of this scale.

My first aim in this dictionary is to make the subject as accessible as possible. Many of the works on organized labor frequently make implicit assumptions about the level of knowledge of their readers, which may be difficult for beginners. Those unfamiliar with the topic should consider reading first the introduction and then the entries on the **United Kingdom, France, Germany, Italy**, the **United States**, and **Japan**. The appendixes and the bibliography are designed to complement the entries and to act as signposts for finding out more about subjects that I have neglected in the body of the dictionary.

My second aim is to show the variety of labor studies. Economists, political scientists, sociologists, and lawyers have long been well represented in this field, often long before historians showed any interest. These disciplines have much to offer historians either by asking new questions about the subject or developing improved frameworks for analysis. Similarly, industrial relations, although a comparatively recent addition to academic disciplines, has much to offer by its synthetic approach even though its focus is typically on the present rather than the past.

My third aim is to encourage a greater international outlook on the topic than is apparent in most works on organized labor. In an era of globalization, the need for this may seem self-evident, but studies of organized labor are still prone to stress the special features of the country being studied rather than show how they fit into and shape global trends.

Apart from the limitations of space—which means that there is no alternative to being brutally brief about so many important subjects—I found the scale of this work daunting. I take solace in knowing that no one individual knows all there is to know about organized labor but am grimly aware that its sheer scale means that the possibilities for errors and misleading statements are enormous; where these occur I take full responsibility and would appreciate being made aware of them. For the provision of statistics, it is my pleasure to thank Christine Vanhaekendover of the International Confederation of Free Trade Unions and the British Department of Employment. For moral support on my statistical efforts in this field, I would also like to thank Malcolm Fairbrother at Berkeley.

James C. Docherty

ABBREVIATIONS AND ACRONYMS

AATUF   All-African Trade Union Federation (1961-1973)

ACTU   Australian Council of Trade Unions (1927)

ACWA   Amalgamated Clothing Workers of America (1914)

AEU   Amalgamated Engineering Union (United Kingdom: 1920)

AFL-CIO   American Federation of Labor-Congress of Industrial Organizations (1955)

AFRO   African Regional Organisation of the International Confederation of Free Trade Unions (1960)

AFSCME   American Federation of State, County, and Municipal Employees (1932)

ALP   Australian Labor Party (1891)

ALU   American Labor Union (1898-1905)

AMWU   Amalgamated Metal Workers' Union (Australia: 1973)

APLN   Asia-Pacific Labour Network (1995)

APRO   Asian and Pacific Regional Organisation of the International Confederation of Free Trade Unions (1984)

ASCJ   Amalgamated Society of Carpenters and Joiners (United Kingdom: 1860)

xv

ASE   Amalgamated Society of Engineers (United Kingdom: 1851-1920)

AWU   Australian Workers' Union (1894)

CCOO   *Confederación Sindical de Comisiones Obreras* (Union Confederation of Workers' Commissions) (Spain: 1960s)

CEC   *Confédération européenne des cadres* (European Confederation of Managers) (1989)

CEF   *Confédération internationale des fonctionnaires* (International Confederation of Public Servants) (1955)

CEOSL   *Confederación Ecuatoriana de Organizaciones Sindicales Libres* (Ecuadorian Confederation of Free Trade Unions (1962)

CESI   *Confédération Européenne des Syndicats Indépendants* (Confederation of Independent European Trade Unions) (1990)

CETU   Confederation of Ethiopian Labor Unions (1963)

CGIL   *Confederazione Generale Italiana del Lavoro* (General Confederation of Italian Labor) (1944)

CGL   *Confederazione Generale di Lavoro* (General Confederation of Labor) (Italy: 1906-1924)

CGS   *Confederación General de Sindicatos* (General Confederation of Trade Unions) (El Salvador: 1958)

CGSL   *Confédération Gabonaise des Syndicats Libres* (Confederation of Free Trade Unions of Gabon) (1992)

CGT   *Confédération Générale du Travail* (General Confederation of Labor) (France: 1895); *Central Geral dos Trabalhadores* (General Confederation of Labor) (Brazil: 1986); *Confederación General del Trabajo* (General Confederation of Labor) (Argentina: 1930); *Confédéra-*

tion Générale du Travail-Force Ouvrière (General Confederation of Labor-Workers' Strength) (France: 1948)

CI   Communications International (1997-2000)

CIF   *Confédération internationale des fonctionnaires* (International Confederation of Public Servants) (1955)

CIO   Congress of Industrial Organizations (United States: 1933-1955)

CIT   *Confederación Interamericana de Trabajadores* (Interamerican Confederation of Workers: 1948-1951)

CITUB   Confederation of Independent Trade Unions of Bulgaria (1944)

CNSLR   *Confederatia Nationala a Sindicatelator Libere din România* (National Free Trade Union Confederation of Romania) (1990)

COHSE   Confederation of Health Service Employees (United Kingdom: 1946-1993)

CPUSTAL   *Congreso Permanente de Unidad Sindical de Los Trabajadores de America Latina* (Permanent Congress of Trade Union Unity of Latin American Workers) (1964)

CROM   *Confederación Regional Obrera Mexicana* (Regional Confederation of Mexican Wage Earners) (1918)

CSEU   Confederation of Shipbuilding and Engineering Unions (United Kingdom: 1891)

ČS-KOS   *Česka a Slovenská Konfederace odborových* (Czech and Slovak Confederation of Trade Unions) (1989)

CSTC   *Confédération Syndicale des Travailleurs du Cameroun* (Union Confederation of Cameroon Workers)

CTAL   *Confederación de Trabajadores de America Latina* (Confederation of Latin American Workers) (1938-1962)

CTM   *Confederación de Trabajadores de Mexico* (Confederation of Mexican Workers) (1936)

CTV   *Confederación des Trabajadores de Venezuela* (Confederation of Workers of Venezuela) (1936)

CUT   *Central Unica de Trabajadores* (Chile: 1953-1973); *Central Unitaria de Trabajadores* (Chile: 1988); *Central Unica dos Trabalhadores* (United Workers' Center) (Brazil: 1983)

CWU   Communications Workers' Union of America (1945)

DAF   *Deutsche Arbeitsfront* (German Labor Front) (1933-1945)

DGB   *Deutscher Gewerkschaftbund* (German Trade Union Federation) (1947)

DMV   *Deutscher Metallarbeiter-Verband* (German Metal Workers' Union) (1891-1933)

EI   Education International (1993)

ETUC   European Trade Union Confederation (1973)

EU   European Union (1993)

FICSA   Federation of International Civil Servants' Assocations (1952)

FIET   *Fédération internationale des employés, techniciens et cadres* (International Federation of Commercial, Clerical, Professional, and Technical Employees) (1921)

FIOM   *Federazione Italiana Operai Metallurgici* (Italian Union of Metal Workers: 1901-1924; 1944-1972)

FTU-B   Federation of Trade Unions-Burma (1991)

GFJTU   General Federation of Jordanian Trade Unions (1954)

GFTU	General Federation of Trade Unions (United Kingdom: 1899)
GFWTU	General Federation of Workers' Trade Unions (Yemen: 1990)
GLU	Gambia Labour Union (1928)
GMWU	General and Municipal Workers' Union (United Kingdom: 1924)
GTUC	Ghana Trades Union Congress (c.1956)
GUF	Global Union Federations (called International Trade Secretariats to January 23, 2002)
GWU	Gambia Workers' Union (1958)
IBT	International Brotherhood of Teamsters, Chauffeurs, Warehousemen, and Helpers of America (1903)
ICATU	International Confederation of Arab Trade Unions (1956)
ICEM	International Federation of Chemical, Energy, Mine, and General Workers (1964)
ICFTU	International Confederation of Free Trade Unions (1949)
IFBWW	International Federation of Building and Woodworkers (1934)
IFCTU	International Federation of Christian Trade Unions (1920)
IFFTU	International Federation of Free Teachers' Unions (1928)
IFJ	International Federation of Journalists (1952)
IFPAW	International Federation of Plantation, Agricultural, and Allied Workers (1960)

IFTU	International Federation of Trade Unions (1901-1945)
IFWPAU	International Federation of Workers in Public Administration and Utilities
IGF	International Graphical Federation (1949)
IG Metall	Industriegewerkschaft Metall (Metal Workers' Industrial Union) (Germany: 1950)
ILGWU	International Ladies' Garment Workers' Union (United States: 1900-1992)
ILO	International Labour Organisation (1919)
IMF	International Metalworkers' Federation (1904)
ISAMMETU	International Secretariat for Arts, Mass Media, and Entertainment Trade Unions (1965-1995)
ITF	International Transport Workers' Federation (1898)
ITGLWF	International Textile, Garment, and Leather Workers' Federation (1970)
ITS	International Trade Secretariats (called Global Union Federations after January 23, 2002)
ITU	International Typographical Union (United States: 1869)
IUF	International Union of Food, Agricultural, Hotel, Restaurant, Catering, Tobacco, and Allied Workers' Associations (1994)
IUFAWA	International Union of Food and Allied Workers' Associations (1920)
IWW	Industrial Workers of the World (United States: 1905)
KOR	Komitet Obrony Robotnikow (Workers' Defense Committee) (Poland: 1976)

LIGA	Democratic League of Independent Trade Unions (Hungary: 1989)
LO	*Landsorganisationen i Sverge* (Labor Union Federation of Sweden) (1898); *Landsorganisasjonen i Norge* (Labor Union Federation of Norway) (1899)
MEI	Media and Entertainment International (1995-2000)
MSzOSz	*Magyar Szakszervezetek Országos Szövetsége Tagszervezeteinek Címlistája* (National Confederation of Hungarian Trade Unions) (1990)
MWF	Mineworkers' Federation of Great Britain (1890-1945)
NALC	Negro American Labor Council (1960)
NALGO	National and Local Government Officers' Association (United Kingdom: 1946-1993)
NEA	National Education Association (United States: 1857)
NLU	National Labor Union (United States: 1866)
NSZZ	*Solidarnosc Niezalezny Samorzadny Zwaiazek Zawodowy* (Independent, Self-Governing Trade Union Solidarity) (Poland: 1980)
NUPE	National Union of Public Employees (United Kingdom: 1928-1993)
OATUU	Organization of African Trade Union Unity (1973)
OBU	One Big Union
OECD	Organization for Economic Cooperation and Development
OPZZ	*Ogolnópolskie Porozumienie Zwiazków Zawodowych* (All-Poland Alliance of Labor Unions) (1984)

ORIT   *Organización Regional Interamericana de Trabajadores* (Inter-American Regional Organization of Workers) (1951)

ÖTV   *Gewerkschaft Öffentliche Dienste, Transport und Verkehr* (Public Service, Transportation, and Traffic Labor Union) (Germany: 1896-1933; re-founded in 1949)

PAFL   Pan-American Federation of Labor (1918-1940)

PSI   Public Services International (1935)

PTTI   Postal, Telegraph, and Telephone International (1920-1997)

PTUC   Pacific Trade Union Community (1980)

SAF   *Svenska Arbetsgivaresöforreningen* (Swedish Employers' Confederation) (1902)

SAK   *Suomen Ammattiliittojen Keskusjärjestö* (Central Organization of Finnish Trade Unions) (1930)

SGB   *Schweizerischer Gewerkschaftsbund* (Swiss Labor Union Confederation) (1880)

SSF   *Syndicats sans Frontières* (Trade Unions without Borders) (Switzerland: c. 1997)

SZOT   *Magyar Szakszervezetek Országos Tanácsá* (Central Council of Hungarian Trade Unions) (1948)

TGWU   Transport and General Workers' Union (United Kingdom: 1922)

TUAC   Trade Union Advisory Committee to the Organization for Economic Cooperation and Development (1948)

TUC   Trades Union Congress (United Kingdom: 1868)

TUCAMW   Trade Union Confederation of Arab Maghreb Workers (1991)

UAW	United Auto Workers [official title: United Automobile, Aerospace, and Agricultural Implement Workers of America, International Union] (1935)
UFCW	United Food and Commercial Workers' International Union (United States: 1979)
UGT	*Unión General de Trabajadores* (General Union of Workers) (Spain: 1888)
UGTA	*Union Générale des Travailleurs Algériens* (General Workers' Union of Algeria) (1956)
UGTT	*Union générale tunisienne de Travail* (General Tunisian Union of Labor) (1946)
UGTU	*Union Syndicale des Travailleurs de Centralafrique* (Labor Union of Central African Workers) (c. 1978)
UMWA	United Mine Workers of America (1890)
UNI	Union Network International (2000)
UNTC-CS	*União Nacional dos Trabalhadores de Cabo Verde-Central Sindical* (National Union of United Workers of Cape Verde-Central Union) (c. 1990)
USWA	United Steelworkers of America (1942)
Ver.Di	*Vereinte Dienstleistungsgewerkschaft* (United Services Labor Union) (Germany: 2001)
WCL	World Confederation of Labor (1968)
WCOTP	World Confederation of Organizations of the Teaching Profession (1952)
WFTU	World Federation of Trade Unions (1945)
WLU	Western Labor Union (United States: 1898)
WU	Workers' Union (United Kingdom: 1898-1929)

CHRONOLOGY

1152 B. C. Egypt: the pharaoh's tomb makers refuse to work over the failure of the pharaoh's officials to supply them with grain.

A.D. 301 Roman Empire: Emperor Diocletian issues an Edict of Maximum Prices, which also sets maximum wage rates.

544 Byzantine Empire: Emperor Justinian forbids laborers, sailors, and others to demand or accept wage increases on penalty of having to pay the treasury three times the amount demanded.

1345 Florence: Cinto Brandini is hanged for attempting to form an organization among woolcombers.

1351 England: The Statute of Labourers prohibits laborers from demanding wage increases and employers from granting them.

1383 England: Early use of the term "journeyman" to describe a group of London saddlers who had combined to raise their pay.

1387 England: A group of London journeymen cordwainers (shoemakers) attempt to form a union.

1393 France: Strike by vineyard workers in Burgundy.

1411 England: Colchester municipal authorities outlaw payment in kind for weavers.

1448 England: Maximum wage law.

1490 Genoa: Shipbuilding employees organize to resist wage reductions; they did so again in 1526.

1504 Venice: Labor dispute in printing.

1524 England: Municipal authorities in Coventry fix maximum wage rates in the textile industry, specify payment in money, and forbid payment in kind.

1539 France: Strike by printing employees in Lyon over long hours. They form a union and attack strikebreakers.

1548 England: Parliament passes the Bill of Conspiracies of Victuallers and Craftsmen which introduces the concept of combinations as conspiracies into English law.

1560 England: Some London saddlers combine to raise their pay.

1562 England: The Statute of Artificers gives justices of the peace the power to set the wages of artisans and laborers and provides penalties for breach of contract by employers and employees. It also requires a seven-year apprenticeship as a qualification to be a journeyman.

1675 Genoa: Uprising by 10,000 silk workers over the introduction of French ribbon-looms, which enable a single worker to weave 10 to 12 ribbons at a time.

1696 England: Organized journeymen felt makers in London try to resist a wage cut.

1701 England: Payment in kind outlawed in the textile and iron industries.

1706 England: Journeymen weavers in the west accused of trying to force their employers to only employ members of their union.

1718 England: The free emigration of skilled artisans and skilled operatives prohibited by law; similar legislation was again passed in 1750 and 1765.

1721 England: London journeymen tailors accused by their employers of forming a "combination" of 7,000 to raise their wages and reduce their work day by one hour.

1726 England: Parliament passes an Act to Prevent Unlawful Combinations of Workmen Employed in the Woollen Manufactures.

1731 England: First recorded use of the "round robin" in the British navy as a method of voicing grievances.

1765 England: First sign of organization among coal miners at Newcastle in northeast England.

1768 England: Parliament passes the Tailors' Act, which imposes jail terms of two months on any London journeyman who demand pay above the legal maximum and on any master who pays a higher amount.

1769-1773 England: Unrest among London's silk workers over mechanized looms and French competition. Workers' clubs evolve into unions, which threaten industrial sabotage to gain standardized wages. They gain the Spitalfields Act in 1773, which provides a procedure for the setting of wages and piece-rates.

1772 England: London journeymen tailors petition parliament for higher pay because of rising living costs.

1773 Scotland: Trial of 12 leaders of weavers from Paisley, near Glasgow. Thousands had taken part in the strike and used force to prevent the use of strikebreakers. The leaders threaten to take their followers to North America if their demands were not met. Seven are found guilty. London cabinetmakers and tradesmen in the royal dockyards go on strike for higher pay.

1773-1776 England: A government register of emigrants to North America shows that of the 6,190 emigrants whose occupations were known, 49 percent were artisans, mechanics, or craftsmen.

1780s United States: Formation of trade societies by journeymen in Philadelphia to meet annually with masters to settle the price of their labor.

1786 United States: First strike of employees in a single trade (Philadelphia printers).

1790 France: Journeymen carpenters in Paris form a union. Following complaints by employers, it was suppressed by the law *Le Chapelier* (1791), which was also applied to employers' organizations and made strikes illegal.

1791 United States: First recorded strike in the building trades by Philadelphia carpenters.

1792 England: Seamen's strike in the northeast.

1794 United States: Formation of the Federal Society of Journeymen Cordwainers (shoemakers) in Philadelphia; the society lasts until 1806. **England:** Rises in the cost of living because of the war with Napoleon lead to some successful strikes for higher pay by London journeymen tradesmen between 1794 and 1813.

1796 England: Debate in the House of Commons concerning a proposal to permit justices of the peace to fix a minimum wage.

1797 England: Henry Maudslay invents a metal cutting lathe with a slide rest; perfected in 1800, the lathe plays a major role in shaping the working conditions of metal workers.

1798 Canada: First union formed.

1799 England: Parliament passes the first Combination Act. This act, and the second act of 1800, outlawed labor disputes but did not prohibit employees from improving wages and conditions. **Scotland:** Abolition of serfdom for coal miners.

1800 England: Parliament passes the second Combination Act. The act includes provision for arbitration in labor disputes.

1810 France: The Penal Cole prohibits strikes.

1812 Canada: In Saint John, New Brunswick, building unions attempt to exclude American immigrants to maintain the shortage of skilled labor. **England:** Frame breaking made an offense punishable by death in a move aimed at the Luddites, who continue to attack woolen machinery for the next two years.

1813 England: Repeal of the wage clause of the Statute of Artificers of 1562.

1814 England: Repeal of the apprenticeship clause of the Statute of Artificers of 1562. One of the petitions to parliament opposing its repeal was signed by 30,517 journeymen.

1817 England: Suppression of the "Blanketeers" march planned from Manchester to London.

1818 United Kingdom: Robert Owen requests the Congress of Aix-la-Chapelle to urge governments to legally limit ordinary working hours of employees in manufacturing.

1819 England: "Peterloo" Massacre at Manchester.

1824 England: Repeal of the Combination Acts of 1799 and 1800.

1825 England: Outlawing of picketing by the Combination of Workmen Act. Repeal of a law that had prohibited the emigration of artisans to continental Europe. **United States:** Boston construction workers strike unsuccessfully to reduce their work day to 10 hours; they strike again, unsuccessfully, in 1830.

1826 England: Formation of Journeymen Steam Engine Makers' Society in Manchester; known as "Old Mechanics," it was the forerunner of the Amalgamated Society of Engineers (1851).

1827 United States: Journeymen in Philadelphia form the Mechanics' Union of Trade Associations, the first citywide federation of local unions in the United States. **England:** Carpenters and joiners form a general union.

1829 Australia: Formation of a labor union by shipwrights in Sydney, New South Wales.

1833 United States: Formation of the General Trades Union in New York; it was a confederation of tradesmen that was copied by more than 12 other American cities; it lasted until 1837. **England:** The Factory Act outlaws the employment of children under nine and sets a maximum of nine hours work per day for employees aged between nine and 13 years. The act appoints inspectors to enforce its provisions and was the ancestor of modern factory laws. The National Regeneration Society in Lancashire advocated general strikes for the eight-hour work day.

1834 England: Six agricultural laborers (the "Tolpuddle Martyrs") sentenced to transportation to Australia for forming a union (March

18). **France:** Revolt by silk workers in Lyon, after the government attempted to suppress labor unions (April 9-13).

1839 England: The Chartist Convention votes in favor of a national strike to achieve its objectives (July 28).

1841 France: First factory legislation; it regulates child labor.

1842 United Kingdom: Formation of Miners' Association of Great Britain and Ireland; it claimed 70,000 members, or a third of the coal mining industry. **United States:** A Massachusetts judge rules that it was not illegal for a union to strike for higher pay, in *Commonwealth v. Hunt.*

1843 France: First collective agreement; it sets wage rates for printers.

1844 Ireland: Formation of Dublin Regular Trades' Association; it perished in the 1847 depression. **England:** Four-month coal miners' strike in Durham and Northumberland; the strike was unsuccessful.

1845 United Kingdom: The National Association of United Trades for the Protection and Employment of Labour advocates Boards of Trade, that is, bodies to conciliate and arbitrate in labor disputes. **Prussia:** Labor unions prohibited.

1846 Chile: Artisans form a mutual aid society.

1847 United Kingdom: William Dixon and W. P. Roberts, two of the leaders of the Miners' Association, become the first union officials to stand for election to parliament. The Miners' Association collapsed the next year.

1848 Germany: Formation of the first national German labor union, the National Printers' Association (*Nationaler Buchdrucker-Verein*). **France:** Government forcibly closes down the national workshops that had been set up to provide employment; several thousand are killed and thousands of others arrested during the "June Days." **England:** Marx and Engels publish the *Manifesto of the Communist Party.*

1849 United States: Organization of the first labor union in the anthracite coalfields of Pennsylvania by an English immigrant, John Bates.

1850 United States: Police kill two picketers in New York, the first labor fatalities in a United States strike.

1851 United Kingdom: Formation of the Amalgamated Society of Engineers in England.

1852 United States: Formation of the National Typographical Union, the first national labor union in the United States. **United Kingdom:** William Newton, a leader of the Amalgamated Society of Engineers, stands for election to the British House of Commons.

1857 Argentina: Mutual aid society among the printers; the society was made into a union in 1877. **United States:** Formation of the National Education Association.

1858 Scotland: Formation of the Glasgow Trades' Council.

1859 United Kingdom: Molestation of Workmen Act makes "peaceful" picketing lawful. A strike by London building employees leads to the formation of the London Trades Council in 1860.

1860 United Kingdom: Formation of the Amalgamated Society of Carpenters and Joiners.

1861 Germany: Lifting of the legal ban on labor unions in Saxony, followed by Weimar (1863), and the North German Confederation (1869), but there was no legal right to form unions.

1862 United Kingdom: A delegation of French workers, allowed to visit the London Exhibition, demand freedom of association and the right to strike on their return.

1863 England: Foundation of the Co-operative Wholesale Society at Manchester.

1864 United Kingdom: Formation of the International Workingmen's Association, or the First International, in London (September 28). **France:** Lifting of the legal ban on strikes.

1866 United States: Formation of the National Labor Union in Baltimore (August); 77 labor union delegates claimed to represent 60,000 members; the union lasts until 1872. **Netherlands:** Formation of unions by printers and diamond cutters.

1867 United Kingdom: Second Reform Act gives the vote to the better-off urban working class. A Conciliation Act also becomes law.

1868 United Kingdom: Formation of the Trades Union Congress at Manchester (June 2-6).

1869 United States: Formation of the National Colored Labor Union (December) by black intellectuals and labor leaders; it tried to affiliate with the National Labor Union but was refused.

1870 Austro-Hungarian Empire: Legalizing of labor unions in what is now Austria.

1871 United Kingdom: Labor unions legalized (June 29), but objections by organized labor led to an improved law in 1876. **Spain:** Formation of a printers' union in Madrid. **Canada:** Formation of first local trade assemblies (councils).

1872 United Kingdom: Joseph Arch founds the Agricultural Labourers' Union.

1874 United Kingdom: Election of Alexander Macdonald and Thomas Burt, two coal mining labor leaders, to the House of Commons. **France:** A factory law introduces a system of inspectors and outlaws child labor and women working underground.

1877 United States: Nationwide railroad strikes (July 16 to August 5) marked by rioting and use of the U.S. Army and state guards.

1878 United States: Formation of the International Labor Union. **New Zealand:** Legalizing of labor unions.

1879 France: Formation of first national labor union by hatters. **Australia:** First Intercolonial Trade Union Congress held in Sydney; subsequent congresses were held in 1884, 1886, 1888, 1889, 1891, and 1898.

1880 Switzerland: Formation of the *Schweizerischer Gewerkschafts-bund* (Swiss Labor Union Federation) by socialist labor unions.

1881 South Africa: The Amalgamated Society of Carpenters and Joiners forms a branch at Cape Town. **Canada**: The Knights of Labor forms its first assembly. **Spain:** After the legalization of labor unions, the *Federación de Trabajadores de la Región Española* (Federation of the Workers of the Spanish Region) is formed. **United States:** Formation of the Federation of Organized Trades and Labor Unions of the United States and Canada, the forerunner of the American Federation of Labor, in Pittsburgh.

1883 United States: First attempt to form an industrial union in the railroad industry, the Brotherhood of Railroad Trainmen. **Bulgaria:** Formation of a printers' union.

1884 France: Legalizing of labor unions (March 21).

1886 Canada: Formation of the Canadian Trades and Labour Congress. **France:** Formation of the first national trade union center, *Fédération Nationale des Syndicats Ouvriers* (National Federation of Workers' Unions). **United States:** Labor riots in Chicago (May 4); founding of the American Federation of Labor (December 8). **Scandinavia**: Beginning of regular conferences between labor leaders of Sweden, Denmark, and Norway.

1887 United States: Burlington railroad strike (February 27, 1888 to January 5, 1889). **France:** First Catholic labor union formed among white-collar workers.

1888 United Kingdom: Strike by women match workers in London for higher pay and improved health and safety. **Denmark:** Blacksmiths and Ironworkers' Union formed. **Spain:** Formation of the *Unión General de Trabajadores* (General Union of Workers). **United Kingdom:** International labor union conference held in London; it claimed to represent 850,000 British union members and 250,000 union members in Europe. The conference was a failure.

1889 France: Formation of Second International in Paris. **Germany:** Strikes for higher wages and regulation of women's and children's work. **United Kingdom:** London longshoremen's strike (August-September).

1890 Australia: 50,000 workers take part in the Maritime Strike (August-December) over freedom of contract; the strike, which extended to New Zealand, failed. **Switzerland:** The Canton of Geneva legally recognizes agreements between employers and unions; it was one of the first laws of its kind. **Austro-Hungarian Empire:** Formation of the Austrian Union of Metalworkers and Miners formed.

1891 Germany: Defeat of a strike by 20,000 German coal miners in the Ruhr; formation of the *Deutscher Metallarbeiter-Verband* (German Metalworkers' Union), Germany's first industrial union. **Norway:** Formation of Iron and Metal Workers' Union. **Australia:** Labor unions form the Labor Party in New South Wales and South Australia. **France:** First collective agreement in the mining industry.

1892 France: Voluntary conciliation and arbitration law. **United States:** Major labor dispute at the Homestead Steel plant near Pittsburgh (June-November). **France:** Foundation of the National Federation of Labor *(Bourses du Travail)*. **Germany:** Labor unions hold their first national congress. It resolves to encourage the formation of national unions and agrees to work for the formation of industry-based unions.

1893 Belgium: General strike (April). **United States:** First successful biracial strike, in New Orleans.

1894 United Kingdom: Beatrice and Sidney Webb publish *The History of Trade Unionism*, the first scholarly investigation of labor unions. **Ireland:** Formation of the Irish Trades Union Congress. **Australia:** Formation of the Australian Workers' Union. **New Zealand:** Becomes the first country in the world to introduce compulsory conciliation and arbitration for labor disputes. **United States:** Pullman railroad strike.

1895 China: Formation of the first unions in the Canton region. **France:** *Confédération Générale du Travail* (General Confederation of Labor) founded in France; it absorbed the National Federation of Labor *(Bourses du Travail)* in 1902.

1896 Uruguay: Formation of the first union federation.

1897 Japan: Steelworkers form a union. **United Kingdom:** Workmen's Compensation Act; the law applies only to blue-collar employees. Formation of the Scottish Trades Union Congress. **Austro-Hungarian Empire:** Formation of the Czechoslovak Trade Union Federation.

1898 United Kingdom: Workers' Union formed. **France:** Failure of first general railroad strike. **Korea:** Longshoremen form a union.

1899 Austro-Hungarian Empire: The Hungarian Trade Union Council (formed 1891) is set up on a permanent basis. **Australia:** First Labor Party government in the world in Queensland; it lasted one week. **France:** Formation of the first company union. **Egypt:** Formation of the first labor union among cigarette workers.

1900 Japan: Formation of unions by employees in metalworking, printing, railroads, teaching, and firefighting; they are suppressed by legislation later in 1900.

1901 United Kingdom: The House of Lords upholds an appeal by the Taff Vale Railway Company against the Amalgamated Society of Railway Servants which cost the society £23,000 in damages (July). **Denmark:** International labor union conference in Copenhagen (August 21); the conference set up the International Secretariat of the National Trade Union Federations, which was officially renamed the International Federation of Trade Unions in 1919. **Argentina:** Formation of the first union federation; it soon split into anarchist, syndicalist, and socialist factions, foreshadowing similar splits in Chile, Brazil, Uruguay, and Paraguay. **Italy:** Italian Metal Workers' Union (*Federazione Italiana Operai Metallurgici*) formed. **Albania:** First strikes among shoemakers and waterfront workers.

1902 United States: A major strike by anthracite coal miners results in the appointment of a presidential arbitration commission by President Theodore Roosevelt. **Philippines:** Creation of a national federation by craft labor unions.

1903 Brazil: Strike by textile workers in Rio de Janeiro. **Netherlands:** Major strikes by railroad and longshoremen. **Switzerland:** White-collar unions form their own federation. **Canada:** Formation of the National Trades and Labour Congress by organizations excluded by the Trades and Labour Congress (that is, by the Knights of Labor and unions not part of American unions).

.

1904 Australia: First national Labor government, with Protectionist support (April 27 to August 12). **Bulgaria:** Creation of socialist and Marxist labor union federations; the two bodies merged in 1920.

1905 United States: Creation of the Industrial Workers of the World in Chicago. **Dutch East Indies** (modern **Indonesia**): Formation of first labor union by Dutch and indigenous railway employees. **Nigeria:** Formation of first substantive labor union of indigenous employees in Africa (civil servants in Lagos). **Russian Empire:** Meeting of All-Russian Conference of Trade Unions.

1906 Russian Empire: Unions made legal (March), but a government crackdown follows after 1907. **Bolivia:** Formation of the first labor union. **Italy:** Foundation of the *Confederazione Generale di Lavoro* (General Confederation of Labor). **France:** The *Confédération Générale du Travail* adopts the radical Charter of Amiens, which advocates the general strike to eliminate capitalism and affirms the independence of trade unions from political parties. **Germany:** The Mannheim Agreement declares the equality of unions and the Social Democratic Party in providing leadership for the working-class movement. **United Kingdom:** The Trades Disputes Act protects unions from prosecution by employers over breach of contract under common law.

1907 Canada: The Industrial Disputes Investigation Act enables the federal government to appoint a tripartite board to try to resolve labor disputes on application by the employers or the unions. **Argentina:** General strike in Buenos Aires by 93,000 employees. **Switzerland:** Catholic unions form their own federation.

1909 Hong Kong: Formation of first labor union. **Sweden:** General strike by 300,000 employees. **Spain:** Over 175 shot in riots led by revolutionary syndicalists in Catalonia over the calling up of reservists for the war in Morocco during "Tragic Week" (July); attacks on churches and convents. Government executes anarchist leader, Francisco Ferrer. **United Kingdom:** House of Lords upholds the Osbourne Judgement declaring political levies by labor unions illegal (December 2).

1910 Spain: Formation of the *Confederación Nacional del Trabajo* (National Confederation of Workers) by anarchists. **France:** First old age pension law.

1911 United Kingdom: First national railway strike; it lasted for two days.

1912 United States: The Lloyd-LaFollette Act and other legislation forbids American federal employees from going on strike. **Italy:** Syndicalists form their own labor federation. **Japan:** Bunji Suzuki forms a labor union.

1913 France: Clerical workers form the first national Catholic union. **United Kingdom:** Syndicalists from 12 countries attempt to form a Syndicalist International in London.

1916 United States: American Federation of Teachers formed (April).

1917 Russia: Bolshevik Revolution (November).

1918 India: B. P. Wadia forms the Madras Union. **Greece:** Formation of the General Confederation of Greek Labor. **Germany:** November Pact (Stinnes-Legien Agreement) made between major employers and organized labor. **United States:** Formation of Pan-American Federation of Labor in Texas (November 13).

1919 Argentina: The army suppresses a general strike with much bloodshed. **France:** Formation of the *Confédération Française des Travailleurs Chrétiens* (French Confederation of Christian Workers) representing 100,000 Catholic workers in 321 unions (November); formation of the International Labour Organisation (ILO) from the Versailles Peace Treaty. Formation of the International Organisation of Employers in 1920 also results from the creation of the ILO. **United Kingdom:** Seven-day national railroad strike; it resulted in the employees gaining the eight-hour work day in 1920. **British Guiana:** Formation of the British Guiana Labour Union. **United States:** Defeat of general steelworkers' strike. **Soviet Union:** Formation of the Third International (Communist); known as the Comintern, it was disbanded in 1943. **Canada:** Six-week general strike in Winnipeg; sympathetic strikes also occur in other Canadian cities, notably in Vancouver.

1920 United Kingdom: formation of the Amalgamated Engineering Union. **France:** The split in the Socialist Party results in the formation of the Communist Party. **India:** Formation of All-India Trades Union

Congress (AITUC) representing 64 unions with about 150,000 members. **France:** Railroad and general strike fails.

1921 Canada: Formation of the Catholic Confederation of Labour in Quebec.

1921-1922 France: The *Confédération Générale du Travail* splits. The Communists and syndicalists form the *Confédération Générale du Travail Unitaire*, which joins the Red International of Labor Unions in 1923.

1922 South Africa: Army kills 230 strikers. **Hong Kong:** Successful general strike by seamen against an attempt to suppress their union. **United Kingdom:** Formation of Transport and General Workers' Union.

1924 Italy: Abolition of nonfascist labor unions (January 24). **United Kingdom:** Formation of the General and Municipal Workers' Union.

1925 China: Formation of the All China General Labor Federation.

1926 France: Syndicalists form their own labor federation. **Portugal:** The government dissolves the *Confederaçao Geral de Trabalho* (the peak labor organization formed in 1913). **United Kingdom:** General (May 4-12) and coal mining (May-November) strikes.

1927 Australia: Formation of the Australian Council of Trade Unions. **China:** Chiang Kai-shek purges the communists from organized labor in Shanghai and kills about 5,000 (April). **Canada:** Formation of the All-Canadian Congress of Labour.

1928 Colombia: Army kills several hundred strikers during a dispute with the U.S.-owned United Fruit Company.

1930 United Kingdom: British government begins to encourage the development of labor unions in its colonies in Africa, Asia, and the Caribbean (September). **Argentina:** Formation of the *Confederación General del Trabajo* (General Confederation of Labor). **Colombia:** Labor unions made legal.

1931 Dutch East Indies (Indonesia): Confederation of native employees joins the International Federation of Trade Unions.

1932 United States: Anti-Injunction (Norris-LaGuardia) Act provides freedom of association to organized labor.

1933 Germany: Labor unions suppressed (May 2); imprisonment of labor leaders in Dachau concentration camp. **United States:** Section 7(a) of the National Industrial Recovery Act gives unions the undisputed legal right to recruit employees and collectively bargain for employees.

1934 France: First successful general strike over the need to resist fascism.

1935 Norway: Conclusion of basic agreement between organized labor and employers. **United States:** National Labor Relations Act (Wagner Act) protects the right of labor unions to organize and engage in collective bargaining.

1936 France: Syndicalists, communists, and other labor organizations hold a unity congress (March). The election of the Popular Front leads to new laws on a 40-hour work week, paid holidays, collective bargaining, and compulsory conciliation and arbitration (this last law was suspended in 1939). The Matignon Agreement provides for the unions' right to organize, an end to antiunion practices, collective bargaining, pay increases of 7 to 12 percent, and the election of shop stewards (June 7). **New Zealand:** Amendments to the Industrial Conciliation and Arbitration Act makes union membership compulsory for any employee subject to a registered award of industrial agreement; this provision remained part of New Zealand law until 1991.

1937 France: A decree legalizes labor unions in the French colonies of West and Equatorial Africa (March 11). **New Zealand:** Formation of the Federation of Labour. **British East Africa:** Banning of the Labour Trade Union of East Africa. **French-speaking Africa:** White-collar workers form the first labor unions in Tunisia, in Bamako (Mali), and in Dakar (Senegal). **Switzerland:** An accord between employers and unions in the engineering industry eventually became the model for a national social partnership in Swiss industrial relations.

1938 Sweden: Saltsjobaden Agreement between unions and employers. **United States:** Formation of the Congress of Industrial Organizations (CIO); John L. Lewis becomes president. **Caribbean:** The West

Indies Royal Commission (Lord Moyne) recommends the encouragement of organized labor.

1939 Canada: Expulsion of the Canadian branches of the CIO international unions from the Trades and Labour Congress. **Cuba:** Formation of the *Confederación de Trabajadores de Cuba* (Confederation of the Workers of Cuba). **France:** The *Confédération Générale du Travail* expels communist affiliates over their support of the Soviet pact with Nazi Germany. **United States:** The Hatch Act prohibits federal employees from active participation in federal election campaigns and from providing organizational support for candidates.

1940 United Kingdom: The Colonial Development and Welfare Act 1940 links the payment of assistance funds to fostering labor unions in British colonies. **Canada:** The expelled CIO unions and the All-Canadian Congress of Labour merge to form the Canadian Congress of Labour. **Japan:** Suppression of all independent labor unions and employers' organizations (June). **France:** Dissolution of all three national labor organizations (November 9).

1942 Egypt: Legalizing of labor unions.

1943 Canada: The Order-in-Council P.C. 1003 creates a legal framework for collective bargaining and mechanisms for resolving disputes.

1944 France: The provisional government restores free labor unions (July).

1945 United Kingdom: Representatives from 53 countries attend the World Trades Union Conference in London, (February 6-17). The conference led to the creation of the World Federation of Trade Unions (WFTU) in Paris on September 25. The International Federation of Trade Unions ceased to exist after December 31. **Austria:** Formation of the *Österreichischer Gewerkschaftsbund* (Austrian Federation of Trade Unions) (April 13). **Germany:** Resurgence of labor unions at the factory level in West Germany (March-August). By August 1945, nearly one million union members had been officially recognized in unions in the British zone. **Netherlands:** Formation of a permanent union-employer policy body, the Foundation of Labor (May).

1946 **United Kingdom:** Major dispute in the transportation industry over the closed shop. **Belgian Congo:** Legalizing of Africans forming labor unions; European labor unions had been permitted in the Congo since 1921. A multiracial labor federation was formed in 1951 but split along racial lines. **Canada:** Rand Formula introduced into industrial relations.

1947 **France:** General strike. **United States:** Taft-Hartley Act outlaws political levies by labor unions and the closed shop (June 23). The act provides for the immediate dismissal of striking American federal government employees and prohibits their re-employment by the government for three years.

1948 **Peru:** Formation of the *Confederación Interamericana de Trabajadores* (Interamerican Confederation of Workers) (January 10) in Lima. **France:** Strike by coal miners accompanied by much violence; 30,000 troops sent in by the government. **West Germany:** The number of union members reaches five million. **Japan:** Public sector employees forbidden to strike. **International:** International Labour Organisation Convention No. 87 (Freedom of Association and Protection of the Right to Organize). The Universal Declaration of Human Rights proclaims the right of individuals to form and join trade unions to protect their interests (Article 23, Part 4).

1949 **International:** International Labour Organisation Convention No. 98 (Right to Organize and Collective Bargaining). **United States:** Introduction of the General Schedule, in its present form, for white-collar employees of the American federal government; its origins go back to pay reforms of 1923, which were based on pay legislation of the 1850s. CIO expels communists. **United Kingdom:** Formation of the International Confederation of Free Trade Unions (December), which claims 54 million members. **Australia:** Communist-led coal miners' strike. The federal Labor government sends in troops to mine the coal (June 26 to August 15).

1950 **Kenya:** Army crushes a general strike in Nairobi. **Germany:** Formation of *IG Metall* (Metal Workers' Industrial Union). **International:** The International Confederation of Free Trade Unions establishes the European Regional Organization (November).

1951 **Mexico:** Formation of the *Organización Regional Interamericana de Trabajadores* (Inter-American Regional Organization of

Workers) in Mexico City (January). **Guatemala:** Castillo Armas, with U.S. support, overthrows President Jacobo Arbenz, executes labor organizers, and suppresses the country's 533 unions.

1955   United States: The American Federation of Labor (AFL) and the Congress of Industrial Organizations (CIO) agree to merge with George Meany as president to form the American Federation of Labor-Congress of Industrial Organizations (AFL-CIO).

1956   Canada: The Trades and Labour Congress and the Canadian Congress of Labour merge to form the Canadian Labour Congress. **Japan:** First *Shunto* or Spring Offensive.

1959   United States: Wisconsin legislature passes the first public-sector bargaining law which gives state employees the right to join unions.

1960   International: The International Confederation of Free Trade Unions establishes the African Regional Organization to represent organized labor in Africa (November). **Canada:** Merger of the Canadian and Catholic Confederation of Labour to form the Confederation of National Trade Unions. **United States:** *Labor History* journal begins publication in New York.

1963   International: International Confederation of Free Trade Unions hold its first World Youth Rally in Vienna, Austria (July 9-19).

1964   United Kingdom: House of Lords upholds the original decision in the *Rookes v. Barnard* case. This loophole in the Trades Disputes Act (1906) made union officials liable for damages for threatening to strike in breach of contracts of employment; it was closed by the Trades Disputes Act (1965).

1967   United States: The Taylor Act in New York State imposes penalties on public-sector employees who went on strike; the penalties were increased in 1969, 1974, and 1978 and have been enforced.

1968   International: The International Federation of Christian Trade Unions renamed itself the World Confederation of Labor. **United Kingdom:** Report of the Royal Commission on Trade Unions (Donovan Commission).

1969 United States: The AFL-CIO disaffiliates from the International Confederation of Free Trade Unions (February) and sets up the Asian-American Free Labor Institute with U.S. State Department support.

1970 United States: The Pay Comparability Act applies the principle of pay comparability with the private sector to American federal government employees in its present form. A successful national strike by postal workers leads to the Postal Reorganization Act 1970, which separates pay determination in the postal service from the rest of federal employment, outlaws strikes, gives the unions the right to engage in collective bargaining, and provides for compulsory arbitration in case of disputes. President Richard Nixon attempts to delay the statutory federal pay adjustment deadline during his freeze on pay and prices; the National Treasury Employees Union (founded in 1938) took its case to the Supreme Court and won what has been claimed to be the largest back pay award in history: $600 million. **European Economic Community:** Creation of the Standing Committee of Employment, the first formal European-level committee of its kind to include representatives from organized labor (December).

1972-1973 South Africa: Strikes by black workers in Durban leads to the arrest of the leaders and the suppression of black unionism.

1973 International: Formation of the European Trade Union Confederation; it claimed 37 million members.

1974 United Kingdom: Labour Party and the Trades Union Congress agree to a Social Contract. **India:** Strike by railway workers.

1976 West Germany: Extension of the Co-determination Law to companies with 2,000 or more employees. **Poland:** Formation of an Organizing Committee for Free Trades Unions in Silesia and an independent labor union committee following a strike wave.

1977 Spain: Organized labor gains minimum legal; full legal freedom was not granted until 1985. **Soviet Union:** Vladimir Klebanov and five others announce the formation of an Association of Free Trade Unions of Workers in Moscow (November).

1979 International: First United Nations resolution calling on member countries to release any person detained "because of their trade union activities." **South Africa:** The government appoints the Wiehahn Commission to investigate trade unionism; the commission successfully recommended that black labor unions be legally recognized. **Romania:** A dissident, Paul Goma, announces the formation of the Romanian Workers' Free Union. **United States:** The AFL-CIO and President Jimmy Carter reach a national accord under which the unions agree to restrain wage claims in return for a package of economic and social measures (September).

1980 **Brazil:** Five-week strike by metalworkers. **Turkey:** A military coup results in restrictions on labor unions. **Sweden:** National lockout by employers (May). **Poland:** Formation of Solidarity (September 22).

1981 **Chile:** Formation of a centrist labor union. **United States:** A strike by the Professional Air Traffic Controllers' Organization (August 3) leads to the firing of strikers and their replacement by military controllers and civilian controllers who returned to work. **International:** Reaffiliation of the AFL-CIO with the International Confederation of Free Trade Unions (November).

1982 **Germany:** 500,000 join in union protests about cuts to social services. **Turkey:** Trial of 52 labor leaders (February-March). **United States:** Federal government takes away air traffic controllers' union's right to bargain collectively (February) after its defeat in the 1981 strike.

1983 **Australia:** The Australian Council of Trade Unions and the Australian Labor Party negotiate an accord covering economic policy to be followed if the Labor Party won the federal election (February). The accord operates between March 1983 and March 1996.

1984 **United Kingdom:** The Employment Act requires secret ballots for labor union officials and for strikes. **International:** The International Confederation of Free Trade Unions conducts the first survey of violations of trade union rights in the world. **New Zealand:** Abolition of access to compulsory arbitration in interest disputes except in "essential" industries. **Germany:** Introduction of 38-hour work week in the steel industry. **Spain:** The government and the *Unión General de Trabajadores* (General Union of Workers) agree to a social and economic pact to control wage claims as an anti-inflationary measure. The pact breaks down after 1986.

1985 United States: Hormel strike, Austin, Minnesota.

1986 United Kingdom: Defeat of London printing unions over the introduction of new technology at Rupert Murdoch's Wapping plant. **Germany:** *Neue Heimat* affair; the mismanagement of the cooperative housing project damaged the prestige of labor unions.

1987 Germany: *IG Metall* gains the 37-hour work week for members from April 1, 1988; other unions also gained reductions in their working time. **Ireland:** Government, unions and employers agree to the Programme for National Recovery (April). **Taiwan:** Formation of a Labor Party (November) after the lifting of martial law.

1988 International: The International Trade Secretariats sign the first framework agreement with a multinational corporation, Danone.

1989 Japan: Merger of two major labor federations, *Rengo* and *Sohyo*, to form *JTUC-Rengo* (November 21), with 7.6 million members.

1990 Italy: Strikes in a wide range of essential services legally prohibited (June). **United States:** The Federal Employees Pay Comparability Act signed into law by President George Bush (November 5).

1991 Albania: Formation of the first independent labor unions and national labor federation (February). **New Zealand:** The Employment Contracts Act abolishes the arbitration system and the system of compulsory union membership, which had operated since 1936. **Cuba:** Formation of the Independent Cuban General Workers' Union (October 4); it continues to be denied official recognition by the government. **Morocco:** Creation of the Trade Union Confederation of Arab Maghreb Workers.

1992 China: Suppression of the China Free Trade Union Preparatory Committee (formed at the end of 1991). **International:** Signing of European Union Treaty in Maastricht (February 7); it includes a social policy agreement that gave European-wide labor and employer federations an enhanced formal role in the social policy of the European Union. **Georgia:** Formation of Georgian Trade Union Amalgamation (December 18).

1993 European Commission: Formal recognition of the European Trade Union Confederation, EUROCADRES, and the *Confédération*

Européene des Cadres as "social partners" for European-wide dialogue on social policy matters. **International:** Formation of Education International. **Poland:** Strikes by Solidarity over low pay and staff cuts (May). **United Kingdom:** The Trade Union Reform and Employment Rights Act becomes law (July 1). **Indonesia:** Government bans the first congress of the independent Indonesia Prosperity Labor Union (August). The union, formed in November 1990, claimed 50,000 members but had twice been refused official registration by the Department of Manpower. **India:** National strike by millions of employees against the national government's economic reforms (September 9).

1994 International: The International Labour Organisation adopts a Convention and Recommendation designed to protect the conditions of part-time workers. The International Confederation of Free Trade Unions launches a campaign against child labor (June).**Vietnam:** A new labor law requires every foreign joint enterprise to establish a labor union within six months (June). **Indonesia:** Muchtac Pakpahan, the leader of the independent Indonesia Prosperity Labor Union, is sentenced to three years in jail for allegedly inciting riots in Medan in April (November 7); his sentence is extended to four years in January 1995. **European Commission:** European Commission's White Paper on Social Policy recognizes employers' organizations, unions, and voluntary associations as partners in the development of social policy (August).

1995 International: The International Confederation of Free Trade Unions announces that 528 union activists were murdered during 1994 (June). Merger of the Miners' International Federation and the International Federation of Chemical, Energy, and General Workers' Unions to form the International Federation of Chemical, Energy, Mine, and General Workers' Unions (November). The International Confederation of Free Trade Unions forms the Asia-Pacific Labour Network. **United States:** The United Steelworkers, the United Auto Workers, and the International Association of Machinists agree to a merger (July). Lane Kirkland steps down as president of the AFL-CIO (August) and is replaced by John J. Sweeney (October).

1996 International: International unions inaugurate the first International Commemoration Day for Dead and Injured Workers to focus attention on occupational health and safety (April 28). Campaign by the International Federation of Commercial, Technical, and Clerical

Employees for union recognition by the U.S. firm Toys "R" Us in 60 countries. **South Korea:** Labor law changes ending job security guarantees (December) produce a wave of strikes in 1997.

1997 India: Murder of Bombay union leader Datta Samant (January 16). **China:** At least three labor protests in Sichuan province over job losses in state-owned industries; two labor activists in Shenzhen are sentenced to three and a half years in jail for setting up an independent trade union in May 1994 (June). **Canada:** Strike by public high school teachers (October 27-November 10) and by postal workers (November). **Israel:** National labor strikes over privatization (November). **United States:** End of the longest strike ever, at Las Vegas; the strike began in 1991 over the rehiring of 550 employees.

1998 Ukraine: Strike by coal miners over unpaid wages (May 4). **Russia:** Blockades and strikes by coal miners over unpaid wages (May). **South Korea:** Unions agree to economic reform laws in return for concessions (increasing unemployment payments, allowing unions to engage in politics, and allowing public sector teachers to form unions) (February 14); auto workers' strike over mass layoffs and privatization (July 14-15). **Greece:** Public sector strikes over labor market reform (July 23). **Russia:** General strikes in main cities over unpaid wages and low pay (October 7). **Peru:** National strike (October 30). **France:** Introduction of a 35-hour working week for enterprises that employed 20 or more employees.

1999 International: International Labour Organisation adopts the Worst Forms of Child Labour Convention (No. 182). **Germany:** Creation of the Alliance for Jobs, Training, and Competitiveness, a national forum of labor unions, employers, and government.

2000 International: Creation of Union Network International (January 1). International Confederation of Free Trade Unions' Annual Survey of Violations of Human Rights shows that 209 union activists were killed in 2000 compared to 140 in 1999. **Russia:** Three labor union federations with a total of 30 million members affiliate to the International Confederation of Free Trade Unions (November). **France:** Organized labor gains a 35-hour working week law.

2001 Germany: Creation of *Ver.di*, the world's biggest labor union (March 21). **United States:** President George W. Bush signs Executive Orders that direct employers to notify union members that they could opt out of dues collected from members that were used for political activity and forbade "project labor agreements" whereby only unionized companies can bid for government contracts. The Bush Administration also indicates that it would overturn workplace safety rule laws on ergonomics (March).

2002   United Kingdom: Formation of Amicus from merger of the Amalgamated Engineering and Electrical Union and the Manufacturing, Science and Finance Union (January). **Italy:** General strikes over planned labor reforms to remove reinstatement of employees for wrongful dismissal (April 16). Labor protests over the giant auto company, Fiat (established in 1899), laying off 20,000 employees (November 26). **Germany:** *IG Metall* conducts a successful series of strikes that gain an immediate 4 percent pay rise and a further 3.1 percent rise from June 1, 2003. **India:** Unions lead 10 million to protest government plans to privatize state-run companies (April 16). **United States:** Lockout of longshoremen shuts down all ports on the West Coast over introduction of new technology and job security (September 29-October 9). **South Africa:** Two-day general strike over the government's privatization policy (October). **Portugal:** General strike over government spending cuts required to meet the financial requirements of membership of the European Union (mid-November). **France:** Dilution of 35-hour week labor law (December). **Venezuela:** Strike by oil workers protesting over president Hugo Chávez remaining in office leads to general strike (December 2-February 3, 2003).

2003   International: International Confederation of Trade Unions calls for the World Confederation of Labor to join with it in building a unified global trade union movement to meet the challenges of globalization (May). A United Nations convention protecting the rights of migrant workers comes into force (July 1); among other things, it guarantees migrant workers the right to trade union representation. **France:** Rolling transport strikes over government plans to reform the state pension scheme (May and June). **Austria:** General strike over government cuts to state pensions (June). **Germany:** Strikes in the chemical and metals manufacturing industries in the east in support of the 35-hour week (June). **Nigeria:** Violence during a general strike over oil price rises (July).

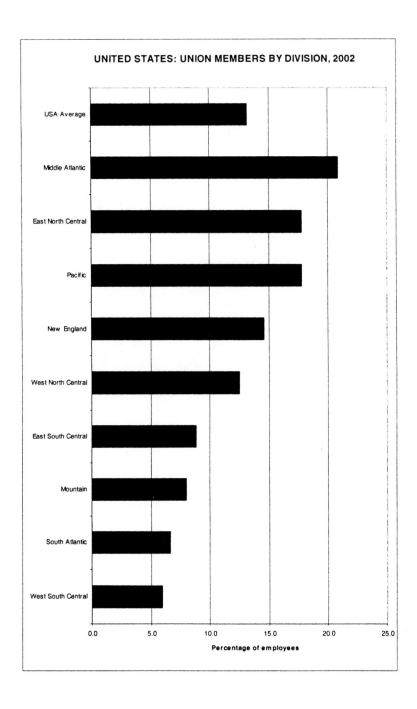

UNITED STATES: UNION MEMBERS BY DIVISION, 2002

INTRODUCTION

Organized labor is about the collective efforts of employees to improve their economic, social, and political position. It can be studied from many different points of view—historical, economic, sociological, or legal—but is fundamentally about the struggle for human rights and social justice. As a rule, organized labor has tried to make the world a fairer place. Even though it has only ever covered a minority of employees in most countries, its effects on their political, economic, and social systems have been generally positive. History shows that when organized labor is repressed, the whole society suffers and is made less just.

This dictionary could be seen as a study in the failure of success, for having succeeded in achieving so much, organized labor now seems no longer needed. Since 1980, organized labor in most Western countries has faced falling membership, defeats by employers, and a general loss of direction and power. There has been much questioning about the need for labor unions and their prospects for survival.

Against this often gloomy contemporary background, it is timely to take stock of the history of organized labor, to see where it came from and where it has been. This introduction presents a general view of the development and growth of organized labor as a historical movement in a global perspective, explores some of the characteristics of organized labor, and analyzes the main trends since 1980.

LABOR IN HISTORY

The Beginnings of Organized Labor in an Unfree World

Labor unions are usually defined as voluntary organizations of employees created to defend or improve the pay and conditions of their members through bargaining with their employers. As institutions, labor unions have existed only in the last 200 years—that is, with the advent of the Industrial Revolution—but in fact organized labor has existed throughout history. It is simply that in a documentary record

1

dominated by the powerful, labor, unless it caused trouble, was hardly mentioned.

Bargaining between rulers and the ruled has always occurred to some degree. Often this bargaining took the form of petitions by labor to their rulers complaining about some matter in the hope of redress. In 1152 B.C. the Egyptian pharaoh's tomb makers struck work over the failure of their rulers to supply them with grain; it was history's first recorded labor dispute. The Old Testament records that during the Israelites' Egyptian bondage, their foremen complained to the pharaoh about the lack of straw they needed to make their quota of bricks. The Old Testament also records the pharaoh's haughty dismissal of their complaints (Exodus 5:6-23).

Rulers from ancient times saw any unauthorized gatherings or organizations as a threat to social order. This can be shown by two examples from the Roman Empire. In about A.D. 54, there was a disturbance among the silversmiths of Ephesus over the threat to the trade in cult objects for the worship of Diana caused by the preaching of St. Paul. A local official pointed out that the gathering was illegal and could lead to the use of force by the Romans (Acts, 19:23-40). A second example occurred in about A.D. 110 when Pliny the Younger, the governor of the troubled province of Bithynia, requested permission from the emperor Trajan to allow a fire brigade of 150 members to be organized. Trajan denied the request on the grounds that the brigade might become a focus for political opposition as had happened elsewhere in Asia Minor.

With most of the labor performed by tied labor forces or slaves, there was little scope for the formation of a large body of free individuals who earned their living by their labor in the societies of classical Greece and Rome. Indeed, the concept of "labor" as a general function in these societies scarcely existed. Both the Greek and Latin words for work (ἔργον and labor) were associated with unremitting toil, compulsion, and slavery. The purpose of the government was to maintain the social and economic order. The Roman emperor Diocletian's well-known edict of maximum prices of A.D. 301 laid down maximum **wages** as well.

Despite government policy, some groups did engage in rudimentary forms of collective bargaining. Evidence for this comes from the early Byzantine Empire. In A.D. 544, one of the "new" laws of the emperor Justinian I forbade sailors and laborers from demanding or accepting pay increases on penalty of having to pay the treasury three times the amount at issue.

Although distant in time, these precedents showed the attitudes of the rulers towards their subjects that were held until fairly recently in recorded history. In the absence of political bargaining, most groups often had to resort to rebellion to make their presence felt. Usually they had no agenda for social reform, although the Mazdakite movement in sixth century A.D. Persia, with its curiously modern call for redistribution of wealth, was an exception.

During the Middle Ages in Western Europe, religion could also be an outlet for those seeking social change, as shown by the activities of revolutionary millenarians. It is interesting to note it was the radical wing of organized labor that was to continue the millenarian tradition through its imagery of a bright and shining tomorrow (*see* **Iconography**). Organized labor emerged very slowly from the economic and urban population growth of Western Europe from about A.D. 1200. The money economy began to assume greater importance, as signaled by the revival of regular gold coin production at Florence and Genoa in 1252. Although the broad pattern of economic and social development across Western Europe differed widely, some common elements were present. Of particular significance was the rise of a wage-earning group in the population, whose existence is documented in Portugal as early as 1253. Wage earners, especially skilled members, were the founders of the first labor unions.

The Birth of Organized Labor in England

Among the Western nations, England can claim special importance because it was there that many of the institutions and much of the lexicon of organized labor had their origins. From about A.D. 1100, guilds or societies of masters and journeymen were the main agents of economic regulation. They could fix the price of their products, had responsibility for maintaining their quality, and controlled entry into their trade through an **apprenticeship** system. The guilds could also set the wages of journeymen. The word "wages" was known to be in use in England by about 1330.

Journeymen were men who, having served an apprenticeship and become qualified in their trade, were employed by a master. Once qualified, they could find themselves in an awkward position in the medieval labor force: They were conscious of being in a socially superior position compared to peasants but could suffer from changes in price levels through being tied to the money economy of the towns. At the same time, opportunities for advancement to a master could be limited or nonexistent.

These conditions gave rise to persistent attempts by journeymen in many trades to organize themselves for higher pay from as early as 1381, when the Corporation of the City of London forbade congregations or alliances among the trades. In 1383, some journeymen saddlers of London were accused of having formed "covins" (a term of conspiratorial suggestion first recorded in 1330) to raise their pay.

With the decline of the guilds after 1500, the English parliament started to make laws covering a wider range of economic regulation. In 1548 parliament passed a general law prohibiting combinations among artisans and laborers. This law, the Bill of Conspiracies of Victuallers and Craftsmen, was significant for introducing the concept of combinations as conspiracies into English law. Other laws passed in the 1550s were designed to preserve the economic order; they applied to the textile industry (one of the first industries to employ large concentrations of employees) and restricted how many looms a person could own and outlawed gig-mills. In 1562, the Statute of Artificers gave justices of the peace the power to set the wages of artisans and laborers and provided penalties for breach of contract by employers and employees. The statute also laid down that a seven-year apprenticeship was required for a man to become a journeyman.

England's economic growth, and particularly its rate of technological change from 1700, made the intent of the 16th-century labor laws increasingly difficult to apply to an increasingly dynamic economy with its fluctuating levels of real wages. It was also an economy with a growing labor force employed in manufacturing. In 1980, P. H. Lindert used samples from burial registers to gauge occupation change in England before 1800. His revised estimates, although tentative, suggest that the importance of commercial and industrial occupations in the pre-1800 economy had been underestimated by Gregory King, who used hearth tax returns and other sources. Lindert estimated that between 1700 and 1803, the number of males employed in manufacturing doubled from 155,000 to 324,000, a modest rate by later standards but impressive for the time. These developments also provided unintended fertile soil for the germination of labor unions. Despite the antiunion laws, journeymen and others continued to form secret labor unions and, from at least 1717, to conduct strikes, a term that had acquired its modern meaning as early as 1763. By 1769, settling **labor disputes** had become an important part of the duties of justices of the peace.

In his 1980 study, C. R. Dobson documented 383 labor disputes in Britain between 1717 and 1800 that covered more than 30 trades; of these, most occurred among wool combers, weavers, and wool spinners (64), seamen and ships' carpenters (37), tailors and staymakers (27), bricklayers, carpenters, and building laborers (19), and coal miners (18). Disputes over wages and working hours accounted for 71 percent of disputes; 9 percent were over the employment of apprentices or other persons; and 6 percent were over innovation and machinery.

The evidence assembled by Dobson is important for showing that even before the start of the Industrial Revolution, labor disputes and labor organizations were established, if unwelcome, features of British society. The evidence also showed that the groups who took part in disputes were similar to those who were to play a prominent role in later periods—weavers, coal miners, and building workers—and that the issues that concerned them most were wages and working hours. In this period, labor unions had no legal standing but were clearly a presence even if shadowy as organizations.

It was no accident that 56 percent of all the disputes between 1717 and 1800 were over **wages**. Real wages fluctuated considerably from year to year in the 18th century, making it all too easy for the living standards of groups of employees to fall behind the cost of living. Falls in the standard of living were most conducive to increased activity by organized labor, especially during the 1790s when England's wars with France caused real wages to fall by 42 percent and led to some successful strikes for higher pay by London journeymen. Parliament responded to the labor unrest by the Combination Acts of 1799 and 1800, which, it has been argued, were largely wartime security measures aimed primarily at labor disputes rather than labor unions as such.

The next 25 years were difficult for organized labor. The Industrial Revolution gathered pace, and with it came a host of technological changes that benefited some groups in the labor force and destroyed the livelihood of others. The legal suppression of strikes encouraged illegal outlets, such as the organized destruction of machines in the woolen industry by the Luddites between 1811 and 1813. Parliament and organized labor differed fundamentally on economic policy. Organized labor wished to preserve the preindustrial economic order with its extensive regulations. Parliament was determined to move towards a free enterprise economy with minimal government regulation. The triumph of the new economic order based on manufacturing was symbolized by the repeal of the wages clause of the Statute of Artificers (1562) in 1813 and the apprenticeship clause in

1814. There was opposition to both actions. One petition presented to parliament opposing the repeal of the apprenticeship clauses was signed by 30,517 journeymen (13,000 in London and 17,517 outside it), an action that gave some indication of the extent of organized labor at the time.

Organized labor and social protest were closely allied. Much of the social protest of the period was economic in origin and intent. Two well-known examples were the planned march to London by some Manchester weavers (the "Blanketeers") of 1817, who were dispersed by the government after the arrest of their leaders, and the "Peterloo" Massacre at Manchester when a militia charge killed 11 people in a crowd that had gathered for a political demonstration for parliamentary reform in 1819.

Although the Combination Acts were repealed in 1824, they were replaced by new legislation in 1825 that effectively prohibited strikes. Despite this, labor unions continued to survive. Francis Place estimated that in this period there were about 100,000 journeymen in London, all potential candidates for union membership. The word "union" itself seems to have come into use at this time in its modern sense in the shipping and shipbuilding industries. By 1834, the term "employee" had also come into use.

During the first half of the 19th century, two elites were evident among the artisans who comprised organized labor in England: an older elite of carpenters, tailors, potters, and curriers and a new elite in ironworking, engineering, and the new manufacturing industries. Other occupations, most notably those of handloom weavers, were destroyed by mechanization of their trade. New unions began to emerge: journeymen steam engine makers (1826), carpenters (1827), a national union of coal miners in 1842 which claimed 70,000 members for a time, carpenters and joiners (1860), and, most famous of all, the **Amalgamated Society of Engineers** (1851).

According to the first directory of British labor unions published in 1861, there were 290 trades with unions in London alone, nearly all of them in manufacturing or construction. How many members of labor unions there were in England before 1860 is not known with precision, but the available evidence suggests it was small and the numbers varied widely depending on the state of the economy. The Grand National Consolidated Trades Union in 1834 is thought to have had only about 16,000 members. Even well-known unions had relatively small memberships. Both the Amalgamated Society of Engineers and the Friendly Society of Operative Stonemasons had only 5,000 members each in 1850-1851. These and other figures suggest that total union membership for Britain in the early 1850s was about 50,000 and fell to about 40,000 in 1860. There was significant growth in the membership of skilled unions in the 1860s. The Amalgamated Engineers grew from 21,000 members in 1860 to 35,000 by 1870, the Ironfounders from 8,000 to 9,000, and the newly formed **Amalgamated Society of Carpenters and Joiners** from 618 to 10,200. At the 1869 meeting of the **Trades Union Congress** there were 40 unions represented claiming a total membership of 250,000.

The Example of England

Outside of Britain before 1835, labor unions seem to have existed only in **France**, the **United States**, **Canada**, and the colony of New South Wales in **Australia**. After the French Revolution in 1789, journeymen carpenters in Paris formed a union that aroused complaints by employers; the union was suppressed by the law *Le Chapelier* (1791), which was also applied to employers' organizations. Strikes were forbidden by the Penal Code of 1810. In North America, the idea of labor unions was imported from England by journeymen immigrants. A British register of American emigrants maintained between 1773 and 1776 showed that of the 6,190 emigrants whose occupations were known, 49 percent were artisans, mechanics or craftsmen. The first American union was the Federal Society of Journeymen Cordwainers (or shoemakers) in Philadelphia; formed in 1794, the society lasted until 1806. In Canada, unions in the building industry made their presence felt at Saint John, New Brunswick, as early as 1812 when they tried to exclude American immigrants to maintain the shortage of skilled labor. In Australia, at least two unions were formed by 1835: one among Sydney shipwrights (1829) and the other among cabinetmakers (1833).

In this period, governments often made little distinction between social unrest and calls for greater democracy and labor unions. The spirit of the age was shown by a revolt by silk workers in Lyon, France, in 1834 after the government attempted to suppress labor unions. Yet despite the harshness of its laws, the environment in England was, in practice, much freer than elsewhere in Europe. For example, in 1825 the British government repealed a law that had prohibited the emigration of artisans to continental Europe, legislation that had been in English statutes since 1718. If they could survive the severe economic fluctuations of the period and the social consequences of technological change brought by industrialization, labor unions could succeed.

European visitors to England in the 1860s were impressed by its labor unions. In 1862, a deputation of French labor leaders was allowed by Napoleon III to visit the London Exhibition. They returned with a high opinion of English working conditions and unions and asked to be granted freedom of association and the right to strike, freedoms that were not really available under English law.

In 1869, the Comte de Paris (Louis Philippe d'Orleans) published a sympathetic study, *The Trade Unions of England*, which was translated into English; it had previously been reprinted six times in French and a German translation was prepared as well. In 1868, Max Hirsch, a German mechanical engineer, toured England and was much influenced by what he saw of the skilled unions, particularly their attempts to settle disputes amicably, and by their independence from political parties. On his return he organized a new group of liberal unions known as **Hirsch-Duncker Trade Associations**, which were based on these ideas. Similarly, the constitution of the **Trades Union Congress** provided the model for the American Federation of Organized Trades and Labor Unions of the United States and Canada, the forerunner of the American Federation of Labor. In Australia, New Zealand, and Canada, British immigration reinforced Britain as the model for organized labor throughout most of the 19th century.

It was no accident that England, as the first industrial nation in the world, should have been the birthplace of organized labor. In European, if not American, terms it was a land of liberty, as underscored by the Second Reform Act of 1867, which gave the vote to the better-off urban working class, that is, to most of the union members of the time. This early accommodation of labor by the political system, expressed through its alliance with the Liberal Party, marked England off from the rest of Europe and held back the formation of a purely labor party. In other parts of Europe, the political wing of labor was often stronger than its industrial wing.

There were other important differences between the history of British organized labor and that of many other parts of the world. First, British society was divided primarily by social class rather than religion, race, or ethnicity, a fact that eased recruiting. Second, as the center of a global empire up to 1939, British unions were freed from the need to participate in any struggle for national independence. Third, they operated in an advanced and relatively wealthy society, even though the distribution of that wealth was highly uneven.

The Role of the State

The spread of the Industrial Revolution, population growth, and rising literacy during the 19th century gave rise to the well-studied phenomenon of the "rise of the working class." Crude repression, the traditional method used by governments to maintain control, continued in many countries such as **Russia**, but from about the 1860s onwards the need for skilled workers gradually made this option less acceptable. What was needed was a way of encouraging working-class demands and protests into acceptable constitutional channels. By a process of trial and error, organized labor gradually became accepted by a number of governments as one way of achieving this goal. In various ways, often unintentional, the form of organized labor was influenced by the state. This can be shown by the responses of governments to the growth of organized labor in a number of countries.

In Britain, the supportive response of the British government to the moderate trade unionism of the 1860s and 1870s (as indicated also by the Trade Union Act of 1871) contrasted with its hostility to the radicalism of Chartism in the 1840s. It was this moderation that earned the labor unions the scorn of Karl Marx and Friedrich Engels. The growth of unions, especially moderate ones, seems to have been implicitly encouraged by governments in a number of European countries with the object of reducing support for socialism. In France, the government legalized labor unions in 1884 and provided financial assistance to the *Bourses du Travail* (the coordinating centers for local unions) provided they remained out of the control of extremists. This was in the starkest contrast to the state's violent suppression of the unemployed during the "June Days" in 1848 and the bloodshed of the Paris Commune in 1871. In **Germany**, the labor unions operated in a legal twilight but operated nevertheless if they avoided politics; as well, Bismarck attempted to undercut the threat of socialism not just by banning the Social Democratic Party (1878) but also by a number of social reforms such as sickness insurance (1883). In this sense, organized labor, far from operating in a political void, was the target of manipulation by the political culture.

Even benign actions by the state affected organized labor. For example, the introduction of compulsory conciliation and arbitration procedures in Australia and **New Zealand** assisted the growth of unions by easing the process of gaining recognition from employers for bargaining but also encouraged an unduly large number of unions.

The spread of the Industrial Revolution from about 1870 and the economic and social changes it brought challenged the social order.

Industrial and urban growth fed the growth of organized labor and raised awkward questions about the distribution of wealth, political reform, and, ultimately, what form future society should take. Radical political creeds arose to offer answers—anarchism, socialism, **syndicalism**, and Marxist-Leninism—creeds that continued to stimulate and divide organized labor throughout most of the 20th century and made them a continuous object of attention by the state. During World War I governments needed the active cooperation of organized labor to maintain the high level of armaments production to fight the war. In the United Kingdom, France, Germany, and the United States, organized labor enjoyed a degree of acceptance by the state that it had not previously enjoyed. In the United Kingdom, France, and the United States, organized labor was courted by the highest levels of government and co-opted into the war effort.

The economic difficulties of the 1920s and 1930s brought new pressures to bear on the relations between the state and organized labor that were resolved by widely differing methods. In France (1936), formal accommodations between government, employers, and unions were agreed to, which had long-lasting results for organized labor. In **Norway** (1935), **Switzerland** (1937), and **Sweden** (1938), employers and organized labor came to agreements that had the support of their governments.

Fascism was the other response to the economic problems of the interwar years. With its emphasis on centralized control justified on the grounds of maintaining national unity, fascism was hostile to any independent source of political power. As such, organized labor was a leading victim of fascist repression. German labor leaders were among the first inmates of Dachau concentration camp. In **Italy** (1924), Germany (1933), and **Japan** (1940), organized labor was incorporated into the apparatus of totalitarian government, examples that were copied by **Brazil** (1931), **Greece** (1931), **Portugal** (1933), and **Yugoslavia** (1935). That said, fascist policies had an enduring impact on organized labor. In Italy, the fascist legacy to organized labor consisted of the legal recognition of unions, a unitary labor organization, compulsory financial contributions, and legally binding collective agreements. In Germany, the forcible organization of labor into national industry groups was a powerful precedent for the simplified labor union structure of the post-1945 era.

During the Cold War, democratic governments intervened in the affairs of organized labor, overtly and covertly, throughout the world to resist communist influence in countries like Italy. Of lasting significance in this period was the creation of the **International**

Confederation of Free Trade Unions in London in November 1949 as a counter organization to the communist **World Federation of Trade Unions**. In these ways organized labor has been shaped by the actions of governments (*see* **Government Control of Organized Labor**).

The Growth of Organized Labor

The growth of organized labor is one of the unsung success stories of modern world history. In 1870, there were about 790,000 labor union members in the world; in 1900, there were about 5 million; in 1970, there were 98 million; and, in 2001 there were 166 million. As these figures exclude communist and other authoritarian countries where unions are not allowed to bargain freely, they are all the more impressive. Few other world movements have grown so much without the use of force or direction from above.

Of the 790,000 union members in the world in about 1870, most lived in Britain (289,000) or the United States (300,000). France had about 120,000 members and Germany plus the Austro-Hungarian Empire had about 81,000. Labor unions also existed in Australia and Canada, but their membership was tiny, probably no more than 10,000 in total. Union growth after 1870 was neither steady nor sure. The original base of recruitment, the skilled trades, was expanded to include employees in mass employment such as the railroads, laborers, and the less skilled and finally, from 1890 onwards, groups like **women** and white-collar employees. Even so, the rise in world union members was heavily dependent upon the condition of the trade cycle and upon events peculiar to countries with large memberships. For instance, in the United States, union membership reached its pre-1900 peak in the mid-1880s with about a million members—or 53 percent of the world total—but then fell to 869,000 by 1900. This collapse was brought about by internal conflict over what form organized labor should take, in particular, the fight between the **American Federation of Labor** and the **Knights of Labor**. In contrast, union membership in Britain advanced from 581,000 in the mid-1880s to 2 million by 1900.

The 20th century opened with a blossoming of organized labor. Between 1900 and 1905 labor unions appeared in Japan (although they were quickly suppressed) and among indigenous workers in Africa (Lagos, Nigeria), the **Philippines**, and in the Dutch East Indies (**Indonesia**). Union membership grew also in Southern and Eastern Europe until, by 1913, there were 14 million union members in the world, a remarkable development compared to 50 years before even if organized labor remained a largely European movement. Of the 14 million union members in 1913, 76 percent were in Europe; of the remaining 3 million, most were in North America or Australia. This meant that unionism was essentially European in structure and outlook. Although the International Federation of Trade Unions tried to build up a truly international membership, in practice it remained a largely European organization during its life from 1901 to 1945.

Less obvious, but more serious, was the relatively small proportion of employees enrolled by organized labor in most countries. In 1913, only Australia (31 percent) had more than 20 percent of its employees in labor unions. Within Europe, the highest levels of union enrollment of employees were in Germany (18 percent), Netherlands (17 percent), and Britain (16 percent). With 9 percent of its employees in labor unions in 1913, the United States was comparable with Sweden and Norway (each with 8 percent). Not only did organized labor embrace a small minority of employees, its membership was heavily concentrated in mining, manufacturing, construction, and transportation. Further, the vast majority of union members were males in blue-collar occupations.

Between 1913 and 1920, there was an explosion in world union membership based on high inflation—largely caused by military expenditure—falling real wages, and the recruitment of large numbers of white-collar workers such as teachers. It was a period of wartime dislocation and political revolution. By 1920, organized labor could claim 44 million members worldwide, three times what it had been in 1913. Of the gain of 30 million, 18 million occurred in Western Europe, 8 million in Eastern Europe, and less than 4 million in the Americas. For the first time too, organized labor emerged in India and Japan.

The year 1920 was a high point in the strength of organized labor, with about half of the employees in Germany, Austria, and Britain belonging to unions, a reflection of their governments' need to enlist the support of organized labor to fight World War I. Considered by region, 63 percent of union members were in Western Europe, 19 percent in Eastern Europe, and 15 percent in the Americas.

Organized labor's new importance was officially recognized by the formation of the **International Labour Organisation** in 1919. After 1920, the fortunes of organized labor fell considerably. By 1930, it could claim only 31 million members worldwide, a net loss of 13 million members. The economic crisis of the 1920s and the revived hostility of the employers cost labor dearly. Those countries where organized labor had grown the most in the period from 1913 to 1920 were those that suffered the largest losses after 1920: Germany (3.6 million), Italy (3.4 million), United Kingdom (3.5 million), and United States (1.6 million). In all, European unions lost 16 million members in the 1920s and North America lost 1.6 million. These losses were only partly offset by membership gains in Latin America, Asia, and Australasia of 3.6 million.

With the rise of fascism and the onset of the Depression, the growth of organized labor ceased. In Italy, the unions' declining labor membership enabled their suppression by Mussolini in 1924. In 1933, the free unions of Germany with their 5.6 million members were snuffed out and many of their leaders arrested and imprisoned. In both Italy and Germany, the fascist government suppressed labor movements that were already in decline. The remaining independent labor unions of Japan were suppressed in 1940. Ironically, it was the 1930s that saw a rebirth of American labor unions, whose membership during the decade rose from 3.2 to 7.9 million between 1930 and 1940, even though this growth only restored the proportion of employees in unions to about where it had been in 1920. The other main areas of labor union membership growth were in Britain and Scandinavia.

After World War II, organized labor became embroiled in Cold War politics. In 1945, the former international body of organized labor, the International Federation of Trade Unions, dissolved itself and was replaced by the World Federation of Trade Unions, which was the first truly global organization of labor unions. It lasted in this form until 1949, when the noncommunist countries withdrew and set up their own international body, the International Confederation of Free Trade Unions, whose membership rose from 48 million at its formation to 156 million by 2001. Meanwhile, the World Federation of Trade Unions continued as an organization.

What happened to these international labor bodies was probably unavoidable given the international climate of the times, but what was more significant and encouraging was the strong revival of organized labor in Germany, Italy, and Japan. By 1950 these three countries had a total labor union membership of 16 million or a quarter of the world's membership. The United States also continued to have a growing labor union membership: from 7.9 million in 1940 to 13.4 million in 1950.

The 30 years from 1950 to 1980 marked another high point in the history of organized labor, with world membership growing from 64 to 118 million. The industries where organized labor was traditionally strong, such as manufacturing and other areas of mass employment, grew to meet the demands of postwar economies. Labor also enjoyed a far more sympathetic political environment, particularly in Western European democracies where **social-democratic, socialist, and labor parties** governed or were major political players. Yet even in the time of its greatest strength, the structural problems that have always bedeviled organized labor remained. Since the 1960s, much of the growth in the labor force has been in the service sector—that is, those industries other than agriculture, mining, and manufacturing—industries with many women and white-collar workers, groups that organized labor either neglected or found difficult to recruit.

Two broad observations may be made about the course of the history of organized labor between 1870 and 1980. First, union membership has grown mightily, if unevenly, from lowly beginnings in hostile political and legal environments to a position of strength where governments had to take account of its views. This growth was achieved by democratic means. Unlike communism, organized labor has come from below rather than being imposed from above. Second, through its political struggles, organized labor has helped change society for the better by fighting for improved working conditions and greater sharing of the gains of economic growth. These successes need to be remembered in any assessment of the history of organized labor. It is also vital to appreciate the many internal difficulties faced by organized labor, which are the subject of the next section.

THE CHARACTER OF ORGANIZED LABOR

The Divisions of Organized Labor
So far, it has been convenient to view organized labor as a single entity to show how it developed and spread as a world movement. But organized labor has never been a single entity, and its divisions are as important as its similarities both within and between countries. Organized labor has always reflected faithfully its country of origin in all important respects.

The most widespread division in the history of organized labor has been that between the skilled and the less skilled (*see* **Craft Unions**). As has already been mentioned, the strongest labor unions developed among groups of skilled men, and it was these groups that were largely responsible for its survival before the 1880s. Skilled men, of course, had many advantages over the less skilled; they could command higher pay, were harder to replace, and so had more bargaining power with an employer. Further, they had already made a substantial investment of time and effort in their employment through the apprenticeship system.

As a result, it was all too easy for the skilled to look down on or fear the less skilled, rather than make common cause with them. At the same time, the less skilled presented a potential threat to skilled men, especially when technological change reduced the skills needed for a job and opened the way for the less skilled to be trained to replace them.

This problem has been a critical issue for organized labor throughout much of its history. It came to the forefront spectacularly with the Knights of Labor in the United States in the 1880s; the Knights were the first labor organization in the world to recruit the unskilled as well as the skilled. The problem gave rise to debate about how organized labor should be organized, by industry or by occupation. An industry-based union implied that all within that industry could be eligible to be recruited into a union, whereas unions based on craft or skilled occupations implied that many employees within the industry would be left out (*see* **Industrial Unions**). As labor unions emerged among the traditionally less skilled, new problems arose. The American Federation of Labor, for example, the body that only accepted affiliates organized along craft lines, also included unions of unskilled employees even in the late 19th century. With union growth came the problem of which unions had the right to recruit which employees. With no clear answer in many cases, there was often much conflict between unions about who had recruitment rights. As a result, national labor federations often had to adjudicate in interunion disputes.

The second divide in organized labor was between **blue-collar** and white-collar workers and the distinctions of social class this implied. In late 19th-century Germany, it was called the *Kragenlinie* or collar line. Although white-collar unionism began to emerge in a number of countries in the 1900s, it was generally moderate in character and aloof from manual union organizations and their concerns until after 1945 (*see* **White-Collar Unionism**).

As well as these sources of division, organized labor has been and is divided by religion. Before World War II, organized labor in Western Europe (apart from Britain) was divided by religion, specifically into Catholic and non-Catholic movements, with the non-Catholic unions largely being socialist in outlook. Since 1945, with the exception of Germany and Austria, this division has persisted in continental Europe despite efforts to unify the movements in France, Belgium, the Netherlands, and Switzerland (*see* **Catholicism**).

Politics has been a fourth source of division in organized labor. Before 1920, the dominant form of political division was between socialists (of varying degrees) and nonsocialists. After 1920, communism became an important and sometimes dominant element in labor union politics. More generally, the persistent political division in labor unions was between right wing and left wing. **Race and ethnicity** has been, and is, a fifth source of division in organized labor. In some countries, notably South Africa, it assumed huge proportions up to the 1990s.

Ways and Means: Achieving Objectives

Since the late 19th century, organized labor, despite its divisions, has sought to change the rules by which work is governed. The means for achieving this goal has been through **collective bargaining**, preferably to have as an outcome a signed, legally enforceable agreement that sets out wages and conditions of employment. Although labor disputes attract publicity and may be dramatically or even violently conducted, in democratic societies the process of collective bargaining is more usually slow, detailed, and dull. When organized labor is unable to secure a collective agreement, it may resort to a withdrawal of labor (the strike), but this is a relatively rare event outside of certain industries such as mining, transportation, and metals manufacturing.

Where collective bargaining is not permitted or fails, organized labor may turn to politics for assistance to achieve its objectives. It may seek to lobby parties—for example, the use of political action committees in the United States—or, if this fails to deliver satisfactory outcomes, to form its own political parties, as happened in Australia, Britain, and Scandinavia (*see* **Australian Labor Party**; **British Labour Party**). Since the 1950s, international labor organizations have become adept in forming specific organizations to lobby larger political organizations to seek a voice for labor or to press particular claims (*see*, for example, **Asia-Pacific Labour Network**).

For most of the past century, organized labor has not tried to change the essential features of capitalism, but it has tried to mitigate its worst effects. By slowly chipping away at the economic system though improved labor laws and collective agreements, organized labor has brought about incremental, but important economic and social changes that have provided benefits that extend well beyond its immediate membership. Indeed, organized labor is one of the principal forces for economic fairness in most democratic societies.

An Assessment of Organized Labor

Given the divisions within organized labor and the other formidable obstacles it has had to face, it is surprising that it has survived and grown at all. The key to its success may be found in its continual concern with the practical and attainable rather than the theoretical or ideal. Although the history of organized labor is punctuated by widespread and often short-lived social eruptions, to survive as organizations, labor unions have to become recognized, to make rules and agreements governing how work is be performed and paid, and to seek change in an incremental rather than revolutionary fashion. This is the discipline of reality, of having to deal with the world as it is rather than how it ought to be, as advocated by political or social theorists. This is not to say that organized labor has not been often profoundly influenced by ideas, but it typically assesses those ideas in terms of their practicality.

Whether they admit it or not, labor unions are political beings. By definition, they represent a potential challenge to the existing distribution of power, goods, and services in society, which accounts for their repression by government throughout much of history. They might be won over by government, but that implicit challenge is always present. Their participation in the political process can take many forms such as lobbying governments or simply providing career stepping stones for upwardly mobile middle-class aspirants, as has happened through labor parties in countries such as Britain and Australia or in a number of African nations since the 1960s.

Unions are also primarily defensive in character. Typically, they work to preserve and protect the pay and conditions of members. Strikes are generally a last resort of unions and occur when other measures have failed. Periods of inflation are especially productive of labor disputes because they upset the distribution of real wages across and within the employed labor force. This was particularly evident in most countries between about 1910 and 1920, and in the 1970s. Similarly, in periods of rising prosperity, unions seek to gain what they see as their share through strikes for improved pay and conditions.

Union membership size, although important, is no guide in itself to bargaining strength with employers. Some numerically large unions representing relatively poorly paid employees may have little bargaining power, while others, particularly those in key industries such as transportation and communications, may have a lot. Even so, few unions are powerful enough in their own right to be able to bargain effectively on a large scale (for example, with governments).

Organized labor learned long ago to cooperate through national bodies (*see* **Trades Union Congress**). None of this is to say that labor unions are ideal organizations. Like any institution they can become corrupt if their leaders pursue their own or some other body's interests to the neglect of their members. Where this has occurred, such as in the celebrated case of the **Teamsters** in the United States in the 1950s and 1960s, it receives widespread attention but, by and large, these are exceptions. Despite all the dire predictions to the contrary, unions continue to go about their work and have remained democratic institutions. This is not to say that all members participate in their activities all of the time; usually union activities are confined to the committed few, but unions do offer the possibility for all to participate if they choose to do so. As Germany and Austria since 1945 show, organized labor can also be a powerful force for promoting and sustaining democracy.

ORGANIZED LABOR SINCE 1980

Global Economic Change and the "Crisis of Labor"

Since 1980 organized labor in most of the Western world has been on the defensive. The topic that has received the most publicity and pessimistic academic study has been the "crisis of labor," that is, the decline of union membership and power in Western countries, particularly in the United States and the United Kingdom. The recession of 1981-1982 greatly reduced employment in industries where organized labor had traditionally been strong, such as **coal mining**, steel, and manufacturing as a whole. General economic problems enabled organized labor to be blamed by conservative governments and their economic advisers in the United States and the United Kingdom as barriers to economic efficiency. There is a fundamental cultural clash between the advocates of free-market forces as an economic policy with its emphasis on deregulation, and organized labor, which is passionately in favor of regulation and government intervention to counteract market failures.

Many economic trends adverse to organized labor since 1980 have been evident. They include a fall in the proportion of well-paid, full-time jobs with benefits; the end of reliable career ladders or long-term employment outside of government service; the increasing use of contractors and the decline of the employer/employee legal relationship; competition from Third World countries (especially from their **export processing zones**) to employees in Western economies and the broader phenomenon of **globalization**; and major shifts in employment away from manufacturing towards the service sector and away from blue-collar workers to white-collar/managerial jobs. The period has also seen a decline in the quality of working life, characterized by longer working hours and greater insecurity of employment. Technological change in the form of the better use of computers in the workplace has brought rising productivity but also a spread of the likelihood of unemployment to white-collar employees.

Ironically, against this gloomy background there has been a considerable improvement in the quality of statistical information about the membership of organized labor (*see* **Labor Statistics**). Household surveys in Australia, Canada, the United Kingdom, and the United States show consistently that from the 1980s to the present, union members have been a relatively privileged part of the labor force. They tended to have higher incomes, higher levels of benefits, and were more likely to work for government or larger enterprises than nonunion members.

Earnings data for Australia, Canada, and the United States show that employees who are union members earn more than nonunion members, although the differential is far higher in the United States (*see* **Union Wage Differential**). In 2002, full-time male employees in Australia who were union members had a median income that was 7 percent more than nonunion members, compared to 16 percent in the United States. For women, these differences were even greater. Australian full-time female employees who were union members had a median income that was 9 percent above those of nonunion employees in 2002 compared to 24 percent in the United States (*see* Appendix F, Table 15). It has been suggested that this large differential in earnings has been one of the reasons for the steep fall in the proportion of employees who belong to unions in the United States. In 2002, only 13.2 percent of United States employees were union members, a level comparable with that of 1935.

The net outcome of all these trends has been a significant fall in the number of union members in Western countries. Between 1980 and 2001, the number of union members in Western Europe fell from 49.3 to 39.6 million and in North America from 23.5 to 19.3 million.

Although the general economic trends of the past 20 years have been unfavorable to organized labor, they are not the sole reason for the declining density of union membership among employees. All too often the leadership of organized labor has made the defense of the labor union as an organization their first priority. Amalgamations of unions protect the edifice of organizations by making them more efficient but may be detrimental to the interests of the members at the grassroots. Similarly, unduly close relationships between the leadership or organized labor and government of the day can too easily lead to the neglect of the interests of members. In the final analysis, the only resource organized labor can trade is the wages and working conditions of its members.

The Third World: Some Cause for Optimism

Organized labor has always faced huge, if not impossible, obstacles in Third World countries, and the economic difficulties of the 1980s provided a convenient excuse for the repression of unions as impediments to economic growth. In 1984, the International Confederation of Free Trade Unions began to conduct annual surveys of violations of trade union rights in the world. These reports make for harrowing reading; they document the murder, torture, and imprisonment of union leaders and the denial of official recognition of labor unions that are not controlled by the government.

Needless to say, those countries with the worst record of human rights also have appalling records of the violation of trade union rights. Despite all this, organized labor has grown in many Third World countries over the past 20 years. In Africa, organized labor grew from 1.1 to 12.9 million members between 1980 and 2001; in Asia, membership growth was from 23.4 to 34.0 million. In Latin America, membership growth was from 14.6 to 17.6 million. There are indications that governments may come to realize that political freedom is an indispensable condition to sustained economic growth.

Eastern Europe: The Unexpected Revival

Eastern Europe has been the unexpected chapter in the history of international organized labor since 1980. In 1920, there were about 8.5 million union members in Eastern Europe or about 19 percent of the world's total. There were only 2.5 million by 1930, and thereafter independent organized labor effectively disappeared in a welter of repression first by fascism and then by communism.

The formation of "Solidarity" in September 1980 was a milestone in the emergence of independent organized labor, not just in Poland but for what it foreshadowed for Eastern Europe as a whole. The 1990s saw the demise of communism and the emergence of organized labor in the Baltic States and in Russia itself, developments barely imaginable in 1980. In 2001, there were 37.5 million union members in Eastern Europe or about 23 percent of the world's total, that is, comparable with its share in 1920. In November 2000, the

International Confederation of Free Trade Unions made the historic decision to admit three labor federations as affiliates with their combined membership of 30 million. It was the first time that any Russian labor unions had been admitted to membership of a democratic, international labor organization.

In summary then, despite a sea change of adverse economic trends and well-publicized declines of organized labor members in Western economies, the world membership of organized labor has increased from 118 to 166 million—a rise of 41 percent—between 1980 and 2001. A loss of nearly 10 million members in Western Europe in this period has been more than offset by gains of 37 million in Eastern Europe, 11 million in Africa, 10 million in Asia, and 3 million in Latin America. Of course, this membership growth will take time to translate into the kind of power and favorable institutional arrangements enjoyed by unions in Western Europe and quite possibly may never eventuate at all. Nevertheless, this unpublicized growth testifies to the dynamism of organized labor in a global economy that has undergone huge changes since 1980.

CONCLUSION

By any measure, organized labor has had an extraordinary history in the 20th century. Certainly, the facts of its growth are undeniable. In 1900, there were just 5 million union members, but 166 million by 2001. In 1900, Western and Eastern Europe accounted for 82 percent of these members, but only 48 percent by 2001. The Americas held 16 percent of the world's union members in 1900 and 22 percent by 2001. Outside of Europe and the Americas, organized labor has grown impressively from 133,000 in 1900 to 52 million by 2001, taking its share of world membership to 31 percent.

Labor unions came into existence because they were wanted. As economies industrialized, so the stress on society grew. The upsetting of power relationships and the redistribution of wealth that came in the wake of industrialization brought friction. Everything that has happened to organized labor since 1980—membership decline, defeats in major strikes, a feeling that it is no longer needed, the threat of technological change, the transferring of jobs to low-wage countries—has all happened before in some form. One thing that seems constant in the history of organized labor is the temptation for employers and conservative governments to take advantage of its weaknesses to attack unions, a policy that can sometimes revive them.

Organized labor is essentially about economic democracy, and how governments treat labor unions is usually a fair indication of the real level of democracy in their society. True, organized labor can cause disruption through strikes, but the economic cost pales before the cost of industrial accidents, high labor turnover, and the lower productivity of sullen employees. Properly consulted, unions can be a force for higher productivity and economic achievement through reducing labor turnover and making for more contented employees. Industrial society has many built-in conflicts that create the demand for unions. Organized labor can be, and has been, frequently suppressed, but unless the mainsprings of its grievances can be satisfied, it will not go away.

There is nothing new in the unions' quest for a more just world. In Greek mythology, Plutos was the god of wealth. To punish mankind, Zeus, the ruler of the gods, blinded Pluto so that he would distribute wealth without regard to merit. In his last extant play, the ancient Greek playwright Aristophanes considered what would happen if Pluto were cured of his blindness; in the play the cured god distributes his benefits only to the deserving. Two and a half millennia later, the attainment of a fairer world still eludes us.

THE DICTIONARY

-A-

ACCORD. *See* UNION-GOVERNMENT AGREEMENTS.

ACTIVITIES. *See* COLLECTIVE BARGAINING; OCCUPA-TIONAL HEALTH AND SAFETY; POLITICAL ACTION COMMITTEES; POLITICS; SOCIAL-DEMOCRATIC, SOCIAL-IST, AND LABOR PARTIES.

AFGHANISTAN. There is no history of organized labor in Afghani-stan, as the country has lacked all of the prerequisites for its devel-opment, being economically backward, politically repressive or un-stable, and with a society based largely on ethnic and tribal loyalties. It has never been represented in the **International Con-federation of Free Trade Unions** (ICFTU).

AFRICAN REGIONAL ORGANIZATION (AFRO). AFRO is an international regional labor organization established by the **Inter-national Confederation of Free Trade Unions** (ICFTU) to repre-sent its affiliated members in Africa. The idea for AFRO originated from a recommendation of the fifth congress of the ICFTU, which was held in Tunis, **Tunisia**, in 1957, but AFRO was not formally established until November 1960. In December 1997, AFRO held a pan-African conference on **child labor**. In 2001, the ICFTU had 45 country affiliates in Africa with a combined membership of 12.9 million. *See also* TRADE UNION CONFEDERATION OF ARAB MAGHREB WORKERS.

AGRICULTURE. Despite its historical importance as an employer of labor in most countries, labor unions have been a relatively minor feature of labor relations in agriculture in 20th-century history.

23

Only a few percent of labor union members in the **United Kingdom** were employed in agriculture between 1900 and 1950; in 2001, it was only 0.4 percent. In contrast, labor unions among plantation workers in Central and South America have been an important part of national labor movements. Agricultural labor in these countries has been traditionally characterized by low pay and poor working conditions, and subject to frequent violence by employers and military governments. *See also* INTERNATIONAL FEDERATION OF PLANTATION, AGRICULTURAL, AND ALLIED WORKERS.

ALBANIA. Ruled by the Ottomans to 1912 and economically backward, organized labor in Albania emerged only from 1901 when shoemakers at Shkodra and longshoremen at Durrës conducted localized strikes. In 1920, Albania finally became independent and the first national labor union was formed among teachers in 1924. In the 1930s, Korça became the center of organized labor in Albania. Further development of organized labor was stifled by Italian and German occupation (1939-1944) and by the establishment of a severe Stalinist regime under Enver Hoxha. Although the constitution of 1946 encouraged the formation of labor unions, this trend was reversed in 1950 when the constitution made the unions subordinate to the ruling communist party.

The totalitarian regime began to crumble in 1985. In 1990, the ruling communist oligarchy agreed to the creation of other parties. In December 1990, there was a round of strikes and in January 1991 strikes were legalized. In February 1991 the first independent labor unions were formed as well as a national labor federation. In October 1991, the legal status of unions and their contracts with employers were upheld by legislation. The right to strike was restricted by labor laws in 1991, and the government arrested strikers in 1993. However, the economic backwardness of Albania continued. A mission to Albania by the **International Confederation of Free Trade Unions** (ICFTU) estimated unemployment at about 25 percent. There was a **general strike** on September 16, 1996, over price rises and demands for pay increases linked to inflation. In 2002, Albania was not a member of the ICFTU.

ALGERIA. A colony of **France** from 1830 to July 3, 1962, the first labor unions were formed by French settlers and their example provided the model for the emergence of organized labor among native

Algerians from the 1940s. The *Union Générale des Travailleurs Algériens* (General Workers' Union of Algeria), (UGTA) was formed in 1956 and affiliated with the **International Confederation of Free Trade Unions** (ICFTU) in the same year. It remained an affiliate until 1963 when it withdrew; in this affiliation period the UGTA claimed a membership of 8.9 million. In 1959, Aissar Idir, the first general secretary of the UGTA, died in a French military prison following his detention and torture. From 1963 to 1988, the UGTA was under the control of the *Front de Liberation National* (National Liberation Front), the political party that ruled Algeria. The UGTA restored internal democracy and asserted its autonomy by breaking all links with political parties. The ICFTU sent several missions to Algeria between 1989 and 1995. In 1996, the UGTA was readmitted to the ICFTU as a national, genuinely independent, and democratic organization with 1,350,000 members. The independent stance of the UGTA, particularly its calls for social justice, has made it the object of attacks by Islamic fundamentalists and the government. Between 1992 and 1994, 300 members of the UGTA were killed by Islamic fundamentalists. On January 28, 1997, Abdelhak Benhamouda, aged 51, the staunchly democratic leader of the UGTA, was assassinated outside the organization's headquarters. In 2001, the UGTA declared a membership of 1.4 million to the ICFTU. In 2002, the ICFTU's survey of **violations of trade union rights** noted that the state of emergency decree of 1992 was still in force and the right to strike was limited. It also noted that labor unions could only be formed with the approval of the government.

ALLIANCE FOR LABOR ACTION. The Alliance for Labor Action was the name of a campaign initiated by **Walter Reuther**, the president of the **United Auto Workers**, in alliance with the **Teamsters**, to recruit new union members among **white-collar** employees and in service industries in 1968. The Alliance was formed outside of the **American Federation of Labor-Congress of Industrial Organizations** (AFL-CIO), from which the United Auto Workers had disaffiliated (July 1968) and from which the Teamsters had been expelled (1957). Based in Altanta, Georgia, the Alliance's campaign had poor results, partly because of hostility from the AFL-CIO, which regarded the Alliance as a rival organization. After Reuther's death in an airplane crash in 1970, the Alliance lost momentum and was disbanded in December 1971.

AMALGAMATED ENGINEERING UNION (AEU). The AEU was formed in the **United Kingdom** from the **amalgamation** of the Amalgamated Society of Engineers (ASE) and several other smaller unions on July 1, 1920. For most of its history, the ASE had only admitted skilled engineering employees, that is, men who had completed an **apprenticeship**, but in 1926 it began to admit lesser skilled workers, mainly because of the effects of technological change and also to counter competition from unions such as the **Workers' Union.** By 1939, it had 390,900 members compared to 168,000 in 1933. World War II boosted the demand for engineering workers. In 1942, **women** were admitted to the ranks of the AEU for the first time; by 1943 they made up 139,000 of its 825,000 members. In 1943 too, the AEU became Britain's second largest union, a position it retained for most of the postwar period.

The AEU continued to grow with the economy and also through amalgamation with other unions, notably with the 72,900 strong Amalgamated Union of Foundry Workers (formed in 1946) in January 1968. Between 1962 and 1979, the membership of the AEU rose from 982,200 to a peak of 1,483,400. In 1971, the Technical, Administrative, and Supervisory Section (TASS) joined the AEU, which renamed itself the Amalgamated Union of Engineering Workers; in 1988 the TASS left to join the Association of Scientific, Technical, and Managerial Staffs to form the Manufacturing, Science and Finance Union and the AEU reverted to its former title. During 1991, the AEU and the other members of the **Confederation of Shipbuilding and Engineering Unions** won a campaign that reduced the working week from 39 to 37.5 hours for many of its members. On May 1, 1992, the AEU merged with the Electrical, Telecommunications, and Plumbing Union to become the Amalgamated Engineering and Electrical Union. Between 1986 and 1994, the membership of the AEU fell from 858,000 to 781,000. In 2001, the AEU had a membership of 728,200 before it merged with the Manufacturing, Science, and Finance Union to form **Amicus** in January 2002. *See also IG METALL.*

AMALGAMATED METAL WORKERS' UNION (AMWU). The AMWU has been one of the strongest labor unions in **Australia**. It began as the New South Wales branch of the English-based **Amalgamated Society of Engineers** in 1852 with 27 members. From 1920 to 1973, it was called the Amalgamated Engineering Union and the AMWU from 1973 to 1990. Its members were skilled metal workers, and it was one of the few unions to offer members sickness, accident, unemployment, and strike payments. From 1915, it began to admit lesser skilled metal workers into its ranks. Between 1920 and 1969, its membership rose from 16,000 to 149,300. In 1968, it formally severed its links with its British parent union. After 1945, the AMWU was one of the leading unions in gaining higher pay and better conditions for its members though **labor disputes**. From 1972, it grew by **amalgamation** with other unions, namely the Association of Drafting, Supervisory, and Technical Employees (1990) and the Vehicle Builders Employees' Federation (originally formed in 1912) in 1993. In February 1995, it merged with the Printing and Kindred Industries Union (formed in 1916) and was renamed the Australian Manufacturing Workers' Union, which claimed a membership of 200,000 in 2000.

AMALGAMATED SOCIETY OF CARPENTERS AND JOINERS (ASCJ). A British, and international union, the ASCJ was formed in London in June 1860 with 618 members following a strike in 1859-1860 to win the nine-hour working day. The employers responded with a lockout and a demand that the strikers sign an undertaking that they not join a labor union. The strong financial support given by the other unions, particularly the **Amalgamated Society of Engineers**, caused the employers to withdraw their demand. Membership of the ASCJ rose to 10,178 by 1870 and to 17,764 by 1880, making it one of the most powerful craft unions.

The ASCJ was also an international union; it established branches in Ireland (1866), **United States** (1867), Scotland (1871), **Canada** (1872), **New Zealand** (1875), **Australia** (Sydney, 1875; Adelaide, 1878; and Melbourne, 1879), and **South Africa** (1881). In Australia, the New South Wales branch of the ASCJ claimed 33,000 members in 1890. In the United States the ASCJ provided a model for the formation of the Brotherhood of Carpenters and Joiners in Chicago in 1881 by Peter J. McGuire. The Brotherhood proved to be far more successful than the ASCJ in recruiting members. In 1923, the Canadian branches of the ASCJ were closed and merged with the American Brotherhood. In 1911, the English ASCJ merged with the Associated Carpenters and Joiners' Society of Scotland (founded in 1861). Further amalgamations followed that transformed the original **craft union** into an **industrial union** that eventually gave rise to the Union of Construction and Allied Technical Trades in 1971. In Australia, the ASCJ retained its separate identity until 1992.

AMALGAMATED SOCIETY OF ENGINEERS (ASE). Since 1851, engineering unions have played a central role in the history of organized labor in the **United Kingdom**. The first continuous labor organization in the engineering industry was the Journeymen Steam Engine, Machine Makers, and Millwrights' Friendly Society formed in Manchester in 1826 and known as "Old Mechanics." The ASE was largely formed from the merger of "Old Mechanics" and the Smiths' Benevolent Sick and Burial Society in 1851. Membership began at 5,000 and reached 11,000 by the end of 1851. The formation of the **Amalgamated Society of Engineers** (ASE) in 1851 was hailed as a pivotal event in the history of organized labor by Beatrice and Sidney James Webb as marking the first of "model" unions with well-developed organizations, high contribution fees, and sickness, unemployment, superannuation, and funeral benefits. The ASE was the target of a nationwide lockout by employers in 1852. Defeated, some members left Britain to form a branch of the ASE in New South Wales, **Australia**, in 1852. In 1851 the ASE founded its first branch in **Ireland**; it also set up branches in **Canada** (1853), the **United States** (1861), **New Zealand** (1864), and **South Africa** (1891). With the creation of these branches, the ASE became an international as well as British union, an example later followed by the **Amalgamated Society of Carpenters and Joiners**.

In 1897-1898, the ASE suffered an important defeat by a lockout organized by the engineering employers, an event that led it to become a prime mover in the formation of the **General Federation of Trade Unions** in 1899. During the lockout over £28,000 was given by European unions (half came from German unions) and overseas branches of the ASE. Faced with intense competition from American unions, the ASE closed down its American branches in 1920, whereas in Australia, the ASE went on to become one of the major unions as the **Amalgamated Metal Workers' Union**. In 1913, the ASE had 17,000 members (or about 10 percent of its total membership) in nine countries outside of Britain. In Britain, the membership of the ASE grew from 100,000 in 1910 to 174,300 in 1914. As a result of the demand for munitions during World War I, membership reached 298,800 in 1918. In 1916, George Nicoll Barnes (1859-1940), a former secretary of the ASE, joined Lloyd

George's wartime government as minister for pensions. From 1905, the ASE supported the creation of a single union for the engineering industry and in 1918 persuaded 17 unions in the industry to conduct ballots for **amalgamation**; nine of these bodies agreed to amalgamate to form the Amalgamated Engineering Union. In 1920, the ASE had 423,000 members. *See also DEUTSCHER METAL-LARBEITER-VERBAND; FEDERAZIONE ITALIANA OPERAI METALLURGICI.*

AMALGAMATION. Amalgamation, that is, the merging of a labor body with one or more other labor bodies, has been an important feature of the history of organized labor in most countries. In the **United Kingdom** and in countries where organized labor had British roots (**United States, Canada, Australia,** and **New Zealand**), there were by the late 19th century relatively large numbers of unions organized by occupation or **craft**. As these unions tried to recruit new members, they soon came into conflict with other unions, and one of the functions of national labor federations such as the **Trades Union Congress** and the **American Federation of Labor** was often to adjudicate in jurisdictional (or demarcation) disputes between unions. One solution to this problem was amalgamation, which had the added advantage of better-funded union administrations. A number of large unions have grown by amalgamation, notably the British **Transport and General Workers' Union** and the Australian Federated Miscellaneous Workers' Union.

Amalgamation has accounted for much of the general fall in the number of unions in English-speaking countries. In **Australia**, the number of unions officially recorded fell from 573 in 1911 to 132 in 1996. In the **United Kingdom**, the peak number of unions was reached in 1920 when there were 1,384 unions; by 2001 there were only 226 unions. In **New Zealand**, the number of unions was greatest in 1937 at 499, but by 1973 this figure had dropped to 309 and between 1985 and 2000 from 259 to 134. Because of its longer tradition of **industrial unions**, the decline in the number of unions in **Germany** has been comparatively low. In the **United States**, the number of unions affiliated with the **American Federation of Labor-Congress of Industrial Organizations** (AFL-CIO) was only 66 in 2001, compared to 139 in 1955. Between 1956 and 1994, there were 133 union amalgamations, of which 40 occurred between 1986 and 1994. Since the recession of the early 1980s, there has been continual economic pressure on unions generally to maintain their strength through amalgamation. Although amalgamations may benefit labor unions as organizations, it can be detrimental to their relations with their members at the grassroots level. *See also* table 13, appendix F.

AMERICAN FEDERATION OF LABOR (AFL). The AFL was the leading federation of American organized labor from the early 1890s. It grew out of the Federation of Organized Trades and Labor Unions of the United States and Canada, which was formed in Pittsburgh in 1881. Based on the British **Trades Union Congress**, it represented 50,000 members and gave autonomy to affiliated unions. It faced strong competition for members from the **Knights of Labor**. Interunion fighting prompted **Samuel Gompers** to lead a campaign by craft unions that resulted in the setting up of the AFL in Columbus, Ohio, on December 8, 1886. The AFL was based on craft unions, not unions based on industries. This led to jurisdictional or demarcation disputes between member unions over which organizations had the right to recruit certain members, particularly in coal mining, which the **United Mine Workers of America** declared as its preserve in the "Scranton Declaration" in 1901. During World War I, the AFL became the recognized spokesman of American organized labor, and it had the support of the National War Labor Board. By 1920 the AFL represented four million employees, but this gain rapidly fell away in the face of a sustained offensive by employers for the "open shop." The Depression reduced the AFL to only 2.1 million members by 1933. The membership was disproportionately concentrated in coal mining, railroads, and construction. Gompers, the AFL president since its formation (with one short break in 1894), died in 1924 and was succeeded by **William Green**, who was president until his death.

Reflecting its craft union roots, the AFL was always a conservative organization, and dissatisfaction with its neglect of mass production workers enabled **John L. Lewis**, the president of the United Mine Workers' Union, to set up a rival to the AFL based on **industrial unions**, the Committee of Industrial Organizations, in 1935, which officially became the **Congress of Industrial Organizations** (CIO) in 1938. In 1937, the AFL had 3.4 million members compared to 3.7 in the CIO, and in 1938 all CIO member bodies of the AFL were expelled in the **United States** and in **Canada**. Competition for members with the CIO, compounded by its less conservative policies, ensured that rivalry continued with the AFL into the late 1940s. In 1952, **George Meany** was elected president of the AFL, and a formal merger with the CIO occurred in December 1955.

AMERICAN FEDERATION OF LABOR-CONGRESS OF INDUSTRIAL ORGANIZATIONS (AFL-CIO). The AFL-CIO was formed by the merger of the two rival national labor federations in the **United States** in December 1955. The **Taft-Hartley Act** of 1947 and the worsening political climate for organized labor encouraged the two bodies to consider joining forces. The deaths of the presidents of both bodies in 1952 (**William Green** of the American Federation of Labor and **Philip Murray** of the Congress of Industrial Organizations), who were bitter rivals, also made the amalgamation of the two organizations far easier. **George Meany**, who replaced Green as AFL president, worked hard to achieve unity, as did his counterpart in the CIO, **Walter Reuther**. Meany became president of the AFL-CIO, a post he held until 1979. In 1957, the AFL-CIO expelled the **Teamsters** and the Laundry Workers and the Bakers' Union for corruption.

Although officially nonpolitical, the AFL-CIO has always been closely associated with the Democratic Party. In its international dealing in labor affairs, the AFL-CIO has followed conservative policies, as shown by its withdrawal from the **International Confederation of Free Trade Unions** (ICFTU) between 1969 and 1981. Since the early 1980s the AFL-CIO has petitioned the United States government to exclude **China**, **Malaysia**, and **Thailand** from the generalized system of preferences for their abuses of **human rights** and labor union freedom. In 1979, **Joseph Lane Kirkland** succeeded Meany as AFL-CIO president and held the post until 1995. He was succeeded by **John J. Sweeney**.

In 1973, the AFL-CIO had 114 affiliated unions with a total membership of 13.4 million. Between 1991 and 2001, the number of its affiliated unions fell from 89 to 66 and the total membership they represented fell from 13.9 to 13 million. In 2002, the AFL-CIO stated as its mission: "to bring social and economic justice to our nation by enabling working people to have a voice on the job, in government, in a changing global economy and in their communities."

AMERICAN FEDERATION OF STATE, COUNTY, AND MUNICIPAL EMPLOYEES (AFSCME). The AFSCME was founded in 1932 by a small group of **white-collar**, professional state employees in Madison, Wisconsin, as the Wisconsin State Administrative, Clerical, Fiscal and Technical Employees Association. In 1935, with help from the **American Federation of Labor** (AFL), the Association successfully resisted through lobbying and demonstrations draft state legislation aimed at dismantling the state's civil service system and was granted an AFL charter. By the end of 1936, AFSCME had emerged as a national labor union recognized by the AFL and with 10,000 members. Before the 1970s, the AFSCME grew steadily rather than quickly, from 73,000 in 1946 to 237,000 in 1965. In 1958, the AFSCME succeeded in obtaining an executive order from New York City Mayor Robert Wagner that granted **collective bargaining** rights to unions representing city employees. In 1961, President John F. Kennedy issued Executive Order 10988, which legitimized **collective bargaining** for federal employees and helped create a favorable atmosphere for similar demands from all public employees. These developments worked to the advantage of the AFSCME, which used them to get collective bargaining frameworks established in a number of states. Its membership rose from 647,000 in 1975 to a million by 1985 and to 1.3 million by 2002. The AFSCME has a history of using the political process and lobbying to achieve its goals. A survey of AFSCME members in March 2001 found that 53 percent were **women**, 29 percent had household incomes of $60,000 or more, and 31 percent had college or postgraduate education.

AMERICAN FEDERATION OF TEACHERS (AFT). Although formed in April 1916, the origins of the AFT can be traced to the Chicago Federation of Teachers, which was formed in 1897. Faced with a hostile environment, particularly the lack of a framework for **collective bargaining** until the 1960s, membership growth was slow and uncertain, falling from 9,300 to 3,700 between 1920 and 1924. Opportunities for growth in the 1930s were hampered by an internal struggle with **communism**. During World War II, the AFT was able to negotiate contracts with educational authorities in Montana and Washington states and conducted its first strike in St. Paul, Minnesota, in 1946. Between 1939 and 1955, the membership of the AFT grew from 32,100 to 46,000. An early affiliate of the **American Federation of Labor-Congress of Industrial Organizations** (AFL-CIO), the AFT achieved a major success in the early 1960s when its New York locals gained collective bargaining rights and, in 1963, the AFT dropped its no-strike policy. Against a background of discontent over the failure of teachers' salaries to keep up with the private sector, the membership of the AFT climbed from 97,000 to 396,000 between 1965 and 1975 and to 499,00 by 1987. The AFT faced a formidable competitor in its efforts from the **National Education Association** (NEA), which had opposed collective bargaining for teachers before 1963. Efforts to merge the two unions nationally failed because of the affiliation of the AFT with the AFL-CIO. Finally, in 2001, the AFT and the NEA signed the NEAFT Partnership, a pledge by both organizations to "work together on behalf of our members and on behalf of all those whom our members serve." The Partnership recognized the independence of both unions and their commitment "to nurturing and improving public education above all. We are determined to fight for family needs, which must be met in order to make our public schools the equalizer they have been and should be for society. This encompasses quality of life issues, such as health care for all Americans, safe neighborhoods and a caring government." In 2002, the AFT claimed a membership of one million.

AMERICAN LABOR UNION (ALU). The ALU was a short-lived radical organization formed by the Western Federation of Miners in 1898 as the Western Labor Union to supplement the eastern-dominated **American Federation of Labor** (AFL). A **socialist** organization, the ALU attempted to recruit employees ignored by the AFL, that is, the lesser skilled, **women**, and immigrants. The Western Labor Union was fiercely opposed by the AFL and changed its name to the ALU in 1902 to compete directly with the AFL, as advocated by Eugene V. Debs. The ALU also advocated **industrial unions** not **craft unions**, which were the basis of the AFL. Despite its wider recruiting ambitions (it claimed 100,000 members), the core of the ALU was the Western Federation of Miners. The ALU was one of the parent organizations of the **Industrial Workers of the World**, which continued its main aims after 1905, after which time the ALU ceased to exist.

AMICUS. Amicus, from the Latin meaning "friend" or "ally," was formed in the **United Kingdom** from the merger of the Amalgamated Engineering and Electrical Union and the Manufacturing, Science and Finance Union in January 2002. With 1.1 million members, it became the second largest British labor union, after **UNISON**.

ANARCHISM. The term anarchism was derived from an ancient Greek word meaning without government. As a political philosophy, it owed much to Pierre-Joseph Proudhon (1809-1865), who regarded the state as a negative element in society which should be abolished. Mikail Alexandrovich Bakunin (1814-1876), an extremist Russian political thinker, propagandist, and activist, absorbed Proudhon's ideas and was one of the leading anarchists of the nineteenth century. Anarchism, as envisaged by Bakunin, sought the overthrow of the state by a **general strike** and its replacement by democratically run cooperative groups covering the whole economy. It attracted support from certain intellectuals and in rural areas where the local political and economic system was repressive and ignored demands for reform. It drew much support from **Spain** and **Italy**, where it formed a strand of political thinking with **syndicalism**. Because of their association with political violence, anarchists were excluded from mainstream socialism from 1896. **Immigration** spread anarchist ideas to Latin America; in 1919, the anarchists attempted to form a federation covering the whole of Latin America.

In Spain, the anarchists formed their own federation, the *Confederación Nacional del Trabajo* (National Confederation of Labor), and anarchists remained important until their destruction during the Spanish Civil War (1936-1939). From 1940 to about 1990, anarchism failed to attract a significant following, but in the 1990s began to grow again. Much of the violence that occurred in the protests about **globalization** from the late 1990s was committed by self-styled anarchists. *See also* ARGENTINA; CHILE; COMMUNISM; SYNDICALISM.

ANARCHO-SYNDICALISM. *See* ANARCHISM; SYNDICALISM.

ANGOLA. Collective bargaining and strikes were forbidden when Angola was a colony of **Portugal** up to 1974, although organizations among European employees existed from 1897. In the 1960s, the *Liga Geral dos Trabalhadores de Angola* (General Union of Angolan Workers) was an affiliate of the **International Confederation of Free Trade Unions** (ICFTU), but only as an organization in exile. Angola was admitted to full affiliation with the ICFTU in 2002 and claimed 51,000 members. In 2002, the ICFTU's survey of **violations of trade union rights** reported that there was little respect either for independent unions or the right to strike in Angola.

ANTIGUA AND BARBUDA. A colony of the **United Kingdom** to 1981, the legal right to register a labor union was granted in 1939. The Antigua Trades and Labour Union, a labor union and a political party, was the first Antiguan labor organization to take advantage of this law; it registered in 1939 and claimed 7,000 members by 1975. The Antigua Trades and Labour Union was an affiliate of the **International Confederation of Free Trade Unions** (ICFTU) by 1975. In 2001, there were 4,400 union members in Antigua and Barbuda.

APPRENTICESHIP. Apprenticeship is a system of vocational training for teenagers characterized by on-the-job instruction and technical training. In England, apprenticeship was first regulated in the 14th century, and a seven-year apprenticeship was set down in law in 1562; this was repealed in 1814, despite protests from organized labor. Apprenticeship has historically been favored by organized labor as a way of maintaining skill standards for craft occupations and as a means of controlling the supply of labor, both unqualified as well as skilled. Apprenticeship has largely been a feature of specialist craft occupations, particularly in **manufacturing**, but has also been extended to service occupations such as hairdressing. In the 20th century, technological change and rising education levels have diminished the importance of apprenticeship. As a method of trade training, apprenticeship has the disadvantage of being less available to school leavers during low points in the trade cycle because that is usually the time when employers cut down on the number of new apprentices to lower their wages cost. *See also* YOUTH.

ARBITRATION. *See* CONCILIATION AND ARBITRATION.

ARGENTINA. Argentina has one of the oldest labor movements in Latin America; in 1857 printers formed a mutual benefit society which they made into a union in 1877. The first union federation, the *Federación Obrera Regional Argentina* (Federation of Workers of Argentina) was formed in 1901, but it soon split into anarchist, syndicalist, and **socialist** factions. Like North America and Australasia, the population of Argentina was built on **immigration**; in the case of Argentina, the bulk of the immigrants up to the 1960s came from **Italy** and **Spain**. Despite its early beginning, union membership was low in the 19th century. In 1908, a government survey estimated that there were only 23,400 union members in Buenos Aires, and even by 1920, national membership had only reached 68,000. Despite these low membership figures, Argentina experienced a **general strike** in 1907 in which 93,000 took part. By 1930, when the *Confederación General del Trabajo* (CGT), (General Confederation of Labor), was formed, the number of union members had grown to 280,000. Other rival labor federations were formed by **socialists, anarchists,** and **syndicalists**. From 1943 the CGT became an active participant in **politics** through Colonel Juan Perón. In the turmoil that followed Perón's removal in 1955, the CGT was disbanded and   forced underground but reemerged in 1963.

     Thereafter, political rather than industrial concerns dominated Argentinean labor as governments both military and democratic attempted to deal with the country's severe economic problems; these policies produced factional divisions within the CGT. The legal status of the CGT was restored in 1986 following intervention by the **International Labour Organisation**. In 1988, Law 23551 established a framework for the administration of labor unions, **collective bargaining**, and **labor disputes**. In 2001, there were claimed to be 4.4 million union members in Argentina compared to 2.5 million in 1990. In 2001-2002, the country's economic crises threatened to undermine political stability and the relatively favorable status of organized labor. Despite the severity of the crisis in 2002, the ICFTU's survey of **violations of trade union rights** reported that labor unions had managed to survive surprisingly well.

ARMENIA. Part of the former Soviet Union from 1920 to September 1991, there is no history of organized labor in Armenia, and there have been no noteworthy efforts to create an independent labor movement since independence. The economy remains undeveloped and the population poor, providing no opportunity for labor unions to emerge.

ASIAN AND PACIFIC REGIONAL ORGANISATION (APRO). APRO is an international regional labor organization formed by the **International Confederation of Free Trade Unions** (ICFTU) in

1984. It began in Karachi, Pakistan, in May 1951, as the Asian Regional Organisation. It was later moved to **India** and then to **Singapore**, where it remains. In 2001, APRO had affiliates in 26 countries and represented 28.7 million members.

ASIA-PACIFIC LABOUR NETWORK (APLN). APLN was formed by the **International Confederation of Free Trade Unions** (ICFTU) in 1995 to lobby for social dialogue with the governments of the Asia-Pacific Economic Cooperation Forum (formed 1989) on economic and social issues such as debt, corruption, structural imbalances, and **child labor**. To date, its overtures have been rejected. APLN has 15 country members.

AUSTRALIA. The first labor unions in Australia arose among shipwrights in 1829, but it was not until after the gold rushes in the 1850s that organized labor became more important. Before the 1880s, most unions were formed by employees in a limited range of occupations, but in the 1880s there was an upsurge of "new" unionism, which embraced a wider range of occupations. By 1890 there were about 200,000 union members covering about 23 percent of all employees, giving Australia, briefly, the highest level of union density in the world. Between 1878 and 1900, the six colonies that made up Australia—there was no national government until 1901—passed laws that recognized labor unions. In 1879 the labor unions held their first intercolonial congress in Sydney; subsequent congresses were held in 1884, 1886, 1888, 1889, 1891, and 1898. Between August and December 1890, 50,000 workers in Australia and **New Zealand** took part in the great Maritime Strike over freedom of contract; the strikers suffered defeat. Between July and September 1894, the unions suffered a second major setback as a result of the wool shearers' strike in Queensland. The depression of the early 1890s, which was aggravated by a severe drought, retarded economic growth and caused union membership to fall to 97,000 (or about 9 percent of employees) in 1901.

The unions also used **politics** to improve their position. Following the introduction of public payment of a salary to members of parliament in New South Wales in 1889, the Sydney Trades and Labour Council resolved to support labor candidates, a decision that resulted in the election of 35 labor members to parliament at the 1891 election, an event which marked the birth of what later was called the **Australian Labor Party**. Greatly assisted by the introduction of compulsory **conciliation and arbitration** as a means of settling labor disputes—a system that eased the process for unions to **collectively bargain** with employers by granting them legal recognition—union **membership** rose to 498,000 or 31 percent of employees in 1913, the highest density level of any country at the time. As in other countries, **white-collar** unions began to organize during the 1900s, but most union members continued to be predominantly male **blue-collar** employees. With the establishment of the Federated Miscellaneous Workers' Union in 1915 (a union that recruited employees not recruited by other unions), the structure of organized labor remained relatively unchanged until the late 1980s. Australian labor unions have been a mixture of large and small organizations since the 1890s. Between 1913 and 1995 the proportion of unions with less than 1,000 members fell from 80 to 49 percent and the number of unions fell from 432 to 142.

After 1913, union membership rose and fell according to the state of the economy and the distribution of employment by industry. Unionism was strongest among blue-collar workers and skilled tradesmen. It was weakest among casual employees and white-collar workers. As a proportion of employees, unions reached their height in Australia in 1953, when 63 percent of employees were members; by 2001, it had fallen to 25 percent.

Since the early 1980s, the structure and size of union membership in Australia has changed considerably, affected by the economy and politics. Between 1983 and 1996, the federal Labor government and the **Australian Council of Trade Unions** (ACTU) worked closely to achieve economic growth and other objectives through a series of **accords**. The pay rises this process delivered to all employees reduced the necessity to join unions, and between 1982 and 1996 the number of union members fell from 2,567,600 to 2,194,300, and the proportion of employees who were union members fell from 49 to 31 percent. With the election of the conservative Liberal-National government in March 1996, the special relationship between organized labor and the federal government ended abruptly. In 1996, the government passed the Workplace Relations Act, which curbed labor unions and restricted the right to strike. In 2002, only 23 percent of all employees were union members; in the private sector, only 18 percent of employees were union members.

AUSTRALIAN COUNCIL OF TRADE UNIONS (ACTU). The ACTU is the national body representing labor unions in **Australia**. The idea of a single body representing Australian labor unions was first suggested by William Gutherie Spence (1846-1926) at the 1884 Inter-colonial Trade Union Congress, but it failed to attract support although subsequent congresses considered ways of federating the various peak labor bodies in the various colonies. The creation of a national government in 1901 and a federal system of **conciliation and arbitration** in 1905 created a new incentive to form a national body. But despite further national congresses in 1902, 1907, 1913, and 1916, it was not until the national conference of 1921 that the first steps were taken to form a peak national labor body, and even then two further conferences were needed (in 1922 and 1925) before the ACTU was formed in Melbourne, Victoria, in 1927. The ACTU was invited to join the **International Federation of Trade Unions** (IFTU) in 1936 but did not accept. Until the late 1950s, the powers of the ACTU were limited, with real power continuing to reside with the state trades and labor councils.

It was not until 1943 that the ACTU created its first salaried position, and it was only in 1949 that it had its first full-time president, Albert E. Monk, who held the post until 1969. In 1953, the ACTU joined the **International Confederation of Free Trade Unions** (ICFTU) and remains its largest member in Oceania. The growing importance of national wage cases and the convenience for national governments of dealing with a single labor body further strengthened the ACTU. In 1968, the then largest labor union, the **Australian Workers' Union**, affiliated with the ACTU. In 1980, the Australian Council of Salaried and Professional Associations joined the ACTU, as did the other major white-collar body, the Council of Australian Government Employees, in 1981. By 1981, all significant unions and union groupings had become affiliated with the ACTU, that is, it represented about 2.5 million employees.

The ACTU was at its greatest influence when the **Australian Labor Party** (ALP) was the national government from March 1983 to March 1996. At the March 1983 national election, the ALP won office and the former ACTU president from 1970 to 1980, Bob Hawke, became prime minister. Although the ACTU remains based in Melbourne, most large labor unions have their headquarters in Sydney. Between 1986 and 1993 the number of unions affiliated with the ACTU fell from 162 to 94, largely in response to a campaign led by the ACTU for the **amalgamation** of unions. In 2001, the ACTU had 44 affiliated unions and represented 1.8 million members. The ACTU has had an affirmative action policy for many years and elected its first female president, Jennie George, in 1996. After George stepped down, she was replaced by Sharan Burrow in May 2000. In 2002, half of the ACTU executive's members were **women**. In recent years, the ACTU has conducted "living wage" campaigns for lower-paid employees and against long **working hours**. It has also played a significant role in promoting democracy and trade unionism in the Pacific and South East Asia. The objectives of the ACTU for 2002-2003 were to double redundancy pay from eight to 186 weeks' pay; to double unpaid maternity leave from one year to two years and to have 14 weeks of paid maternity leave. *See also* PACIFIC TRADE UNION COMMUNITY; UNION-GOVERNMENT AGREEMENTS.

AUSTRALIAN LABOR PARTY (ALP). The ALP is one of the oldest and most successful continuous political parties based on organized labor in the world. It had its beginnings in a decision of the Sydney Trades and Labor Council in January 1890 to support candidates in the 1891 election following the introduction of state payment of the salaries of members of parliament in 1889. Support for a direct role in **politics** by organized labor was boosted by its defeat in the Maritime Strike of 1890. Labor unions have continued to provide the basis of the ALP ever since. It represented the culmination of efforts to elect working-class representatives to parliament, which began in the late 1870s. It drew part of its inspiration from the British Liberal Party, the main political outlet for the organized English working class in the 19th century. By the mid-1900s, the ALP had been set up in all Australian states. Its features of a platform of policies and disciplined voting by its elected members began a new era in Australian politics. Though usually represented by its opponents as a "leftwing" party, the ALP has always been a moderate social democratic party, though it did contain some radical groups. There have been two major splits in the ALP. The first was in 1916-1917 over military conscription, and the second occurred in 1955 over attitudes to communism.

The ALP formed national governments in 1908-1909, 1910-1913, 1914-1915, 1929-1932, 1941-1949, 1972-1974, and 1983-1996, but its longest terms of government success have been in the states. Notable ALP prime ministers have been William Morris Hughes, James H. Scullin (1929-1932), John Curtin (1941-1945),

Ben Chifley (1945-1949), Gough Whitlam (1972-1974) and Bob Hawke (1983-1991); before becoming prime minister, Hawke was president of the **Australian Council of Trade Unions** (ACTU) from 1970 to 1980. In September 2002, the federal parliamentary ALP leader, Simon Crean (1949-), a former ACTU president, succeeded in reducing bloc voting by organized labor at ALP state conferences from 60 to 50 percent.

AUSTRALIAN WORKERS' UNION (AWU). From the 1900s to 1969, the AWU was the largest labor union in **Australia**. It began as a sheep shearers' union in Ballarat, Victoria, in 1886. In 1894, the AWU was founded in Sydney, New South Wales, from the **amalgamation** of shearers' and laborers' unions, with a claimed membership of 30,000. The membership of the AWU was open to all employees. The AWU expanded by amalgamation with other unions, first with the rural laborers' union in 1894 and then with unions of semiskilled workers in rural, general laboring, and mining occupations between 1912 and 1917. By 1914, the AWU had 70,000 members.

The AWU has been a powerful but conservative force in Australian organized labor and in the **Australian Labor Party**. In the 1950s the AWU had about 200,000 members. Structural changes in industries and occupations, as well as internal disputes, have reduced the AWU membership since 1970 from 160,000 to 115,500 by 1990. In November 1993, the AWU amalgamated with the Federation of Industrial Manufacturing and Engineering Employees (FIMEE), formerly the Federated Ironworkers' Association (formed in 1911) and was officially renamed the AWU-FIME Amalgamated Union. It had a membership of about 170,000 in 1999.

AUSTRIA. Labor unions were legally tolerated within the present borders of Austria in 1870; the unions claimed 46,600 members by 1892 and 119,000 by 1900. Union growth was hampered not just by political and religious divisions in Austrian society but also by the large proportion of the labor force employed in **agriculture**. In 1920, 41 percent of the labor force was employed in agriculture, a proportion that had only dropped to 32 percent by 1934. Even so, as in other Western European countries, union **membership** grew substantially after 1913 from 263,000 to a million by 1920, when it reached 51 percent of employees, a level comparable with **Germany**. To a large extent, the union growth that occurred just after

World War I was the result of legislative change. The newly created Austrian Republic, following the German example, sought to tie organized labor into the new political order by laws in 1919-1920, which set up chambers of labor (modeled on the chambers of commerce) within the works' council law of 1919; these laws set up an ordered industrial relations system with compulsory union membership. By 1930, union membership had declined to 38 percent of employees in response to the economic dislocation of the 1920s and the Depression. Unions were also caught up in the turmoil of Austrian **politics**. After a short civil war in 1934, the **socialist** unions along with the Social Democratic Party were repressed and placed under the control of a labor federation run by the Catholic unions. After the annexation of Austria by Germany in 1938, all Austrian organized labor was incorporated into the *Deutsche Arbeitsfront*. The end of World War II saw the immediate rebirth of free organized labor in Austria. Wartime imprisonment of all labor leaders by the Nazis encouraged the Catholics, socialists, and communists to bury their differences and form the *Österreichischer Gewerkschaftsbund* (Austrian Federation of Labor Unions) in April 1945. Comprised of 15 **industrial unions**, the *Österreichischer Gewerkschaftsbund* has worked with government to promote economic growth and a stable democratic government. The laws of 1919-1920, which set up works' councils, were the basis of the "social partnership" which became characteristic of the corporatist approach to organized labor followed by Austria throughout the post-1945 period. In 2001, there were 1.4 million union members in Austria compared to 1.6 million union members in 1994; over this period, union membership among Austrian employees fell from 49 to 43 percent.

AZERBAIJAN. Independent of the former Soviet Union since August 1991, organized labor in Azerbaijan has progressed despite the government's use of Soviet-era laws. In 1993, an independent journalists' union was formed after two journalists were beaten up on government orders. Azerbaijan became an affiliate of the **International Confederation of Free Trade Unions** (ICFTU) in 2000. In 2001, there were 735,000 union members in Azerbaijan. In 2002, the ICFTU's survey of **violations of trade union rights** reported that there was little respect for collective bargaining in Azerbaijan even though it had been legal to form labor unions since 1994.

-B-

BAHAMAS. A colony of the **United Kindgom** to 1973, labor unions emerged in the Bahamas after 1943 when unions were, in effect, legalized; the law was broadened in 1958. By 1969, the Bahamas had became an affiliate of the **International Confederation of Free Trade Unions** (ICFTU). In 2001, there were 2,500 union members in the Bahamas.

BAHRAIN. In 2001, there were no independent labor unions in Bahrain. In 1983, the government introduced a joint work council system that included elected workers' representatives, who in turn elect 11 members to the General Committee of Bahrain Workers. About 60 percent of the labor force is expatriate even though official policy is to replace them with Bahraini workers.

BALTIC STATES. *See* ESTONIA; LATVIA; LITHUANIA.

BANGLADESH. Called East Pakistan until December 1971 when it forcibly seceded from West Pakistan, organized labor in Bangladesh dates from the 1920s, mainly in cotton manufacturing. After the creation of **Pakistan** in 1947, Indian labor unions set up a labor union federation in East Pakistan to mirror the All-India Trade Union Congress, but under Indian tutelage. Despite ratification of **International Labour Organisation** conventions 87 and 98 relating to the right to **collective bargaining** and the right to **strike** respectively, organized labor in East Pakistan was effectively muzzled. The creation of Bangladesh did not lift the restrictions on organized labor, and labor relations remained turbulent, reflecting the poverty of Bangladesh and its political instability. By 1975, organized labor in Bangladesh was divided among three national labor federations; two were affiliated with the communist-led **World Federation of Trade Unions** (WFTU) and the third, the Bangladesh Jatio Sramik League, was an affiliate of the **International Confederation of Free Trade Unions** (ICFTU). By 1989, there were four national labor organizations affiliated with the ICFTU. In 2001, these affiliates had a combined **membership** of 888,700. The ICFTU and the **Global Union Federations** have urged the labor federations of Bangladesh to work closely together. In 2002, the ICFTU's survey of **violations of trade union rights** reported that there were still many legal restrictions on organized labor and that a climate of political violence towards labor unions continued.

BARBADOS. A colony of the **United Kingdom** to November 1966, the framework for labor relations in Barbados was created in 1939 with the implementation of the Trade Disputes (Arbitration and Enquiry) Act. The Barbados Workers' Union was registered in 1941 and claimed 15,000 members by 1975. Barbados has been an affiliate of the **International Confederation of Free Trade Unions** (ICFTU) since 1951. In 2001, these affiliates had a combined **membership** of 15,000.

BASQUE COUNTRY. Although part of **Spain**, the Basque Country has been a recognized affiliate of the **International Confederation of Free Trade Unions** (ICFTU) since 1951 through the *Solidaridad de Trabajadores Vascos* (Solidarity of Basque Workers), formed before the Spanish Civil War (1936-1939), declared illegal after the War, and forced to be an exiled organization until the end of the dictatorship of General Francisco Franco in 1975 and the legalizing of labor unions in Spain in 1977. In 2001, the Basque Country remained affiliated with the ICFTU; in 2001, it claimed a **membership** of 110,000.

"BATTLE OF THE OVERPASS." The "battle of the overpass" was the name given to a violent incident on May 26, 1937, on an overpass to the Ford Motor Company between **Congress of Industrial Organizations** organizers and Ford's private **police** force. The organizers, who included **Walter Reuther** and Richard Frankensteen, had planned to hand out leaflets at Ford. Ford refused to recognize unions and ordered the organizers to leave. In the fight that followed, Reuther and Frankensteen were beaten up by Ford's police in front of the press. The incident was the subject of some famous photographs in the *Detroit News* and typified the violence of U.S. labor relations in the 1930s. *See also* UNITED AUTO WORKERS.

BECK, DAVID (1894-1993). Beck was one of the main figures in the **Teamsters** from the mid-1930s to the mid-1950s. Born in Stockton, California, he joined the Teamsters in 1914 and, after service in World War I, was elected to his first position within the union in 1923. He became a full-time organizer for the union in 1927 for the Northwest. In 1940, he became an international vice president. In

1949, he was the fraternal delegate of the **American Federation of Labor** (AFL) to the British **Trades Union Congress** (TUC). In 1952, he was elected international president of the Teamsters. He supported Dwight D. Eisenhower's campaigns in the 1950s and became a vice president of the **American Federation of Labor-Congress of Industrial Organizations** (AFL-CIO) between 1953 and 1957. In 1957, he was accused of corruption and embezzlement of union funds by Senator McClellan and expelled from the AFL-CIO. Beck served a 30-month jail term between 1962 and 1965 for federal income tax evasion. He later became a millionaire from real estate dealings in Seattle, Washington.

BELARUS. Independent of the former Soviet Union since August 1991, Belarus has remained the closest of the former Soviet territories to its authoritarian past. An independent trade union movement was begun by miners and workers in the capital, Minsk. In November 1993, the Free Trade Union of Belarus and the Belarussian Independent Trade Union formed a **strike** committee and together with political opponents of the government called a strike for February 15, 1994. The government declared the strike illegal and imprisoned and harassed the organizers. Under the 1996 constitution, the president of Belarus has, in effect, a monopoly of political power and rules by decree. In January 1999, all previously registered labor unions had to re-register or be banned. The Labor Union law of January 2000 violates trade union rights, according to the assessment of the **International Confederation of Free Trade Unions** (ICFTU) in 2002. In 2002, the ICFTU's survey of **violations of trade union rights** reported that the government had forced the Federation of Labor Unions of Belarus under its control and that its violations of trade union rights were the worst in Europe.

BELGIUM. The first Belgian unions were organized by spinners and weavers in the cotton industry in 1857, but organized labor was weak and divided by religion and ethnicity. Nevertheless, this did not mean the absence of working-class discontent; in April 1893, about 200,000 employees took part in a national **strike**. Catholic and **socialist** labor unions emerged in the 1880s, but even their combined efforts at recruitment yielded poor results. By 1900, there were only 42,000 union members or 3 percent of all employees. Only 10 percent of employees were unionized by 1913 but, in common with other Western European countries, union growth was substantial to 1920, when there were 920,000 union members or 45 percent of employees, a level not exceeded until 1950. Since 1960, the Catholic labor federation (*Confédération des Syndicats Chrétiens*, formed in 1909) and the socialist labor federation (*Fédération Générale du Travail de Belgique*), formed in 1937 from a labor body set up in 1898, have developed a closer working relationship to strengthen their bargaining position with employers. In 1990, about 53 percent of Belgian employees were members of labor unions. In 2001, Belgium had 1.2 million labor union members, covering 40 percent of Belgian employees. *See also* CATHOLICISM.

BELIZE. A colony of the **United Kingdom** to September 1981, the National Trade Union Congress of Belize has been an affiliate of the **International Confederation of Free Trade Unions** (ICFTU) since 1992, when it claimed 2,400 members.

BENIN. A colony of **France** before August 1960 when it was called Dahomey, a national labor organization existed in Benin in the 1950s, when it joined the *Union Générale des Travailleurs de l'Afrique Noire* (General Union of Workers of Black Africa) in 1957. After independence, organized labor in Benin became intertwined with **politics**. In 1969, the Benin labor body the *Confédération nationale des Syndicats libres* (National Confederation of Free Trade Unions) was admitted to membership of the **International Confederation of Free Trade Unions** (ICFTU). The ICFTU was concerned about the efforts of the Benin military government to form a single national labor organization under its control. In 1973, the *Confédération nationale des Syndicats libres* merged with the *Union Générale des Syndicats du Dahomey* (General Union of the Trade Unions of Dahomey), which had been formed in 1964. Through this body, Benin remained a member of the ICFTU, but continued being a hostage to political instability and poverty.

BERMUDA. A British dependent territory, the foundations of a labor relations system were laid by the Trade Union and Trade Disputes Act (1946). After the introduction of this law, the Bermuda Industrial Union was formed in 1946, drawing most of its **membership** from black residents; by 1975, it claimed 6,000 members. Bermuda has been a member of the **International Confederation of Free Trade Unions** (ICFTU) since 1969 and had 5,000 union members in 2001.

BEVIN, ERNEST (1881-1951). Bevin was the greatest leader to emerge from organized labor in the **United Kingdom** in the 20th century. Born into poverty in Somerset, he held a number of lowly jobs until finding work as a van driver in 1901. His formal education was very limited. Like other labor leaders of his generation, he was a Methodist. He gained some further education from the Quaker Adult School and joined the Socialist Party in Bristol, where he became a speaker and an organizer. In 1908, he became active in the Right to Work movement for the unemployed. During the **strike** by dockers (longshoremen) at Avonmouth, he organized the dock carters as part of the Dock, Wharf, Riverside, and General Workers' Union so they could not be used as strikebreakers. In 1911, Bevin became a full-time official of the Dockers' Union. An outstanding negotiator, Bevin became one of the Union's three national organizers in 1913. He realized that strong, centralized authority was as vital for unions as rank-and-file support.

In 1915-1916, Bevin was sent as the fraternal delegate of the **Trades Union Congress** (TUC) to the **American Federation of Labor** (AFL), a trip that gave him an international outlook on the world of organized labor. In 1920, his brilliant advocacy for the dock workers before the Industrial Court won him national recognition, as did his leadership of the Council of Action's campaign to boycott the supply of military equipment to **Poland** for use against the Russian revolutionaries. In 1921, Bevin was the pivotal figure in the **amalgamation** of 14 unions to create a new mass union, the **Transport and General Workers' Union** (TGWU), which by the late 1930s had grown to be the largest union in Britain and, for a brief time, the largest in the world.

In 1925, Bevin became a member of the general council of the TUC, a position he held until 1940; in 1937, he was chairman of the TUC. During the 1930s, Bevin successfully fought communist influence within the TGWU. In 1937-1938, he conducted a tour of the British Commonwealth and was able to bring about improved labor relations. In 1940, he was made minister for labor, a position responsible for organizing Britain's labor force during World War II. Bevin's last official position was foreign secretary from 1945 to just before his death. *See also* DEAKIN, ARTHUR.

BLACK LABOR MARKET. The black labor market refers to employment in jobs where the income is not declared for taxation and social security. It is a subset of the term "black economy," which came into use in the late 1970s. This form of labor came into use in the late 1970s. This form of labor engagement often removes workers from occupational health and safety protection as well as being a traditional source of low pay. In 1999, it was estimated that 10 million employees in Europe worked in the black labor market. Labor unions oppose the black labor market as its lower labor costs threaten the pay and conditions of their members. *See also* BONDED LABOR.

BLUE-COLLAR/WHITE-COLLAR. Blue-collar and white-collar are terms to describe manual occupations (meaning literally to work with the hands) and nonmanual occupations (meaning to work with the brain rather than the hands). Although of U.S. coinage, both terms have entered general English usage, although the color blue—whether of caps or coats—was associated with servants and other menial occupations in England from the 17th century. The term "white-collar," meaning a clerical occupation, was used in the U.S. from about 1920; "blue-collar" was coined in about 1950 and was in general English usage by the 1960s.

One of the outstanding features of the labor force in Western economies in the 20th century has been the shift away from blue-collar to white-collar occupations. The trend in the British labor force seems to have been typical for other countries. Between 1911 and 1951, the proportion of blue-collar jobs in the labor force fell from 75 to 64 percent and has continued to decline ever since. By 2000, only about a third of the labor force in Western economies worked in blue-collar jobs.

Historically, these terms have strong connotations of social class: A manual occupation was the membership badge of the working class and a white-collar occupation indicated middle-class membership. These social distinctions were reinforced by labor laws and from about 1910 were reflected in the occupational classifications of population censuses, which presented a carefully graded hierarchy of occupations from managers at the top to laborers at the bottom. The *Code de Travail* (Code of Labor) in **France**, which was published between 1910 and 1936, and distinguished between the superior intellectual qualities of white-collar work and that required for blue-collar jobs. Labor laws passed in **Greece** (1920), **Italy** (1926), and France (1924, 1935) defined the division between blue- and white-collar jobs and provided for different systems of payment. Blue-collar workers received wages; white-collar workers were paid salaries. White-collar workers were paid more but less frequently and received preferential treatment in the case of their employers' bankruptcy. Although the legal distinction between blue-collar and white-collar employees has tended to lessen since the 1950s, it remained a feature of labor law in most Western European countries in the late 1990s.

Organized labor worldwide reflected the social division between blue-collar and white-collar workers. In 1900, less than 10 percent of union members worked in white-collar jobs, but after 1910 the proportion of white-collar members began to slowly rise. Even so, the **iconography** of organized labor tended to pay homage only to blue-collar work ("real" work) as opposed to the work performed at a desk by a white-collar employee. Heavy manual work was more amenable to being presented as heroic rather than working in safety and comfort at a desk. Generally not welcome in organized labor, white-collar unions and their federations tended to remain outside its ranks until the 1960s.

Since the 1970s, technological change has blurred the social distinction between blue- and white-collar jobs. A white-collar job no longer carries the social status it did 50 years ago. Over the same period, the proportion of blue-collar jobs in the labor force has declined and the proportion of white-collar jobs has risen as a result of changes in types of work and through social mobility. In 2000, the British Department of Trade and Industry recognized these changes when it ceased to publish statistics on union **membership** divided by blue- and white-collar jobs following the introduction of a new classification of occupations. For organized labor, these trends have meant that a substantial part of its membership in most Western economies works in white-collar jobs. In 2001, 48 percent of union members in the **United States** were employed in white-collar jobs, and 45 percent were in **Australia**. In both countries, employees in blue-collar jobs were more likely to be union members than were white-collar employees. *See also* WHITE-COLLAR UNIONISM.

BÖCKLER, HANS (1875-1951). Böckler was one of the leading architects of the revived post-1945 labor movement in **Germany**. The son of a coachman, he qualified as a gold and silver smith and joined the *Deutscher Metallarbeiter-Verband* (German Engineering Union) and the Social Democratic Party in 1894. After being wounded in 1916, he left the army to become an official of the Engineering Union. In 1927, he became the Düsseldorf area chairman of the General German Trade Union Federation and was elected to the Reichstag in 1928. In 1944, Böckler managed to avoid capture by the Nazis for his part in the July Plot to kill Adolf Hitler. After the Nazis' defeat, the Allies adopted different policies on the revival of the labor unions. The British policy, following the Potsdam Agreement, which encouraged organized labor, was to allow the revival to come gradually from the local level first and to be carefully supervised, whereas leaders like Böckler preferred to organize centralized democratic unions quickly using the organizational framework of the former Nazi *Deutsche Arbeitsfront*. Böckler and other leaders were advised on the future structure of organized labor by a delegation from the British **Trades Union Congress** (TUC) in 1945. The individual independent labor unions that had been approved set up the *Deutscher Gewerkschaftbund* (German Trade Union Federation) in the British zone on April 22-25, 1947, with Böckler as its head. Realizing the need for the labor movement to be better informed, Böckler was the prime mover in 1946 in creating the Institute for Economic Science to give organized labor expert advice for its policies and positions. Also in 1946, Böckler, in an address to the first labor conference in the British zone, made clear his support for the unions to be represented on the managing and supervisory boards of companies, thereby laying the foundation for the introduction of *Mitbestimmung* (codetermination). In October 1949 the federations of German labor unions in the British, American, and French zones of occupation were merged into the present *Deutscher Gewerkschaftbund*, and Böckler was elected chairman by 397 out of 474 votes, a position he held until his death.

BOLIVIA. Organized labor in Bolivia has a violent history. The first trade union in Bolivia was formed in 1906, but organized labor was torn by political ideologies—socialism, **anarchism** and, later, **communism**—as well as facing opposition from the government, and handicapped by the poverty of Bolivia's people. The first national Bolivian national congress was held in 1927. The Bolivian miners' unions federated in June 1944. Following the successful revolution of the National Revolutionary Movement, organized labor formed the *Central Obrera Boliviana* (Bolivian Central Workers') or COB in 1952. Until 1963, the COB worked with the leftist government and gained significant advantages, notably concession of its demand for "workers' control" of mines. A military coup in November 1964 ended the alliance between the government and the COB. Thereafter, Bolivia's labor unions were the focus of government repression. A **general strike** led by the COB in May 1965 resulted in hundred of deaths. In 1974, the COB and organized labor generally were banned by the government. There were widespread violations of human rights in Bolivia in the 1970s, which were exposed after a secret mission to the country by the British National Union of Miners in April 1977. The leftwing COB was not an affiliate of the **International Confederation of Free Trade Unions** (ICFTU), preferring affiliation with the communist **World Federation of Trade Unions** (WFTU). Bolivia's membership of the ICFTU in the 1950s and 1970s was through one its smaller unions. Civilian government was restored in Bolivia in 1982. In 1993, the government introduced free-market reforms, which resulted in a wave of **strikes** during 1995. In 2001, Bolivia and **Uruguay** were the only South American countries not to be members of the ICFTU. In 2002, the ICFTU reported that the general climate for organized labor in Bolivia continued to be repressive.

BONDED LABOR. Bonded labor is a form of **forced labor** in which a worker is bonded to an employer, often to repay a debt lent to the worker at an inflated interest rate. Bonded or indentured labor was a feature of the labor force of colonial North America. It was common in Asia, particularly in **India**. Since 1945 bonded labor has been illegal in India but widespread in practice; it has been estimated that there were 10 million bonded laborers in India in 1999. The **International Confederation of Free Trade Unions** (ICFTU) has been associated with Anti-Slavery International since 1997. In 2001, the United Nations Working Group on Contemporary Forms of Slavery estimated that there were 20 million workers of both sexes and all ages working as bonded labor. *See also* SLAVERY.

BOSNIA-HERZOGOVINA. One of the six republics that made up the former **Yugoslavia**, Bosnia-Herzogovina has been a separate nation since 1991. The country's war-torn history in the 1990s has precluded the emergence of organized labor. Bosnia-Herzogovina was not a member of the **International Confederation of Free Trade Unions** (ICFTU) in 2001, and in 2002, the ICFTU noted that although some efforts were being made to create a comprehensive framework for labor unions and **collective bargaining**, this was not yet in place.

BOTSWANA. A colony of the **United Kingdom** up to September 1966, there were some labor unions in Botswana before independence, but their **membership** was slight; even by 1974, Botswana's unions had a total of only 1,400 members. By 1986, the membership of the Botswana Federation of Trade Unions—as indicated by its returns to the **International Confederation of Free Trade Unions'** (ICFTU)—had risen to 14,000 and to 18,000 by the 1990s. Unlike most other post-independence African countries, Botswana has remained a stable democracy, a condition that has maintained organized labor and reflected its relatively prosperous economy.

BRAZIL. The first labor unions were formed in Brazil in the 1900s but, as in other countries founded by **Portugal** or **Spain**, organized labor developed along the political and religious divisions of the mother country, as shown by the formation of **Catholic, socialist, anarchist,** and **communist** unions. Although Brazil claimed 270,000 union members by 1930, these divisions allowed the government of Getúlio Vargas to force all unions to become officially registered in 1931, a move that Vargas used to outlaw the communist and anarchist unions. Vargas, who ran the government until 1945, used the example of fascist **Italy** to build a corporatist state in which unions were controlled by government nominees or supporters and received their finances from compulsory contributions by all employees regardless of whether they were union members. Since 1945, as in other Latin American countries, the labor unions have played a central role in the campaign against authoritarian government and in favor of democracy, although their efforts have been hampered by internal political divisions. The 1950s and 1960s were marked by a high level of labor disputes and the growth of communist support. In 1964, an antiunion military junta seized government.

It was not until August 3, 1986, that the first national labor federation, the *Central Geral dos Trabalhadores* (General Confederation of Labor) (CGT), was formed after the reintroduction of civilian government in 1985. In 1991, three Brazilian labor federations were members of the **International Confederation of Free Trade Unions** (ICFTU): the CGT with 4 million members, the *Central Unica dos Trabalhadores* (Single Workers' Center) (CUT) (formed in 1983) with 3.8 million members, and the *Força Sindical* (Union Strength) (formed in 1991) with 2.1 million members. In 2001, there were 8.9 million labor union members in Brazil covering 21 percent of employees. On October 27, 2002, Luiz Inacio "Lula" Da Silva (1945-), a former leader of the metal workers' union in the 1970s, was elected president, the first occupant of the position with a background in organized labor. His election raised hopes for improvement in the treatment of organized labor in Brazil.

BRENNER, OTTO (1907-1972). One of the main post-1945 labor leaders in **Germany**, Brenner was born in Hanover and began his working life as a general laborer but eventually worked his way up to electrical engineer. He joined the *Deutscher Metallarbeiter-Verband* (German Metal Workers' Union) in 1922. He was a co-founder of the *Sozialdemokratische Arbeiterpartei* (Social Democratic Workers' Party) in 1931. Arrested by the Gestapo in 1933, he was jailed for two years and was under **police** surveillance until 1945. With Hans Brümmer, he was joint leader of *IG Metall* from 1952 to 1956 and then led the union alone until his death. Under Brenner's leadership, *IG Metall* led the movement in West Germany for **shorter working hours**. In 1958, Brenner warned of the dangers of unemployment caused by technological change. In 1969, he was elected president of the European Confederation of Free Trade Unions, the forerunner of the **European Trade Union Confederation** (ETUC).

BRITAIN. *See* UNITED KINGDOM.

BRITISH GENERAL STRIKE. The British General Strike, which took place between May 4 and 12, 1926, was the largest single confrontation between the government and organized labor that has ever occurred in the **United Kingdom**. The immediate background to the **strike** was the government's decision in 1925 to return Britain to the gold standard, a move that increased the price of British exports and encouraged employers to instigate pay cuts to maintain their position in world trade. At the center of the strike were grievances by the coal miners over wage cuts and their efforts to gain the support of other unions. Although employees gave a high level of support to the strike—a record 162 million working days were lost through labor disputes in 1926—the Stanley Baldwin government was well prepared and used special constables, university students, and other volunteers to take the place of strikers. The coal miners remained on strike until August, when they admitted defeat and returned to work on the employers' terms.

As a result of the strike, the **Trades Union Congress** (TUC) issued an invitation for talks on the reform of British industrial relations in 1927. Although the offer was ignored by the employers' association, the offer was taken up by Sir Alfred Mond, the chairman of Imperial Chemical Industries, who met with Ben Turner of the TUC in a series of talks that ran into 1928; these talks led to the Mond-Turner Report, which suggested that organized labor should have a role in making national economic and industrial relations policies. The idea was rejected by the **employers' organizations** and the talks were abortive. The government enacted the Trade Disputes Act in 1927, which outlawed the secondary boycott and strike, the mechanisms on which the strike had been based. This law, although not used, was repealed by Clement Attlee's Labour government in 1946. *See also* GENERAL STRIKES; LABOR DISPUTES.

BRITISH LABOUR PARTY. Formed in 1900 as the Labour Representation Committee, the British Labour Party has been one of the leading continuous political parties in the world to be based on organized labor. Labor officials first began contesting British parliamentary elections in 1847, but none were successful until 1874 when Alexander Macdonald (1821-1881) and Thomas Burt (1837-1922), two coal miners' leaders, were elected to the House of Commons. In 1867, the franchise was widened to include relatively well-off urban working-class males. Because of its ability to work with the Liberal Party for labor objectives, the **Trades Union Congress** (TUC) was slow to see the need for organized labor to support its own political party. In 1892, Keir Hardie (1856-1915) succeeded in having a resolution for separate labor representation carried at the TUC, but no action followed. It was the **Taff Vale Case** that galvanized organized labor into supporting a separate labor party; in 1906, the Labour Representation Committee was renamed the Labour Party. Membership was at first open only to unions, but in 1918 individuals were allowed to join. During World War I a number of Labour members were participants in the government.

In 1918, the Labour Party adopted a socialization objective that called for government control of most of the economy and, in 1922, became the official opposition party for the first time. In 1923-1924, the Labour Party formed a minority government under Ramsay MacDonald. In the 1930s the Labour Party fared badly in elections and directed its policies towards producing detailed reformist programs. During World War II, members of the Labour Party, such as **Ernest Bevin**, participated in Winston Churchill's government. In 1945, Labour, under Clement Attlee (who had been leader of the party since 1935), won government for the first time and proceeded to implement wide-ranging reforms. Labour was defeated in 1951 and did not win government again until 1964. Thereafter, the Labour Party's electoral record in national British politics was mixed: Labour lost power in 1970, regained it in 1974, lost it again in 1979, and spend 18 years in the political wilderness before winning a landslide victory in 1997 under Tony Blair. It won a second victory in June 2001. However, despite these wins, relations between the Blair government and organized labor have been cool. The government has shown no obvious bias in favor of organized labor and has been accused by organized labor's left of being too close to big business. Certainly the election of the Labour Government in 1997 has done little to arrest the slow decline in the **membership** of organized labor. Although the number of British union members rose 2 percent (140,000) to 7.3 million between 1997 and 2001, the proportion of employees who were union members fell from 30.2 to 28.8 percent, a fall that reflected the failure of unions to recruit additional males in **full-time employment**. *See also* UNITED KINGDOM.

BULGARIA. The first labor union in what is now Bulgaria, but was then part of the Ottoman Empire to 1908, was formed in 1883 by printers. Other unions were formed after that date, and a Socialist Party was set up in 1893. In 1904, two labor federations were formed: one socialist and one Marxist. Despite its small membership (there were 2,700 members in 1904 and about 29,000 union members in 1911), organized labor conducted 537 **strikes** up to 1910, of which 161 won gains for the strikers. During World War I, Bulgarian organized labor developed a revolutionary character; in 1920, when the two labor federations merged, union **membership** reached 36,000 and attained its pre-1945 peak of 49,800 in 1923. Bulgaria was an affiliate of the **International Federation of Trade Unions** (IFTU) from 1904 to 1913 and from 1921 to 1933. A military coup in June 1923 brought a fascist-style government to power, which banned many labor unions. Although there was some revival of organized labor after 1927, union membership had fallen to 18,900 by 1933. After the withdrawal of the Nazis in 1944, the

Confederation of Independent Trade Unions of Bulgaria (CITUB) was formed; it became a pillar of the communist regime and was given a range of responsibilities concerning labor administration. Bulgaria was a model of communist orthodoxy until the late 1980s. In February 1989, some members of the intelligentsia formed an independent labor union, *Prodrepka* ("Support"). In spite of the imprisonment of some of its leaders, it claimed 100,000 members by December 1989 and played a central part in the popular uprisings which broke the communist political monopoly. The challenge posed by *Prodrepka* for the leadership of organized labor prompted the CITUB to reform itself and call a **general strike** in December 1990, a move that helped to cause the fall of the government. As in **Poland**, disputes over the ownership of union assets have been a major issue since the end of communism. In December 1991, the democratically elected government seized the assets of the Communist Party, including those of the CITUB. In June 1992, the CITUB and *Prodrepka* agreed that union property should be returned to organized labor and divided between them. In 1993, *Prodrepka* was a member of the **International Confederation of Free Trade Unions** (ICFTU) with 321,200 members. By 2001, these two affiliates had a combined membership of 555,350. In 2002, the ICFTU was critical of government policies towards organized labor, citing harassment of union officials and members and obstruction of **collective bargaining**.

BURKINA FASO. Originally called Upper Volta, Burkina Faso was a colony of **France** up to 1960. As in other French colonies, organized labor followed the example of French settlers and reflected divisions within French organized labor. In 1947, the first national union federation was formed as a branch of the French *Confédération Générale du Travail* (CGT or General Confederation of Labor). In the 1960s, the *Organisation Voltaique des Syndicats Libres* (Organization of Free Trade Unions of Volta) was established and was admitted to membership of the **International Confederation of Free Trade Unions** (ICFTU); it claimed 6,000 members by 1966. Organized labor remained fragmented and weakened by too many unions. Nevertheless, in January 1966, the unions successfully conducted a **general strike** to bring down the government. Burkina Faso has continued to be a member of the ICFTU. Following the suspicious death of the journalist Norbert Zongo in 1998, a Workers' Front was formed to defend organized labor and basic

human rights generally; the Workers' Front was the target of government repression in 2000. In 2001, the ICFTU reported that there were still many restrictions on organized labor, particularly over the government's ability to use public sector employees to break **strikes**. There were 59,500 union members in Burkina Faso in 2001. In 2002, the ICFTU reported that a climate of government intimidation towards organized labor prevailed in Burkina Faso.

BURMA. Part of British India from 1886 to 1937, and independent of the **United Kingdom** since 1947, organized labor in Burma emerged among Indian and Chinese imported workers in the 1920s. In 1926, the British administration legalized labor unions, and this principle was incorporated into the 1948 constitution. By 1961, there were 173 registered unions with a total membership of 64,000, but thereafter Burma's history was dominated by political instability, leftwing politics, military repression, and rebellious ethnic groups. In 1964, the Socialist Program Party government abolished independent organized labor and, in 1968, set up its own system of grassroots committees to control labor. Following thousands of deaths in student riots in 1988, the military took power, renamed the country Myanmar, and all vestiges of organized labor were suppressed.

In 1991, the Federation of Trade Unions-Burma (FTU-B) was formed in secret in **Thailand** and is forced to operate along the borders of Burma because of the severity of military repression. By 1997, the FTU-B claimed to have an underground national network of sympathizers within Burma. Virtually all factories in Burma are owned by the military government. **Forced labor** is a general feature of the labor force, despite Burma's ratification of **International Labour Organisation** (ILO) Convention No. 87—Forced or Compulsory Labor (1930). The **International Confederation of Free Trade Unions** (ICFTU) has consistently drawn attention to the government of Burma as one of the worst human rights offenders in Asia. Burma has never been a member of the ICFTU.

-C-

CAMEROON. Cameroon was under French administration for the United Nations to 1960. Accordingly, its labor unions developed along French lines with the usual French ideological divisions.

Cameroon has been represented in the **International Confederation of Free Trade Unions** (ICFTU) since 1953. By 1975, there were about 40,000 union members. The first union federation was formed in 1948 and, in 1971, Cameroon's four union federations agreed to merge. Labor unions were regulated by law in 1974. The 1992 labor code required government approval for workers to form a trade union. Between December 1993 and January 1994 there was a **strike** caused by large pay cuts in the public sector; the strike was defeated by violence and intimidation. A delegation to Cameroon by the ICFTU and its **African Regional Organization** (AFRO) was able to get an assurance from the government that it would not interfere in the internal affairs of the country's labor federation, the *Confédération Syndicale des Travailleurs du Cameroun* (Union Confederation of Cameroon Workers) (CSTC). The 1992 Labor Code permits labor unions to be formed, but the ICFTU has complained about government interference in the internal affairs of unions. In contrast to other Third World countries, the ICFTU found that the country's **export processing zones** generally conformed with internationally recognized labor standards. In 2001, there were 385,000 labor union members in Cameroon.

CANADA. Labor unions in Canada were first formed in 1798, and seven are known to have existed by 1829. They made their presence felt at Saint John, New Brunswick, as early as 1812 when they tried to exclude American immigrants to maintain the shortage of skilled labor in the building industry. Up to the early 1870s, the **United Kingdom**, through **immigration**, was the dominant influence on the shaping of Canadian organized labor as shown by the establishment of Canadian branches of British unions such as the **Amalgamated Society of Engineers** in 1853 and the **Amalgamated Society of Carpenters and Joiners** in 1872. The first local trade assemblies were formed in 1871.

With the growth of the United States economy after the Civil War and its greater interrelationship with the Canadian economy after the early 1870s, the U.S. increasingly came to dominate the politics and structure of organized labor in Canada. The **Knights of Labor** set up their first assembly in Canada in 1881, the same year that saw the formation of the Federation of Organized Trades and Labor Unions of the United States and Canada in Pittsburgh. Its successor, the **American Federation of Labor** (AFL), soon established a presence in Canada. Conflict arose with the Knights of Labor and, in 1902, the Canadian Trade and Labour Congress (formed in 1886) expelled the Knights and all other unions that were not part of an American (or "international") union. The excluded unions formed their own federation, the National Trades and Labour Congress, in Canada in 1903, which was renamed the Canadian Federation of Labour in 1908. In 1906, the **Industrial Workers of the World** (IWW) created its first organization in Canada; as in the United States, it largely recruited the lesser-skilled employees. **Catholic** unions in Quebec created a provincial federation in 1921. In common with other countries Canada experienced a wave of **labor disputes** after World War I, notably the **general strike** in Winnipeg in 1919. The **One Big Union** movement also found support at the same time. Despite the growth of organized labor, the proportion of employees enrolled in unions remained low. In 1920, for example, only 15 percent of Canadian employees were union members compared to 17 percent in the **United States,** 42 percent in **Australia,** and 26 percent in **New Zealand.** Union density rose to 33 percent in 1950 but remained relatively unchanged thereafter; unlike other countries, Canada did not suffer a sharp decline in union **membership** during the 1980s.

For most of the 20th century, about half of Canada's union members have been members of American unions, a feature that ensured that the political divisions and events of the United States, such as the formation of the **Congress of Industrial Organizations** (CIO), were also part of the history of Canadian organized labor. This particular chapter was closed in 1956 when the Trades and Labour Congress (the Canadian equivalent of the AFL) and the Canadian Congress of Labour (the Canadian equivalent of the CIO) merged to form the Canadian Labour Congress, which remains the largest labor federation in the country, with 1.5 million members in 2001. Since 1974, a number of Canadian unions have split from the American unions to be fully independent in **collective bargaining.** In 2001, there were 3 million union members in Canada, compared to 3.9 million in 1995. Canada has always been a member of the **International Confederation of Free Trade Unions** (ICFTU), and despite the country's excellent **human rights** record, the ICFTU has been critical of restrictions on trade union rights imposed by some provincial governments, particularly in the **public sector.**

CAPE VERDE. An independent nation from **Portugal** since July 1975, the first labor union was formed in Cape Verde in 1976. Cape

Verde was not represented in the **International Confederation of Free Trade Unions** (ICFTU) until 1990, when its affiliate, the *União Nacional dos Trabalhadores de Cabo Verde-Central Sindical* (National Union of Workers of Cape Verde-Central Union) (UNTC-CS), claimed 15,000 members. In December 1991, the government closed part of the social center building of the UNTC-CS and handed the keys to a rival labor organization. The dispute continued for three years and led to calls for intervention by the ICFTU. In 2001, there were 15,000 union members in Cape Verde.

CARIBBEAN CONGRESS OF LABOUR. This regional international labor organization was formed in 1960 to lobby Caribbean governments on labor issues and to provide training and research. Between 1990 and 2001, the number of employees it represented rose from 122,600 to 500,000 in 17 countries. Most of its country members are also members of the **International Confederation of Free Trade Unions** (ICFTU).

CATHOLICISM. Catholics and Catholicism have played a major role in shaping the history of organized labor. Because the growth of **socialism** in Western Europe was often associated with anti-clericalism, it led to a Catholic reaction. At Ghent, an Anti-Socialist League was set up in 1878. In **France**, the first Catholic labor union was formed among **white-collar** workers in 1887. The papal encyclical *Rerum Novarum* (Of New Things) rejected socialism but recognized and supported the need for social justice within industrial society, thereby encouraging Catholics to participate in labor unions. In **Germany**, the first Catholic unions were formed in 1894 and, by 1919, had a combined membership of one million. In France, the first national Catholic union was formed among clerical workers in 1913. In **Switzerland**, Catholic unions formed their own federation in 1907. A French Catholic labor federation, *Confédération Française des Travailleurs Chrétiens* (French Confederation of Christian Workers), was formed in 1919; it claimed to represent 100,000 employees. An international body, the International Federation of Christian Trade Unions (the forerunner to the **World Confederation of Labour**), was formed at The Hague in 1920, the culmination of efforts begun in 1908. Although Catholic labor organizations were important, they did not represent the full extent of Catholic activity in organized labor, for Catholics were also active in the non-Catholic organizations, which generally retained their numerical superiority over the purely Catholic ones.

The emergence of **communism** from the early 1920s presented Catholicism with its greatest ideological challenge of the century, as it had many of the features often associated with a religion. Communism was officially condemned by the Vatican in the encyclical *Domini Redemptoris* (Redemption of the Lord) in 1937. From that time onwards, Catholics were important as a group in fighting communist infiltration of organized labor in the 1940s and 1950s. Catholic unions remain a feature of organized labor in Western Europe, but in Germany and **Austria** their support is limited because the pre-World War II divisions within organized unions were seen as contributing to the success of fascism. Catholicism has been the driving force behind the **World Confederation of Labour** (WCL).

CENTRAL AFRICAN REPUBLIC. Independent of **France** since 1960, organized labor had about 2,000 members in the Central African Republic at independence. The government of Jean-Bédel Bokassa brought the unions under the control of one organization in 1964. The Central African Republic has been represented in the **International Confederation of Free Trade Unions** (ICFTU) since 1980 by the *Union Syndicale des Travailleurs de Centrafrique* (Labor Union of Central African Workers) (USTC). **Strikes** in the Central African Republic, such as those conducted by public sector employees in April 1994 over unpaid salaries, have been met by government military forces. Despite the establishment of a democratic government in 1993, relations between the government and organized labor remain difficult. In 1999, the general secretary of the USTC, Sony Colé, was arrested and beaten up by the presidential security unit. In 2001, there were 15,000 union members in the Central African Republic. In 2002, the ICFTU reported that there had been strikes in the Central African Republic over unpaid salaries for **public sector** employees and they continued to occur.

CHAD. Independent of **France** since August 1960, organized labor in Chad began as branches of French unions; they claimed 1,500 members by 1960. In 1962, the government required official approval before a trade union could be formed and banned any political activity by unions. The unions were brought under government control by one union body in 1965. In 1975, **strikes** were banned, and in 1976 **public sector** employees were forbidden to form trade unions. Despite the hostile legal and political environment, Chad has been represented in the **International Confederation of Free Trade Unions** (ICFTU) since 1987 by the *Union des Syndicats du Tchad* (Federation of Chad Labor Unions) (UST). Strikes in the public sector over the government's failure to pay salaries in 1994 and 1995 were met with violence by the government; at least five union leaders were murdered in 1994. In July 1994, the government and the UST agreed to a social pact that resulted in an agreement to pay the salaries due; the International Monetary Fund warned the government that the pact was a serious violation of its aid package and could result in its cancellation. There were 30,000 union members in Chad in 2001. In 2002, the ICFTU remained critical of the lack of government respect for trade union rights in Chad.

CHILD LABOR. The elimination of child labor was a general objective of organized labor in the 19th century, not just on the grounds of the protection of children but also to reduce their competition with adults. As children were cheaper to employ than adults, they tended to reduce the wages of adults. Early 19th-century British social reformers like Robert Owen (1771-1858) opposed the employment of children. Union pressure for legislation to regulate factory employment and exclude child labor effectively began in 1833 in England, but progress was slow and grudging. In the **United States**, **Samuel Gompers**, although generally suspicious of government labor laws, supported them if they were aimed at eliminating child labor. The National Child Labor Committee (formed in 1904) induced most states to pass child labor legislation, but Supreme Court opposition delayed the passing of a national law to directly prohibit child labor until 1949. The **International Labour Organisation** (ILO) has sought to reduce the incidence of child labor but with limited success outside of Western economies. The first ILO Convention concerning child labor was adopted in 1919: the Minimum Age (Industry) Convention, 1919 (No. 5). It was followed by the Minimum Age for Employment Convention 1973 (No. 138).

The **International Confederation of Free Trade Unions** (ICFTU) has been campaigning against child labor since 1986. Child labor remains widespread in Third World countries, with many poor families seeing child labor as essential for their economic survival. On January 8, 1995, the Indian National Trade Union Congress and the Centre of Indian Trade Unions signed a pact with the ILO to work towards the elimination of child labor. In 1999, the ILO adopted the Worst Forms of Child Labour Convention (No. 182), which was based on the ICFTU's Child Labor Charter released in 1998. *See also* BONDED LABOR; MINIMUM AGE; SLAVERY.

CHILE. The first labor organizations in Chile were founded as mutual aid associations by artisans in 1847. The growth of unions was slowed by hostile governments, which violently suppressed **strikes** in 1890 and 1907; the 1907 strike was led by nitrate employees, of whom over 2,000 were killed by the army. The first national labor federation in Chile was set up in 1909. **Anarchism** attracted a wide following, and an anarchist labor federation existed between 1931 and 1936. The number of union members was claimed to be 150,000 by 1923 and 204,000 in 1927. A new labor federation was created in 1936, but during 1946-1947 it split into **communist** and **socialist** factions. A reformed national labor federation, the *Central Unica de Trabajadores* (CUT), was established in 1953; leftwing in character but independent of any political party, it became affiliated with the **International Confederation of Free Trade Unions** (ICFTU). During the 1960s, there was a general rise in labor unrest, a reflection of the deep divisions in Chilean society. In 1970, Salvador Allende, the leader of the Popular Unity Coalition, was elected president with the CUT as his major ally. In September 1973, Allende was assassinated in a military coup that had the backing of the administration of Richard Nixon in the **United States**. Not only were unions and **collective bargaining** suppressed, but 13,000 people were arrested and at least 2,200 were executed.

Labor unrest during the 1980s gave rise to a new, broad-based labor federation, the *Central Unitaria de Trabajadores* (Unified Workers' Center) or CUT in August 1988, which actively worked for the restoration of democratic government (achieved in 1990) and labor law reform. In 1992, there were about 720,000 union members in Chile (about 24 percent of employees) of whom 425,000 were affiliated with the CUT. Between 1983 and 1993, the number of unions in Chile rose from 4,401 to 11,389. In 1994, the CUT was admitted to membership of the ICFTU. In 2001, it was estimated that about 12 percent of Chilean employees were union members. On September 11, 2001, the senate of Chile adopted a labor union rights law; the ICFTU has complained that the law does not go far enough, but noted that for the first time in the history of Chile, 10 military officers were found guilty of the murder of a labor union official, that of Tucapel Jiménez, under the dictatorship of General Augusto Pinochet.

CHINA. The first Chinese labor unions were formed in the Canton region from 1895; they were followed by a union of seamen formed in the British colony of **Hong Kong** in 1909, who successfully defended their union by a **strike** in 1922 against an attempt to suppress it. In the same year, the first national congress of Chinese labor was held, which led to the formation of the All China General Labor Federation in 1925. Organized labor drew much of its support from the industrial city of Shanghai. In 1927, Chiang Kai-shek purged the **communists** from organized labor in Shanghai, which resulted in the killing of about 5,000 people. In 1930, there were said to be 2.8 million labor union members in China, but free labor bodies were never able to get established primarily because neither the communists nor the Kuomintang supported an independent labor movement.

In 1950, the communist government adopted a labor union law that recognized only the All-China Federation of Trade Unions under the control of the communist party; the law was amended in 1992 and October 2001, but has not led to the recognition of any independent labor organizations. In 1989, there was an attempt to form independent labor unions but these bodies and the Free Trade Union Preparatory Committee (formed at the end of 1991) were suppressed by the government in 1992. China has never been a member of the **International Confederation of Free Trade Unions** (ICFTU). On January 1, 1995, a labor law came into effect that set down minimum general conditions of employment for the first time. The absence of an officially recognized labor movement has not meant the absence of **labor disputes** in China, which are known to have occurred on a large scale, particularly following the **privatization** of many state-owned enterprises in the 1990s. In 2002, the ICFTU was particularly critical of abuses of trade union rights in China and noted a wave of **strikes** during March to May 2002, particularly in the northeastern provinces. *See also* TAIWAN.

COAL MINING. With engineering, coal mining was one of the main pillars of organized labor in most Western countries. Between the mid-1900s and the late 1930s coal miners' unions were the largest single labor unions in both the **United Kingdom** and the **United States**. Within both countries, labor unions among coal miners emerged on a regional basis after 1840, but their attempts to form effective national bodies floundered until the 1890s. The similarity in the two countries was explained not just by the geographical separation between coalfields but also by the presence of British immigrants among the union leaders in the early history of coal mining in the United States. The first labor union in the anthracite coalfields of Pennsylvania was organized by an English immigrant, John Bates, in 1849. Later, Daniel Weaver and Thomas Lloyd, both immigrant miners from Staffordshire, formed the American Miners' Association in 1861.

Between 1854 and 1902, nearly 191,000 miners of all kinds emigrated from Britain; of the 184,000 whose destinations are known, 109,200 went to the United States, 11,000 to **Canada**, and 24,900 to **Australia** and **New Zealand**. The bulk of this migration occurred between 1854 and 1871, when 70,400 British miners emigrated. In 1890, 58 percent of coal miners in Pennsylvania were foreign-born; in Australia, 76 percent of coal miners in the largest coalfield, at Newcastle, New South Wales, were foreign-born in 1891.

Because coal was the main source of energy up to the 1950s, coal miners' unions were able to command considerable influence within organized labor, but since that time, technological changes have reduced the number of miners needed and other sources of energy have lessened the reliance on coal. Between 1910 and 1940, the amount of energy supplied to the U.S. economy from coal fell from 85 to 50 percent. Coal mining had also been a major source of **labor disputes** in Australia, Britain, and the United States before 1950. (*See also* IMMIGRATION; MINEWORKERS' FEDERATION OF GREAT BRITAIN: UNITED MINE WORKERS OF AMERICA; table 14, appendix F).

CODETERMINATION. *See MITBESTIMMUNG.*

COLLECTIVE BARGAINING. Collective bargaining is the decision-making process whereby employers and unions negotiate the wages and conditions of employment. This process may also include governments. The form of collective bargaining varies. Unions and employers may bargain directly with each other or through a third party, such as an independent negotiator or a tribunal established by the government. Bargaining structures can vary also. Bargaining can take place with just a single enterprise or across a whole industry or a whole country. The types of collective bargaining that are used reflect the particular histories and cultures of the countries concerned. For example, collective bargaining in the private sector in the **United States** and the **United Kingdom** is generally done without any government participation, whereas in **Australia** government industrial tribunals continue to play an active part in the bargaining process. *See also* UNION-GOVERNMENT AGREEMENTS.

COLOMBIA. Associations of employees were formed in Colombia from the 1850s, but the first unions did not appear until around 1909. A **strike** by banana laborers in December 1928 resulted in the deaths of over a hundred strikers. Unions and **collective bargaining** were fostered by a law of 1931. A union federation was formed in 1935 but soon split between **socialists** and **communists**. It was reunited as the *Confederacion de Trabajadores de Colombia* (the CTC or Confederation of Colombian Workers) in 1938. Colombia had two union federations affiliated with the **International Confederation of Free Trade Unions** (ICFTU) by 1951, the CTC and the Catholic *Union de Trabajadores de Colombia* (Union of Workers of Colombia), formed in 1946, but they were rivals and it was not until 1958 that the two bodies, with the support of the ICFTU, agreed to work together.

Although collective bargaining and trade unions were legalized in 1975, organized labor in Colombia has had a difficult history marked by political instability and repression, a reflection of the country's narrow economic base and poor economic performance. In its annual surveys of **violations of trade union rights**, the ICFTU has consistently made special mention of the savagery of labor relations and **human rights** abuses in Colombia, specifically the killing of labor union activists. Between 1986 and 1994, at least 1,020 union activists were killed in Colombia; in 2002, 184 were killed, compared to 185 in 2001.

COMMONWEALTH TRADE UNION COUNCIL. This international body, based in London, was formed in 1979 to promote the interests of employees in the 50 countries that make up the Commonwealth, that is, the former British Empire. In 2001, there were 30 million employees in the Council's member countries. In 2001 and 2002, one of the main concerns of the Council was the violation of trade union and **human rights** in **Zimbabwe** following the parliamentary elections in June 2000 and organizing an appeal for the Zimbabwe Congress of Trade Unions.

COMMUNICATION WORKERS' UNION OF AMERICA (CWU). The CWU is the largest telecommunications union in the world. It grew out of the organization of telephone workers in the 1890s by the International Brotherhood of Electrical Workers and the Commercial Telegraphers' Union. The modern union began as the National Federation of Telephone Workers, which was formed at Chicago in June 1939 with 45,000 members. By 1945, the Federation had grown to 170,000 members. Following a failed strike against the American Telephone and Telegraph Company, the Federation renamed itself the Communication Workers' Association in 1947 and was reorganized along more central lines. In 1949, it joined the **Congress of Industrial Organizations** (CIO) to avoid further jurisdictional or demarcation disputes with other unions in the telecommunications industry and became affiliated with the **American Federation of Labor-Congress of Industrial Organizations** (AFL-CIO) in 1955. **Membership** of the CWA rose from 180,000 in 1950 to 260,000 in 1960 and to 573,000 by 1983. Between 1992 and 2002, its membership increased from 700,000 to 740,000 in the **United States** and **Canada**. *See also* POSTAL, TELEGRAPH, AND TELEPHONE INTERNATIONAL.

COMMUNICATIONS INTERNATIONAL (CI). The CI was named the **Postal, Telegraph, and Telephone International** until August 1997. The change in name was made in response to mergers and other changes in the organization of global telecommunications. On January 1, 2000, the CI merged with the **International Graphical Federation,** the **Media Entertainment International**, and the *Fédération internationale des employés, techniciens et cadres* (International Federation of Commercial, Clerical, Professional, and Technical Employees) to form the **Union Network International** (UNI).

COMMUNISM. The establishment of the Bolshevik regime under Vladimir I. Lenin following the revolution in the former Russian Empire in 1917 and the formation of communist parties in other parts of the world after 1918 began a new era in the history of organized labor. Underlying these changes was an upsurge of working-class discontent based on sharp inflation during and after World War I and the economic slump of the early 1920s. Following Lenin, communist theory and practice regarded labor unions as the primary vehicle of working-class organizations and, as such, ideal for infiltration and mobilization on behalf of revolution; this was the purpose of the Comintern, which was established in March 1919. Noncommunist bodies that proved resistant to infiltration, notably the **International Federation of Trade Unions** (IFTU), were made the targets of propaganda wars of ridicule and scorn.

As organizations, labor unions were often poorly equipped to deal with communist infiltration because of the low proportion of members who usually attended union meetings. As well, many communists gained election to union posts because of their dedication and hard work. The communist presence was notable in the leadership of certain industries such as **coal mining**, engineering, transportation, and the waterfront; during the Depression of the early 1930s communists were often the leaders of moves to mobilize the unemployed into movements. With Hitler's attack on the Soviet Union in June 1941, the communist parties in the West were instructed to cooperate with their governments. In 1943, the Comintern was officially disbanded.

The end of World War II and the start of the Cold War saw a renewal of the Russian-led campaign to infiltrate organized labor, a campaign that brought about a split of the **World Federation of Trade Unions** (WFTU) and the creation of the **International Confederation of Free Trade Unions** (ICFTU) in 1949. The improvement in the world economy after the early 1950s and determined campaigns to remove communists from key union positions (often, but not entirely, led by Catholics) largely eliminated communism as a major force within organized labor in the West. Nevertheless, individual communist leaders continued to be important in organized labor until the 1980s. With the collapse of the Soviet Union in 1991, the threat of communism largely disappeared, and the former labor union federations in Russia and Eastern Europe converted themselves into organizations that professed to be democratic to compete with the emergence of new labor union organizations that had no history of being run by communist governments. In Western Europe, few communist-oriented labor federations remain, the only notable exception being the *Confédération Générale du Tra-*

vail (CGT) or General Confederation of Labor, in France. *See also* CATHOLICISM; SOCIALISM.

CONCILIATION AND ARBITRATION. Conciliation and arbitration are two methods that can be used for settling **labor disputes**. Following legislation in 1562 to fix maximum levels of wages, local courts in England acted as industrial tribunals and as wages boards. By 1769, conciliation in labor disputes had become an important part of the work of English magistrates. The Combination Act of 1800 included an arbitration clause. During the 19th century, conciliation and arbitration gradually became features of the method of resolving labor disputes in England.

Conciliation refers to the voluntary use of a mediator, who tries to reach a settlement that both employer and employees would accept. Failing that, resort could be made to arbitration, where a settlement would be proposed by a board or individual. The first conciliation legislation was passed in Britain in 1867, but the system had mixed success. In the wave of labor disputes in the late 19th and early 20th centuries, governments considered making conciliation and arbitration compulsory, that is, the parties in dispute would be legally compelled to accept the settlement of a board or tribunal. In the **United Kingdom**, labor unions generally opposed compulsory conciliation and arbitration. Nevertheless, compulsory arbitration as a means of settling disputes was used in **Germany** (1923-1928), **France** (1915-1919, 1936-1939), and 1940-1951), Kansas, (1920-1923), **Norway**, (1945-1952), and **Turkey** (1947-1963, 1980-1982).

Compulsory conciliation and arbitration achieved its most lasting success in **Australia** and **New Zealand**. In 1894, New Zealand introduced compulsory arbitration into its legal system, and it remained there until removed by far-reaching reforms in 1991. In Australia, industrial tribunals were established under federal and state laws between 1896 and 1912. In the early 1900s, there was considerable interest in these labor experiments from the United Kingdom, France, and the **United States**. In 1907, the British government sent Ernest Aves (1857-1917) on a fact-finding mission to Australia and New Zealand to investigate compulsory conciliation and arbitration; he reported that these systems seem to work well in their particular environments but concluded that the different legal and economic environment of the United Kingdom made their adoption inappropriate. Since the mid-1980s both federal and state governments in Australia have encouraged greater reliance on **collective bargaining**, although the essentials of the conciliation and arbitration system remain intact.

CONFEDERACIÓN DE TRABAJADORES DE AMERICA LATINA* (CTAL)**. The CTAL, or Confederation of Latin American Workers, was formed in 1938 by Vincente Lombardo Toledano, a Mexican Marxist. A left wing international federation, it had close links with the **Congress of Industrial Organizations** (CIO). During World War II, the CTAL actively promoted organized labor in Latin America and supported the work of the **International Labour Organisation** (ILO). In 1945, the CTAL joined the **World Federation of Trade Unions** (WFTU) and became its regional affiliate for Latin America. The CTAL remained with the WFTU after the withdrawal of its noncommunist members in 1948. In 1962, the CTAL was officially disbanded and replaced by the ***Congreso Permanente de Unidad Sindical de los Trabajadores de America Latina (Permanent Congress of Trade Union Unity of Latin American Workers).

CONFEDERACIÓN INTERAMERICANA DE TRABAJADORES* (CIT)**. The CIT, or Interamerican Confederation of Workers, was the successor body to the Pan-American Federation of Labor. Formed on January 10, 1948 in Lima, **Peru**, the other founding member countries of the CIT were **Bolivia, Brazil, Chile, Colombia, Costa Rica, Cuba, El Salvador**, Dutch Guiana, **Mexico, Panama, Puerto Rico**, and the **United States**. The **American Federation of Labor** (AFL), represented by **George Meany** and others, was the prime mover in the creation of the CIT, which also had the support of the U.S. Department of State in its efforts to insulate Latin America from European fascism. The CIT soon fell victim to regional and international politics. In 1949, it was expelled from Peru by the government crackdown on organized labor and was then caught up in the politics of the Cold War. In 1951, the CIT reorganized itself into the ***Organización Regional Interamericana de Trabajadores.

***CONFÉDÉRATION EUROPÉENNE DES CADRES* (CEC)**. The CEC (European Confederation of Managers), also known as EUROCADRES, was formed in 1989 to represent the interests of managers, executives, and professional staff. Since December 1993, it has been formally recognized by the **European Union** as a "social partner" for European-level dialogue on social policy matters. In 2001, the CEC represented 1.5 million employed managers in Europe, compared to 800,000 in 1993. The CEC supports professional equality between men and **women** and programs to improve their access to jobs involving supervision, responsibility, and autonomy; the specific presence of a representation of executives and managerial staff in all the information, consultation, and participation bodies in the company; and adaptations to supplementary pensions in Europe to promote the free movement of labor.

CONFÉDÉRATION EUROPÉENNE DES SYNDICATS INDÉ-PENDANTS (**CESI**). The CESI, or European Confederation of Independent Trade Unions, was created in 1990 to represent the interests of a range of independent labor organizations. Its country membership in 1993 consisted of **Belgium, Germany, Iceland, Italy,** the **Netherlands, Portugal, Spain,** and the **United Kingdom** as well as **Sweden, Norway** (to July 1994), the **Czech Republic** and **Slovakia,** and the **Public Services International.** Since 1994, the CESI had admitted affiliates from **Bulgaria, Hungary, Poland,** and **Romania.** The CESI has not been granted "social partner" status for European-level dialogue on social policy matters by the European Commission. Even so, in 2001 the CESI claimed to represent seven million members, compared to five million in 1993. *See also CONFÉDÉRATION EUROPÉENNE DES CADRES;* EUROPEAN TRADE UNION CONFEDERATION.

CONFÉDÉRATION GÉNÉRALE DU TRAVAIL (**CGT**). The CGT, or General Confederation of Labor, has been the oldest continuous peak labor organization in **France** since its formation at Limoges in 1895; it absorbed the National Federation of *Bourses du Travail* in 1902. In 1906, the CGT adopted the radical Charter of Amiens, which called for wage increases and **shorter working hours** by dispossessing the "capitalist class" and supported the **general strike** as a means of achieving that end; the charter also made the CGT independent of any political party or philosophy. Between 1914 and 1920 the number of union members represented by the CGT grew from 400,000 to 2.5 million but, as before 1914, the CGT was riven by tensions between its right and left wings. In 1921-1922, the CGT split when the **communists** and **syndicalists** formed their own federation, the *Confédération Générale du Tra-*

vail Unitaire, which joined the Red International of Labor Unions in 1923. In 1936, the CGT and the *Confédération Générale du Travail Unitaire* held a unity congress that resulted in its readmission to the CGT. Membership of the CGT soared to between four and five million by 1936. Nevertheless, tensions between the communists and noncommunists remained.

In 1948 many of the noncommunists in the CGT left to form their own body, the *Confédération Générale du Travail-Force Ouvrière* (CGT-FO), leaving the CGT effectively under the control of the French Communist Party (formed in 1920). The CGT has been the most important Western European affiliate of the communist **World Federation of Trade Unions** (WFTU) since 1949, but its power has been declining since the 1970s. Between the early 1970s and 1988, the membership of the CGT fell from 2.3 million to 800,000 and to 650,000 by 1999. In November 2001, the CGT was the only major national labor federation in Western Europe that was not an affiliate of the **International Confederation of Free Trade Unions** (ICFTU).

CONFÉDÉRATION INTERNATIONALE DES FONCTION-NAIRES **(CIF).** The CIF (International Confederation of Public Servants) is a Paris-based labor organization that was formed in 1955. In 2001, it had 11 members in eight countries and was associated with the *Confédération Européenne des Syndicats Indépendants.*

CONFEDERATION OF HEALTH SERVICE EMPLOYEES (COHSE). The COHSE was a British health workers' union that was formed in 1946 from the merger of the Mental Hospital and Institutional Workers' Union (founded in 1910) and the Hospital and Welfare Services Union (founded in 1918). Between 1948 and 1982, its membership grew from 25,000 to 230,000. In 1993, it merged with two other labor unions to create **UNISON**.

CONFEDERATION OF SHIPBUILDING AND ENGINEERING UNIONS (CSEU). The CSEU began in 1891 as the Federation of Engineering and Shipbuilding Trades. It provided a forum for **collective bargaining** for British white- and **blue-collar** unions in shipbuilding and engineering. In its present form, it was constituted in 1936, but until World War II it was not a fully representative body. Wartime cooperation with the Foundry Union and the **Amal-**

gamated **Engineering Union** (AEU) on the national negotiating body, the National Engineering Joint Trades Movement (formed in 1941) helped to allay suspicions and, in 1944, the Foundry Union joined the CSEU, followed by the ASE in 1946. In 1989, the CSEU had 22 affiliated organizations representing 2 million members. In 2001, the CSEU represented about 1.2 million union members.

CONGO. The administration of French Equatorial Africa allowed Africans to form unions in 1944 and legalized them in 1952. The present territory of Congo was granted independence by **France** in 1960. In August 1963, the unions successfully resisted the attempts of the Fulbert Youlou government to impose a one-party state. The unions formed a national labor federation in 1964. A comprehensive labor law was introduced in 1975 to regulate the unions; union **membership** was then about 22,000. By 1995, Congo was represented in the **International Confederation of Free Trade Unions** (ICFTU) by two affiliates with a combined membership of 80,800.

CONGO (DEMOCRATIC REPUBLIC). A colony of **Belgium** to 1960, labor unions existed only among Europeans before 1945. Called Zaire from 1971 to 1997, organized labor among Africans claimed 325,000 members by 1965, according to the returns by its four affiliates of the **International Confederation of Free Trade Unions** (ICFTU), of whom 300,000 were members of the *Confédération des Syndicats libres du Congo* (Confederation of Free Trade Unions of the Congo), formed in 1961. Thereafter, the fortunes of organized labor in the Congo (Democratic Republic) have reflected its unstable and violent political history. There was no representation from the Congo in the ICFTU between 1965 and 1995. When the Congo (Democratic Republic) was again represented in the ICFTU; its affiliates claimed a combined **membership** of 526,500. In 2002, the ICFTU reported that although trade union rights existed on paper, they were ignored in practice against a background of fragile peace following the civil war and economic collapse.

CONGRESO PERMANENTE DE UNIDAD SINDICAL DE LOS TRABAJADORES DE AMERICA LATINA (CPUSTAL). The CPUSTAL or Permanent Congress of Trade Union Unity of Latin American Workers was an international labor federation formed in 1964 with 18 countries from Latin America and the Caribbean. It

succeeded the *Confederación de Trabajadores de America Latina.*
Closely associated with the **World Federation of Trade Unions**
(WFTU), it had 25 member countries in 1990 and claimed 20 mil-
lion members. The CPUSTAL faced much opposition from right-
wing governments and was defunct by 2001. *See also ORGANI-
ZACIÓN REGIONAL INTERAMERICANA DE TRABAJADORES.*

CONGRESS OF INDUSTRIAL ORGANIZATIONS (CIO). The
CIO was a national labor federation in the **United States** from 1935
to 1955. Unlike its competitor, the **American Federation of Labor**
(AFL), the CIO practiced **industrial unionism** and sought to organize the unskilled. Although there had been earlier attempts to recruit
the unskilled into the ranks of organized labor, notably by the
Knights of Labor and the **Industrial Workers of the World**
(IWW), the results of their efforts had been short-lived. The AFL
only supported unions based on "craft" or occupation and ignored
the unskilled and those employed in the mass production industries
which emerged after 1900. During the 1920s, the membership of
American unions declined in the face of company unionism, well-
organized campaigns for the open shop, and an unsympathetic political and legal environment. In 1929, a group of **socialists** and
progressive labor unionists led by A. J. Muste set up the Conference for Progressive Labor Action to win the AFL over to industrial
unionism and recruitment of the unskilled, but their efforts failed.

The possibility for success came in 1933 in the form of Section
7(a) of the National Industrial Recovery Act, which provided for
the right of employees to form unions for **collective bargaining**
free from employer interference. Despite the known existence of a
high level of support for unionism in mass production industries,
the leadership of the AFL successfully resisted all efforts to charter
new industrial unions at its 1934 convention. **John L. Lewis,** the
president of the **United Mine Workers of America**, itself an industrial union, assumed the leadership of the dissidents to the AFL
policy and, along with **Sidney Hillman** of the Amalgamated Clothing Workers, **David Dubinsky** of the **International Ladies' Garment Workers' Union**, and five other labor leaders, formed the
Committee for Industrial Organization in November 1935. In August 1936, the 10 unions that had affiliated with the CIO were suspended by the AFL following successful organizing drives by the
CIO in the steel, automobile, radio, and rubber industries.

The CIO unions went on to win three major industrial victories for union recognition. The first was achieved by a large-scale sit-down **strike** at the Goodyear Tire and Rubber Company, which won union recognition for the CIO's United Rubber Workers in 1936. In March 1937 the CIO won an unexpected major victory by negotiating union recognition for the Steel Workers Organizing Committee from U.S. Steel. The committee negotiated a 10 percent pay rise, an eight-hour day, and a 40-hour week. The third victory for union recognition was won by the **United Auto Workers** (UAW) against the General Motors Corporation, also in 1937. In 1938, the CIO was expelled from the AFL. The last major victory by the CIO was the gaining of recognition by the UAW from the Ford Motor Company after a 10-day strike in 1941. By 1939, the CIO claimed that its affiliated unions had a combined membership of 1.8 million compared to 3.9 million for the AFL. World War II more than doubled the membership of the CIO to 3.9 million, making it equal to that of the AFL.

However, the CIO never again regained the recruiting initiative it had seized in the late 1930s because the AFL began to recognize industrial unionism within its own ranks, as shown by the conversion of large affiliates like the **Teamsters** into industrial unions and by the defection of John L. Lewis and his United Mine Workers of America from the CIO in 1940. The Cold War also harmed the CIO, which had always been a more militant body than the AFL. On November 5, 1955, the two organizations agreed to merge as the **American Federation of Labor-Congress of Industrial Organizations** (AFL-CIO). At the time of its merger, the CIO had an affiliated membership of 4.6 million.

COOK ISLANDS. A dependency of **New Zealand**, the Cook Islands have been an affiliate of the **International Confederation of Free Trade Unions** (ICFTU) since about 1993 through their Cook Islands Public Service Association Inc., which has a **membership** of 1,120.

COSTA RICA. The first unions in Costa Rica were created in the early 1920s. In 1943, non-Catholic and **Catholic** union federations were formed. Despite its democratic government, union growth has been limited by the narrow basis of the economy and by unemployment as well as by political and religious divisions. By 1976, the three national labor federations had only about 30,000 members. Between 1958 and 1991, the **membership** of the Catholic federation increased from 12,000 to 56,700. Costa Rica has been represented in the **International Confederation of Free Trade Unions** (ICFTU) since 1951 and claimed 45,000 members in 2001. In 2002, the ICFTU reported that a repressive political climate continued to prevail over organized labor in Costa Rica.

CÔTE D'IVOIRE. See IVORY COAST.

COUNCIL OF NORDIC TRADE UNIONS. An international labor organization representing **Denmark, Finland, Iceland, Norway,** and **Sweden,** this Council has existed since 1972 in its present form, but its origins date back to 1886. The purpose of the Council is to provide a forum for topics of mutual interest and to exchange information. In 2001, the Council represented 8 million members, compared to 7.2 million in 1990.

CRAFT UNIONS. Historically, craft labor unions have been based on craftsmen, that is, those skilled **blue-collar** occupations requiring the completion of an **apprenticeship** to attain a formal qualification of competency. Because of their relatively high pay and strategic position in the workplace to disrupt production, craft unions have often been able to exercise economic power disproportionately greater than their numbers and were at the forefront of the leadership of organized labor in the **United Kingdom** and the **United States** in the 19th century. Up to the 1960s, craft unions had especially been a feature of **printing** and metals **manufacturing.** Generally, **membership** of craft unions was closed to employees who had not completed a relevant apprenticeship, and craft unions attempted to regulate their working environment closely by upholding unwritten work rules, such as reserving particular jobs for skilled workers. Notable examples of craft unions have included the **Amalgamated Society of Engineers,** and craft unions have often been leaders in the establishment of national union federations such as the British **Trades Union Congress** (TUC) and the **American Federation of Labor** (AFL). Technological change since the 1960s has effectively brought about the end of craft unions, which usually **amalgamated** with other unions. *See also* INDUSTRIAL UNIONS.

CROATIA. Organized labor emerged in Croatia in 1904, and in 1907, Croatia became a member of the **International Federation of Trade Unions (IFTU).** By 1913, membership of the country's unions had grown to 7,000. From October 1918 to its dissolution in June 1991, Croatia's labor movement was intertwined with the violent history and ethnic politics of the republic of **Yugoslavia.** However, the situation changed with independence. The largest labor organization in Croatia, the Union of Autonomous Trade Unions (UATUC), applied to join the **International Confederation of Free Trade Unions** (ICFTU) in 1992 and was admitted in January 1997 with 650,000 members; in 2001, it claimed a membership of 345,900. In 2001, the ICFTU reported that although the legal framework for organized labor had improved, much remained to be done.

CUBA. The first Cuban labor union was formed among tobacco employees in 1868, and over the next 15 years a number of **craft unions** were set up. A congress of Cuban employees was held in 1892 and passed resolutions calling for independence from **Spain** and the eight-hour day. **Anarchism,** as in other Latin American countries, was an important force within organized labor; an anarchist labor federation was created in 1925. In 1933, there was a **general strike** that succeeded in gaining some progressive legislation, but a second general strike in 1935 was repressed and organized labor crushed. It revived in 1938 and, in January 1939, the *Confederación de Trabajadores de Cuba* (Confederation of Workers of Cuba) was formed. Fidel Castro's triumph over Fulgencio Batista was greatly assisted by a general strike in 1959. With Castro's victory, organized labor was gradually deprived of its independence; Cuba then had 1.2 million union members. Cuba was represented in the **Confederation of Free Trade Unions** (ICFTU) from 1951 to 1959. In October 1991, an Independent Cuban General Workers' Union was created, but it has always been denied recognition by the government. In 2002, the ICFTU reported that promised labor law reforms had not been made and that the government continued to persecute independent organized labor.

CURAÇAO. The southern group of islands that make up the Netherlands Antilles, Curaçao has been a member of the **International Confederation of Free Trade Unions** ICFTU since at least 1957.

Union **membership** in Curaçao fell from 9,000 in 1957 to 6,000 in 1988 and to 5,100 in 2001.

CYPRUS. Organized labor in Cyprus emerged in 1910, four years before the island was annexed by the **United Kingdom**. The first trade union law was enacted in 1932, but comprehensive labor laws were only introduced during World War II. The first labor federation was established in 1941. Organized labor was part of the struggle for independence, which was gained in 1960. From 1963, divisions between Greeks and Turks on Cyprus became evident and were formalized after the division of the island with the Turkish invasion in 1974. Cyprus has been represented in the **International Confederation of Free Trade Unions** (ICFTU) since 1951. In 2001, its affiliate, the Cyprus Workers' Confederation, claimed a membership of 66,000.

CZECH REPUBLIC. The Czech Republic was created in 1993 from the division of **Czechoslovakia**. It has been represented since the division in the **International Confederation of Free Trade Unions** (ICFTU) by the Czech-Moravian Chamber of Trade Unions, which claimed a **membership** of 883,000 in 2001. In January 2001, a new labor code was introduced which strengthened the legal position of organized labor but excluded the **public sector** from **collective bargaining**. In 2002, the ICFTU was critical of the right to strike in the Czech Republic.

CZECHOSLOVAKIA. Before 1918, Czechoslovakia was part of the Austro-Hungarian Empire. The first labor union was set up by journeymen drapers at Liberec in 1870 and had 3,500 members after a year. Unions became part of the political struggle for independence as well as pursuing industrial objectives. A labor federation was formed in 1897, some of whose members attended as observers at the conferences of the **International Federation of Trade Unions** (IFTU) in 1901 and 1902. Reflecting the diversity of the society, unions were divided along national, political, and religious lines. In 1905, the unions made their presence felt through protests for the eight-hour day as well as for the universal franchise. By 1913, there were 318,000 union members; some were in German unions and others were members of **Catholic** or Protestant unions. In 1919, the Czech and German labor federations became affiliates of the IFTU and remained affiliated until 1938. By 1920, there were 1.7 million union members in the Czechoslovak Republic. Unlike most of its neighbors, Czechoslovakia had a large industrial base; in 1921, 37 percent of the labor force was employed in **manufacturing**. Union **membership** peaked at 1,738,300 in 1928, when there were 583 unions. Under the Nazi occupation (1938-1945), free unions were suppressed and compliant ones created. As a result of their leadership of the partisans during World War II, the **communists** gained much popular support. In 1945, the communists formed their own labor federation, the Central Council of Trade Unions. Noncommunist unions reestablished themselves, but their independence was short-lived and, from 1948, the communist federation was the sole national labor center. During the "Prague Spring" in 1968, the unions actively supported Alexander Dubček's program of reforms. The 12 industrial unions were divided into 58 new unions with a high degree of independence. After the Soviet invasion and the fall of Dubček in April 1969, these initiatives were suppressed. After the collapse of the communist regime in November 1989 in the so-called Velvet Revolution, organized labor carried out its own internal reforms, which produced a united federation of Czech and Slovak unions, *eska a Slovenská Konfederace odborových* (ČS-KOS), with a membership of six million. Following the peaceful division of the country into the **Czech Republic** and **Slovakia** in 1993, the ČS-KOS was also divided along Czech and Slovak lines. At the time of the division, there were 2.6 million members in the Czech Republic and 1.2 million in Slovakia.

-D-

DEAKIN, ARTHUR (1890-1955). One of the leading British labor leaders in the 1940s, Deakin was born in Sutton Coldfield, Warwickshire, and moved to Wales in the early 1900s where he worked in a steel plant. During this period he became a Primitive Methodist and a teetotaler. In 1910, he moved to north Wales where he was a member of several unions including the **Amalgamated Society of Engineers** but transferred to the Dock, Wharf, Riverside, and General Workers' Union and became a full-time organizer for the Union in 1919. When the Union became part of the **Transport and General Workers' Union** (TGWU) in 1922, Deakin became, in effect, its manager for north Wales. After holding various local government positions, he became national secretary of the General Workers' part of the TGWU and moved to London, where his abilities were recognized by the general secretary, **Ernest Bevin**, who made Deakin his protégé. When Bevin joined Winston Churchill's War Cabinet in 1940, Deakin became the acting general secretary of the TGWU; he became permanent in the position with Bevin's retirement in 1946. In the same year he also became president of the **World Federation of Trade Unions** (WFTU) and, like his patron, Bevin, strongly opposed the communists, who were against the Marshall Plan for aiding postwar Europe. Indeed, Deakin played a central role in the foundation of the **International Confederation of Free Trade Unions** (ICFTU) in 1949. Deakin continued to play an important part in fighting **communism** within the **Trades Union Congress** (TUC), of which he was president in 1951-1952.

DENMARK. Organized labor developed relatively strongly in Denmark from the mid-1850s after the abolition of the guilds. By 1890, there were 218 unions with about 31,000 union members; in 1900, there were 96,000 union members or about 14 percent of employees, a level comparable with the **United Kingdom** (13 percent). This strength owed much to an agreement reached between the Federation of Danish Trade Unions (the *Landorganisationen i Denmark* or LO, formed in 1898) and the government in 1899 over the right to organize; the unions were also given the task of running the unemployment insurance program. This agreement enabled Danish unions to enjoy a privileged position within European countries of the time and continued to sustain them thereafter. In the post-1945 period, Denmark continued to have a high level of union **membership**; it rose from 52 percent of employees in 1950 to 80 percent in 1980 and even by 1991 remained at 81 percent. In 2001, there were two million union members covering 83 percent of employees.

DEUTSCHE ARBEITSFRONT **(DAF).** The DAF (German Labor Front) was set up by the Nazis to control the German labor movement between 1933 and 1945. After November 1933, the DAF also included all employers. The DAF covered the whole labor force and by 1939 had control of about 20 million people. During World War II, it was used to maintain production of war materials and to settle **labor disputes**. The members of the DAF were organized among 18 *Reichbetriebsgruppen* or industrial groups. Although not a free labor organization, the structure of the DAF foreshadowed the 16 industrial groups (*Industriegewerkschaften*) in West Germany which were created between 1948 and 1950. *See also* BÖCKLER, HANS; *DEUTSCHER GEWERKSCHAFTSBUND.*

DEUTSCHER GEWERKSCHAFTSBUND (DGB). The DGB (German Trade Union Federation) is the leading labor union federation of **Germany**. The first German union federation, the *Allgemeiner Deutscher Gewerkschaftsbund* (General German Trade Union Federation), was formed in 1868 and claimed to represent 142,000 employees but was able to achieve little as a result of Otto von Bismarck's repressive Anti-Socialist Laws, which were in force from 1878 to 1890. In 1890 a new labor federation, the *Generalkommission der Gewerkschaften* (General Council of Trade Unions), was formed with **Carl Legien** as its president.

In 1919 this body was reorganized as the *Allgemeiner Deutscher Gewerkschaftsbund* (General German Trade Union Federation), a title it retained until its suppression by the Nazis in 1933. After Germany's defeat in 1945, unions were at first only allowed to organize within state boundaries but, with the lifting of this restriction, the *Deutscher Gewerkschaftsbund* was set up in the British zone under the leadership of **Hans Böckler** in April 1947. With the agreement of the Americans and French, the DGB was allowed to extend into their zones in West Germany and in their sectors cf Berlin in October 1949. By 1950, the DGB had a total **membership** of nearly 5.5 million, of whom 83 percent were **blue-collar** employees and 15 percent were **women**. Until 2001, one union, *IG Metall*, accounted for about a quarter of its total membership. Although not formally affiliated with the German Social Democratic Party, the DGB has been closely associated with it in practice. Following the formal reunification of Germany in October 1990, the membership of the unions affiliated with the DGB rose from 7.8 to 9.8 million members between 1989 and 1994. Its membership in 1994 consisted of 62 percent blue-collar workers and 31 percent women. Since 1994, the DGG has experienced a decline in the membership of its affiliates, prompting greater moves toward **amalagamation**. In 1996, the DGB abandoned its long-standing support for the nationalization of key industries.

In 2002, the DGB consisted of eight industry unions (compared to 16 in 1994), but its power over its larger affiliates was very limited. The eight industrial groups covered by its affiliated unions were construction, **agriculture**, and environment; mining, chemicals, and energy; private transportation and communications; **education** and science; metal manufacturing; food beverages and catering; **police**; and the four industry groups covered by *Ver.di* (commerce, banking and insurance; media and the arts; public services and transportation; and postal workers).

DEUTSCHER METALLARBEITER-VERBAND **(DMV).** The DMV (German Metal Workers' Union) was the first **industrial union** to be formed in **Germany**. The first German metal workers' unions were formed in 1868-1869, but **membership** growth was slow before 1891, when representatives of a number of separate metal unions formed a single industrial union, the *Deutscher Metallarbeiter Verband* (DMV) with 23,200 members. Because it recruited unskilled as well as skilled workers, the DMV was regarded with suspicion by the older craft metal unions. For instance, the Berlin metal workers did not join the DMV until 1897 and then only on the condition that they retain their independence. For an industrial union, the growth of the DMV was slow, 50,000 in 1896, 100,000 in 1901, and 554,900 by 1913, largely because the DMV was denied recognition by employers in the new large-scale heavy industry plants. Granted recognition during World War I in 1916, the membership of the DMV rose to 786,000 by 1918 and to 1.6 million in 1919, a level it held until 1923, making it briefly the largest single union in the world. The DMV proved incapable of retaining these gains after 1924 because of the economic crisis and also internal weaknesses. In particular, it failed to recruit the young; between 1919 and 1931, the percentage of members under 20 fell from 23 to 12 percent. By 1928 membership had fallen to 944,000. The DMV was to the left of most of the German labor movement. It was dissolved by the Nazis on May 2, 1933, and many of its leaders were imprisoned. *See also* BRENNER, OTTO.

DJIBOUTI. A colony of **France** to June 1977, labor unions were scarce. Apart from local branches of French unions, only two unions existed by 1975. The French Overseas Labor Code of 1952 remained in force in 1994, despite the government's promise to update the country's labor laws. In July 1993, the secondary school teachers formed a union that received legal recognition; it called a **strike** in January 1994 over the nonpayment of salaries, prompting a round of government repression and intimidation. Djibouti has been represented in the **International Confederation of Free Trade Unions** (ICFTU) since 1994 by the *Union Djiboutienne du travail* (Djibouti Labor Union), which claimed 15,000 members. In 2002, the ICFTU reported that there was considerable interference with organized labor by the government of Djibouti.

DOMINICA. Independent of the **United Kingdom** since November 1978, organized labor in Dominica had emerged by the late 1940s, and Dominica was an affiliate of the the **International Confederation of Free Trade Unions** (ICFTU) by 1951. By 1995, it reported a union **membership** of 1,900. The government since the 1990s has severely curtailed the right to strike. In 2001, there were about 1,800 union members in Dominica.

DOMINICAN REPUBLIC. Organized labor emerged during the U.S. occupation between 1916 and 1924. A union federation was formed in 1930. The dictator General Rafael Trujillo tried to suppress the federation, but it survived despite much loss of life. In 1946, Trujillo set up a union federation controlled by the government. Following a mission to the Dominican Republic in 1957, the **International Confederation of Free Trade Unions** (ICFTU) boycotted the oppressive Trujillo government; Trujillo was assassinated in 1961. In 1962, organized labor split along political lines, with the moderate bodies setting up the *Confederación Nacional de Trabajadores Libres* (National Confederation of Free Workers); it was affiliated with the ICFTU by 1965. The militant union bodies opted to resist the government. Civil war in 1965-1966 resulted in U.S. occupation. The political environment for organized labor only began to improve after the 1978 elections. A labor code introduced in 1992 provided legal protection for labor unions and required that a union had to have a **membership** of more than half of the employees at an enterprise for it to be recognized as the representative for **collective bargaining**. Economic reforms from the 1980s led to the establishment of **export processing zones**, in which unions were, in effect, not permitted, and working conditions and pay were substandard. In 2002, the ICFTU reported that although workers could form labor unions, they are effectively excluded from export processing zones and sugar plantations. The government remains repressive towards organized labor.

DONOVAN COMMISSION. The Donovan Commission was the popular term for the British Royal Commission on Trade Unions and Employers' Associations, which reported to the government in 1968. Named after its chairman, Lord Donovan, it made a comprehensive investigation of industrial relations and institutions. The commission found that Britain had two systems of labor relations, a formal and an informal system. The formal system, based on law and official institutions, was less important than the informal system, based on the behavior of unions, shop stewards, and employers. It argued that **collective bargaining** should be extended with the agreement of employers and unions and that legislative reform of the formal system was not a practical option. Despite the commission's findings, which were the product of careful research including some pioneering survey investigations, British conservative governments since 1980 have placed primary reliance on the law as a means of controlling and reducing the power of organized labor. The lasting legacy of the Donovan Commission was the inauguration of official workplace surveys, the most recent being conducted in 1998. *See also* EMPLOYMENT ACTS; *ROOKES V. BARNARD.*

DUBINSKY, DAVID (1892-1982). A leading U.S. labor leader, Dubinsky was born in Russian **Poland**, and began his working life as a baker. He took part in a successful **strike** in 1907, after which he spent 18 months in jail. Exiled to Siberia, he escaped on the way and went underground until he gained an amnesty in 1910. In 1911, he emigrated to the **United States** and joined the **International Ladies' Garment Workers' Union** in New York. From 1918, he occupied various senior offices in Local 10 of the union and became secretary-treasurer in 1929 and president in 1932, a position he held until 1966. Thereafter, Dubinsky emerged as one of the main labor leaders in the United States. He was a labor adviser to the National Recovery Administration from 1933 to 1935 and an executive council member of the **American Federation of Labor** (AFL) in 1935 but resigned after the suspension of the **Congress of Industrial Organizations** (CIO) in 1937. Nevertheless, Dubinksy opposed the CIO as an independent body. In 1940, he reaffiliated his union with the AFL and, in 1945, was again on its executive council. He also took an active part in labor **politics** and was a founder of the American Labor Party in 1936. Dubinsky was a participant in the formation of the **International Confederation of Free Trade Unions** (ICFTU) in 1949.

-E-

ECUADOR. Organized labor emerged in Ecuador in its main port of Guayaquil in 1920, mainly as a result of the rise in the cost of living caused by the inflation of World War I. Although union protests over the cost of living were suppressed, the unions formed a federation to campaign for rights; its efforts led to the labor law of 1928. A national **Catholic** federation was formed in 1938 and, in June 1944, the **industrial unions** set up their own labor federation. A third national federation was formed later and was affiliated with the **International Confederation of Free Trade Unions** (ICFTU) by 1953; by 1975 this organization was renamed as the *Confederación Ecuatoriana de Organizaciones Sindicales Libres* (Ecuadorian Confederation of Free Trade Unions (CEOSL). In 1964, the military government denied the unions the right to **strike**, but they and students successfully forced the government to resign. Despite their differences, the three labor federations have tended to cooperate to try to achieve common goals such as a larger social security system and the nationalization of the petroleum industry. Internal division aside, slow economic growth as well as political hostility have made it difficult for organized labor to accomplish significant gains since the 1970s.

A fresh challenge came in the 1990s with government efforts to reform the economy along free market principles. In 1991, the labor law was amended to discourage the formation of unions in small enterprises that are an important part of the economy of Ecuador. There was a strike wave over government policies, particularly over petrol price rises and redundancies. In 1994, there was a nine-week strike by teachers that was only brought to an end by the government threat to declare a state of emergency and subject teachers to military discipline. Hyperinflation in 2000 and a fall in gross domestic product of 7.5 percent led to widespread labor protests in January 2001, which were met by government repression and the unlawful detention of the leaders of organized labor, including José Chávez, the president of the CEOSL. During demonstrations by teachers in June 2001, four people were shot dead. In 2002, the ICFTU reported that there was routine intimidation and violence towards organized labor and that there was no right to strike in practice.

EDUCATION. Labor unions in education have historically concerned school teachers. In the **United Kingdom**, the National Union of Elementary Teachers was formed in 1870; it renamed itself the National Union of Teachers in 1888 and conducted its first **strike** in 1914 against the Education Authority in Herefordshire. In 1919, the union agreed to admit uncertificated teachers as members, gained a national pay scale, and adopted an equal pay for **equal work** policy. In **Australia**, the first teachers' union was formed in Victoria in 1878. Other teachers' bodies were formed in Queensland in 1889 and New South Wales in 1895. The New South Wales Teachers' Association was formed in 1918 and formally registered as a labor union in 1919. The first teachers' strike occurred in Western Australia in July 1920 when they joined the majority of the **public sector** in a three-week strike for increased pay to compensate for inflation; the strike was largely successful. The first teachers' strike in Victoria occurred in 1965 and in New South Wales in 1968.

In the **United States**, the Chicago Federation of Teachers was formed in 1897 and affiliated with the **American Federation of Labor** (AFL) in 1902. In 1916, the **American Federation of Teachers** (AFT) was created and grew to 9,300 members by 1920. Thereafter, it had a difficult history marked by a fall of **membership** in the 1920s (down to 3,700) and an internal struggle with **communists** in the 1930s. Even by 1940 only about 3 percent of teachers were members of the federation. Despite a national no-strike policy up to 1963, teachers did strike at the state level from 1946 largely because of the failure of teachers' salaries to keep pace with comparable occupations in the private sector. The AFT faced strong competition from the **National Education Association** (NEA) from 1960; since 1987 the NEA has been the largest labor union in the U.S. and in 2001 was the second largest union in the world. *See also* WHITE-COLLAR UNIONISM.

EDUCATION INTERNATIONAL (EI). The EI was formed in 1993 from the merger of the **International Federation of Free Teachers' Unions**, (formed in 1928) and the World Confederation of Organizations of the Teaching Profession (formed in 1952). It is based in Brussels and has 311 affiliated unions in 153 countries representing 25 million members, mostly **women**. Its president since 1997 has been Mary Hatwood Futrell of the **National Education Association** (NEA). At its July 2001 congress, EI delegates passed resolutions relating to the role of education and new technology in the global economy, particularly the pay and conditions of teachers.

EGYPT. The first Egyptian labor union was formed among cigarette workers in 1899, and by 1911 there were 11 unions claiming a total of 7,000 members. As often happened in other colonial societies, labor unions became part of the movement for independence. They participated in the revolution of 1919, which led to the formation of a monarchical government in 1922. In the early 1920s the unions were led by the Egyptian Socialist Party (formed in 1921), but an attempted **general strike** in 1923 was suppressed. During the 1930s Egyptian organized labor became intertwined with **politics**. Unions were legalized in 1942. After the overthrow of the monarchy in 1952 under Colonel Gamal Abdel Nasser, organized labor and the political system became increasingly integrated. In 1962, the president of the Egyptian Federation of Labor (formed in 1956) was made minister of labor, a trend later followed by **Guinea** and **Tanzania**. Strikes do occur in Egypt, but they are regarded as a form of public disorder and are illegal. The government response to strikes is to use the **police** to repress them violently. Because there is no independent organized labor in Egypt, it has never been a member of the **International Confederation of Free Trade Unions** (ICFTU).

EL SALVADOR. Organized labor formed its first national federation in El Salvador in 1922; a reformed federation was set up in 1924 and drew support from plantation workers. A revolt in 1932 against the dismissal of the elected government by the military dictatorship of Maximiliano H. Martinez was savagely repressed with the slaughter of up to 20,000 peasants, an event that cowed organized labor until the mid-1950s. In 1957, the *Organización Regional Interamericana de Trabajadores* (Inter-American Regional Organization of Workers) (ORIT) held a congress that resulted in the foundation of the *Confederación General de Sindicatos* (CGS) or General Confederation of Labor Unions in 1958 and its swift affiliation to the **International Confederation of Free Trade Unions** (ICFTU). Although some liberalization was extended to organized labor by the government from 1962, mainly in response to fears caused by the communist revolution in **Cuba**, progress was limited by the inequitable distribution of land ownership, unemployment, and vigilante violence as well by the dependence of the economy on a few staples such as coffee for its growth. The country was torn apart by civil war from 1980 to 1992. Since 1992, organized labor has continued to face hostility from the government and legislative restrictions; for example, El Salvador still had not ratified International Labor Convention No. 87 (Freedom of Association and Protection of the Right to Organize) by 2001. In 2002, the ICFTU reported that there had been no improvement in the political and economic environment for organized labor in El Salvador.

EMPLOYERS' ORGANIZATIONS. Employers' organizations, like labor unions, have existed at least since Adam Smith's well-known discussion of their secret activities in *The Wealth of Nations* (Book I, Chapter VIII) in 1776. As shapers of national labor policy or participants in **collective bargaining**, formal employers' organizations in most countries emerged after 1880 partly in response to the rise of organized labor. The general pattern was usually for employers in an industry to organize first and create a national body later. In the **United Kingdom**, the ship owners formed a national federation in 1890, as did the engineering employers in 1896; the engineering federation organized two lockouts in 1896 and 1922 and defeated the unions both times. In 1919, the British Employers' Confederation was formed. In 1965, the Confederation of British Industry was created from a merger of the British Employers' Confederation, the Federation of British Industries, and the National Association of British Manufactures. The Chambers of Commerce remained separate from these bodies. In the **United States**, the shoemakers' employers organized an association as early as 1789. In 1899 the National Metal Trades Association was formed. The National Association of Manufacturers was set up in 1895, and in 1903 it adopted an "open shop" policy to fight unions. The Chamber of Commerce of the United States was founded in 1912.

In **France**, the *Le Chapelier* law of 1791 banned organizations by employees and employers but was largely enforced only against labor unions. The legislation that legalized unions in 1884 also legalized employers to form organizations, but those organizations that were created were confined to particular industries. A national employers' organization was only created in 1919 and even then was set up at the behest of the government; it was dissolved in

1940. The present principal employers' organization in France, the *Conseil National du Patronat Français*, was created in 1945. In **Germany**, a national federation of employers in manufacturing (*Vereinigung der Deutschen Arbeiterverbände*) was formed in 1913; it was joined by another national body (*Reichsverband der Deutschen Industrie*) in 1919. The **November Pact (Stinnes-Legien Agreement)** of 1918 encouraged the formation of employers' organizations by making such associations responsible for representing employers in **collective bargaining**. In the 1930s, the Nazis incorporated the employers' organizations into the *Deutsche Arbeitsfront*.

In 1950, the West German employers created the first comprehensive national employers' organization, the *Bundesvereinigung der Deutschen Arbeitgeberverbände* (Confederation of German Employers' Associations) to conduct national collective bargaining. In **Italy**, a national employers' organization was established in 1910; it became known by its shortened title *Confindustria* (Confederation of Industry) after 1920. In 1923, *Confindustria* successfully opposed a proposal by the fascist government of Benito Mussolini to integrate employers and unions in one body; it retained its autonomy and went on to remain a part of industrial relations in Italy after 1945.

In **Japan**, a national federation of chambers of commerce was formed in 1892. In 1917, the Japan Economic Federation was formed to prevent the legal recognition of labor unions. In 1938, the government set up the Greater Japan Patriotic Industrial Association (known as *Sampō*); all employers' organizations and unions were forced to join this body as part of the war effort in June 1940. *Nikkeiren*, the Japanese Federation of Employers' Associations, was formed in 1948.

In **Australia**, the first employers' organizations designed to deal with unions were formed by coal mine owners in 1872. The first national body was formed by building employers in 1890. In 1903, the various State Chambers of Manufactures formed a national body. Until the 1970s, employers' organizations were largely state-based and relatively ineffective as national organizations. In 1977, the first national umbrella employer organization, the Confederation of Australian Industry, was formed as a counterpart to the **Australian Council of Trade Unions**; in 1992, this body merged with the Australian Chamber of Commerce to form the Australian Chamber of Commerce and Industry. The Business

Council of Australia, a group of large employers, was created in 1983 to shape industrial policy. In **New Zealand**, the New Zealand Federation of Employers' Associations was formed in 1902. In 1992, the New Zealand Employers' Federation had 10,000 individual employer members and 51 affiliated business organizations as members. The New Zealand Business Roundtable, an employer body made up of large firms, was created in the mid-1970s to discuss and prepare general economic policies.

The International Organization of Employers, formed in 1920, is the only international body of its kind; it provides the employers' representatives to the **International Labour Organisation** (ILO).

EMPLOYMENT ACTS. Between 1980 and 1993, Conservative governments in the **United Kingdom** introduced a number of laws to limit the power of labor unions, following the **"winter of discontent."** The Employment Act 1980 limited **picketing** to employees who were directly engaged in a **strike**, expanded the exemptions from the closed shop, introduced public funding for secret ballots for the election of full-time union officials, and required secret ballots before unions engaged in strikes. The idea of strike ballots was first suggested in the Conservative Party's policy paper, *Fair Deal at Work*, which was published in 1968 and was also recommended for certain kinds of strikes in a **British Labour Party** policy document, *In Place of Strife*, published in 1969. The Employment Act 1982 outlawed the pre-entry closed shop and demanded that post-entry closed shops must be supported by 85 percent of employees in a ballot. The secret ballot provisions of the 1980 act were boycotted by the **Trades Union Congress** (TUC) and had little effect.

In 1984, the government published a Green Paper (a statement of government proposals) on proposed changes to the industrial law, which reintroduced the debate about public funding for secret ballots for the election of full-time union officials and before industrial disputes. This was followed by a White Paper (a statement of government intentions) and the Trade Union Act 1984, which required secret ballots for the election of full-time officials and for the holding of strikes not more than four weeks before they were due to start; the strike provision came into force on September 26, 1984. The Employment Act 1988 enabled a union member to apply to the court for legal action against the union if it engaged in industrial action without the support of a ballot. The Employment

Act 1990 provided for a right of complaint to an industrial tribunal for any employee refused employment because he/she did or did not belong to a union; made unions potentially liable for common law actions if any of their officials (including shop stewards) initiated industrial action without written repudiation; and employers were given greater power to dismiss employees who engaged in unofficial industrial action. This act has been interpreted as a return to the **Taff Vale Case**.

The Trade Union Reform and Employment Rights Act 1993 became law on July 1 and built on the trends evident in British labor law since 1980. Among other things, the law created a new legal right that enabled any individual, employer, or union member whose supply of goods and services was affected by a dispute that did not meet these conditions to initiate civil law proceedings against the union. The legislation also required unions about to engage in a labor dispute to conduct first an independently scrutinized postal ballot among members and to provide the employer with at least seven days' written notice.

The election of the **British Labour Party** in May 1997 did not result in the repeal of these employment acts, and although the level of labor disputes in the United Kingdom was low in the 1990s, this decline seems to have been caused by economic circumstances rather than the legislative environment. *See also* DONOVAN COMMISSION.

EQUAL PAY FOR EQUAL WORK. Equal pay for equal work refers to **women** receiving the same pay as men provided they perform work of equal value. In the **United States**, equal pay for women was raised as early as 1837. In the **United Kingdom**, the **Trades Union Congress** (TUC) passed resolutions in support of equal pay for women in the 1890s. Union support for equal pay, although based on **human rights** concerns, was also influenced by the desire to prevent women from being used to undercut union wage rates. The entry of large numbers of women into jobs traditionally done by men was generally only tolerated in wartime such as in transportation or metal working, but they were expected to leave these jobs at war's end. In the United Kingdom, women were only admitted to the **Amalgamated Engineering Union** in 1942. In **Australia**, industrial tribunals set women's pay rates at 55 percent that of men's in the 1920s and 1930s and raised them to 75 percent in 1950.

In 1951, the **International Labour Organisation** (ILO) adopted the Equal Remuneration Convention (No. 100), which called for equal pay for men and women for work of equal value. In 1958, the Australian state of New South Wales introduced "equal pay for equal work" legislation, which was followed by the other states by 1968. In 1969 and 1972, the Australian federal industrial tribunal handed down decisions in favor of equal pay for equal work for employees covered by federal **awards**. In 1970, the United Kingdom government introduced the Equal Pay Act. Despite these changes, women's pay in the private sector still lags behind men's.

EQUATORIAL GUINEA. Independent of **Spain** since October 1968, organized labor in Equatorial Guinea never had the opportunity to develop, either under Spanish rule or since independence. In 1976, the London-based Anti-Slavery Society published a report on **forced labor** and **slavery** in Equatorial Guinea. In 1990, the independent Equatorial Guinea Trade Union was formed, but failed to gain legal recognition or any reform of the country's denial of trade union rights. The Independent Services Trade Union in the **public sector** has also been unable to secure legal recognition since 1995. Despite the government's ratification of the eight core labor standards of the **International Labour Organisation** (ILO) in 2001, it has suppressed all attempts to create independent labor unions in 2002, according to the **International Confederation of Free Trade Unions** (ICFTU). Equatorial Guinea was not represented in the ICFTU in 2002.

ERITREA. Eritrea was formed as an independent nation in 1993 after a 30 years' war against **Ethiopia**. By 1995, the National Confederation of Eritrean Workers had been admitted to affiliation to the **International Confederation of Free Trade Unions** (ICFTU); it claimed 18,000 members and was a member in 2001.

ESTONIA. Organized labor was only able to emerge in Estonia after it gained independence from **Russia** in 1921; previously it had been part of the Russian Empire. By 1923, there were 30,000 union members and a national labor federation had been formed by 1927 and joined the **International Federation of Trade Unions** (IFTU). The number of union members reached 50,000 by 1932, and the national labor federation retained its membership of the IFTU until

1939. In 1940, an independent labor movement ceased to exist in Estonia, when like the other **Baltic states** it was annexed by the Soviet Union. From 1957 to 1994, the Estonian Seamen's Union was accorded membership in exile by the **International Confederation of Free Trade Unions** (ICFTU).

In the late 1980s, the Soviet Union began to fragment, allowing organized labor to reemerge. In 1989, the communist labor federation of Estonia joined the independence movement. In March 1990, Estonia and the other Baltic states declared their independence from the Soviet Union. Nevertheless, the political climate remained dangerous, as was shown by the murder of two visiting Swedish union officials who made contact with the independent labor movement. In 1994, Estonia became the first Baltic state to be represented in the ICFTU by the Confederation of Estonian Trade Unions; it claimed 57,000 members in 2001.

ETHIOPIA. Although a member of the **International Labour Organisation** (ILO) from 1923, Ethiopia did not legally recognize labor unions until 1962 and unions had to form and operate secretly. The first union was formed among the railroad workers in 1947. In 1954, the unions formed the first national labor federation, which was reformed into the Confederation of Ethiopian Labor Unions (CETU) in 1963. Assisted by both the **International Confederation of Free Trade Unions** (ICFTU), which it joined, and the **American Federation of Labor-Congress of Industrial Organizations** (AFL-CIO), the membership of the CETU grew from 28,000 in 1964 to 85,000 in 1974, but organized labor fell foul of the military council (the Dergue) that replaced Emperor Haile Selassie. The Dergue regime formed its own labor federation. Strikes were forbidden and the CETU was caught up in a policy of government hostility and prolonged civil war, economic destruction, and famine. In 1994, the CETU reaffiliated with the ICFTU, but ceased its membership by 1997 as it was brought increasingly under government control. In 2002, the ICFTU reported that there had been no improvement in the conditions for organized labor in Ethiopia.

EUROPEAN TRADE UNION CONFEDERATION (ETUC). The ETUC is the major international labor organization of Western Europe. Although the **International Federation of Trade Unions** (IFTU) was mainly a European body for most of its life between

1901 and 1945, the first moves to form a regional labor federation of European bodies were made in November 1950 when the **International Confederation of Free Trade Unions** (ICFTU) established the European Regional Organization. The creation of the European Coal and Steel Community prompted a number of national labor federations as well as the **International Metalworkers' Federation** and the **Miners' International Federation** to form the Committee of Twenty-One to represent the interests of organized labor. Following the creation of the European Commission by the Treaty of Rome in 1958, the ICFTU formed the European Trade Union Secretariat, which incorporated the Committee of Twenty-One.

Further changes in the structure of Western European organized labor were also prompted by wider changes in the supranational European political framework. In 1968, the ICFTU members of the Free Trade Area set up the Trade Union Committee for the European Free Trade Area. In 1969, the European Trade Union Secretariat reshaped itself as the European Confederation of Free Trade Unions. In February 1973, these two bodies agreed to merge as the European Trade Union Confederation (ETUC). Up to 1991, the membership of the ETUC was largely confined to noncommunist labor bodies in Western Europe, but since that time, the ETUC has admitted affiliates from Eastern European countries.

The ETUC has always operated as a lobbying body for organized labor, but at its 1991 congress it resolved to take an active role in **collective bargaining** for the whole of Europe. Its role assumed added significance after the signing of the **European Union** Treaty (February 7, 1992); appended to the treaty was a social policy agreement which gave European-wide labor and **employers' organizations** an enhanced formal role in preparing and implementing the social policy of the European Union. In December 1993 the ETUC was one of three European-wide labor bodies that were granted formal "social partner" status by the European Commission for European-wide dialogue on social policy matters.

Although both the Commission and the ETUC wanted to advance this dialogue to collective bargaining, this course has been opposed by the Union of Industrial and Employers' Confederations of Europe even though the ETUC had reached an agreement with the European Center of Public Enterprises for such a move in September 1990. In 1994, the ETUC claimed 46 million members (compared to 37 million in 1973) in 21 countries. In 2002, the

ETUC had 74 national labor federations as affiliates from a total of 34 European countries representing a total of 60 million members. The most recent achievements of the ETUC have been the signing of agreements with European Union employers' organizations concerning parental leave and part-time work, agreements that are legally enforceable. *See also CONFÉDÉRATION EUROPÉENNE DES CADRES.*

EUROPEAN UNION (EU). The EU has its origins in the European Economic Community in 1957; its present title dates from November 1, 1993. The rise of the EU has been paralleled by changes in the **European Trade Union Confederation** (ETUC), the primary lobby group for European organized labor. Although not a labor body, the EU's concern with economic and social issues, particularly since the 1970s, has made it an increasingly important vehicle through which European labor can achieve its objectives. The European Union Treaty signed at Maastricht on February 7, 1992. appended a social policy agreement that gave European-wide organized labor and **employers' organizations** an enhanced formal role in the social policy of the European Union. In 1993, the European Commission formally recognized the ETUC, and the *Confédération Européenne des Cadres* as "social partners" for European-wide dialogue on social policy matters. In August 1994, the European Commission's White Paper on Social Policy recognized employers' organizations, labor unions, and voluntary associations as partners in the development of social policy. In 1996, the European Commission directive on European Works' Councils came into force; it meant that any company with more than 1,000 employees, of whom at least 150 worked in a minimum of two EU member countries, had to set up a work's council or at least a formal procedure for informing and consulting staff about matters affecting their working lives. In 1999, a European Commission directive setting a limit on **working hours** became operational in the **United Kingdom**. In February 2002, the EU, after much lobbying by the **International Confederation of Free Trade Unions** (ICFTU), incorporated trade union rights in its regulations on tariff preferences for 2002-2004.

EXPORT PROCESSING ZONES (EPZ). Also known as Free Trade Zones or *maquiladores* or *maquilas* (assembly plants), the term EPZ refers to areas designated by governments in Third World countries since the 1960s where foreign companies can produce goods and services with minimal taxation and without the legal restraints of the labor regulations that might apply elsewhere in the country. In practice, export processing zones are generally zones of exploitation for their employees, characterized by low wages and poor working conditions. EPZs were first set up in northern **Mexico** on the U.S. border in 1965. The first EPZ in Africa was established in **Mauritius** in 1970 and was followed by Asian countries, beginning with the Philippines. Labor unions are either prohibited or actively discouraged by violence, as, for example, in **Guatemala**. Excluding **China**, there were about 850 EPZs in the world in 1999. In 2002, the **International Confederation of Free Trade Unions** estimated that about 80 percent of employees in EPZs were **women** and that they earned about half of what their male counterparts were paid.

-F-

FALKLAND ISLANDS. A British dependency, which was successfully retaken by the **United Kingdom** after the Argentine invasion in June 1982, the Falkland Islands has only one labor union, the General Employees Union; formed in 1943, it has been an affiliate of the **International Confederation of Free Trade Unions** (ICFTU) since 1949. Between 1975 and 1990, the membership of the General Employees Union fell from 450 to 150.

FÉDÉRATION INTERNATIONALE DES EMPLOYÉS, TECHNICIENS ET CADRES **(FIET).** The FIET, or the International Federation of Commercial, Clerical, Professional, and Technical Employees, was an **international trade secretariat** formed in 1921 from a failed earlier international clerical body that had operated from Hamburg, **Germany**, between 1909 and 1914. The FIET was primarily a European body until 1949, after which time it expanded into other continents. The main industries represented by the FIET were in the **service sector**: banking, insurance, commerce, retailing, and social services. Between 1976 and 1994, the affiliated membership of the FIET rose from 6.2 to 11 million. It is based in Geneva. In January 2000, the FIET merged with **Communications International**, the **International Graphical Federation**, and the **Media Entertainment International** to form the **Union**

Network International (UNI). *See also* WHITE-COLLAR UN-IONISM.

FEDERATION OF INTERNATIONAL CIVIL SERVANTS' AS-SOCIATIONS (FICSA) Founded in 1952, the FICSA represents the staff employed by the United Nations and its specialized agencies, including the **International Labour Organisation** (ILO). Based in Geneva, the FICSA had 27 affiliated associations or unions in 2001 representing about 30,000 union members. *See also* WHITE-COLLAR UNIONISM.

FEDERAZIONE ITALIANA OPERAI METALLURGICI **(FIOM).** The FIOM (Italian Union of Metal Workers) was formed in 1901 and operated until 1924, when it was suppressed by the fascist government along with the other free unions in **Italy**. Its membership growth was slow, a reflection of the slow industrialization of the Italian economy. In 1906, it signed the first collective agreement in **Italy**, which gave the union the closed shop and the right of employees to elect members to grievance committees. From 10,000 members in 1913, it had only reached 40,000 by 1918, but by 1920 it had grown to 152,000, a rise that reflected the demands of World War I. By 1923 its membership had fallen to 20,000. It was revived in 1944. A union known for its militancy in the 1960s, its **membership** grew from 167,000 in 1968 to 278,700 in 1972, when it merged with two other metal unions to form an **industrial union** for the metal industry.

FIJI. Labor unions were first formed in Fiji in 1939 but had an unstable history, largely in response to the ethnic tensions between Indians and native Fijians, with unions tending to be either ethnically Indian or native Fijian. In 1957, the Fiji Industrial Workers' Congress, which had been formed in 1952, was admitted to membership of the **International Confederation of Free Trade Unions** (ICFTU), thereby becoming the third part of Oceania to be a member after **New Zealand** and **Australia**. In 1966, the Fiji Industrial Workers' Congress was reformed as the Fiji Trade Union Congress; by 1975 it had 23,000 members. In 1970, Fiji became an independent democratic nation from Britain, but by the late 1980s economic difficulties fed racial tensions between native Fijians and the economically better-off Indian Fijians, who made up about half the population. Two military coups in support of the rights of native

Fijians in 1987 resulted in restrictions on labor unions and the reintroduction of the Tripartite Forum, made up of unions, employers, and government representatives. Fiji's poor economic performance undercut efforts to attain political stability. There was another coup in May 2000 by elements of the military, although civilian rule was restored with military support in July 2000. In 2002, the ICFTU reported that although **collective bargaining** and the right to **strike** are legally recognized, there was a general failure by the government to enforce these rights.

FINLAND. Organized labor in Finland emerged on a significant scale in the 1900s. In 1907, at the initiative of the Social Democratic Party, 18 unions held a congress that claimed a total membership of 25,000 out of 175,000 nonagricultural employees. Strongly influenced by Marxism, this body was banned by the government in 1930, and the Social Democratic Party reorganized a noncommunist body, the Confederation of Finnish Trade Unions. In 1922, a separate **white-collar** federation was formed to restore real pay levels, which had been sharply eroded by the inflation that followed World War I; the white-collar federation, unlike the other labor federation, was politically independent. In the 1920s, organized labor collapsed; union density dropped to 5 percent in 1930 compared to 25 percent in 1920 but recovered strongly after 1944 with the improvement of the political climate for labor.

Between 1965 and 1970, union **membership** in Finland rose from 642,900 to 945,300, causing the density level to rise from 42 to 57 percent, an increase brought about by diminished internal conflict within organized labor and the introduction of a centralized **collective bargaining** system. The *Suomen Ammattiliittojen Keskusjärjestö* (SAK), or Central Organization of Finnish Trade Unions, remained the dominant labor federation in the post-1945 period; in 2001, it had one million members. In the same year, the proportion of employees who were union members remained among the highest in the world, about 85 percent. In addition, Finland has the highest level of association between **politics** and organized labor of any country; at the 1997 elections, 118 out of the 200 elected to parliament were union members.

FLAGS OF CONVENIENCE. An international system of merchant ship registration whereby a ship owner in a country with a Western economy registers ships in a Third World country to avoid paying high taxes and wages and providing good working conditions; the system began in the 1920s when U.S. ship owners began registering ships in **Panama**. Since the 1970s, the share of global merchant shipping sailing under flags of convenience has risen from 20 to over 50 percent. The **International Transport Workers' Federation** (ITF) has denounced the flags of convenience system since 1948. Often poorly maintained, flags of convenience ships are more prone to accidents that cause environmental damage. In 2000, twice as many flags of convenience ships were shipwrecked as other ships. The ITF has estimated that about 2,000 merchant sailors a year die in accidents at sea, mainly in flags of convenience ships. In 2002, the top flags of convenience countries were Panama, **Liberia**, **Malta**, **Bahamas**, and **Cyprus**. The top ship ownership countries of flags of convenience were **Greece**, **Japan**, **United States**, **Norway**, and **Hong Kong**. In January 2001, the ITF achieve two significant global agreements with the International Maritime Employers' Committee covering basic pay and conditions on 1,200 ships.

FORCED LABOR. Throughout recorded history, the performance of the work needed by society has been linked with coercion. Labor in classical Greek and Roman society depended heavily on agricultural laborers tied to the land and **slavery**. With the rise of market economies in Western Europe after 1300, the first free labor forces in the modern sense of the term began to emerge slowly on a significant scale. Although most working people had effectively little economic freedom, the Industrial Revolution brought a far greater range of choices of employment and the crude notion of a forced labor force receded, although pockets of feudal arrangements remained even in the **United Kingdom**; for example, Scottish coal miners were not fully emancipated from lifetime bondage until 1799. Slavery was abolished in the British Empire in 1807, in the United States in 1865, and was the target of an international conference in 1890. Serfdom in Russia was abolished in 1861. Forced labor in a legal sense in Britain became confined to convicts, who were exported from Britain to North America from 1655 to 1776 and Australia until 1868. Within British prisons, labor was regarded by the authorities as therapeutic and useful for offsetting administrative costs. Before World War II, forced labor in some form and to varying degrees was a feature of the African colonies of **Belgium** and **France**.

Organized labor has generally been hostile to prison labor because it could be used to undercut the price of goods produced by union members. In 1934, the U.S. Supreme Court denied the state of Alabama an injunction to stop the sale of goods made by prisoners. Nazi Germany and Japan both made extensive use of forced labor by civilians as well as by prisoners of war. Forced labor has also been a feature of communist regimes, notably in the former Soviet Union. The **International Labour Organisation** (ILO) passed a Convention against Forced Labor (No. 29) in 1930. During the 1990s, the **International Confederation of Free Trade Unions** (ICFTU) has repeatedly denounced the use of forced labor in a number of countries, most notably **Burma**.

FRANCE. Early forms of labor organization existed in France long before the effects of the Industrial Revolution became evident during the 19th century. For example, there is a record of a **strike** by vineyard workers in Burgundy as early as 1393 and by printers at Lyons in the 16th century. As in Britain, journeymen were the leaders in forming labor unions. Following the revolution in 1789, journeymen carpenters in Paris took advantage of its promise of political freedom by forming a union in 1790, but the employers objected and it was suppressed by the law *Le Chapelier* (1791), which was also applied to **employers' organizations** and made strikes illegal. Despite the legal prohibition on strikes, there was a revolt by silk workers in Lyons after the government attempted to suppress labor unions in April 1834. Some progress towards peaceful labor relations occurred in the early 1840s, as evidenced by the making of a collective agreement in the printing industry in 1843, but otherwise the government was quick to use force against the working class, as shown by the "June Days" in 1848, when it shut down employment workshops for the unemployed, a move that resulted in some thousands of deaths and the arrest of thousands of others.

In 1862, a deputation of French labor leaders was allowed by Napoleon III to visit the London Exposition. They returned with a high opinion of English working conditions and unions and asked to be granted freedom of association and the right to strike. Strikes were legalized in 1864 but although legalizing unions was considered in 1868, nothing was done. In 1869, the Comte de Paris published a sympathetic study, *The Trade Unions of England,* which was reprinted six times, but the official attitude towards unions was colored by the bloodshed of the Paris Commune (1871).

By the 1880s, the government realized that there were advantages to encouraging labor unions as a means of tempering revolutionary tendencies by the working class. In 1884, it legalized labor unions and provided financial assistance to the *Bourses du Travail* (the coordinating centers for local unions) provided they remained out of the control of political extremists. The first national trade union center (the *Fédération Nationale des Syndicats Ouvriers*) was opened in 1886. A **Catholic** labor union was formed among **white-collar** workers in 1887, the first sign of an important division within French organized labor; the Catholic unions went on to form their own national labor federation in 1919. **Collective bargaining** began in the **coal mining** industry in northern France but remained limited in scope because of the importance of small enterprises in the economy. In 1895 a new national labor federation, the *Confédération Générale du Travail* (CGT), was formed; it absorbed the National Federation of *Bourses du Travail* (founded in 1892) in 1902. **Syndicalism**, a doctrine that had its origins in the revolutionary tradition of France, became an important influence on organized labor, particularly with its emphasis on the use of **general strikes**.

Yet French organized labor never attained the strength of its counterparts in other major European countries. In 1920, a highwater mark for organized labor in Europe, only 12 percent of French employees were members of unions, compared to 53 percent in **Germany**, 39 percent in **Italy**, and 48 percent in the **United Kingdom**. Subsequently, French labor was weakened by divisions caused by **communists**. Despite the **Matignon Agreement** in 1936, which provided for the unions' right to organize, an end to antiunion practices, collective bargaining, pay increases, and the election of shop stewards, French organized labor remained relatively weak even though an impression of strength might have been created by dramatic events such as the national disturbances of May 1968. Although the reasons for the weakness of French organized labor since 1945 are complicated, they stem in large part from its deep political and religious divisions. Aside from the Catholic labor federation, the *Confédération Française des Travailleurs Chrétiens* (French Confederation of Christian Workers, formed in 1919), the most important division occurred in April 1948 when the noncommunist unions of the CGT withdrew and formed their own federation, the *Confédération Générale du Travail-Force Ouvrière* (CGT-FO) (General Confederation of Labor-Workers' Strength). A third national labor federation, the *Confédération Française Démocratique* (CFDT) or French Democratic Confederation of Labor, was formed in 1964. From a high point of 38 percent of employees in unions in 1950, there was a steady decline thereafter to 21 percent in 1960 and 17 percent in 1980. Between 1989 and 2001, union density in France fell from 11 to 9 percent, the lowest level for any Western industrialized country. Also, unlike most other Western industrialized countries, France still has no single, dominant national labor federation. In 2001, organized labor was divided between three national federations: the CGT (650,000 members), the CGT-FO (300,000 members), and the CFDT (765,000 members). Yet, despite its very low level of union membership, France has experienced a high level of **labor disputes** in recent years compared to Germany and the United Kingdom, particularly surrounding the introduction of the 35-hour week in February 2000. In May and June 2003, the unions conducted rolling strikes in protest over government plans to reform the government pensions scheme.

FREEDOM OF ASSOCIATION. The **International Labour Organisation** (ILO) first considered drafting a Convention on Freedom of Association to protect labor unions in 1925, a concern prompted by the incorporation of unions under government control in fascist **Italy**. Among the ILO member countries of the time, there were two main kinds of laws relating to unions. Under the first kind of law, unions were unlawful unless their formation and operation were authorized by the government. Under the second kind of law, unions were legally recognized and operated without government control. Examples of countries following this second kind of law were the **United Kingdom** (1871), **New Zealand** (1878), and **France** (1884). However, the 1925 proposal failed, mainly because the representatives of organized labor within the **International Federation of Free Trade Unions** (ICFTU) were unable to agree on a course of action, with some fearing that such a convention could limit the freedoms the unions already had. The present ILO Convention (87) on Freedom of Association and Protection of the Right to Organize was not passed until 1948. It was augmented by Convention No. 98 (Right to Organize and Collective Bargaining) in 1949. The ILO established the Freedom of Association Committee to monitor the operation of these conventions in 1951.

FRENCH POLYNESIA. Acquired piecemeal by **France** by 1889, organized unions in this group of south Pacific islands were mainly overseas branches of French unions. In 1990, a Polynesian union based on Tahiti, *A Tia I Mua*, was admitted to membership of the **International Confederation of Free Trade Unions** (ICFTU) as the affiliate for French Polynesia with 5,000 members, although the largest labor union in French Polynesia is the Confederation of Workers' Union of Polynesia.

FULL-TIME/PART-TIME EMPLOYMENT. Before the 1960s, most employees were employed full-time, that is, they worked about 40 or 44 hours a week. Part-time employment emerged in the early 1930s as a temporary expedient to cope with the Depression. With the entry of more **women** into the labor force, particularly married women, there was a growth in demand for fewer working hours. Official labor force household surveys in many countries collect statistics on full-time and part-time employment—with full-time employment defined as 35 hours or more a week—and these have shown a general rise in part-time employment since the 1970s. In 1994, the **International Labour Organisation** (ILO) adopted a convention to protect the conditions of part-time workers.

Organized labor has generally found it difficult to recruit part-time workers as members, as was shown by results from labor force surveys in 2002. In the **United States**, 15 percent of full-time employees, but only 7 percent of part-time employees were union members. In Australia, 26 percent of full-time employees were union members compared to 17 percent of part-time employees. In the **United Kingdom**, 32 percent of full-time employees were union members compared to 21 percent of part-time employees. *See also* WORKING HOURS.

-G-

GABON. Independent of **France** since 1960, indigenous organized labor developed along the French model. One of its labor federations was an affiliate of the **International Confederation of Free Trade Unions** (ICFTU) by 1965, with 6,100 members. In 1964, Gabon became a one-party state and formed a single labor federation under party control from the country's 70 unions in 1969; the 1978 labor law reaffirmed this system. By 1992, the *Confédération*

Gabonaise des Syndicats Libres (Confederation of Free Trade Unions of Gabon) (CGSL) had become affiliated to the **International Confederation of Free Trade Unions** (ICFTU) and gained government recognition as Gabon's second labor federation. The CGSL conducted an unsuccessful **general strike** in February 1992 over inflation and falling living standards. By 1994, the CGSL had a membership of 14,100 and it has remained an affiliate of the ICFTU. In 2002, the ICFTU complained that although the right to strike was recognized in Gabon, in practice this did not occur, and migrant workers were discouraged from forming labor unions.

GAMBIA. Independent of the **United Kingdom** since 1965, organized labor in Gambia began effectively in October 1928 when the Gambia Labour Union (GLU) was formed by Edward Francis Small (1890-1957) and conducted the first **strike** in Gambia in 1928. In 1935, the GLU was officially registered under the 1932 Trade Union Act. By 1953, the GLU was affiliated with the **International Confederation of Free Trade Unions** (ICFTU). By 1965, the Gambia Workers' Union (GWU), founded in 1958, had replaced the GLU as Gambia's ICFTU affiliate; its **membership** was small, being only 3,000 by 1988. The GWU remained a member of the ICFTU in 2002, and Gambia was remarkable for being one of the few African countries not named in the ICFTU's 2002 annual report on **violations of trade union rights**.

GENERAL AND MUNICIPAL WORKERS' UNION (GMWU). The GMWU was one of the largest labor unions in the **United Kingdom** from its formation on July 1, 1924, following the **amalgamation** of three unions: the National Union of General Workers, which was founded by Will Thorne (1857-1946) in 1889 as the National Union of Gasworkers and General Labourers of Great Britain and Ireland (it had 202,000 members in 1924); the National Amalgamated Union of Labour, which had about 53,000 members in 1924; and the Municipal Employees' Association, which was founded in 1894 and had about 40,000 members in 1924.

Known officially as the National Union of General and Municipal Workers, the GMWU drew the bulk of its **membership** from lesser skilled employees, particularly those in the gas industry and local government. There was much overlap between the kinds of employees it recruited and those of similar general unions, particularly the **Transport and General Workers' Union**.

At its creation, the GMWU had 298,200 members. This number fell during the Depression to 207,700 in 1932, but by 1940 the GMWU had 493,740 members and 715,460 by 1950. Between 1945 and 1992, the GMWU was Britain's third largest union in most years. Membership rose to 786,140 by 1962 and to a peak of 964,800 in 1979. An important feature of this growth was the share of **women** members. Between 1924 and 1940, the proportion of women members in the GMWU rose from 9 to 18 percent and to 20 percent by 1950. By 1976, 34 percent of the total membership were women, a proportion that had increased to 36 percent in 1994. In 1972, the GMWU set up a new section to recruit **white-collar** employees.

Between 1963 and 1979, the GMWU absorbed five small unions. In 1982, it combined with the Amalgamated Society of Boilermakers, Shipwrights, Blacksmiths, and Structural Workers (itself a production of **amalgamation** with other unions, the oldest of which was formed in 1834) to create the General Municipal, Boilermakers' and Allied Trades' Unions. In 1989, this union amalgamated with the Association of Professional Executive, Clerical, and Computer Staff (originally formed as the National Union of Clerks in 1890) to form a union known simply as the GMB. In 2001, the GMB had 683,900 members, compared to 790,000 in 1994.

GENERAL FEDERATION OF TRADE UNIONS (GFTU). The GFTU was formed in Manchester, England, in January 1899 by a number of relatively large unions, including the **Amalgamated Society of Engineers** (ASE) with 85,000 members, the Gas and General Labourers' Union (with 48,000 members), the National Amalgamated Union of Labour with 22,000 members, and the National Union of Boot and Shoe Operatives (with 22,000 members). A moderate body, the purpose of the GFTU was to provide mutual support and resolve **labor disputes**. At its formation, its constituents had about 310,400 members or about a quarter that of the **Trades Union Congress** (TUC), which regarded the GFTU as a competitor. Although the GFTU aspired to be a large organization, it found it difficult to move beyond representing **craft unions**, a feature that won it respect and support from **Samuel Gompers**. The number of members it represented rose from 884,000 in 1912 to over a million by 1920, but the withdrawal of the ASE in 1915 and other unions severely weakened the GFTU. The general secretary of the GFTU from 1907 to 1938 was William A. Appleton (1859-

1940). As well as its useful role in **labor dispute** settlements and labor **politics**, the GFTU was Britain's representative in the **International Federation of Trade Unions** (IFTU) until it was supplanted by the TUC between 1918 and 1922. In 2001, the GFTU had 34 affiliates, mainly smaller, skilled unions, and represented 252,000 members, compared to 277,900 in 1988.

GENERAL STRIKES. General strikes, in the sense of a widespread **labor dispute** that affects a city, region, or country, feature prominently in the history of organized labor; there is no hard-and-fast definition because these labor disputes can assume a variety of forms. The followers of **anarchism** and **syndicalism** in the late 19th century and early 20th centuries saw the general strike as a means of overthrowing the existing social order and replacing it with a fairer one. The strike wave of the late 19th century was often an expression of working-class discontent, with many participants not being members of labor unions, as occurred in **Belgium** in 1893. A general strike could also be international in its effects; the Maritime Strike that was called by unions in eastern Australia in 1890 was also supported by unions in **New Zealand**. After 1900, general strikes were usually called by labor unions.

General strikes have also occurred in cities (for instance, Philadelphia in 1910, Brisbane, Australia, in 1912, Seattle in 1919, and Winnipeg, Canada, in 1919), and countries (such as Sweden in 1909 and Argentina in 1909 and 1919). The 1920s were a highpoint of the use of the general strike: **Portugal** (1919, 1920, and 1921), **France** (1920), **Norway** (1921), **Hong Kong** (1922), **Egypt** (1923), **South Africa** (1922), and the **United Kingdom** (1926). Usually these general strikes were suppressed (for example, in **Cuba** in 1935 or in **Kenya** in 1950) by military force or led to punitive legal actions by the government (for instance in **South Korea** in 1946-1947). On occasions the general strike has achieved some improvements (for instance in Cuba after the general strike in 1933). Although general strikes have continued to occur in Western Europe since 1945—for instance in France (1947, 1968) and Denmark (1973)—their incidence has declined. Yet they remain an option for labor in an intolerable political environment, as happened in **Bulgaria** in 1990 and **Bangladesh** in 1994. In the 1990s, general strikes, such as in Greece in 1998, have often centered on labor market reforms or **privatization**. Others, such as in **Venezuela** between December 2002 and January 2003, have had purely political objectives. *See also* BRITISH GENERAL STRIKE; "WINTER OF DISCONTENT."

GEORGIA. Part of the Russian Empire to November 1917, Georgia briefly enjoyed independence to 1921, when it was forced to join the Soviet Union. Always strongly nationalistic, Georgia's people began to demand independence from 1988. In June 1990, Georgia's labor unions seceded from the Soviet trade unions and declared their political independence. Over the next three years, the Georgian labor unions fought against attempts by the communist government of Zviad Gamsakhurdia to take control of organized labor for his own ends. Finally, on December 18, 1992, Georgia's labor unions formed the Georgian Trade Union Amalgamation, consisting of 26 of the country's 30 unions. The Georgian economy in the first half of the 1990s was weakened by the victory of the separatist movement in Abkhazia (which resulted in an influx of 200,000 refugees), high inflation, and the general disruption caused by the transition to a free-market economy. In 2001, Georgia was admitted to affiliation with the **International Confederation of Free Trade Unions** (ICFTU). In 2002, the ICFTU reported favorably on the legal environment for organized labor in Georgia but claimed it was restrictive in practice and subject to government interference.

GERMANY. In terms of historical importance and influence in Europe, organized labor in Germany has been second only to the **United Kingdom**. This importance derived not just from the numerical size of Germany's labor unions during the first two decades of the 20th century but also from the pivotal role German labor leaders played in promoting international labor unionism. Organized labor came relatively late to Germany. The first national German labor union, the National Printers' Association (*Nationaler Buchdrucker-Verein*), was not established until 1848. Despite the spread of industrialization after 1850, political repression retarded the growth of unions. In 1861, the legal ban on labor unions was lifted in Saxony, followed by Weimar (1863) and the North German Confederation (1869), but there was no legal right to form unions. In 1863, Ferdinand Lasalle (1825-1864) founded the German Workingmen's Association, which had as one of its aims the legalizing of labor unions. Yet by 1869 there were only 77,000 union members, of whom 30,000 were enrolled in **Hirsch-Duncker Trade Associations**. Further progress of organized labor was retarded by Otto von Bismarck's Anti-Socialist Laws of 1878, which were not repealed until 1890.

In 1892, German labor unions held their first national congress at which they agreed to encourage the formation of national and **industrial unions**. In 1894, the **Catholics** began organizing their own unions, a step that marked the beginning of the third division of pre-1933 German organized labor, along with the conservatives (the Hirsh-Duncker Trade Associations) and the **socialists** (the Free Trade Unions). By 1913, the Free Trade Unions had 2.5 million members, the Catholic unions 218,200, and the Hirsh-Duncker Trade Associations 106,600. **White-collar** unions were formed after 1900, and their **membership** grew from 567,700 in 1906 to 941,300 by 1913. **Collective bargaining** also emerged during the 1900s; by 1913, two million employees were covered by agreements negotiated by collective bargaining. In 1913 too, Germany had nearly three million labor union members, the second highest figure in the world after the United Kingdom. World War I boosted membership to 10.5 million in 1920, but the hyperinflation of the war and the economic disruption that followed it made this level unsustainable. Nonetheless, the labor unions were largely responsible for the defeat of the rightwing Kapp *putsch* in Berlin in 1920.

In 1923, the government created an **arbitration** service to deal with **labor disputes** and even made the service compulsory if the parties could not agree. The legitimacy of organized labor was not accepted by many large employers in the late 1920s. Between October and December 1928, 220,000 engineering employees were locked out by their employers in the Ruhr; and although the dispute was settled by mediators, the employers were harshly critical of their efforts. The economic downturn turned into full depression by 1931, and its resultant very high unemployment (44 percent by 1932) destroyed the power of organized labor and made its suppression by Adolf Hitler a relatively easy matter. On May 2, 1933, Germany's unions were suppressed and many of their leaders were sent to the Dachau concentration camp.

In reviewing the relative political weakness of German organized labor before 1933, it is important to realize that for all the industrial growth after 1850, a large part of the German economy remained in **agriculture**; even in 1933 the proportion of the labor force employed in agriculture was 29 percent.

The revival of organized labor in western Germany began with the advancing Allied armies being petitioned for permission to form labor unions in March-April 1945. By August 1945, nearly one million union members had been officially recognized in unions in the British zone, where official policy was favorable to their growth as a means of promoting democracy. In this they were very successful, for Germany's labor unions went on to play a fundamental role in promoting and sustaining democracy in West Germany.

Determined to avoid the mistakes of the past, German unions were to be organized along industry lines, sectarian divisions were to be avoided, and unions were to have a say in the decision-making process of large enterprises, a policy that made it possible for Germany to put pressure on the South African government to permit black labor unions. Despite the impressive gains made by organized labor since 1950, only 33 percent of employees were union members by the late 1980s, which was below the levels of neighboring **Austria**, **Belgium**, and **Denmark**.

Although the formal reunification of Germany in October 1990 opened up new recruiting opportunities for organized labor, it also presented many problems because of the economic backwardness of the former East Germany. At first there were impressive gains in membership, but these had been largely lost by 1999 as a result of the recession of the early 1990s, the lackluster performance of the German economy, persistently high unemployment, and the high cost of the economic integration of the former East Germany. In 2001, only 30 percent of German employees were union members, but organized labor continues to carry much political weight in Germany, particularly after the reelection of the federal Social Democratic Party-Green coalition in September 2002. *See also* BÖCKLER, HANS; BRENNER, OTTO; *DEUTSCHE ARBEITS-FRONT*; *DEUTSCHER METALLARBEITER-VERBAND*; *DEUTS-CHER GEWERKSCHAFTSBUND*; HIRSH-DUNCKER TRADE ASSOCIATIONS; *IG METALL*; LEGIEN, KARL; *MITBESTIM-MUNG;* UNION GOVERNMENT-AGREEMENTS.

GHANA. Independent of the **United Kingdom** since March 1957, organized labor in Ghana began in the 1920s and gained legal regulation in 1941. In 1945, the Gold Coast Trades Union Congress was formed and was an affiliate of the **International Confederation of Free Trade Unions** (ICFTU) by 1953 with 74,000 members; later it was renamed the Ghana Trades Union Congress (GTUC). As in other African colonies and territories, organized labor was aligned with movements for independence. By 1965, the GTUC had ceased to be a member of the ICFTU and did not rejoin until 1992; in 1993, it claimed 556,501 members. Since 1965, the right to **strike** has been virtually illegal in Ghana, but despite the country's post-independence political and economic difficulties, the environment for organized labor has remained positive. The ICFTU's annual survey of **violations of trade union rights** for 2002 reported that there were still legislative restrictions on forming labor unions in Ghana.

GLOBAL UNION FEDERATIONS (GUF). Before January 23, 2002, GUFs were known as **International Trade Secretariats** (ITS). In 2001, there were nine GUFs, compared to 16 ITS in 1995. They were **Educational International** (EI); **International Federation of Building and Woodworkers** (IFBWW); **International Federation of Chemical, Energy, Mine, and General Workers' Unions** (ICEM); **International Federation of Journalists** (IFJ); **International Metalworkers' Federation** (IMF); **International Textile, Garment, and Leather Workers' Federation; International Transport Workers' Federation** (ITF); **International Union of Food, Agricultural, Hotel, Restaurant, Catering, Tobacco, and Allied Workers' Associations** (IUF); **Public Services International** (PSI); and **Union Network International** (UNI). *See also* GLOBALIZATION.

GLOBALIZATION. Globalization came into general use in the late 1990s to describe the process of acceleration in the interdependence of the international economy since about 1980, particularly with reference to trade, technological transfers, and information. Supporters of globalization hail its general economic benefits, such as increasing the volume of world trade, reducing poverty, and keeping prices down. Opponents of globalization complain about its potential threat to the sovereignty of nations, and international and regional organized labor has been long concerned about job losses from advanced industrial economies to the Third World.

In November-December 1999, organized labor took part in the protests about globalization at the World Trade Organization meeting in Seattle, but because it conducted its protest peacefully, it received little publicity in the mass media compared to the violence used by anarchist and other anticapitalist groups. Led by the **International Confederation of Free Trade Unions** (ICFTU), organized labor called for the inclusion of social justice issues in the debate about globalization and for the inclusion of **International Labour Organisation** (ILO) standards in tariff agreements. Symbolic of the need by international organized labor to address globalization directly was the renaming of the **International Trade Secretariats** as **Global Union Federations** (GUF) in January 2002.

In March 2002, the ICFTU presented a submission to the first meeting of the ILO World Commission on Globalization in which it acknowledged that globalization had "created unprecedented wealth and resources" but at the price of "a still-widening gap in incomes both inside and between countries and enduring unacceptable levels of absolute poverty." It cited an associated growth in human rights abuses with globalization, such as **forced labor, child labor,** and the exploitation of **women** workers in **export processing zones** throughout the Third World. The ICFTU was especially critical of the lack of social responsibility shown by the World Trade Organization, the International Monetary Fund, and the World Bank in addressing the need for ILO **international standard-setting** for labor as well as the need by multinational corporations to exercise due social responsibility and accountability.

The ICFTU and the GUFs continue to lobby the United Nations, the World Bank, the International Monetary Fund, and regional economic groups on behalf of the rights of workers. On May 28, 2003, the ICFTU's general secretary, **Guy Ryder**, called for the religious international labor body, the **World Confederation of Labour**, to join with the ICFTU in building a unified global trade union movement capable of better meeting the challenges of globalization.

GOMPERS, SAMUEL (1850-1924). Gompers was the outstanding national labor leader in the **United States** from the late 1880s until his death. He was also an important figure in international labor. Born in London, he and his family arrived in New York in 1863, where he began work as a cigar maker and attended night classes to improve his education. He joined the Cigarmakers Local 15 in 1864 and made the union the basis of his career. Gompers was one of the principal founders of the Federation of Organized Trades and Labor Unions of the United States and Canada in 1881 and of its successor, the **American Federation of Labor** (AFL) in 1886; he became the first president of the AFL, a position he held, with the exception of 1894, until his death. Although originally attracted to **socialist** ideas in the early 1870s, Gompers turned to unionism as the means to improve the position of labor. He was an admirer of English unionism and used it as a model for reorganizing the Cigarmakers' Union, particularly its emphasis on high membership fees and unemployment, sickness, and death benefits. He based the Federation of Organized Trades on the British **Trades Union Congress** (TUC). He and the socialists became enemies.

By the late 1870s, Gompers had developed the set of beliefs—later known as the doctrine of **voluntarism**—that he applied throughout his labor career. He believed that unionism, organized along occupational rather than industrial lines and using **strikes**, was the correct path to improving the position of employees. He distrusted the state as a means of achieving this end and opposed not only unions supporting political parties but also laws designed to set maximum hours and **minimum wages** and establish health and unemployment insurance. At the same time, he supported the state legislating to restrict **child labor**. Voluntarism, as espoused by Gompers, made the United States a notable exception to the views held by organized labor in other countries and led to friction with the **International Federation of Trade Unions** (IFTU). With the collapse of the Knights of Labor from the late 1880s, Gompers and the AFL became the undisputed national center of American organized labor, but it was a narrow movement based on better-off employees that largely ignored the unskilled and the immigrants. Gompers's ideas prevailed until the Depression and the rise of the **Congress of Industrial Organizations** in the 1930s. Gompers also played a significant role in setting up the **International Labour Organisation** (ILO).

GOVERNMENT CONTROL OF ORGANIZED LABOR. Since 1920, governments that have been unwilling to tolerate an independent organized labor movement have generally suppressed them first and then set up their own labor organizations as agents of control. In communist countries, governments have suppressed independent organized labor on the grounds that, as **communism** represented the working class, an independent labor movement was not needed. By 1922, organized labor in **Russia** had been brought under the complete control of the communist party. In 1924, nonfascist labor unions were suppressed in **Italy**, an example followed by

Greece (1931), **Brazil** (1931), **Germany** (1933), **Portugal** (1933), **Yugoslavia** (1935), and **Spain** (1940). In the 1960s, it was common for newly independent countries in Africa and Asia to bring organized labor under government control through the creation of single national labor organizations, even though organized labor typically played an active role in independence movements. *See also DEUTSCHE ARBEITSFRONT;* EGYPT; POLITICS; UNION-GOVERNMENT AGREEMENTS.

GOVERNMENT EMPLOYMENT. *See* PUBLIC SECTOR.

GREECE. The development of organized labor in Greece was hampered by the country's lack of economic growth and dependence upon **agriculture**; in 1920, half the Greek labor force was employed in agriculture. The first union was formed by carpenters at the Syros shipyard in 1879, but it was not until 1918 that the General Confederation of Greek Labor was founded. Throughout the 1920s, conflict between **socialists** and **communists** weakened organized labor. Beginning in 1914, legislation was passed to regulate unions, and from 1931 to 1936, the state brought organized labor under its control, using the example of fascist **Italy**. This was obvious in 1946 when the government nominated the executive of the General Confederation of Greek Labor. Between 1967 and 1974, Greece was run by a military government, which seized control by a coup.

In 1968, sections of organized labor formed a group to work for the restoration of democracy. With the collapse of the military government, this group continued its activities but redirected its focus at improving democracy within organized labor, particularly with respect to the General Confederation of Greek Labor. Following organized labor's complaints to the **International Labour Organisation** (ILO) over government interference in the confederation, a new leadership took over and conducted a **strike** against proposed antistrike legislation in 1990, in which more than a million participated. Even so, the General Confederation of Greek Labor has been continuously represented in the **International Confederation of Free Trade Unions** (ICFTU) since 1951. In the 1990s, Greek unions have engaged in **labor disputes** over the **privatization** of government businesses and moves to reform the labor market. In 1998, there was a **general strike** by **public sector** employees over labor market reforms. In 2001, there were about 580,000 union members in Greece, covering about 26 percent of employees.

GREEN, WILLIAM (1872-1952). Green succeeded **Samuel Gompers** as president of the **American Federation of Labor** (AFL) in 1924 and held the post until his death. Born in Cochocton, Ohio, into a **coal mining** family of English-Welsh immigrants, Green became a coal miner, like his father, at 16. He became active in coal mining unionism in 1891 and served as president of the Ohio District of the **United Mine Workers' of America** (UMWA) in 1906. He served two terms in the Ohio Senate for the Democratic Party, where he achieved the passage of a workman's compensation law in 1911. In 1912, he was made the international secretary-treasurer of the UMWA, a post he held to 1922. From 1914, he served in executive positions in the AFL and attended the Paris Peace Conference in 1919, which led to the creation of the **International Labour Organisation** (ILO). Upon Gompers's death on December 3, 1924, Green became president of the AFL with the support of the president of the UMWA, **John L. Lewis.**

As AFL president, Green maintained the policy of backing **craft unions** as the preferred model for organized labor and ignored the need for recruiting union members among lesser skilled workers and **women.** As a result, the employers' organizations were able to continue their offensive against organized labor, assisted by a weakening economy in the late 1920s, culminating in the Depression, with little resistance. By 1930, only 9 percent of U.S. employees were union members, the same level as in 1913, and nearly half of what it had been in 1920. In contrast, Green's career prospered from 1933 under the presidency of Franklin D. Roosevelt. Green served on the National Labor Board in 1934 and on the governing board of the ILO from 1935 to 1937.

The creation of the **Congress of Industrial Organizations** (CIO) by John L. Lewis in 1935 led to Green's resignation from the UMWA in 1938, following the AFL's expulsion of the unions that supported the CIO. Although the two national labor federations supported the Allied effort during World War II, they remained rivals. After World War II, the AFL began to recognize industrial unions. Green died on November 21, 1952, 12 days after the death of his CIO counterpart, **Philip Murray.** The deaths of these rivals greatly assisted the merger of the AFL and the CIO in December 1955. *See also* MEANY, GEORGE.

GRENADA. Independent from the **United Kingdom** since February 1974, organized labor in Grenada followed a British pattern of development. **Collective bargaining** was first regulated by the Labour Ordinance of 1940, which was extended to labor unions in 1951. The unions formed the Grenada Trade Union Council in 1955. Grenada has been represented in the **International Confederation of Free Trade Unions** (ICFTU) since 1951 and had about 7,500 members by 2001.

GUATEMALA. Organized labor in Guatemala began from the 1900s. Efforts were made to form union federations in 1912 and 1928, but under the military dictatorship of General Jorge Ubico all activities by organized labor were suppressed from 1931 to 1944. Yet by 1951 a legal framework had been created in Guatemala that enabled **collective bargaining** to occur. In 1957, Guatemala was admitted to membership of the **International Confederation of Free Trade Unions** (ICFTU) and has retained its representation since. Despite interference in its external affairs by the **United States**, widespread violence against labor unions, and 30 years of murderous civil war from the mid-1960s to the mid-1990s, organized labor declared a **membership** of 150,000 to the ICFTU by 1989. Guatemala has figured largely in the ICFTU's annual survey of **violations of trade union rights** for the murder of labor union leaders, a legal system that discriminates against employees generally, and violence towards efforts to form labor unions in the country's **export processing zones**. In 2002, the right to **strike** remained difficult to exercise in practice, despite some reforms to the labor code in 2001. *See also* INTERNATIONAL UNION OF FOOD, AGRICULTURAL, HOTEL, RESTAURANT, CATERING, TOBACCO, AND ALLIED WORKERS' ASSOCIATION; VIOLATIONS OF TRADE UNION RIGHTS.

GUINEA. Independent from **France** since October 1985, organized labor in Guinea was largely confined to French employees until the 1950s. There were only 2,600 union members in Guinea by 1953, but this had grown to 39,000 by 1955 after a successful **general strike**. After independence organized labor came under the control of the government. Guinea was not represented in the **International Confederation of Free Trade Unions** (ICFTU) until 1997. In 2002, the ICFTU reported that there was a general climate of government intimidation towards organized labor in Guinea.

GUINEA-BISSAU. Only independent of **Portugal** since September 1973, organized labor had to operate in secret before then because of Portuguese rule. A General Union of Guinea-Bissau Workers existed by the 1960s and was an affiliate in exile of the **International Confederation of Free Trade Unions** (ICFTU) from 1965 to 1975. Guinea-Bissau was admitted to membership of the ICFTU in December 1997.

GUYANA. Independent from the **United Kingdom** since May 1966, the first labor union in Guyana was the Guyana Labour Union in 1919, followed by the Manpower Citizens' Association in 1936, which recruited Indian employees of the sugar plantations. In 1940, the unions formed the Guyana Trades Union Congress. In 1942, the colonial administration introduced three ordinances that provided a legal framework for **collective bargaining** and union registration. By 1953, there were 30 unions in Guyana and the country had two unions affiliated with the **International Confederation of Free Trade Unions** (ICFTU), with a combined **membership** of 8,600. Thereafter, political and ethnic tensions polarized organized labor. Guyana did not rejoin the ICFTU until 1965, when the Guyana Trades Union Congress claimed to represent 45,000 members. In 2001, the Guyana Trades Union Congress claimed to represent only 15,000 members. In 2002, the ICFTU reported that that there was political and ethnic discrimination towards organized labor in Guyana and restrictive **strike** legislation remained in place.

-H-

HILLMAN, SIDNEY (1887-1946). An important U.S. labor leader, Hillman was born in **Lithuania**. He studied to be a rabbi until 1902, when he moved to **Russia**; there he studied economics. For his part in labor agitation, he spent eight months in jail. On his release, he emigrated to the **United States** in 1907, where he settled in Chicago. Hillman worked as a clerk for two years, then became a garment cutter and a member of the United Garment Workers' Union of America (formed in 1891). Between September 1910 and January 1911, Hillman was the leader of a **strike** against Hart, Schaffner, and Marx in Chicago. The success of this strike fed discontent with the conservative leadership of the union, and in 1914, Hillman led a breakaway group of members who formed the Amalgamated Clothing Workers of America (ACWA). Hillman became its first president. The second result of the 1910-1911 strike was the setting up of **arbitration** machinery that was extended to other parts of the clothing industry. Hillman was a dedicated supporter of **industrial unionism** and led the ACWA through an industry-wide lockout between December 1920 and June 1921 and the exclusion of racketeers during the 1920s. He served on the federal Labor Advisory Board (1933) and on the National Industrial Recovery Board (1935). In 1935, he became one of the leaders of the **Congress of Industrial Organizations** (CIO). A political moderate, Hillman supported the American Labor Party and the Democratic Party.

HIRSCH-DUNCKER TRADE ASSOCIATIONS. Hirsch-Duncker trade associations were a group of labor unions that operated in **Germany** from 1869 to 1933. They were begun by Max Hirsch (1832-1905), a mechanical engineer, and Franz Duncker, a newspaper publisher. Hirsch made a tour of England in 1868 and came back with the idea that German unions should follow those of England as he believed them to be, that is, independent from political parties and in favor of the amicable settlement of labor disputes and avoiding the use of **strikes**. In 1869, he and Duncker organized a national federation of unions with 30,000 members among eight trade associations. Although the Hirsch-Duncker Associations were exempt from the Anti-Socialist Law of 1878 because of their lack of political affiliation, their growth was slow; it was not until 1902 that their combined membership reached 102,600. Despite claims of political and religious neutrality, the associations were linked with leftwing liberalism, a political area to which other groups could make better claim. After reaching a peak **membership** of 226,000 in 1920, the associations' membership declined to 149,800 by 1931. They were dissolved by the Nazis in 1933 and were not reestablished after 1945.

HOFFA, JAMES P. (1941-). The only son of **James Riddle Hoffa**, James P. Hoffa was born in Detroit, Michigan, and completed his education at the University of Michigan as a lawyer in 1966. He joined the **Teamsters** in 1959 and worked as a laborer in Detroit and Alaska in the 1960s. Between 1968 and 1983, he was a Teamster attorney representing members in workers' compensation cases, social security, and personal legal matters; he also represented Teamster joint councils and local unions. He was administrative assistant to the president of Michigan joint council 43 between 1993 and 1998. In 1999, Hoffa was easily elected general president of the Teamsters on a platform of reform. Under his leadership, the Teamsters conducted an independent, internal investigation of the history and current status of the influence of organized crime in the Teamsters and released it to the public in March 2002. In 2003, Hoffa also held two appointments: the President's Council on the 21st Century Workforce and the Secretary of Energy's Advisory Board.

HOFFA, JAMES RIDDLE (1913-c. 1975). Hoffa was one of the most controversial labor leaders in recent U.S. history. Born in Brazil, Indiana, Hoffa worked in various service sector jobs before he became involved with organized labor in 1931. He became a member of the **Teamsters** in 1934. He advanced steadily in the Teamsters, was made a vice president in 1952, and was president from 1957 to 1971. In the course of his union career, Hoffa developed links with the Mafia. In 1964, he was convicted of jury tampering, fraud, and conspiracy over the disposition of union benefit funds and began a 13-year jail sentence in 1967, which was commuted by President Richard Nixon in 1971. As president, Hoffa's contribution to the Teamsters as a union was to enlarge its **membership** in the transportation and storage industry (under Hoffa, the Teamsters' membership grew from 1,417,400 to 1,789,100); to introduce the first nationwide contract in the industry (1964); and to expand the union's health and medical program. Hoffa disappeared in 1975 and has been presumed to have been murdered by the Mafia. His career was the subject of the 1993 film *Hoffa*, starring Jack Nicholson and Danny DeVito. *See also* HOFFA, JAMES P.

HONDURAS. The first labor union in Honduras was formed in 1917 among tradesmen, but organized labor could make little progress because of government opposition; under the dictatorship of General Tuburcio C. Andino organized labor was suppressed from 1932 to 1949. Between 1950 and 1963, a more favorable political environment enabled the formation of unions. A successful **strike** by 10,000 banana plantation workers against the U.S.-owned United Fruit Company led to union recognition and the country's first collective agreement in 1954 and a general government recognition of labor unions and the right to strike. From 1959 Honduras was represented with the **International Confederation of Free Trade Un-**

ions (ICFTU). In 1963, the military took power and suppressed organized labor; they held power more or less continuously until 1982. By the 1990s, the main concern of the ICFTU with regard to Honduras had turned to harsh working conditions and physical abuse of women workers in the country's **export processing zones,** particularly by Korean-owned firms. A strike in October 2000 was suppressed by the police. The right to strike and to form unions remained tenuous in Honduras in 2002, despite some reform of labor laws.

HONG KONG. A dependent territory of the **United Kingdom** until June 1997 (after which time Hong Kong became a Special Administrative Region of **China**), the first labor union in Hong Kong was formed in 1900, and its waterfront unions conducted a major **strike** in 1922. The first labor federation was formed in 1923. Although strikes were illegal before the ordinance of 1948, the colonial administration appointed an official in 1938 to arbitrate in labor disputes and to regulate unions. The Hong Kong Federation of Trade Unions was formed in 1948, and the Hong Kong and Kowloon Trades Union Council was established in the following year. Hong Kong has been represented in the **International Confederation of Free Trade Unions** (ICFTU) since 1951. Despite being a British colony, the legal status of labor unions in Hong Kong lagged behind that of other British colonies by the 1970s, a state of affairs that drew criticism from the ICFTU and the British **Trades Union Congress** (TUC) in the 1970s. Since June 1997, the ICFTU has been critical of the Hong Kong authorities' failure to create an institutional framework that provided for labor union rights and **collective bargaining.** In 2002, the ICFTU considered that the outlook for organized labor in Hong Kong was likely to be even more restricted.

HUMAN RIGHTS. Organized labor has always supported human rights issues, even if that support has been tinged with economic considerations. The exclusion of children from factory employment, for example, could be justified on the grounds of the protection of their welfare, but the employment of children also posed a threat to adult wages. Similarly, the attempts of the **American Federation of Labor-Congress of Industrial Organizations** (AFL-CIO) to deny tariff preferences to certain countries such as **Indonesia** for abuses of trade union rights could also be interpreted as reducing competition from countries with low wage economies. More clearly, the support for human rights by organized labor was evident in the case of the apartheid system in **South Africa**, where German and Swedish unions were able to exert pressure on the boards of their companies operating in South Africa to adopt progressive codes of conduct that excluded racist practices. In 1985, the **International Confederation of Free Trade Unions** (ICFTU) began to publish annual surveys of **violations of trade union rights** in the world, which document the murder, torture, and imprisonment of union leaders and denial of official recognition of labor unions that are not controlled by the government. Those countries with the worst record of human rights violations also have the worst record of violation of trade union rights. The Middle East usually attracts significant attention in this regard, but of late attention has been given to Asia and Africa. *See also* CHILD LABOR; FORCED LABOR; INTERNATIONAL LABOUR ORGANISATION; SLAVERY.

HUNGARY. Organized labor within the modern borders of Hungary emerged during the 1860s and grew in parallel with the Social Democratic Party, which set up a council of labor unions in 1891; this was reorganized on a permanent basis in 1899. In 1898, there were 126 unions with a combined **membership** of 23,000. In 1907, the unions claimed a combined membership of 130,000, but the hostile political climate reduced this to 112,000 by 1912. Hungary was an affiliate of the **International Federation of Trade Unions** (IFTU) from 1905 to 1939. In 1919, Hungary's political framework was shattered by the attempted creation of a communist republic, which was replaced by a provisional government of labor and **socialists** and then by a right wing counterrevolutionary government led by Admiral Miklós Horthy, who suppressed the left wing of organized labor. The imposition of **communist** rule meant that it was impossible for an independent labor movement to operate until 1986.

By 1995, two national labor federations existed: the *Magyar Szakszervezetek Országos Szövetsége Tagszervezeteinek Címlistája* (MszOSz) or National Confederation of Hungarian Trade Unions, formed in 1990 from the former communist *Magyar Szakszervezetek Országos Tanácsá* (SZOT) or Central Council of Hungarian Trade Unions with 895,000 members, and the Democratic League of Independent Trade Unions (LIGA), formed in 1989 with 98,000 members. The LIGA, MszOSz, and the Autonomous

Trade Union Federation were members of the **International Confederation of Free Trade Unions** (ICFTU) in 2001. Together, their membership was 766,000 or about 29 percent of all employees. A national survey by the MszOSz in 2001 found widespread violations of **freedom of association**, discrimination against organized labor, and breaches of labor law. Amendments to the labor code in September 2002 have improved the legal environment for organized labor in Hungary, but discrimination against unions continues.

-I-

ICELAND. In 1916, two years before Iceland became independent from **Denmark**, seven unions created the Icelandic Federation of Labor with 650 members. The first attempt at forming a labor federation had been made in 1907, but it collapsed in 1910. By 1923, union **membership** had reached 4,000. Between 1925 and 1927, three regional labor federations were created. Despite legal restrictions, many **labor disputes** have occurred in Iceland. State and local government employees organized their own labor federation in 1942. Union membership grew from 4,500 in 1927 to 30,000 in 1960 and to 82,900 in 2001. *See also* COUNCIL OF NORDIC TRADE UNIONS.

ICONOGRAPHY. Throughout its history organized labor has made extensive use of public symbols to express and create unity and to win support. Painted silken banners depicting the activities and aspirations of union members seem to have been derived from coats of arms in Britain and began to be used from about 1807. About three-quarters of the union banners used by organized labor in Britain from 1837 until the 1970s were made by one firm, that founded by George Tutill (1817-1887); Tutill's banners were also exported throughout the British Empire. Banners were carried on May Day or **Labor Day** and to encourage solidarity during **labor disputes**. Common themes in the iconography of organized labor were the appeal to unity (for example, in slogans like "the unity of labor is the hope of the world") and secular millenarianism (the promise of a better future often symbolized by a rising sun) and how it might be achieved through **socialism** or **communism**. Traditionally, the iconography of organized labor has depicted **blue-collar** employment. Union labels have also been used to promote goods produced by union members; they were first used in the **United States** by the Cigar Makers' International Union in 1874. In 1884, the **Knights of Labor** and other unions used union labels as part of their boycott campaign. Organized labor has also used badges and medals to promote **membership**; the **general strike** in Brisbane, Australia, in 1912 was prompted by managements' objections to government street car employees wearing membership badges. Other outlets for the use of union iconography were the labor press from the 1880s and, from the 1930s, film. In 1954, the **International Confederation of Free Trade Unions** (ICFTU) began to create a catalog of films made by organized labor and held screenings at their own film festivals held every two years. *See also* INDUSTRIAL ARCHAEOLOGY.

IG METALL. *IG Metall* was the largest labor union in **Germany** and the largest union in any democratic country in the world between 1950 and 2001. Since 1965, it has had over two million members or a third of Germany's total trade union **membership**. Based on engineering employees, the sheer size of *IG Metall* has made it a major force in post-1945 German labor history. *IG Metall* was formed at a congress in Hamburg, September 18-22, 1950, with a membership of 1.3 million. Its leader between 1954 and 1972 was **Otto Brenner**. *IG Metall* played a prominent part in **labor disputes** and in gaining pay increases and **shorter working hours** for its members. In 1977, the first debates were held within *IG Metall* for gaining a 35-hour work week.

In 1984, *IG Metall* conducted a **strike** that reduced the working hours of its members to 38.5 hours and, in February 1988, signed an agreement that gave many of its members a work week of 36.5 hours. Following the reunification of Germany in 1989, *IG Metall* actively recruited in the former East Germany to raise its membership to 3.6 million by 1992. On April 24, 1994, *IG Metall* negotiated an agreement with the employers' metal trades federation for a 35-hour week to begin on May 1, 1994. In 1994, *IG Metall* had 3 million members, but by 1997, membership had fallen to 2.6 million, of whom 18 percent were **women**. This decline was a reflection of the slow growth of the German economy and the cost of the integration of the former East Germany.

In the mid-1990s, *IG Metall* moved to the forefront of German labor unions in its adoption of policies aimed at combating discrimination on the grounds of **race and ethnicity**. In 1994, about 10 percent of the membership of *IG Metall* were non-German, of whom about half were from Turkey or of Turkish descent. By 2000, membership had increased slightly to 2.7 million. In April 2002, *IG Metall* conducted a successful campaign using warning strikes that gained a 4 percent pay rise and a further rise of 3.1 percent rise from June 1, 2003. *See also DEUTSCHER METALLAR-BEITER VERBAND.*

IMMIGRATION. Immigration from Western Europe has played an important role in spreading organized labor to other countries. In the **United Kingdom**, some sections of organized labor actively encouraged emigration as a way of reducing unemployment. Several English unions, notably the **Amalgamated Society of Engineers** and the **Amalgamated Society of Carpenters and Joiners**, were able to establish branches in North America, South Africa, and Australasia through immigration. As a major source of skilled employees, British immigrants were particularly important in the founding of labor unions in **Canada**, the **United States**, **Australia**, and **New Zealand** before 1900. Similarly, organized labor in Latin America was much influenced by Spanish and Italian immigrants. In the United States immigrants were disproportionately represented in organized labor because they were the backbone of the industrialized labor force in the large cities.

Up to 1890, the industrialized labor force of the United States was dominated by British, Irish, and German immigrants, but thereafter immigrants from **Russia**, Eastern Europe, **Italy**, and Scandinavia assumed greater importance. By 1910, 20 percent of the labor force of the United States was foreign-born. Not only that, 72 percent of immigrants were urban dwellers, compared to 36 percent for the native-born. The occupations that loomed large in the history of organized labor were immigrant-dominated; in 1910, 48 percent of coal miners were foreign-born, as were 45 percent of woollen textile workers, and 37 percent of cotton textile workers. The harsh lot of many immigrant employees—low pay, long hours, and poor and unsafe working conditions—generated justifiable discontent and created a large social divide in American society, whose established unions (because they tended to represent the better-off native-born) proved ill-equipped to heal. Nevertheless, union activity was one source of upward social mobility for the foreign-born. Gary M. Fink estimated in 1984 that of the 80 top labor leaders in the United States in 1900, 40 percent were foreign-born, and that even by 1946 this proportion had only fallen to 20 percent. In Australia, immigration has been a feature of organized labor for over a century, and between 1976 and 1999 a steady 24 percent of union members were born overseas.

In Western Europe, immigration from Eastern Europe, the Middle East, the Caribbean, and Africa since the 1970s has fed the **black labor market** and heightened issues of **race and ethnicity**. Although the leadership of European organized labor officially opposes racism, there are doubts about the degree to which the rank-and-file share their views.

On July 1, 2003, the United Nations Convention on Migrant Workers came into force. Among other things, it required countries that ratified the convention to guarantee migrant workers the right to labor union representation. The **International Confederation of Free Trade Unions** (ICFTU) has expressed concern that none of the countries receiving large numbers of migrants—that is, in North America, Western Europe, Australasia, and the Middle East—have ratified the convention. *See also* COAL MINING.

INDIA. Before 1918, there was very little organized labor in India. Those unions that had been formed were confined to skilled and better-off employees. The industrialization brought by World War I created a more favorable climate for the creation of unions. In 1918, B. P. Wadia created the Madras Union, which was based on textile employees. Stimulated by low wages, wartime inflation, and the rise of the independence movement, the next two years brought an increase in unions and union members. In 1920, the All-India Trades Union Congress was formed, representing 64 unions with about 150,000 members. In the interwar years, India's unions and labor federations became divided between moderates and **communists**. As in other countries, industrial and political aims (that is, support for independence) became mixed. In 1947, the government sponsored a new noncommunist labor federation, the Indian National Trade Union Congress, thereby setting a precedent for the various labor federations to be associated with a particular political party.

Between 1950 and 1970, the number of union members rose from 2.3 million to 4.9 million. Although Indian unions operate in a relatively benign legal environment compared to most other Asian countries, their power to influence governments has been limited. For example, a **general strike** by millions of employees against the national government's economic reforms on September 9, 1993, had no effect on government policy. There were 11.8 million union members in 2001 in India, compared to 10.3 million in 1995. On April 6, 2002, unions led 10 million workers in protests over government plans to **privatize** state-run companies. In 2002, the ICFTU was critical of government efforts to restrict the right to strike, particularly in the state of Tamil Nardu and in **export processing zones** generally. *See also* CHILD LABOR.

INDONESIA. Indonesia was ruled by the **Netherlands** as the Dutch East Indies from the 17th century to 1949. It had no organized labor until 1905, when Dutch and indigenous railway employees formed a union. A labor federation was founded in 1919, but it only lasted until 1921. **Communism** and nationalism were features of organized labor from the 1920s to the 1960s. By 1930, there were 32,000 members of unions in Indonesia and, in 1931, a revived labor federation of indigenous employees was admitted to the **International Federation of Trade Unions** (IFTU). Since independence, labor unions have been bound up with the government. Some sections of organized labor participated in the communist insurgency in the 1950s and early 1960s, but these were suppressed in an extensive crackdown that followed the attempted coup of 1965. Since 1973 labor unions have been incorporated into the apparatus of government, though remaining nominally independent. Although three Indonesian labor federations have been members of the **International Confederation of Free Trade Unions** (ICFTU) since 1969, in the early 1990s their **membership**, and those of a fourth body, was suspended because of their lack of independence from government control.

An independent union, *Sepia Kawan* (Prosperity Labor Union), was formed in November 1990; it claimed 50,000 members in 1993 but has twice been denied registration as a legal body, and its leadership has been harassed by the military. In August 1993 the government banned the union's first congress. There is also another independent labor body, the Center for Indonesian Working-Class Struggle. Muchtar Pakpahan (1958-), a lawyer and the leader of the Prosperity Labor Union, was arrested on August 13, 1994, over riots in Medan, Sumatra, that occurred in April 1994 because of demands for raising the **minimum wage, freedom of association**, the investigation of the death of Rusli (a striker), and compensation for sacked rubber factory workers.

On November 7, 1994, Pakpahan was sentenced to three years in jail, a decision that brought protests from labor leaders in **Australia** and the **United States**. On January 16, 1995, Pakpahan's sentence was increased to four years by the North Sumatra High Court. After the collapse of the Suharto government in May 1998, the government of Bacharuddin Jusuf Habibie released Pakpahan and other labor organizers. It also agreed to ratify **International Labour Organisation** (ILO) Convention 87 on freedom of association and the right to organize labor unions. Although Convention 87 and the other seven core standards of the ILO were ratified by 2001, trade union rights in practice have proved difficult to exercise in Indonesia, and violence and intimidation of organized labor remains commonplace. In 2001, four Indonesian unions were affiliated with the ICFTU with a total membership of 432,600. In 2003, the right to strike and **collective bargaining** were curtailed by new legislation, and violence against union activists continued.

INDUSTRIAL ARCHAEOLOGY. Industrial archaeology is a branch of archaeology devoted principally to the physical remains and technology of the Industrial Revolution. It emerged in the 1960s and is also associated with efforts to recreate the living conditions in industrial centers through open air museums such as those of Beamish in northeast England and at Dudley in the English Midlands. *See also* ICONOGRAPHY.

INDUSTRIAL DEMOCRACY. Industrial democracy is a term with a wide spectrum of meanings but indicating some degree of control by employees in the decisions and processes that affect their working lives. At its most extreme, it can mean that the employees should be the managers of their employment. This has been a particularly popular view in the left wing of organized labor and expressed in the term "workers' control." In its milder forms, especially in the 1970s, it has been used to justify greater consultation with employees as a means for raising labor productivity. *See also MITBESTIMMUNG*; SYNDICALISM.

INDUSTRIAL PSYCHOLOGY. Industrial psychology is primarily concerned with human relations at work. There have been a number of schools of thought within the field reflecting the kinds of employment dominant in the economy. One of the earliest was "scientific management" which was founded by an engineer, Frederick Winslow Taylor (1856-1915), one of the developers of chromium-tungsten high-speed steel, who had been employed by the Midvale Steel Company in the 1880s. Taylor developed his ideas at a time when technological changes in the steel industry enabled managements to break the power of skilled employees and replace them with lesser skilled. Employees were assumed to be relatively unintelligent and motivated largely to earn more by agreeing to close supervision in the performance of monotonous work of low skill content. Scientific management was suitable for industries engaged in high-volume production where the tasks could be broken down into a series of repetitive steps such as assembly lines.

The "human relations" school was founded by an Australian-born psychologist, (George) Elton Mayo (1880-1949), who conducted a series of experiments for the management of the Western Electric Company in Chicago between 1924 and 1927. One of Mayo's findings was the important role played by informal groups in the performance of factory work and their significance for work habits and attitudes.

In 1943, A. H. Maslow published a psychological theory of motivation, which proposed that employees' satisfaction depended upon a hierarchy of needs beginning with the physiological, safety, love or social needs, self-esteem, and ending with self-fulfillment. In the 1950s and 1960s, F. Herzberg built on Maslow's work to stress the need for the work itself to have or produce a sense of achievement, advancement, and responsibility as factors that motivated employees to perform more productively. In the 1970s, "**industrial democracy**" (a term with a variety of meanings) was given more attention in the management literature as a means of promoting higher productivity and lower absenteeism. In practical terms, it has encouraged greater consultation by management of its employees. As a general rule, the results of the research carried out by industrial psychologists have been of far greater interest and use to management than they have to organized labor. This is because the research has often been commissioned by employers and because the research itself often ignored unions and why they might be supported by employees. *See also* EMPLOYERS' ORGANIZATIONS.

INDUSTRIAL SOCIOLOGY. Industrial sociology is a branch of sociology concerned with work, its organization, and its effects. Although there were earlier investigations, industrial sociology had its origins in the work of British pioneers such as Henry Mayhew in the 1850s and 1860s and Charles Booth in the 1890s. These investigators collected data on employment, living conditions, income, and costs among the working class in London. In the **United States**, important studies were carried out of particular groups such as coal miners (for example, by Peter Roberts in 1904) and clothing employees. In the 1930s, studies by industrial sociologists in many countries documented the debilitating effects of long-term unemployment; for example, E. W. Bakke published *Citizens without Work* in 1940. Others published their findings as official government reports. Common themes in industrial sociology in the period from 1945 to 1980 were how the working class was responding to greater affluence, the monotony of mass production, and family relationships.

Labor unions as such were not studied much before the pioneering works of Beatrice and Sidney Webb in the 1890s. In 1952, an American investigator, Joseph Goldstein, published *The Government of British Trade Unions*, which examined the workings of the **Transport and General Workers' Union** and estimated that branch attendance at union meetings never exceeded 15 percent of the **membership**. Subsequent studies have confirmed Goldstein's findings of low membership participation in the affairs of most large unions. Since 1980, industrial sociologists have often been concerned with the social impact of economic change; the effects of steel plant closures on communities, for instance, have been studied in many countries. *See also* LABOR HISTORY.

INDUSTRIAL UNIONS. In theory, industrial unions are labor unions that only recruit their members from a particular industry regardless of whether or not the employees in the industry have completed an **apprenticeship**, in contrast to **craft unions**. The issue of how organized labor should be organized—whether by particular trade or by industry— was often raised in the late 19th century, but assumed greater importance in the early 20th century with the growth of unions. In 1905, the **Industrial Workers of the World** agreed that it should consist of five main industry groups: mining, manufacturing, building, transportation, and public service distribution. Concerned about their autonomy, craft and other smaller labor unions resisted the advocates of industrial unions. In resisted the advocates of industrial unions. In turn, the advocates of industrial unions, particularly drawing on **syndicalism**, regarded craft unions as organizations that maintained divisions among the working class and rendered organized labor vulnerable to attack. The debate assumed urgency in **Germany** after World War II when leaders like **Hans Böckler** succeeded in reestablishing organized labor along the lines of industrial unions. This was possible because of the smashing of the previous mix of craft and industrial unions in Germany by the Nazis, but elsewhere the goal of purely industrial unions has proved elusive for organized labor in democratic societies. The main difficulty with industrial unions has been defining an "industry" for practical purposes. In 2001, organized labor is still characterized, despite numerous **amalgamations** over the past 40 years, by a mixture of types of unions, some organized around an industry (for example, **Education**), or a particular occupation (for example, the U.S. Brotherhood of Railroad Signalmen), or a conglomerate of occupations (for example, **Amicus**).

INDUSTRIAL WORKERS OF THE WORLD (IWW). The IWW, popularly known as the "Wobblies," was the American expression of **syndicalism**, which was influential in international organized labor from the early 1900s until about 1920. Although the works of European theorists such as Karl Marx and Georges-Eugène Sorel were known, the IWW owed its origins to the violent labor environment of the mining industry in the western **United States**. The prime mover in the formation of the IWW was the radical Western Federation of Miners, a body that originated in the Butte Miners' Union, established in 1878. After defeats in disputes in 1903-1904, particularly at Cripple Creek, Colorado, the Western Federation of Miners called a convention in 1904 in Chicago to form a single organization for the working class, which led to the creation of the IWW in 1905. The convention adopted a radical platform that declared that the employers and workers had nothing in common and agreed to build an organization that admitted all employees regardless of sex, **race**, or nationality, an idea dormant in American organized labor since the demise of the **Knights of Labor** in the late 1880s. It also agreed that the IWW should be made up of five main industry groups: mining, **manufacturing**, building, transportation, and public service distribution, an idea that later became very influential in international organized labor.

By 1906, the IWW claimed 14,000 members but was able to mobilize far greater support among poorly paid and exploited workers. It campaigned for free speech in the late 1900s, which provoked vigilante violence, and conducted America's first sit-down **strike** at the General Electric plant at Schenectady, New York, in 1906. The IWW proved adept at mobilizing working class discontent, for example among the largely immigrant textile employees at Lawrence, Massachusetts, in 1912, but not at creating lasting organizations. With the entry of the United States into World War I in 1917, the IWW came under direct attack from the federal government, which raided IWW offices and arrested the bulk of the leadership. Of the 105 leaders arrested, 91 were convicted, including William Haywood (1869-1928). At its height, between 1919 and 1924, the membership of the IWW ranged between 58,000 and 100,000.

Although the IWW continued to live on after 1924, it was no longer a significant force. In its heyday, it led the mobilizing of unskilled workers in **agriculture** and lumber and, more important, drew public attention to their deplorable working conditions. The IWW also provided members for the American Communist Party. Although primarily an American organization, the IWW was an important force in **Canada** and was a focus for leftwing activity in **Argentina**, **Australia**, **Mexico**, **New Zealand**, and **South Africa**; its most lasting legacy was its advocacy of the **One Big Union**. The IWW continues as an organization and maintained a website in 2003.

INDUSTRIEGEWERKSCHAFT METALL. See IG METALL.

INTERNATIONAL BROTHERHOOD OF TEAMSTERS, CHAUFFEURS, WAREHOUSEMEN, AND HELPERS OF AMERICA. *See* TEAMSTERS.

INTERNATIONAL CONFEDERATION OF ARAB TRADE UNIONS (ICATU). The ICATU was formed in Damascus, Syria, in March 1956, by national labor bodies in **Egypt**, **Jordan**, **Lebanon**, **Libya**, and **Syria**. The aims of the ICATU included the improvement of living standards of Arab employees but also support for national struggles for independence against colonial rule. The ICATU promoted training and study courses for union officials from 1969. Two forces weakened the potential effectiveness of the ICATU: the repression of organized labor by Arab governments and the left-wing character of the ICATU. The ICATU split in 1978 and its headquarters were transferred from Egypt to Syria. In 1992, the ICATU had 16 member nations and had close links to the **World Federation of Trade Unions** (WFTU). Although the ICATU held a conference in 2000, it has not developed into an effective international labor organization.

INTERNATIONAL CONFEDERATION OF FREE TRADE UNIONS (ICFTU). The ICFTU has been the largest international body representing organized labor in noncommunist countries since its formation in December 1949. After the replacement of the **International Federation of Trade Unions** (ICFTU) by the **World Federation of Trade Unions** (WFTU) in 1945, there was growing concern over infiltration of the new body by **communist** organizations controlled by the Soviet Union. This concern was strongest in the **United States**, the **United Kingdom**, and the **Netherlands**, which set up the ICFTU in 1949. At its foundation, the ICFTU had members in 51 countries, which represented 48 million union members, of whom 43 percent were in Western Europe and 31 percent in North America. Despite its strong support for independent labor unions from its formation, many of the ICFTU's members in Latin America, Africa, and Asia were guilty of violations of this principle. In 1985, the ICFTU began to publish annual surveys of **violations of trade union rights** in the world. The ICFTU vets applicant organizations carefully to ensure that they are independent and not mouthpieces of their governments.

By the 1960s, the ICFTU had broadened its perspective to include progressive social goals. In 1969, the politically conservative **American Federation of Labor-Congress of Industrial Organizations** (AFL-CIO) withdrew from the ICFTU and did not rejoin until 1981. The absence of the AFL-CIO reduced the budget of the ICFTU by one quarter.

The ICFTU has four regional organizations: the **European Trade Union Confederation** (ETUC), the *Organización Regional Interamericana de Trabajadores* (Inter-American Regional Organization of Workers), formed in 1951; the **Asian and Pacific Regional Organisation**, formed in 1984 from the Asia Regional Organization formed in 1951; and, the **African Regional Organization** formed in 1960.

After 1989, some labor federations from former East European communist countries were admitted to membership of the ICFTU. By 1995, organized labor in Eastern Europe accounted for only 9 percent of the 125 million members in the ICFTU. However, in November 2000, the ICFTU took the historic decision to admit the **Russian** labor federations as affiliates, a move that boosted the union membership represented by the ICFTU by 30 million and the proportion of its members living in Eastern Europe to 24 percent. As well as country members, **Global Union Federations** (GUF) have been associated with the ICFTU although retaining their autonomy. In 2001, the ICFTU had a membership of 156 million or about 93 percent of all global labor union members.

INTERNATIONAL FEDERATION OF BUILDING AND WOODWORKERS (IFBWW). The IFBWW **global union federation** was formed on April 1, 1934, through the merger of the Woodworkers' International (formed in 1904) and the Building Workers' International (formed in 1903). Later in 1934, two other **international trade secretariats**, the Painters' International (formed in 1911) and the Stoneworkers' International (formed in 1904), joined the IFBWW, which has been based in Geneva since 1970. The affiliated membership of the IFBWW was 2.2 million in 1975 and 3.5 million in 1992. In 2001, the IFBWW claimed 11 million members and 281 affiliated labor unions in 124 countries. The IFBWW campaigns for **occupational health and safety** and sustainable forestry development.

INTERNATIONAL FEDERATION OF CHEMICAL, ENERGY, MINE, AND GENERAL WORKERS' UNIONS (ICEM). The ICEM **global union federation** was created in 1964 from the merger of the International Federation of General Factory Workers (formed in 1907) and the International Federation of Industrial Organizations and General Workers' Unions (formed in 1947). The IFCEGW faced competition from the International Federation of Petroleum and Chemical Workers (formed in 1954) until its denouncement by Victor George Reuther as a "front" for the U.S. Central Intelligence Agency, an action that led to the folding of the federation in 1976. Between 1976 and 1992, the affiliated **membership** of the IFCEGW rose from 4 to 6.3 million members. In 1995, it merged with the **Miners' International Federation**. In 2001, ICEM claimed a membership of 20 million and 390 affiliated labor unions in 107 countries. The ICEM seeks to obtain global agreements with multinational corporations on pay and working conditions. Its activities include support for dialogue with the International Monetary Fund, the World Bank, the World Trade Organization, and other similar bodies with the view of making them more accountable to democratic processes.

INTERNATIONAL FEDERATION OF CHRISTIAN TRADE UNION. *See* WORLD CONFEDERATION OF LABOR.

INTERNATIONAL FEDERATION OF FREE TEACHERS' UNIONS (IFFTU). The IFFTU **international trade secretariat** was originally formed as an entirely European body in 1928 but was reorganized as a global labor body in 1951 in Paris. Its **membership** increased from 2.3 million in 1976 to 19 million in 1993. It was based in Brussels. In 1993, it was reorganized as the **Educational International** following its merger with the **World Confederation of Organizations of the Teaching Profession** (WCOTP).

INTERNATIONAL FEDERATION OF JOURNALISTS (IFJ). The first efforts to form an international labor organization among journalists date from 1926. The IFJ was formed in 1952 by noncommunists who split from the communist-dominated International Organization of Journalists. Up to the late 1980s, the IFJ was neither an **international trade secretariat** nor a formal associate of the **International Confederation of Free Trade Unions** (ICFTU), but it was both by 1993. Membership of the IFJ was 81,900 in 1976 and 350,000 in 1994. It is based in Brussels. In 2001, the IFJ claimed a **membership** of 450,000 in 138 labor unions in 101 countries. The IFJ has a particular concern with **human rights** and the freedom of the press. It maintains a list of the names of journalists killed while trying to report on world events. *See also* WHITE-COLLAR UNIONISM.

INTERNATIONAL FEDERATION OF PLANTATION, AGRICULTURAL, AND ALLIED WORKERS (IFPAW). The IFPAW **international trade secretariat** was created in 1960 by the merger of the International Landworkers' Federation, which was formed by some European agricultural labor unions in 1921, and the Plantation Workers' International, which was organized by the **International Confederation of Free Trade Unions** (ICFTU) in

1957 to represent Third World plantation employees; the International Federation of Tobacco Workers joined this body in 1958. Between 1976 and 1992 the affiliated membership of the IFPAW was stationary at three million. In 1988, the IFPAW signed an agreement with the French food multinational, Danone, on **collective bargaining**, one of the first of its kind. In 1994, the IFPAW merged with the **International Union of Food and Allied Workers' Associations**. *See also* AGRICULTURE.

INTERNATIONAL FEDERATION OF TRADE UNIONS (IFTU). The IFTU was the first continuous general international organization of labor unions. Officially called the International Secretariat of the National Trade Unions Federations until 1919, the IFTU was formed in Copenhagen on August 21, 1901, by labor representatives from **Belgium, Denmark, Finland, France, Germany, Norway, Sweden**, and **United Kingdom**. The original impetus for the formation of the IFTU came from J. Jensen, the leader of the Danish labor unions, who had attended a conference held by the **General Federation of Trade Unions** in London in 1900. Its largest affiliates between 1901 and 1913 were the United Kingdom and Germany. The **American Federation of Labor** (AFL) joined the IFTU in 1911 but left officially in 1919; it did not reaffiliate until 1937. Before 1913, the IFTU devoted itself to collecting money to help unions and strikers engaged in **labor disputes**, and to exchanging information. World War I split the IFTU along national lines, and it was not reestablished until 1919. Up to 1919, the IFTU was led by **Carl Legien**.

After 1919, the IFTU participated in European **politics**, a policy that led to the withdrawal of the AFL. The IFTU invited the **Russian** trade unions to its conferences, but these moves were met with hostility from the communist government, which regarded the IFTU as a competitor for the leadership of organized labor. The Russians established Profitern, the labor arm of the Comintern, as a rival to the IFTU. The IFTU continued to aid labor unions in affiliated countries and carried out fact-finding missions of workers' conditions in **Austria** and Belgium (1920) and the Saar and Upper Silesia (1921). Throughout its life, the IFTU was essentially a moderate, European-based organization and the voice of organized labor in the **International Labour Organisation** (ILO). In 1927, the IFTU established an International Committee of Trade Union Women, which lasted until 1937; it considered issues such as **equal**

pay for equal work, domestic service, working from home, and the **women's** peace campaign.

In the 1930s the IFTU tried to widen its membership; **India** joined in 1934, **Mexico** in 1936, **New Zealand** in 1938, and **China** in 1939. The **Australian Council of Trade Unions** was invited to join in 1936 but did not accept. At its conferences in 1931 and 1932, the IFTU adopted the 40-hour work week and a comprehensive social program as objectives. Despite its best efforts, the IFTU was weakened by the suppression of organized labor by fascism and undermined by **communism** and lack of support from the AFL for most of its life. The IFTU gave way to the **World Federation of Trade Unions** (WFTU) and ceased to exist on December 31, 1945. *See also* INTERNATIONAL CONFEDERATION OF FREE TRADE UNIONS; SOCIAL-DEMOCRATIC, SOCIALIST, AND LABOR PARTIES.

INTERNATIONAL GRAPHICAL FEDERATION (IGF). The IGF was founded in Stockholm in 1949 through the **amalgamation** of three international printing and graphical trades bodies—the International Typographical Secretariat (formed in 1889), the International Federation of Lithographers (formed in 1896), and the International Federation of Bookbinders and Kindred Trades (formed in 1907)—and eight British graphical trades labor unions. Based in Brussels, the IGF is mainly a European body. Its affiliated **membership** increased from 806,300 in 1976 to 1.2 million in 1994. In January 2000, the IGF merged with **Communication International,** the **Media Entertainment International,** and the *Fédération internationale des employés, techniciens et cadres* (FIET) or the International Federation of Commercial, Clerical, Professional, and Technical Employees, to form the **Union Network International** (UNI). *See also* PRINTING.

INTERNATIONAL LABOUR ORGANISATION (ILO). Created in 1919 as part of the peace process to end World War I, the ILO is a permanent world organization comprised of representatives of governments, **employers' organizations,** and organized labor whose function is the protection and improvement of working people through the setting of legal minimum standards and technical assistance. The first steps towards the creation of such a body were taken in **Switzerland** in the late 1880s. The Belgian government supported the Swiss initiatives, and the International Congress of

Civil Reforms in Brussels in 1897 called for the setting up of an international body to protect labor. The Swiss-based International Association for Labor Legislation was formed in 1900 and held a number of international conferences, which stimulated government interest in forming a permanent body to protect employment conditions. An important precedent for the creation of the ILO occurred in 1904 when **France** and **Italy** signed a treaty regulating the employment conditions of their nationals working in each other's country.

World War I disrupted these efforts, but the need for the active support of labor to fight the war gave organized labor an enhanced standing with the British, French, and German governments. In 1916, a congress held by organized labor in the **United Kingdom** was attended by representatives from France, Italy, and **Belgium**; it prepared specific proposals to be incorporated into the treaty expected to end the war and suggested an international commission to implement them. In Germany, **Carl Legien**, concerned that the **International Federation of Trade Unions** (IFTU) might be broken up, convened a counter-conference at Berne in 1917. Organized labor in France and **Germany** strongly supported the idea of an international body to safeguard the interests of labor. During the preparations for the Versailles Treaty, a Labor Commission was formed of 15 members drawn from the **United States**, France, United Kingdom, Italy, **Japan**, Belgium, **Cuba**, **Czechoslovakia**, and **Poland** and chaired by **Samuel Gompers**.

Overcoming many political and ideological differences, the commission succeeded in having these principles incorporated in the treaty: respect for labor; the right of association; adequate wages; an eight-hour work day or 48-hour week; abolition of **child labor**; **equal pay for equal work**; migrant workers to be given the same treatment as nationals; and an inspectorate system for protecting labor. Although the final outcome of the peace process was a disappointment for organized labor in Europe, the compromises reflected the political reality of the time. Under the ILO constitution, the governing body was to have 12 representatives from governments, six from employers, and six from employees; although, in practice, employee representation was dominated by the IFTU. The ILO became an affiliated agency of the League of Nations.

The ILO was able to achieve relatively little in its first 20 years. The fascist suppression of free unions in Italy raised the issue of **freedom of association** in a very stark way, but the ILO was unable, as an organization, to agree on a course of action. Its representation was also inadequate; the **United States** did not join until 1935. Its recommendations for reducing the mass unemployment of the early 1930s through increased government spending were ignored by member governments. Despite its difficulties, the ILO succeeded in starting the first continuous collections of international **labor statistics.**

In 1946, the ILO became the first specialized agency to be associated with the United Nations. In the late 1940s the ILO adopted two fundamental propositions regarding organized labor: Convention 87 (Freedom of Association and Protection of the Right to Organise, 1948) and Convention 98 (Right to Organise and to Bargain Collectively). In 1951, the governing body of the ILO set up a standing Freedom of Association Committee to oversee the operation of these and other conventions relating to organized labor. Although there is no specific ILO convention setting down the right to **strike,** Article 3 of Convention 87 stating that unions had the right to "draw up their constitutions and rules, to elect their representatives in full freedom, to organize their administration and activities and to formulate their programmes" has been interpreted as including a right to strike. The extent of ratification by member governments of the ILO of these and similar conventions varies, as does the degree of respect for them among those governments that have. The United States withdrew from the ILO between 1977 and 1980 because of disagreements with its policies.

Organized labor is represented in the ILO by the **International Confederation of Free Trade Unions** (ICFTU) which uses the **international standard-setting** of the ILO, specifically seven core labor standards, in its assessment of **violations of trade unions rights**: forced or compulsory labor (Convention No. 29, 1930); freedom of association and protection of the right to organize (Convention No. 87, 1948); right to organize and **collective bargaining** (Convention No. 98, 1949); equal remuneration for work of equal value (Convention No. 100, 1951); discrimination in employment and occupation (Convention No. 111, 1958); minimum age for employment (Convention No. 138, 1973); worst forms of child labor (Convention No. 182, 1999). *See also* LABOR DISPUTES; OCCUPATIONAL HEALTH AND SAFETY; THOMAS, ALBERT.

INTERNATIONAL LADIES' GARMENT WORKERS' UNION (ILGWU). The ILGWU has played a significant role in the history of organized labor in the **United States**. Formed in New York City in March 1900, the ILGWU received a charter from the **American Federation of Labor** (AFL) three months later. Its **membership** grew from 2,200 in 1904 to 58,400 in 1912, many of whom were Jewish and East European immigrants. Successful **strikes** in New York City in 1909 and 1910 secured the union's future. The 1910 cloak makers' strike gained a 54-hour work week over six days, the closed shop, **arbitration** for the settlement of disputes, and the abolition of home-based work and subcontracting, which were important means of keeping wages in the trade low. Other important initiatives of the ILGWU in this period were union health centers (1913) and the preparation of an employer-funded unemployment plan (1919). By 1920, the ILGWU had grown to 195,400, but this success was undermined by **communists**, who dominated the leadership until 1928.

The newly elected leadership of Benjamin Schlesinger and **David Dubinsky** took over a union with debts of $800,000 and a financial membership of only 40,000. Assisted by the **National Industrial Recovery Act**, the ILGWU was rebuilt; by 1935 its membership had grown to 168,000 and most of the debts had been repaid. Under Dubinsky's leadership, the ILGWU was at the center of the struggle within organized labor to promote **industrial unionism** and in the formation of the **Congress of Industrial Organizations**. It left the AFL in 1938 but rejoined in 1940. In 1973, the union had a membership of 427,600, of whom about 80 percent were **women**. Diversity of **race and ethnicity** remained characteristic of its membership. In 1992, the ILGWU had 143,000 members. In 1995, the ILGWU merged with the Amalgamated Clothing and Textile Workers' Union to form the Union of Needletrades, Industrial, and Textile Employees.

INTERNATIONAL METALWORKERS' FEDERATION (IMF). The IMF was the largest of the **international trade secretariats** until 1995. It began as the International Metallurgists' Bureau of Information in 1893 and took its present name in 1904. In 1921, the IMF accepted a new constitution, which included a call for international cooperation to improve wages and conditions and for workers to take over the means of production. By 1930, the IMF had a **membership** of 1.9 million, but by 1938 the Depression and fascism had reduced its membership to only 190,000. By 1947, its membership had grown to 2.7 million. The IMF played a major role in defeating the attempt of the **communist**-led **World Council of Trade Unions** to absorb the various International Trade Secretariats in 1948-1949 and in the formation of the **International Confederation of Free Trade Unions** (ICFTU) in 1949. In 1994, the IMF claimed 16 million members among its 165 affiliated unions. In 1995, the IMF merged with the International Federation of Chemical, Energy, and General Workers' Unions to form the **International Federation of Chemical, Energy, Mine, and General Workers' Unions** (ICEM).

INTERNATIONAL ORGANIZATION OF EMPLOYERS. *See* EMPLOYERS' ORGANIZATIONS.

INTERNATIONAL SECRETARIAT FOR ARTS, MASS MEDIA, AND ENTERTAINMENT TRADE UNIONS. *See* MEDIA ENTERTAINMENT INTERNATIONAL.

INTERNATIONAL STANDARD-SETTING. International standard-setting refers to the work of the **International Labour Organisation** (ILO) in devising suitable standards for the protection and improvement of working conditions, especially in relation to **working hours**, the protection of **women** and children, adequate wages, social security, **freedom of association**, and vocational and technical education. The framing of such standards is difficult because the standard of living in the member countries of the ILO differs so greatly, as do their politics and economies. At the same time, there is an obvious need for such standards.

INTERNATIONAL TEXTILE, GARMENT, AND LEATHER WORKERS' FEDERATION (ITGLWF). The ITGLWF is a **global union federation** formed in 1970, although international bodies among European textile labor unions dated from 1894, and among shoemakers and leather employees from 1907. In 1960, the Textile Workers' Asian Regional Organization was created with 1.5 million members. Other similar regional bodies were formed, and these were the basis of the ITGLWF. Based in Brussels, the **membership** of the ITGLWF was 5.2 million in 1976, 7 million in 1994, and 10 million in 2001.

INTERNATIONAL TRADE SECRETARIATS (ITS). ITSs have been an important feature of the European labor movement throughout the 20th century and of the international labor movement since 1945. The secretariats represented individual occupations or particular industries. They emerged as formal organizations among hatters (Paris, 1889); cigar makers (Antwerp, 1889); shoemakers (Paris, 1889); miners (Manchester, 1890); glass workers (Fourmies, France, 1892); typographers (Berne, 1892); tailors (Zurich, 1893); metal workers (Winterthur, Switzerland, 1893); textile workers (Manchester, 1894); furriers (Berlin, 1894); lithographers (London, 1896); brewery workers (Berlin, 1896); transportation workers (London, 1897; this secretariat absorbed the railroad workers who had formed a secretariat in Zurich in 1893); foundry workers (1898); stone workers and stone cutters (1902, 1904); building workers (Berlin, 1903); carpenters (Hamburg, 1903); wood workers (Amsterdam, 1904); pottery and china workers (1905, 1906); diamond workers (Antwerp, 1905); bookbinders (Nuremberg, 1907); hairdressers (Stuttgart, 1907); municipal and public services (Mainz, 1906); factory and unskilled workers (this secretariat lasted from 1908 to 1914); postal workers (Marseilles, 1910); hotel and restaurant workers (Amsterdam, 1911); and painters (Hamburg, 1911).

By 1913, the trade secretariats claimed a total membership of 5.6 million, of which the largest were those of the miners (1.2 million), metal workers (1 million), transportation workers (860,000), and textile workers (533,000). By 1939, important new secretariats had emerged among teachers (1928) and government employees (1935).

After 1945, international labor organizations along occupational lines were important among civil servants, journalists, transportation workers, metal workers, miners, teachers, postal workers, textile workers, and plantation and agricultural employees. Despite attempted **communist** infiltration in 1948-1949, the international trade secretariats have preserved their independence. Since 1949 they have been associated with the **International Confederation of Free Trade Unions** (ICFTU). One way in which the ITSs try to improve the conditions of their members is through agreements negotiated with multinational corporations to provide a framework for **collective bargaining**; the first of these was negotiated with the French corporation, Danone, in 1988. In January 2002, the ITSs were renamed **Global Union Federations**.

INTERNATIONAL TRANSPORT WORKERS' FEDERATION (ITF). The ITF is a **global union federation** that grew out of the International Federation of Ship Dock and River Workers, which was formed by Tom Mann (1856-1941) and some European labor leaders in London in 1896. It became the ITF in 1898. World War I disrupted the ITF, and it was reestablished in 1919 though the efforts of Dutch, Swedish, and British labor unions. In 1920, the ITF had 3 million members, all of them in Europe; by 1931 **membership** had fallen to 2.3 million. The ITWF provided valuable services to the Allied war effort during World War II. As of 1948, the ITF began to seek affiliates from outside Europe. Since 1949, the ITF has been working closely with the **International Confederation of Free Trade Unions** (ICFTU) to draw attention to the hazards of the use of **flags of convenience** in world merchant shipping. By 1976, half of the 4.1 million members of the ITF were in developing countries. In 2001, the ITF claimed five million members among its 533 affiliated union members in 136 countries. Because it has many waterfront union affiliates, the ITF can exert considerable power if it chooses. For example, in **Australia** in 1997, it successfully supported the Maritime Union of Australia in two **labor disputes** with the conservative federal government over planned changes to waterfront labor practices.

INTERNATIONAL UNION OF FOOD, AGRICULTURAL, HOTEL, RESTAURANT, CATERING, TOBACCO, AND ALLIED WORKERS' ASSOCIATIONS (IUF). The IUF is a **global union federation** that was formed in 1994 from the merger of the **International Union of Food and Allied Workers' Associations** (IUFAWA) and the **International Federation of Plantation, Agricultural, and Allied Workers** (IFPAW). In 1997, the IUF negotiated an agreement to provide a framework for **collective bargaining** with a number of multinational corporations. In 2001, the IUF had 10 million members in 326 labor unions in 118 countries.

INTERNATIONAL UNION OF FOOD AND ALLIED WORKERS' ASSOCIATIONS (IUFAWA). The IUFAWA was an **international trade secretariat** established in 1920 from the **amalgamation** of the international federation of brewery employees (formed in 1896) and baking and meat employees. Until 1945 the IUFAWA was a European body, but afterwards it expanded into North America (1950), Latin America (1953), Africa (1959), and

East Asia (1961). In 1980, the IUF, with the support of international organized labor, campaigned against Coca-Cola over the exploitation of plantation workers in **Guatemala**. Membership of the Geneva-based IUFAWA was 2.1 million in 1978 and 2.3 million in 1992. In 1994, the IUFAWA merged with the **International Federation of Plantation, Agricultural, and Allied Workers** (IFPAW) to form the **International Union of Food, Agricultural, Hotel, Restaurant, Catering, Tobacco, and Allied Workers' Association**. (IUF).

INTERNATIONAL UNIONS. International labor unions are those that have branches in more than one country. The term is commonly applied to American unions with branches in **Canada**, but could also be applied to **Ireland**. Other international unions have been the **Amalgamated Society of Carpenters and Joiners** and the **Amalgamated Society of Engineers**. *See also* IMMIGRATION.

IRAN. Organized labor began in Iran when printers formed a union in the early 20th century. A national labor federation was formed in 1920 and fought for the eight-hour working day; it claimed 8,000 members by 1922. The first labor legislation was introduced in 1923. Under the right wing regime of Reza Khan, organized labor was forced to operate and grow in secrecy. In 1944, the Unified Trade Union of Iranian Workers was formed, with a membership of about 150,000, and became an affiliate of the **World Federation of Trade Unions** (WFTU). It had about 180,000 members by 1945. Organized labor played an active role in the oil nationalization campaign between 1946 and 1953, and there were large-scale **strikes**. By 1951, the Iranian Trades Union Congress had affiliated with the **International Confederation of Free Trade Unions** (ICFTU) and remained an affiliate until 1959, representing 65,000 union members. The overthrow of the Mohammed Mossadeq government and its replacement by the son of Reza Khan, Mohammad Reza Shah Pahlavi, with secret British and U.S. support, resulted in renewed repression and the outlawing of labor unions that were not controlled by the government. After the fundamentalist Islamic Revolution in 1978-1979, organized labor has remained repressed.

IRAQ. There was no independent organized labor in Iraq in the 20th century. There was only one legal labor organization after 1945, the

General Federation of Trade Unions, which was controlled by the ruling Ba'ath Party until the overthrow of Saddam Hussein in April 2003.

IRELAND. The existence of unions by the 18th century in Ireland is known from a law of 1729, which outlawed combinations among journeymen, with a penalty of three months' hard labor. Similar laws were passed in 1743 and 1757. Despite the intimidating legal climate, unions were formed. In May 1788, journeymen cabinetmakers in Belfast formed a union; their minute book survives, making it one of the oldest documents of its kind. As a part of the **United Kingdom** until 1922, Irish organized labor was much influenced by the English model, but it also took some important initiatives of its own. In 1844, the Regular Trades' Association was formed in Dublin; it perished in the 1847 depression, but it was one of the first city labor councils in Britain. British unions were active in Ireland from 1851, beginning with the **Amalgamated Society of Engineers**. By 1900 about three-quarters of the 67,000 union members in Ireland belonged to British unions; in 1940, this proportion had fallen to 30 percent and was stable at about 14 percent between 1955 and 1985.

In 1894, the Irish Trades Union Congress was formed, with 50,000 members among its affiliates. Originally intended to act as an auxiliary to the British **Trades Union Congress** (TUC), it went its own path from 1901; in 1945, it was challenged by the formation of a new peak labor body, the Congress of Irish Unions, but in 1959 these two bodies merged to become the Irish Congress of Trade Unions. Union membership in Ireland rose from 189,000 in 1922 to 285,000 in 1950 and to 490,000 in 1980. Despite some losses in the 1980s, union membership reached 677,600 by 1995 and 758,800 by 2001, or 59 percent of employees. Irish immigrants have played a significant role in the history of organized labor in the **United States, Australia**, and **New Zealand**.

ISRAEL. Organized labor in what is now Israel began in 1920 with the formation of leagues by both Arab and Jewish workers. The creation of the *Histadrut* (General Federation of Labor in Israel) in December 1920, representing 4,400 workers, was a pivotal event in the history of organized labor in Israel. Unlike the labor federations in most other countries, the socialistic *Histadrut* was a state in miniature with wide political and economic goals within its promotion of Zionism and consumer cooperation. In 1933, there were 35,400 union members within the present borders of Israel. In the next year, some members of the *Histadrut* formed the National Labor Federation, which rejected the idea of class struggle and supported separate þodies for employees and employers. Nevertheless, the *Histadrut* continued to be the dominant labor organization after the declaration of the state of Israel in 1948; in 1945 it claimed 150,000 members and 300,000 by 1995. In 2001, the *Histadrut* had about 450,000 union members and about the same number who were self-employed or housewives. Individuals join the *Histadrut* directly and are then placed in the union that covers their occupation. The *Histadrut* has close ties with the Labor Party, which was formed in 1968 and has been represented in the **International Confederation of Free Trade Unions** (ICFTU) since 1957.

The Palestinian General Federation of Trade Unions was formed in the early 1990s and claimed a membership of 131,000 in the West Bank and the Gaza Strip. The federation became an affiliate of the ICFTU in November 2002, with 215,000 members. Since 1989, the ICFTU has sought to improve relations between the federation and the *Histadrut*. In 2003, the ICFTU reported that although the rights of Israeli employees were fairly well respected, there was legal discrimination against Palestinian workers and no protection for expatriate employees, notably Chinese construction workers.

ITALY. Although organized labor in its modern form developed during the last half of the 19th century, there is evidence of earlier organizations in cities such as Florence from the 14th century. In 1675 an estimated 10,000 silk workers in Genoa rioted over the introduction of French ribbon looms, which enabled a single worker to weave 10 to 12 ribbons at a time; the workers burnt the new looms. Medieval guilds lasted longer in Italy than in other parts of Western Europe and were only abolished piecemeal on a regional basis between 1770 and 1821. At the same time, as in other parts of Western Europe, artisan journeymen were the vanguard of organized labor. In 1853 they held a regional conference of friendly societies, bodies that were forerunners of labor unions. Although the first labor union was formed in the **printing** industry in Turin, and a national printers' body was created in 1872, there was little in the way of unions elsewhere until after 1880.

Nevertheless, the absence of formal unions did not indicate the absence of **labor disputes**; 634 occurred between 1860 and 1878, mainly in the north and mostly over wages. The example of the French *Bourse du Travail* (labor union center*)*, particularly that founded at Marseilles in 1888, was influential in Italy and led to the formation of chambers of labor (*Camera del Lavoro*) beginning in Milan in 1891. By 1893, the chambers had about 41,000 members. Government policy towards organized labor turned hostile in the 1890s, and it tried to suppress the unions between 1894 and 1899.

After a last attempt at official suppression in Genoa in 1900, labor unions began to emerge and create new national organizations, exemplified by the formation of the *Confederazione Generale di Lavoro* (CGL) or General Confederation of Labor in 1906. Although there was impressive national growth in Italian union **membership** after 1900, the labor movement was divided on political and religious lines. Revolutionary **syndicalism** attracted much support from rural workers employed on large estates and claimed 200,000 members in 1908. The syndicalists formed their own labor federation in 1912 and were opposed by the **socialist** unions. As well, the **Catholic** unions, which were first formed in 1894 and claimed 107,600 members by 1910, made up a separate strand of organized labor. In 1920, they formed their own federation, the *Confederazione Italiana dei Lavoratori* (Italian Confederation of Workers), with 1.2 million members of whom 79 percent were employed in **agriculture** or textiles **manufacturing**. The socialist federation, the CGL, had 2.2 million members of whom about 34 percent worked as farm laborers and most of the others in manufacturing.

Politically, Italy was immature in 1920; universal manhood suffrage was only granted in 1912 and there was little opportunity for labor leaders to gain the experience of government they needed. There was much labor unrest in 1919 and 1920, but the Socialist Party failed to translate this into practical political gains and continued to preach revolution; it was further weakened by a split caused by the **communists** in 1921. Divided, organized labor lost support and declined. Between 1920 and 1924, the membership of the CGL collapsed from 2.2 million to 201,000.

On January 24, 1924, Benito Mussolini's fascist government abolished the nonfascist labor unions of Italy. The CGL voted itself out of existence in 1927. The fascist government introduced a number of important principles into Italy's system of industrial relations that were to have lasting consequences. It brought in a centralized system of **collective bargaining** under which unions that were part of the Confederation of Fascist Corporations were legally recognized as partners, as well as a compulsory system of pay deductions for union dues. Italy's example in these areas was imitated by **Germany, Greece, Spain, Portugal**, and **Brazil**.

On June 3, 1944, all three sections of organized labor—socialist, communist, Christian Democrat (Catholic)—agreed to the "Pact of Rome," which provided for the setting up of a new united labor confederation, the *Confederazione Generale Italiana del Lavoro* (CGIL), General Confederation of Italian Labor, which was made up of equal representation from these three groups. This unity did not last; following a wave of **strikes** and unrest led by the communists of the CGIL, the Christian Democratic unions formed their own federation in 1948, as did the republican and democratic socialists in 1949. The Christian Democratic federation, the *Libera Confederazione Generale Italiana dei Lavarotori* or Free General Italian Confederation of Workers, received support for its establishment not only from the Catholic church but also from the **American Federation of Labor-Congress of Industrial Organizations** (AFL-CIO) and the U.S. Central Intelligence Agency as a counter to the communist-dominated CGIL. In 1972, the three labor federations formed an alliance, which collapsed in 1984 and was only partly restored. Rank-and-file dissatisfaction with the three federations in 1987-1988 led to the formation of grassroots committees known as *comitati di base* or "cobas," which sought the repeal of a law of 1970 giving the federations legal rights in **collective bargaining**. In June 1990, the government prohibited strikes in a wide range of essential services. In 1994, Italy's 10 "autonomous" labor unions (which operated mostly in the **public sector**) formed a federation, the *Intesa Sindicati Autonomi* (Pact of Autonomous Unions), which claimed to represent six million employees. In 2001, there were about four million union members in Italy, covering about 27 percent of employees. Italian labor union membership figures have been remarkable since the 1960s for their high proportion of **retired employees**. *See also FEDERAZIONE ITALIANA OPERAI METALLURGICI.*

IVORY COAST. A colony of **France** until 1960, organized labor in the Ivory Coast before the 1950s consisted of overseas branches of French unions. The indigenous unions that emerged after 1950 became associated with the independence movement, but after independence came under pressure to become part of a one-party political system. The Ivory Coast has been affiliated with the **International Confederation of Free Trade Unions** (ICFTU) by the *Union Générale des Travailleurs de Côte d'Ivoire* (General Union of the Workers of the Ivory Coast) since 1992. Under its law, the president of the Ivory Coast can end a strike by compulsory **arbitration**. A strike by 700 workers at a government-owned enterprise over management's refusal to allow democratic trade union elections between May 1993 and April 1995 resulted in the deaths of 14 strikers and their eviction from company-owned housing. Between 1991 and 2001, the number of union members in the Ivory Coast declined from 400,000 to 120,000, and the economy suffered from a civil war in 2003.

-J-

JAMAICA. A colony of the **United Kingdom** until August 1962, the first labor union in Jamaica was formed by longshoremen in 1918 and labor unions were legalized in 1919. Reflecting Jamaican society generally, organized labor in Jamaica has been divided by racial and class conflicts. Important milestone events in the history of organized labor in Jamaica since 1930 have been the formation of the Bustamente Industrial Trade Union in 1938, the Trades Union Congress of Jamaica in 1948, and the National Workers' Union of Jamaica in 1952. Jamaica has been represented in the **International Confederation of Free Trade Unions** (ICFTU) since 1953 and has about 140,000 union members. In 2002, the ICFTU complained that no labor unions had been formed in the country's **export processing zones**, that the right to strike was denied to employees in the **public sector**, and that **collective bargaining** remained restrictive in Jamaica.

JAPAN. The first recorded labor disputes in Japan date from 1870 and the first union was formed among steelworkers in 1897. Other unions were formed among employees in **printing, railroads**, teaching, and firefighting; their total **membership** reached 8,000 in 1900, but they were suppressed by law. Japanese government opposition to unions continued until 1945, and unions were denied legal recognition. Nevertheless, a Japanese labor movement did

emerge from 1912 when Bunji Suzuki formed a labor union called
the *Yuai-kai* (Workers' Fraternal Society); government hostility
forced it to pretend it was a cultural and moral body in its early
years. In 1917, some employers formed the Japan Economic Federation to prevent the legal recognition of labor unions. By 1920,
there had been significant growth in organized labor in Japan, with
total membership reaching 103,000. In 1921, the *Yuai-kai* established Japan's first labor federation, the *Nihon Rodo Sodomei*. In
the 1920s and 1930s, Japanese organized labor was split between
social democrats, **socialists**, and **communists**. In 1940, when all
independent unions and **employers' organizations** were compulso-
rily merged into a body run by the government, there were only
9,500 union members compared to 408,700 in 1935.

As in **Germany**, the end of World War II brought an explosive
growth in organized labor; in December 1945, Japanese employees
were legally allowed to form unions, to engage in **collective bargaining**, and to strike. The release of communists and other radicals
from jail enabled them to rejoin the unions and exploit the hardship
and poverty of the immediate postwar period through **strikes**. In
1948, the right to strike was withdrawn from **public sector** employees. Between 1945 and 1950, the number of labor union members increased from 380,700 to 5.8 million and the number of unions rose from 509 to 29,144. A Japanese delegation attended the
founding congress of the **International Confederation of Free
Trade Unions** (ICFTU) in London in November-December 1949,
and Japan was a full member of the ICFTU by 1951.

Three labor federations were formed in 1946 and multi-
federations based on political as well as industrial differences remained a feature of Japanese organized labor thereafter. The largest
federations were the *Domei* (that is, the Japanese Confederation of
Labor, which evolved out of *Sodomei*, the Japanese Federation of
Trade Unions, originally formed in 1946 to cover private sector
employees) and the socialist, mainly public sector *Sohyo*, General
Council of Trade Unions of Japan. *Sohyo* was formed in 1950 when
the noncommunists split from the communist-dominated *Sanbetsu-
Kaigi* (or Congress of Industrial Unions of Japan, originally formed
in 1946). In 1987, *Domei* and some other federations as well as un-
affiliated unions formed a new private sector federation, now referred to as "old" ***Rengo*** (Japanese Trade Union Federation). In
1989, this body merged with *Sohyo* to create "new" ***Rengo***, which
claimed 7.7 million members by 1992 or about two-thirds of total

labor union membership. New *Rengo* has also engaged directly in **politics** by supporting opposition candidates in elections.

From 1946 to 1960, the level of **labor disputes** in Japan was relatively high; an annual average of 458 working days per thousand employees were lost through labor disputes between 1946 and 1950, 468 between 1951 and 1955, and 437 between 1956 and 1960. In 1956, the *Shunto*, or Spring Offensive, was begun by *Sohyo* and became an annual coordinated drive to gain wage increases. Since the mid-1970s the level of labor disputes in Japan has decreased.

As a proportion of employees, union membership has declined steadily since its peak of 56 percent in 1950 to 22 percent in 2001. This decline has largely occurred in the private sector, with union density remaining high among government employees. Japan continues to be a nation with a large number of labor unions; there were 31,185 unions in 2001, compared to 32,065 in 1995, and 41,561 in 1960. Nevertheless, since 1945 organized labor in Japan has become important in world terms; with 11.5 million members in 2001 Japan accounted for about 7 percent of the membership of the ICFTU. In 2002, the ICFTU complained about the effectiveness of the Japanese legal system in protecting workers against unfair labor practices. *See also* CHINA; SOUTH KOREA.

JOB SHARING. Job sharing generally refers to the splitting of a full-time job into two part-time positions in Western countries. Although first proposed in the 1970s, job sharing is largely a development of the 1980s and has been especially beneficial to **women** employees with young children. Although it came to be accepted by most unions when it was done on a voluntary basis, it was often treated with suspicion at first as a possible threat to the conditions of full-time employees.

JORDAN. Although the first labor union among Arab workers in Jordan was formed in Haifa in 1920, organized labor effectively dates from 1954 with the formation of the General Federation of Jordanian Trade Unions (GFJTU) but has since had a difficult history caused by government restrictions. In 1965 and 1969, Jordan was represented in the **International Confederation of Free Trade Unions** (ICFTU), but not again until 1995, when it was represented by GFJTU, which claimed 200,000 members. In 2002, the ICFTU reported that organized labor faced many restrictions in practice and that Jordan's one million foreign employees were denied the right to join unions.

JORDAN, BILL [WILLIAM BRIAN] (1930-). General secretary of the **International Confederation of Free Trade Unions** (ICFTU) from 1995 to 2001, Jordan was born and educated in Birmingham, England. He began work as a machine tool fitter at the age of 15. In 1966, he became a shop steward convenor with the **Amalgamated Engineering Union** and rose to become the president of the Amalgamated Engineering and Electrical Union in 1986, a post he held until becoming general secretary of the ICFTU. He was a member of the general council of the **Trades Union Congress** (TUC) from 1986 to 1995 and over the same period served on the executive of the **International Metalworkers' Federation** (IMF) and was president of the European Metalworkers' Federation. During his period as general secretary of the ICFTU, there was a sustained offensive against **child labor** and a major increase in the **membership** of the ICFTU (from 126 to 156 million), mainly brought about by the accession of the labor federations of **Russia** in 2000. In 2000, he was made a Baron (life peer) in recognition of his contribution to British and international organized labor.

-K-

KAZAKHSTAN. Independent of the former Soviet Union since December 1991, the emergence of independent organized labor in Kazakhstan was hampered by a 1990 Soviet labor law that required **collective bargaining** to be carried out between management and a "conference" representing employees. However, the law did not define how or by whom the "conference" was to be convened. This omission has enabled the former government-controlled unions to be parties to collective agreements and freeze out independent unions. Despite considerable government opposition, including violence, the coal miners formed an independent labor union in 1992 and conducted a strike in May 1994. In July 1995, a mission from the **International Confederation of Free Trade Unions** (ICFTU) and the **Miners' International Federation** (MIF) visited Kazakhstan but was unable to secure a fair settlement for the coal miners because the judicial system was biased in favor of the former government-run unions. In 2002, the ICFTU reported that antiunion practices by employers were widespread.

KENYA. A colony of the **United Kingdom** until December 1963, labor unions among African workers emerged in the late 1940s and were largely preoccupied with the independence movement. After independence, the government was hostile to the existence of an independent labor movement. For example, on May 1, 1994, the government arrested Joseph Mugalla, the general secretary of the Central Organisation of Trade Unions, over threats to call a **general strike** in support of wage claims. Kenya was represented in the **International Confederation of Free Trade Unions** (ICFTU) from 1953 to 1959 and again since 1991 by the Central Organisation of Trade Unions. In 2001, the ICFTU reported that unions in Kenya were restricted in practice in their right to organize, particularly in the country's **export processing zones.** There were about 233,500 union members in Kenya in 2001. In 2002, the ICFTU complained that the right to strike was subject to much government interference.

KIRIBATI. Independent of the **United Kingdom** since July 1979, the Kiribati Trades Union Congress has been represented in the **International Confederation of Free Trade Unions** (ICFTU) since 1993, when it claimed a **membership** of 2,600.

KIRKLAND, JOSEPH LANE (1922-1999). Kirkland was president of the **American Federation of Labor-Congress of Industrial Organizations** (AFL-CIO) from 1979 to 1995. Born in Camden, South Carolina, he was employed as a merchant marine pilot between 1941 and 1946 and as a nautical scientist in the Hydrographic Office of the U.S. Navy Department between 1947 and 1948. In 1945-1946, he was a member of the International Organization of Masters, Mates, and Pilots (formed in 1887). He graduated with a science degree from Georgetown University in 1948. In the same year he joined the **American Federation of Labor** (AFL) as a researcher and was assistant director of its social security department between 1953 and 1958. His writing ability was recognized in the AFL-CIO, and in 1961 he was made executive assistant to its president, **George Meany.**

In 1969, Kirkland was elected secretary-treasurer of the AFL-CIO. In the 1960s, he coordinated the AFL-CIO's civil rights campaign and fought racial discrimination in unions. He lobbied for a fair employment clause in the Civil Rights Act (1964), played an active role in the war on poverty, and helped to raise over $2 million for the A. Philip Randolph Institute's antighetto programs. In 1979, he negotiated a national accord with the Jimmy Carter administration in which the AFL-CIO promised to restrain wage claims to help control inflation in return for greater measures to protect the poor, limits on corporate profits, and an undertaking not to use unemployment as a means of lowering inflation. As AFL-CIO president, Kirkland followed a more moderate path than Meany. Under him, the AFL-CIO rejoined the **International Confederation of Free Trade Unions** (ICFTU) in 1981. In 1986, Kirkland was elected president of the Trade Union Advisory Committee to the Organization of Economic and Community Development (founded in 1948). In 1995, Kirkland was succeeded by **John J. Sweeney** as AFL-CIO president.

KNIGHTS OF LABOR. The Knights were the first mass labor organization in the **United States** to recruit unskilled workers as well as African-Americans and **women**, and the organization has been described as a form of **sydndicalism**. Originally formed in 1869 as a secret society by some garment cutters in Philadelphia, the Knights rejected the wage system and supported cooperation and education as a means of improving the position of workers. Between 1878, when it became a national body, and 1881, the **membership** of the Knights rose from 9,000 to 19,000 and was open to all who earned their living through manual labor either as employees or as small farmers. Between 1881 and 1893, the Knights were led by Terrence V. Powderly (1849-1924). The Knights supported the abolition of **child labor**, government inspection of mines and factories, and the nationalization of banks and **railroads**. A centralized organization, the membership of the Knights grew from 49,500 in 1883 to a peak of 703,000 in 1886, of which about 10 percent were African-Americans and 10 percent were women. Most of this growth occurred as a result of successful **strikes** against railroad companies in 1884.

After 1886, the membership of the Knights declined rapidly following their defeat in a strike against Jay Gould's South-Western Railroad (1886), factional fighting within the Knights, and a prolonged struggle with the **craft unions** represented by the **American Federation of Labor**. One of the major problems faced by the Knights was the gulf between the expectations of the rank-and-file and the moderation of the senior leadership, a gulf exposed by the leadership's refusal to endorse the nationwide eight-hour campaign in 1886. The Knights were also active outside the United States, forming offshoots in **Canada** (1881), the **United Kingdom** (where they claimed 10,000 members by 1889), **Belgium, Ireland, Australia** (1890), and **New Zealand**. Within the United States, the membership of the Knights ebbed rapidly from 511,400 in 1887 to 220,600 by 1889. Although a spent force after 1890, the Knights claimed 20,200 members in 1900 and continued to publish a journal until 1917. Some of their ideas were carried on by the **Industrial Workers of the World** (IWW) after 1905.

KOREA. *See* NORTH KOREA; SOUTH KOREA.

KUWAIT. Although it is possible to form labor unions in Kuwait, it is very difficult. In 1994, the law required that at least 100 workers were required to form a labor union, of whom at least 15 had to be Kuwaiti nationals. Expatriate workers have to live in Kuwait for at least five years before they can join a labor union, but they cannot hold office or vote in union ballots or at union meetings. Expatriate domestic servants are often mistreated and can be prosecuted if they leave their employers.

KYRGYZSTAN. Independent since August 1991 from the former Soviet Union, of which it had been formally a part since 1924, there is no history of organized labor in Kyrgyzstan. The 1992 Labor Law recognized the right of workers to form unions but the right to **strike** was not specifically protected and strikes were made illegal. The law recognized the right to **collective bargaining**. Kyrgyzstan is not represented in the **International Confederation of Free Trade Unions** (ICFTU), but has independent labor unions. In 2002, the ICFTU noted that labor practices in Kyrgyzstan lagged behind the country's relatively progressive labor legislation.

-L-

LABOR DAY. Labor Day, a public holiday celebrated in the **United States** and **Canada** on the first Monday of September, was begun by the **Knights of Labor** as a march in New York City in 1882;

other marches were held in 1883 and 1884 to celebrate labor. Oregon was the first U.S. state to legislate Labor Day as a public holiday in 1887. The U.S. Congress declared it a public holiday in 1894. Labor day public holidays are also a feature of **Australia** and **New Zealand**, though largely devoid of their original significance.

LABOR DISPUTES. Labor disputes, whether arising from **strikes** or lockouts, are the most consistently visible sign of the presence of organized labor. There have been labor disputes since the earliest times—the first recorded labor dispute occurred in **Egypt** in 1152 B.C. among the pharoah's tomb-makers—and they predate unions as formal, continuous organizations. In 18th-century England, 383 labor disputes were recorded between 1717 and 1800, and these led to the first sustained efforts to create legal mechanisms for their resolution. As the Industrial Revolution developed, labor disputes and other kinds of collective action such as rallies and demonstrations began to replace older forms of social protest such as food riots and tax revolts.

From about 1830, the first systematic efforts were made to collect information on disputes both by officials and by individuals. In France, official monitoring began in 1830 even though strikes were treated as a crime before 1864. Elsewhere in Europe, monitoring of disputes in some form had begun in the **United Kingdom** (1870) and **Italy** (1871), activities that often grew into official national statistical collections by the 1890s. In the **United States**, in 1888, the Massachusetts Bureau of Statistics published a time series for its labor disputes from 1825 to 1886 and continued to publish statistics into the 20th century, as did New York State, even though a national series of U.S. dispute statistics was begun in 1881. Other countries followed: **Denmark** (1897), **Canada** and **Germany** (1901), **Sweden** and **Norway** (1903), **New Zealand** and **South Africa** (1906), **Finland** (1907), **Australia** (1913), and **Japan** (1914). In 1927, the **International Labour Organisation** (ILO) began publishing dispute statistics for all the countries that collected them.

This monitoring was in response to a general rise in the level of disputes in Western Europe and North America from the late 1860s to the outbreak of World War I in 1914 and from 1917 to about 1930. **General strikes** occurred in some countries such as in Belgium (1893), Sweden (1909), Britain (1926), and France (1968). The year 1920 was one of the high points of disputes based on rising inflation and falling real wages. The causes of these waves of disputes included political as well as economic objectives. Before 1890, many employees who were not formally union members took part in labor disputes.

Governments before 1914 were more concerned with disputes as a threat to political stability than as a cost to the economy. Labor disputes are unlike most other social phenomena in that they can change greatly from one year to the next and often occur in waves. There have been three major international waves of labor disputes: 1869 to 1875, 1910 to 1920, and 1968 to 1974. The relationship between labor disputes and the trade cycle is complicated, but there is a clear association between the frequency of disputes and the state of the trade cycle: In good economic times, there are usually more disputes than when the cycle is depressed.

On occasion, particularly intense labor disputes have politicized some of their participants. For instance, two of the thousands of strikers who were victimized after the great railroad strike of 1917 in New South Wales, Australia, were drawn into politics; one was Joseph Benedict Chifley (1885-1951), who was Australia's prime minister from 1945 to 1949, and the other was John Joseph Cahill (1891-1959), who was premier of New South Wales from 1952 to 1959.

In 1984, two Danish economists, Martin Paldam and Peder J. Pedersen, examined data for 18 Organization for Economic Cooperation and Development (OECD) countries between 1919 and 1979 and found a positive link between nominal wage rises and the number of labor disputes. They found that changes in real wages were only negatively related to changes in labor disputes in the United States and that in other countries the relationship was either positive or insignificant They also suggested that there was a cultural-linguistic divide in the labor dispute record of these countries between 1919 and 1979. They distinguished high-conflict countries as belonging to the Anglo-Saxon group (United Kingdom, **Ireland**, United States, Canada, Australia, and New Zealand) or the Latin group (**France** and Italy), low conflict countries as belonging to the German-Nordic group (**Austria**, **Denmark**, Germany, **Netherlands**, Norway, Sweden, and **Switzerland**), and a fourth group that did not fit easily into any category (**Belgium**, **Finland**, and Japan). They could not discern any long-term pattern in the labor dispute levels of the Anglo-Saxon or Latin groups, but in the German-Nordic group there was a strong falling trend of disputes since the peak level of the early 1920s.

Labor disputes are unevenly distributed in the economy. Certain industries, particularly **coal mining**, engineering, and transportation, have frequently accounted for a major part of the disputes in many countries. Since 1980 the number of disputes has fallen to very low levels in most countries, a trend that has been attributed to the decline in the strength of organized labor and profound economic shifts.

The study of labor disputes has been approached from two main directions: the sociohistorical approach, which examined their statistical characteristics within and between countries over time, and the "rational expectations" approach, which treats labor disputes as one possible result of rational decision-making by bargainers with incomplete information. This latter approach has been popular among labor economists since about 1970, although it was first suggested by the economist John R. Hicks in 1932. Although the two approaches proceed from widely different attitudes and assumptions, it is clear that there is no agreed single model that can be applied to labor disputes for all periods.

For all the drama that can accompany large labor disputes, they account for only a tiny proportion of the work days lost in most Western economies compared with other sources of loss such as illness and industrial accidents. The lost production caused by disputes is usually quickly made up. Nevertheless, governments remain sensitive to the level of disputes as an indicator of political stability and the countries' reliability as international traders. Consequently, the legal right to strike is circumscribed in various ways even in many Western countries. Legal notice of a strike is required in Belgium, **Greece**, Netherlands, **Portugal**, Spain, the United Kingdom (since 1984), and New Zealand (since 1991). In Japan, most of the **public sector** is denied the right to strike, as are federal government employees (since 1912) and most state employees in the United States, with the exception of those in Hawaii and Pennsylvania. Finally, the international statistics on disputes for any period must be treated with considerable caution, as many countries understate their true level of disputes and use incomparable definitions. Data compiled by the British department of industry indicated that within the countries of the OECD, the average number of working days lost per thousand employees in 1996 to 2000 was 59, compared to an average of 66 between 1991 and 1995. *See also* BRITISH GENERAL STRIKE; CONCILIATION AND ARBI-

TRATION; GENERAL STRIKES; LABOR STATISTICS; STRIKES; "WINTER OF DISCONTENT."

LABOR HISTORY. Credit for the first truly scholarly investigation of organized labor must go to Beatrice Webb (1858-1943) and Sidney James Webb, (1859-1947). Married in 1892, the Webbs created one of the most productive working partnerships in modern British intellectual history. Committed Fabians, their contribution to the scholarship of organized labor was enormous and included *The History of Trade Unionism* (1894), *Industrial Democracy* (1897), and *The Consumers' Co-operative Movement* (1921). The *History of Trade Unionism* was revised in 1920 and exerted a major influence, particularly in encouraging an institutional approach to labor unions. They defined a labor union as a "continuous association of wage earners for the purpose of maintaining or improving their conditions of employment" a definition that has been criticized for neglecting the role of noncontinuous labor bodies in the history of organized labor.

In the **United States**, John R. Commons (1862-1945) founded the Wisconsin school of labor history, one of the first systematic, scholarly endeavors of its kind anywhere, and published the 10-volume *A Documentary History of American Industrial Society* in 1910-11 and a four-volume *History of Labor in the United States* between 1918 and 1935.

In **Australia**, T. A. Coghlan (1855-1926) published a four-volume general account, *Labour and Industry in Australia from the First Settlement in 1788 to the Establishment of the Commonwealth in 1901,* in 1918. In 1921, J. T. Sutcliffe published *A History of Trade Unionism in Australia.*

However, this impetus was not sustained, and the scholarly examination of the history of organized labor tended to languish in the 1930s and 1940s and did not revive until the 1960s, when it benefited from an upsurge of interest in social and economic history, stimulated by works such as E. P. Thompson's *The Making of the English Working Class* (1963). Academic journals devoted to labor history began in the United States (1960), Australia (1962), and Canada (1976).

LABOR-MANAGEMENT REPORTING AND DISCLOSURE ACT. *See* LANDRUM-GRIFFIN ACT.

LABOR PARTIES. *See* SOCIAL-DEMOCRATIC, SOCIALIST, AND LABOR PARTIES.

LABOR STATISTICS. Most of the earliest labor statistics were collected through the census of population and housing: the **United Kingdom** census included a question on occupation from 1811 and the **United States** census included a question on industry from 1820. From the 1860s, there was growing demand for better statistical information about labor. Several American states, notably Massachusetts (1869), Pennsylvania (1870), and Ohio (1877), established statistical bureaus that collected data on wages, prices, and **labor disputes**.

The demand for better statistics did not just come from governments and employers; sections of organized labor were well aware of the importance of accurate statistics. Aim III of the **Knights of Labor** was the establishment of a Bureau of Labor Statistics "so that we may arrive at correct knowledge of the educational, moral and financial condition of the laboring masses." The U.S. Bureau of Labor was created in 1884 and made an independent organization in 1888. From about 1890, many countries began to publish official statistics on topics, such as labor disputes, trade union **membership**, wages, prices, employment, and unemployment. In 1893, the British government began to issue a national statistical publication with commentary, the *Labour Gazette*, which continues to the present as the *Employment Gazette*. In **Australia**, the federal government began publishing a compendium of national labor statistics, the *Labour Report*, in 1912 and continued it until 1972. The U.S. Bureau of Labor Statistics began to publish the *Monthly Labor Review* in 1915, a publication that continues to the present.

In 1940, the United States began to collect labor force statistics from a regular household survey, an example followed by **Canada** (1954), and Australia (1960) and many other countries since. One important by-product of these surveys has been their ability to match labor union membership with a range of socioeconomic and demographic characteristics. Such information began to be available for the United States in 1973 (although the present survey began in 1983), from 1983 for Australia (with a pilot survey being held in 1976), in 1984 for Canada, in 1987 for **Sweden**, and in 1989 for the United Kingdom.

The main agency for the collection of international labor statistics is the **International Labour Organisation** (ILO), which has been publishing its *Year Book of Labour Statistics* since 1927. ILO Convention 160 (Labor Statistics, 1985) called on member countries to regularly compile and publish statistics on employment, unemployment, earnings, working hours, consumer prices, household expenditure, occupational injury and diseases, and labor disputes. This convention was a revision of Convention 63 (Statistics of Wages and Hours of Work, 1938).

LANDRUM-GRIFFIN ACT. This act, known officially as the Labor-Management Reporting and Disclosure Act, was a major piece of U.S. federal labor law that was passed in September 1959. It was aimed at reducing corruption within unions as exemplified by the **Teamsters**. It set down minimum standards to ensure democratic elections, but it also extended the ban of the **Taft-Hartley Act** on secondary boycotts and allowed the states to assume jurisdiction in relatively minor **labor disputes**.

LATVIA. Organized labor was only able to emerge in Latvia after it gained independence from **Russia** in 1920; previously it had been part of the Russian Empire. In 1921, the labor federation of Latvia joined the **International Federation of Trade Unions** (IFTU) and remained a member until 1933. In 1923, Latvia claimed a trade union **membership** of 23,660. In 1940, an independent labor movement ceased to exist in the Baltic States after their annexation by the Soviet Union.

In the late 1980s, the Soviet Union began to fragment, allowing organized labor to reemerge. During March 1990, Latvia and the other **Baltic states** declared their independence from the Soviet Union. Labor unions were legalized in Latvia in December 1990, although there was conflict over the ownership of the property of the former communist labor federation. The right to **strike** was recognized in 1998, although with limitations. In 1997, the Free Trade Union Confederation of Latvia was admitted to membership of the **International Confederation of Free Trade Unions** (ICFTU) and claimed a membership of 207,400 in 2001. During 2001, the government made efforts to bring Latvia's laws in line with the conventions of the **International Labour Organisation** (ILO) and the **European Union**. In 2002, the ICFTU conceded that progress had been made with Latvia's legal environment for organized labor, but that government did not regard labor unions as partners in social dialogue and that there was much opposition to unions in the private sector.

LAW. *See* EMPLOYMENT ACTS; LANDRUM-GRIFFIN ACT; NATIONAL INDUSTRIAL RECOVERY ACT; RIGHT-TO-WORK LAWS; *ROOKES V. BARNARD*; TAFT-HARTLEY ACT; WAGNER ACT.

LEBANON. An independent nation since 1943; it had been previously administered by **France** under a mandate from the League of Nations. Labor unions in Lebanon were first formed in the 1940s. Reflecting its society, organized labor was fragmented along religious, ethnic, and political lines. Lebanon has been represented in the **International Confederation of Free Trade Unions** (ICFTU) since 1951, but by a number of affiliates since 1965; in 1996, Lebanon had 13 affiliates, the most of any country at the time. Between 1975 and 1990, Lebanon suffered from civil war, which claimed 150,000 lives and inflicted massive economic damage. In 2002, the ICFTU reported that the government continued to interfere in the internal affairs of organized labor.

LEGIEN, CARL (1861-1920). Carl Legien was one of the leading labor leaders in **Germany** before 1914. Born in Marienburg, he was raised in an orphanage after the death of his parents. Apprenticed as a turner in 1875, he settled in Hamburg after military service. He joined the turner's union in 1886 and became its chairman. In 1890, he was elected chairman of the *Generalkommission der Gewerkschaften*, the National Federation of Trade Unions, a position he held until his death. He used his position to build a strong national union organization and to maintain the independence of the union movement from the control of the Social Democratic Party. He was a strong opponent of the **general strike** as advocated by **syndicalism.** He was president and secretary of the **International Federation of Trade Unions** (IFTU) from 1901 to 1919. Ironically, for someone who opposed general strikes, it was Legien who issued the call for the general strike in Berlin that defeated the proto-fascist Kapp Putsch in 1920.

LESOTHO. Independent of the **United Kingdom** since October 1966, organized labor had emerged sufficiently by the 1960s to form the Basutoland Federation of Labour, which was admitted to the **Inter-**

national **Confederation of Free Trade Unions** (ICFTU) in 1979, declaring a **membership** of 12,000. Changing its name to the Lesotho Federation of Trade Unions by 1983, the federation remained in the ICFTU to 1993, against a backdrop of political instability and military rule between 1986 and 1995. The ICFTU has been critical of the environment for organized labor in the 1990s. In 2002, it reported that labor unions in the private sector could not be formed without permission and had to be registered by the registrar of trade unions. Harassment of union activists remained commonplace.

LEWIS, JOHN LLEWELLYN (1880-1969). John L. Lewis was the most important miners' leader in the **United States** in the 20th century. He was born in Lucas, Iowa, and began working as a coal miner at 16. In 1909, he gained his first office with the **United Mine Workers of America** (UMWA), progressing to vice president in 1917 and president in 1920, a position he held until 1960. Lewis was a controversial figure who devoted much of his energies in the 1920s to fighting and expelling rivals from within the union, the membership of which fell from 500,000 to 75,000 between 1920 and 1933. Lewis realized the need for legal support in rebuilding the union and was a prime mover behind Section 7(a) of the **National Industrial Recovery Act** of 1933, which gave employees the right to collectively organize and bargain without employer interference. A supporter of **industrial unions**, Lewis saw the potential for organizing the semiskilled and led the campaign to form the **Congress of Industrial Organizations** (CIO). He served as its president from 1938 to 1940, resigning in opposition to the policies of President Franklin D. Roosevelt. In 1946 and 1948, Lewis led a series of **strikes** that resulted in the coal mine owners paying a bounty on each ton of coal mined, which was used to finance health, welfare, and retirement benefits for miners. Lewis's last major achievement was the first federal Mine Safety Act (1952). *See also* COAL MINING.

LIBERIA. Despite its name and origins as a haven for freed U.S. slaves, Liberia has not enjoyed a history of liberty. There was no legal framework for organized labor or **collective bargaining** until 1963. A national labor union federation was formed in 1960; modeled on the U.S. **Congress of Industrial Organizations** (CIO), it gained affiliation with the **International Confederation of Free Trade Unions** (ICFTU) by 1965 but by 1989 had been replaced as

Liberia's affiliate by the Liberian Federation of Labor Unions. In 2002, Liberia was one of the few African nations not to be mentioned in the ICFTFU's survey of **violations of trade union rights.**

LIBYA. Independent from **Italy** since December 1951, organized labor in Libya only dates from after 1945; under Benito Mussolini's rule, labor unions were outlawed. The Libyan General Workers' Union was formed in 1952 and was an affiliate of the **International Confederation of Free Trade Unions** (ICFTU) from 1953 to 1959, when it amalgamated with another labor federation to form the Libyan National Confederation of Trade Unions. However, after the coup by Colonel Mummar al-Qaddafi in September 1969, organized labor in Libya ceased to function and its affiliation with the ICFTU also ended; at that time Libya had about 35,000 union members. In 2002, the ICFTU reported that Libyan workers were denied any right to organize independent labor unions, and it was particularly critical of the government's disregard of the rights of migrant workers, who contribute considerably to the economy.

LITHUANIA. Organized labor was only able to emerge in Lithuania after it gained independence from **Russia** in 1918; previously it had been part of the Russian Empire since 1795. A labor federation existed in Lithuania by 1926 and was a member of the **International Federation of Trade Unions** (IFTU) until 1927, but after a military government took power, the number of union members fell from 18,500 in 1927 to 1,200 by 1932. In 1940, an independent labor movement ceased to exist in Lithuania and the other **Baltic states** after their annexation by the Soviet Union.

In the late 1980s, the Soviet Union began to fragment, allowing organized labor to reemerge. The first independent labor union in the post-1940 period in the Baltic states was formed in Lithuania in 1988. During March 1990 all three Baltic states declared their independence from the Soviet Union. In Lithuania, an independent workers' union, the Lithuanian Workers' Union, was formed in 1989 and claimed 150,000 members by 1992. In 1991, the Lithuanian government nationalized the property of the **communist** labor federation and introduced the Collective Agreements Law, which hindered the formation of new labor unions. Lithuania was represented in the **International Confederation of Free Trade Unions** (ICFTU) by 1997. In 2001, its two labor federation members claimed a combined **membership** of 91,600. In 2002, the ICFTU was critical of restrictions on the right to join unions and to **strike** in Lithuania, despite the adoption of a new labor code, which came into force on January 1, 2003.

LOBBYING. *See* POLITICS.

LUXEMBOURG. Luxembourg has been a sovereign nation since 1867, when organized labor also began to develop. Like its neighbor, **Belgium**, its organized labor has been divided by religion. The *Confédération Générale du Travail* (General Confederation of Labor), the main labor federation, was formed in 1919. A **Catholic** labor federation was formed in 1920. Union **membership** was 18,000 in 1930. Unions were suppressed by the Nazis and, although an attempt was made to build a unified labor movement after 1944, it had failed by 1948 through the defection of **communists** and Catholics. Luxembourg has always been a member of the **International Confederation of Free Trade Unions** (ICFTU). Between 1970 and 1990 the number of union members in Luxembourg rose from 52,000 to 75,000, divided among labor federations that cater to white- and **blue-collar** unions, Catholic unions, private sector white-collar unions, and **craft unions**.

-M-

MACEDONIA (FORMER YUGOSLAV REPUBLIC). Macedonia was part of **Yugoslavia** until 1991. Unlike **Yugoslavia (Federal Republic)**, there was no significant continuous history of organized labor in Macedonia—though some unions are known to have been formed in 1905—which remains the poorest of the republics that made up the former Yugoslavia.

MADAGASCAR. Independent from **France** since June 1960, labor unions existed in Madagascar by 1937. Madagascar was represented in the **International Confederation of Free Trade Unions** (ICFTU) by 1953 and has retained its affiliation ever since, despite political uncertainty. In 1995, there were about 30,000 union members in Madagascar. In 2002, the ICFTU reported that the government was hostile to labor unions among its own employees and particularly in **export processing zones**.

MALAWI. A former colony of the **United Kingdom**, independent since July 1964, Malawi was previously called Nyasaland. It was unusual among colonies in having an ordinance regulating labor unions in 1932 before there was any real presence of organized labor. The Nyasaland Trades Union Congress was formed in 1956 and was admitted to the **International Confederation of Free Trade Unions** (ICFTU) in 1957; it was reformed as the Trades Union Congress of Malawi in 1964 and has remained an affiliate of the ICFTU ever since. After independence, organized labor fared poorly. Hastings Banda, who led the independence movement and was the first prime minister, declared himself president for life in 1971 and ran a one-party government to 1994 that committed abuses of trade union and **human rights**. By 1995, Malawi had about 45,000 labor union members. In 2002, the ICFTU advised that although labor unions and collective bargaining were legally recognized in Malawi, they were severely regulated and that **strikes** were repressed.

MALAYSIA. The first labor unions in the Malayan Peninsula were created by the Chinese in the **Singapore** area, starting with a union of engineering mechanics in 1875. Other unions were formed later by Indian employees. In 1939, there were 43 unions. By 1947, there were about 200,000 members of labor unions, of which about half belonged to unions controlled by **communists**. The Malaysian Trades Union Congress (originally called the Malayan Trade Union Council) was formed in 1950. The development of Malaysian labor unions was retarded by the economic dominance of **agriculture** until the late 1980s and by the period of the Emergency (1948-1960), which forced governments to devote their efforts to fighting the communist insurgency. Since becoming independent from the **United Kingdom** in 1957, Malaysian governments have tolerated rather than encouraged labor unions. In 1967, the Industrial Relations Act gave the government the power to use compulsory arbitration to settle **labor disputes** if **conciliation** failed. To encourage foreign investment in 1981, labor unions were excluded from **export processing zones**, which mainly produced electronic goods. Under pressure from the **American Federation of Labor-Congress of Industrial Organizations** (AFL-CIO), this policy was relaxed in September 1988 to permit in-house unions in these zones. Malaysia has been represented continuously in the **International Confederation of Free Trade Union** (ICFTU) since 1951.

The ICFTU has been critical of the Malaysian government and policies of hindering **collective bargaining** and the free operation of labor unions. In 2001, there were 404,000 union members in Malaysia, compared to 350,000 in 1992. In 2002, the ICFTU stated that the government kept organized labor under tight control.

MALI. Independent of **France** since September 1960, organized labor in Mali originally consisted of the overseas branches of French labor unions. After independence, organized labor was placed under government control through the *Union Nationale des Travailleurs du Mali* (National Union of Workers of Mali). In 1993, this organization was admitted to membership of the **International Confederation of Free Trade Unions** (ICFTU), when it claimed 130,000 members.

MALTA. Fully independent from the **United Kingdom** since 1964, the first Maltese labor union was formed among waterfront fitters under English influence in 1884, but it was not until 1945 that a legal framework for labor unions and **collective bargaining** was established. Malta has been represented continuously in the **International Confederation of Free Trade Union** (ICFTU) since 1951 by the General Workers' Union (formed 1943); it claimed 36,000 members in 2001. In 2002, the government introduced a law that would allow for compulsory arbitration in **labor disputes**.

MANUAL/NONMANUAL. *See* BLUE-COLLAR/WHITE COLLAR.

MANUFACTURING. Manufacturing, also known as the secondary sector, covers all those economic activities that result in the production of tangible goods. It was the first economic sector where organized labor arose from about 1350, in Western Europe. **Printing** was the earliest part of manufacturing to produce organized labor. With the advent of the Industrial Revolution from 1850, engineering and metal working, together with **coal mining**, became important parts of the backbone of organized labor. In the **United Kingdom**, this was most evident in the **Amalgamated Society of Engineers** (ASE), formed in 1851. Between 1892 and 1970, about 40 percent of all British union members were employed in some area of manufacturing, of whom about half were employed in metal working and engineering. Since the 1970s, the strength of manufacturing unions within organized labor in industrial countries has declined along with employment in the industry. In the United Kingdom, the share of union members employed in manufacturing fell from 45 percent in 1980 to 15 percent in 2001.

MATERNAL PROTECTION. The provision of legal safeguards for employed mothers was recognized by the **International Labour Organisation** by Convention No. 3 (Maternal Protection) in 1919, which was revised in 1952 as Convention No. 103. Paid leave for maternity (that is, during and after pregnancy), however, generally only became a feature of **women's** employment in the 1980s.

MATIGNON AGREEMENT. The Matignon Agreement was a landmark agreement in the history of labor relations in **France**. It was reached between the Socialist government of Léon Blum, the *Confédération Générale du Travail* (General Confederation of Labor) (CGT) and **employers' organizations** on June 7, 1936. The agreement provided for the unions' right to organize, an end to antiunion practices, **collective bargaining**, pay increases of 7 to 12 percent, and the election of shop stewards. One problem with the agreement was that by extending bargaining rights to all representative unions rather than to a single bargaining body, it tended to inhibit the development of strong collective bargaining units representing employees.

MAURITANIA. Independent from **France** since November 1960, organized labor in Mauritania has been under government control since 1971, and the government reserved the right to recognize or dissolve labor unions. Foreign workers do not have the right to form labor unions. On October 16, 2000, a march organized by the Free Confederation of Mauritanian Workers was declared illegal by the government and 40 participants were arrested. In December 2001, Mauritania was admitted to membership of the **International Confederation of Free Trade Unions** (ICFTU). The ICFTU has been critical of the Mauritanian government's failure to make good its promises to reform its labor laws, made to the **International Labor Organisation** (ILO) since 1993. It remained critical of the labor law reforms of 2002.

MAURITIUS. Independent from the **United Kingdom** since March 1968, organized labor in Mauritius developed in the 1940s—as evidenced by the formation of the Mauritius Trades Union Congress in

1946—and came to reflect the country's ethnic and political divisions. Mauritius has been represented in the **International Confederation of Free Trade Unions** (ICFTU) since 1951; between 1951 and 1995, its reported **membership** rose from 10,000 to 67,000 and the Mauritius Labour Congress, which was formed in 1963, has been the country's representative at the ICFTU since 1965. Mauritius established the first **export processing zone** in Africa in 1970. In 2001, the ICFTU was critical of the low level of union membership in the export processing zones of Mauritius, even though such membership is legal; in 2002, it noted that some improvements had been made.

MEANY, GEORGE (1894-1980). Meany was president of the **American Federation of Labor** (AFL) from 1952 to 1955 and of the **American Federation of Labor-Congress of Industrial Organizations** (AFL-CIO) from 1955 until 1979. Born in New York City, Meany completed an **apprenticeship** as a plumber in 1915 and based his union career on the United Association of Plumbers and Steam Fitters of the United States and Canada. In 1939, he was elected secretary-treasurer of the AFL, but it was not until the late 1940s that he could exercise any real power. He was the first director of the AFL's League for Political Education (1948) and served on the executive board of the **International Confederation of Free Trade Unions** (ICFTU) during 1951. A skilled negotiator, he played a major role in the merger of the AFL with the **Congress of Industrial Organizations** (CIO) to form the AFL-CIO in 1955. A Catholic, Meany waged a determined campaign against **communism** and labor rivals such as **Walter Reuther**; he was also opposed to racial or religious discrimination in organized labor. A rightwing Democrat, Meany refused to give the AFL-CIO's endorsement to the leftwing George S. McGovern, the Democratic nominee for president in 1972. Under his leadership, the AFL-CIO left the ICFTU in 1969 over its stance on **politics** and did not rejoin until 1981. Meany was succeeded as AFL-CIO president by a more moderate figure, **Joseph Lane Kirkland**.

MEDIA ENTERTAINMENT INTERNATIONAL (MEI). Originally called the International Secretariat of Entertainment Trade Unions, the MEI was an **international trade secretariat** set up in 1965 in Brussels at a conference of the **International Confederation of Free Trade Unions** (ICFTU). In 1984, it became an autonomous part of the *Fédération internationale des employés, techniciens et cadres* or the International Federation of Commercial, Clerical, Professional, and Technical Employees (FIET). The secretariat was not a success; between 1973 and 1992 its membership fell from 470,000 to 100,000. In 1993, it merged with the International Federation of Trade Unions of Audio-Visual Workers (founded in 1974) to form the International Secretariat for Arts, Mass Media, and Entertainment Trade Unions (ISAMMETU). In December 1995, the ISAMMETU renamed itself the MEI and in January 2000 it merged with **Communication International**, the **International Graphical Federation,** and the FIET to form the **Union Network International** (UNI).

MEMBERSHIP OF ORGANIZED LABOR. The membership of organized labor tends to be drawn from the better-off sections of the labor force or from industries characterized by large employers. The first labor unions were made up of skilled artisans, such as in **printing**, and later by skilled metal workers in **manufacturing**. Unions among large-scale industries such as **coal mining**, textiles, and **railroads** tended to be formed after about 1860. Unions among the lesser skilled employees mostly only began late in the 19th century. The industrial composition of union membership changed considerably in the 20th century in response to shifts in employment. In 1900, about half of all union members in the **United States** were employed either in mining or in manufacturing, but since 1950 the share of union membership has declined. In 2001, only 17 percent of union members were employed in mining or manufacturing in the United States.

Other industries (excluding **agriculture**) have accounted for a growing share of union members, again in response to employment shifts within the labor force. These industries cover a great range of economic activities, from construction to education and from government employment to personal services. Transport and communications accounted for 22 percent of union members in **Australia** and the United States in 1900, but only for 11 percent in the **United Kingdom**. By 2001, the share of union members employed in transport and communications had fallen to about 10 to 11 percent in all three countries.

Household surveys of the labor force since 1980 have shown that the proportion of employees in these industries (sometimes called the tertiary or **service sector**) varies greatly. For example, in

2001, the proportion of employees in wholesale and retail trade who were union members was 4.7 percent in the United States, 15.2 in Australia, and 12.0 percent in the United Kingdom. In contrast, the proportion of employees in government employment in 2001 was consistently high in all three countries: 37 percent in the United States, 59 percent in the United Kingdom, and 48 percent in Australia.

Until the 1960s, **women** made up only about 20 percent of union members but have more than doubled their share in Australia, the United Kingdom, and the United States. An exception to this trend was **Germany**, where the proportion of women members only grew from 18 to 32 percent between 1960 and 1997. Statistics on the ages of union members have only become available with household labor force surveys since the 1970s. These surveys show that younger employees, particularly teenagers, are less likely to be union members than middle-aged employees. In 2002, only 11 percent of employees aged 16 to 24 were union members in the United Kingdom, compared to 36 percent of those aged 35 to 49 years. In the United States, 5 percent of employees aged 16 to 24 were union members compared to 14 percent of employees aged 35 to 44 years. *See also* FULL-TIME/PART-TIME EMPLOYMENT; WHITE-COLLAR UNIONISM; appendix F.

MEXICO. As in Western Europe, the first organizations among workers in Mexico were friendly societies, which were formed in the main urban areas between 1835 and 1864. Although unions emerged after 1876, it was not until after 1900 that organized labor made its presence felt though **strikes** by miners (1905) and textile workers (1906); these were violently suppressed. The Constitution of 1917 recognized labor unions and was a tangible victory from the revolution of 1910. The *Confederación Regional Obrera Mexicana* (Regional Confederation of Mexican Wage Earners or CROM) was established in May 1918 with 75 organizations that claimed a million members. Militant at first, the CROM became more allied with the government, a trend that promoted the creation by **anarchists** of a radical alternative labor federation, the *Confederación General de Trabajo* (General Confederation of Labor or CGT) in 1921. By 1923, union **membership** in Mexico had fallen to about 800,000 but then rose to 2.1 million by 1927.

The Depression reduced union membership to 500,000 by 1932, but by 1934 organized labor in Mexico claimed 2.6 million members. In 1936, a third labor federation, the *Confederación de Trabajadores de Mexico* (Confederation of Mexican Workers or CTM) was formed. Because the CTM had the affiliation of metal workers, railroad employees, and peasants, it became the dominant federation and developed close links with the ruling political party. The other labor federations formed since 1936 have been to the left of the CTM. Mexico joined the **International Federation of Trade Unions** (IFTU) in 1936 and has been an active participant in Pan-American labor bodies such as the **Pan-American Federation of Labor** and the *Organización Regional Interamericana de Trabajadores*. In 1966, the *Congreso del Trabajo* (Congress of Labor) was set up to provide a single voice for organized labor. Mexico has been represented in the **International Confederation of Free Trade Unions** (ICFTU) since 1951. In 1965, the Mexican government established the first **export processing zone** near the U.S. border to assemble goods for foreign-owned companies at low wages. In 2001, Mexico's affiliate in the ICFTU, the CTM, claimed a membership of 1.5 million. In 2002, the ICFTU noted that although the general legal environment for organized labor was acceptable, in practice there were **violations of trade union rights** in the **public sector** and the export processing zones.

MINERS' INTERNATIONAL FEDERATION (MIF). The MIF was set up in **Belgium** in 1890 by representatives of miners' unions from **Austria**, Belgium, **France**, **Germany**, and the **United Kingdom**. Between 1913 and 1931 its claimed **membership** rose from 1.2 to nearly 1.5 million. In the late 1950s, the MIF began to prepare standards for miners; it released a miner's charter in 1957 and a charter for young miners in 1958. In 1976, the MIF had 887,500 members, of whom 628,700 were in Europe, 203,800 in Asia, and 8,800 in the **United States**. In 1994, the MIF had 58 affiliated unions that represented 4.2 million members. In 1995, the MIF merged with the **International Federation of Chemical, Energy, Mine, and General Workers** (ICEM). *See also* COAL MINING.

MINEWORKERS' FEDERATION OF GREAT BRITAIN (MWF). From the early 1890s to the late 1930s, the Mineworkers' Federation (its official title from 1932) was the largest labor union in the **United Kingdom** and the largest single labor union in the world until 1919. The federation grew out of discussions among delegates representing regional groups of employees in **coal min-**

ing who met to coordinate wage claims against the mine owners. The Yorkshire Miners' Association (formed in 1858) took the initiative to form the federation in 1889. In 1890, the MWF showed its strength by leading a campaign that resulted in a 5 percent wage rise. In 1892, the federation claimed 150,000 members among its affiliates, compared to only 36,000 in 1889. Thereafter, the federation's membership grew rapidly as large affiliates joined: the Scottish Miners' Federation joined in 1894, the South Wales Miners' federation in 1898, and, finally, the Durham Miners' Federation in 1908. Originally formed in 1869, the Durham Miners' Federation had 121,800 members when it affiliated with the MWF. Between 1900 and 1910, the membership of the federation rose from 363,000 to 597,000, but it continued to be an umbrella organization covering a multitude of labor unions, often with a regional rather than a national outlook. In 1944, when the federation had 603,000 members, it was made up of no less than 22 largely autonomous districts. Wartime centralization of coal mining organization and bargaining hastened the conversion of the federation into the National Union of Mineworkers in January 1945. *See also* UNITED MINE WORKERS OF AMERICA.

MINIMUM AGE. The legal specifying of a minimum age of employment in an industry has been one way of controlling the exploitation of children and teenagers in the labor force. The first effective factory legislation in England in 1833 outlawed the employment of children under nine years of age. In 1919, the **International Labour Organisation** (ILO) approved Convention No. 5, which set 14 as the minimum age for entry into industrial employment. This convention was revised in 1937 to raise the minimum age to 15 for most forms of employment. Since 1970, the ILO has introduced two additional conventions to address the minimum age and **child labor**: minimum age for employment (Convention No.138, 1973) and worst forms of child labor (Convention No.182, 1999).

MINIMUM WAGE. The term minimum wage refers to the principle that an employee in a country or an industry should be paid a minimum amount. The idea of a minimum (or living) wage was an important aspiration in the history of organized labor, naturally so in the 19th century when wages were often barely adequate to live on, particularly in certain industries such as clothing manufacturing. The first modern minimum wage law was passed in the **United Kingdom** in 1773; this was the Spitalfields Act, which gave English silk weavers a minimum wage that lasted as a principle until about 1820, but other textile employees were not successful. In 1779, English stocking hand-loom workers rioted after a proposed minimum wage law for the industry was rejected by parliament. In 1811 petitions for a minimum wage from weavers in England and Scotland with a total of 77,000 signatures were also rejected by parliament. In 1796, the English parliament debated a minimum wage law that had been proposed by Samuel Whitebread, but the measure failed to attract support.

Pressure for minimum wages caused governments to act in various ways to provide a minimum wage. Some countries (the **United States** in 1938 and **France** in 1950) have provided a minimum wage through national legislation. Others, such as **Australia** and **New Zealand**, have used **conciliation and arbitration** to set minimum wages in particular industries. There was no legal minimum wage legislation in the United Kingdom before 1999; this followed commitments the **British Labour Party** had adopted in the early 1990s but was only able to implement after its victory in the 1997 elections.

The effects of minimum wage laws have been criticized by some economists since the 1970s as hurting rather than helping low-skilled employees. They have argued that such laws raise the cost of their labor above the market rate and thereby increase their unemployment. The economic effect of a minimum wage depends upon the level at which it is set and whether employers have a monopoly on the labor they wish to hire. Too high a minimum wage rate could add to unemployment but, where employers enjoy monopoly conditions, a minimum wage can help low-skilled workers because the additional labor cost could be paid out of profits. *See also* WAGES.

MITBESTIMMUNG. Mitbestimmung is a German term meaning the right to have a voice in the economic decision-making of firms; it is usually translated as codetermination. *Mitbestimmung* was expressed though direct labor representation at the various levels of decision making within a firm. The idea of codetermination came from the desire of organized labor to replace the authoritarian order of pre-1918 **Germany** with one that embodied both political and economic democracy. This goal was given practical expression in the Works' Councils Law of February 1920, which provided for elected employee-employer councils in enterprises employing more than 20 employees and for the election of a works' steward in enterprises with less than 20 employees; the idea for these councils grew out of the government's attempts during World War I to enlist the support of organized labor for the war effort in return for recognition. The principles of codetermination remained popular in German organized labor throughout the 1920s. In 1928, the *Allgemeiner Deutscher Gewerkschaftsbund* (German General Trade Union Federation) formally adopted *Wirtschaftsdemokratie* (or economic democracy), a philosophy designed to counter Leninism. In contrast, what little support there was for codetermination among large employers in the early 1920s rapidly declined as the decade progressed.

With the revival of free German labor unions in 1945, codetermination was widely adopted and was first applied at the Klöckner steel works in early 1946. Codetermination was encouraged in the British occupational zone (but not in the American) as a means of promoting and sustaining democracy in the economy.

An extended form of codetermination, *Montanmitbestimmung*, was applied to companies that derived more than half their income from steel, iron, or coal in 1951. Under legislation passed in 1952 and 1972 all enterprises with five or more employees were able to have works' councils. In 1976, the principle of codetermination was extended to the supervisory boards of enterprises with 2,000 or more employees. Although in theory works' councils are distinct from labor unions, in practice those elected to the councils from the unions are usually shop stewards. Although only 39 percent of German firms had works' councils in 1992, the proportion varied according to the size of the firm, with 13 percent among those with five to 20 employees, 34 percent among those with 21 to 50 employees, 53 percent among those with 51 to 159 employees, 97 percent among those with 151 to 300 employees, and 88 percent among those with more than 300 employees. *See also* AUSTRIA; BÖCKLER, HANS; EUROPEAN UNION; SLOVENIA.

MOLDOVA. Independent of the former Soviet Union since August 1991, organized labor in Moldova has faced considerable economic, political, and social obstacles to its development. Although parliamentary elections have been held in Moldova since February 1994, its labor laws reflect the repressive Soviet era. The Confederation of Trade Unions of the Republic of Moldova has faced official discrimination and the right to **strike** is restricted. High unemployment also restricts the potential of the unions to organize and bargain collectively. Moldova was not represented in the **International Confederation of Free Trade Unions** (ICFTU) in 2002.

MONGOLIA. Independent from **China** since 1921, and a communist state until March 1990, independent organized labor in Mongolia has, of necessity, a brief history. Nevertheless, the Confederation of Mongolian Trade Unions had been formed by November 1994 and was admitted to **membership** of the **International Confederation of Free Trade Unions** (ICFTU) in the same year; it claimed a membership of 450,000 in 2001.

MONTENEGRO. See YUGOSLAVIA (FEDERAL REPUBLIC).

MONTSERRAT. A dependent territory of the **United Kingdom**, the Montserrat Trades and Labour Council was formed in 1948 and was an affiliate of the **International Confederation of Free Trade Unions** (ICFTU) from 1957 to the 1980s, when it was replaced by the Montserrat Allied Workers' Union (formed in 1973); in 2001, it reported a **membership** of 193.

MOROCCO. Independent of **France** since March 1956, organized labor in Morocco dates from 1936 when the colonial administration allowed European workers to form labor unions. However, Moroccan workers were denied the legal right to form labor unions until 1951, although the colonial administration tolerated Moroccan **membership** of unions in 1946. As in other African countries, organized labor in Morocco was associated with the independence movement and Moroccan workers preferred to form their own unions rather than join European ones. The *Union Marocaine du Travail* (Moroccan Union of Workers), formed in March 1955, was admitted to the **International Confederation of Free Trade Unions** (ICFTU) in 1957 but had ceased its membership by 1965; it did not reaffiliate until 1993, when it claimed a membership of 410,600. Since 1994, the right to **strike** has been restricted in Morocco and, by 2002, the ICFTU reported that organized labor had little real legal protection for its activities and spoke of **police** violence against labor demonstrations.

MOZAMBIQUE. Independent of **Portugal** since June 1975, organized labor in Mozambique effectively dates from 1965, when limited rights of **collective bargaining** were granted to bank and railroad employees, even though some European workers there had formed organizations as early as 1898. From 1975 to the early 1990s, the government did not permit an independent labor movement. Mozambique has only been represented in the **International Confederation of Free Trade Unions** (ICFTU) since 1995; it claimed to represent a **membership** of 119,900 in 2001. In 2002, the ICFTU noted that there was discrimination against employees who went on strike in the **export processing zones**.

MURRAY, PHILIP (1886-1952). Murray was the first president of the **United Steelworkers of America**. He was born in Blantyre, Scotland, and began work as a coal miner at the age of 10. His father was a local coal mining union official. In 1902, he emigrated with his family to the **United States**, where he began working as a coal miner in western Pennsylvania. In 1904, he was elected to his first position within the **United Mine Workers of America** (UMWA) and, in 1912, was elected to its executive board. Thereafter Murray sat on a number of important labor bodies, including the National Bituminous Coal Production Committee (1917-1918) and the Labor Industrial Advisory Board of the National Recovery Administration (1933).

In 1936, as a vice president of the UMWA, he was put in charge of the campaign to unionize the steel industry by the UMWA's president, **John L. Lewis**. His efforts eventually led to the formation of the United Steelworkers of America, which Murray led from 1942 to his death. In 1940, he took over the presidency of the **Congress of Industrial Organizations** (CIO) after Lewis's resignation. Lewis had Murray expelled from the UMWA for a combination of personal and political differences; Lewis was a Republican and Murray was a Democrat. After World War II, Murray led major strikes in the steel industry (1946, 1949, and 1952) for better pay and conditions. Murray was also active in community affairs; for example, he was a member of the National Association for the Advancement of Colored People. *See also* COAL MINING; GREEN, WILLIAM.

MYANMAR. *See* BURMA.

-N-

NAMIBIA. Independent of control by **South Africa** since 1989, organized labor in Namibia originally consisted of branches of South African unions, both for European and African workers. In 1962, the Union of South West Africa in Exile was formed and was associated with the movement for independence. The first legal **strike** in Namibia took place in November 1992 in the diamond industry following the introduction of new labor legislation. In December 1995, the government prohibited **public sector** employees from participation in **politics**. In 1995, the government established **export processing zones** in which strikes were prohibited for five years. In December 2001, the National Union of Namibian Workers was admitted to membership of the **International Confederation of Free Trade Unions** (ICFTU) and claimed a **membership** of 65,000. In 2002, the ICFTU noted some improvement in the legal environment for organized labor in settling **labor disputes** outside of the export processing zones.

NATIONAL AND LOCAL GOVERNMENT OFFICERS' ASSOCIATION (NALGO). NALGO was one of the largest unions in the **United Kingdom** from 1946 to 1993. It was founded in 1905 as a provincial federation catering to local government officers and was called the National Association of Local Government Officers (NALGO). Between 1905 and 1946, its **membership** grew from 5,000 to 140,000. In 1946, NALGO broadened its recruitment of members to include those in other parts of the **public sector** such as the National Health Service, gas, and electricity. Its title was officially changed to National and Local Government Officers' Association in 1952 to reflect these changes in membership, but the acronym NALGO was retained. In 1964, when it became affiliated with the **Trades Union Congress** (TUC), its membership had reached 338,300. Like other white-collar unions, NALGO was opposed to **strikes** and connections with the political and industrial aspects of organized labor for most of its life. It was not until 1970 that NALGO authorized its first strike. By 1981, NALGO's membership had reached 706,150; its membership rose to 750,000 by 1986, but had only increased to 760,000 by 1991. In 1993, NALGO merged with the **National Union of Public Employees** to create UNISON. *See also* WHITE-COLLAR UNIONISM.

NATIONAL EDUCATION ASSOCIATION (NEA). Since about 1987, the NEA has been the largest labor union in the **United States**. Formed in 1857 in Philadelphia, it operated as a professional association of school administrators until 1905, when it admitted teachers as members. Despite its conservative reputation until the 1960s, the NEA has displayed its progressive side on a number of occasions. In 1866, it formally admitted **women** to full **membership**. In 1914, the NEA passed a resolution supporting **equal pay for equal work** and, in 1972, the NEA representative assembly voted to formally support the passage of the Equal Rights Amendment.

Before 1963, the NEA opposed unionism and **collective bargaining** for teachers but changed this policy and, since 1963, it has been a participant in collective bargaining, as evidenced by its victories in ballots for exclusive bargaining rights against its industrial rival, the **American Federation of Teachers** (AFT), an affiliate of the **American Federation of Labor-Congress of Industrial Organizations** (AFL-CIO). The affiliation of the AFT with the AFL-CIO has long been an obstacle to efforts to amalgamate the two unions. In 1992, the NEA gained a major civil rights victory, lobbying successfully to pass the Civil Rights Act, which protects individuals against on-the-job harassment and discrimination and allows victims of employment discrimination to collect compensatory damages.

In 2001, the two organizations agreed to form a cooperative partnership to work together on issues of mutual interest while preserving their independence. Between 1995 and 2001, membership of the NEA rose from 2.2 to 2.7 million members, making it the largest white-collar union in the world and the world's second largest labor union after *Ver.di. See also* EDUCATION; WHITE-COLLAR UNIONISM.

NATIONAL INDUSTRIAL RECOVERY ACT. The National Industrial Recovery Act of 1933 was the cornerstone of modern **collective bargaining** in the **United States**. Under Section 7(a), a provision fought for by the miners' leader, **John Llewellyn Lewis**, employees were given the right to organize labor unions to collectively bargain with employers without harassment, provisions that had been included previously in the federal Railway Labor Act (1926). The National Industrial Recovery Act was declared unconstitutional by the Supreme Court in *Schecter Poultry Corporation v.*

U.S. in 1935 and was replaced by the **Wagner Act**. Nevertheless, the shift in the legal environment towards a more favorable view of labor unions indicated by these laws was the basis of a massive recruitment drive by organized labor in the mid-1930s. *See also* AMERICAN FEDERATION OF LABOR; CONGRESS OF INDUSTRIAL ORGANIZATIONS; UNITED STEELWORKERS OF AMERICA.

NATIONAL LABOR UNION (NLU). The NLU was a body created by U.S. organized labor in Baltimore, Maryland, in August 1866, to bring about progressive political reforms. Its agenda included the eight-hour work day, the reduction of monopolies, and producer and consumer cooperatives. The delegates at the inaugural congress represented about 60,000 employees. The main achievement of the NLU was gaining the eight-hour work day law for laborers, workmen, and mechanics working for the federal government. In 1869, it sent a delegate to the first conference of the International Workingmen's Association in Basle, Switzerland. In 1870, the NLU formed a political wing, which created the Labor Reform Party in 1872. The emphasis on **politics** cost the NLU the support of **craft unions** and by 1876 it was defunct. *See also* WORKING HOURS.

NATIONAL LABOUR FEDERATION. The National Labour Federation was formed in Newcastle-upon-Tyne, England, in 1886, with the goal of organizing men and **women** of all trades in contrast to both **craft unions** and **industrial unions**. Any labor union could also join. Its founders were some members of the **Amalgamated Society of Engineers** and Edward R. Pease (1857-1955), a **socialist** and founder member of the Fabian Society. The federation claimed 60,000 members in 1890, mostly in semiskilled jobs in engineering, chemicals, shipbuilding, and construction. By 1892, the federation's membership had fallen to 6,000, and it was dissolved in 1894, largely as a result of the depression of the early 1890s and defeats in **strikes**. *See also* KNIGHTS OF LABOR.

NATIONAL LABOR RELATIONS ACT. *See* WAGNER ACT.

NATIONAL UNION OF PUBLIC EMPLOYEES (NUPE). The NUPE grew out of the London County Council Employees' Protection Society (formed in 1888), which became the basis of the Municipal Employees Association in 1894. As a result of a split in

1907, a new body was created, the National Union of Corporation Workers, with a **membership** of 8,000. In 1928, this body changed its name to the NUPE and set about recruiting all employees working for local governments in the **United Kingdom**, a policy that led to conflict with the **General and Municipal Workers' Union** (GMWU) and the **Transport and General Workers' Union** (TGWU), which managed to exclude the NUPE from affiliation with the **Trades Union Congress** (TUC) until the 1970s. The membership of the NUPE grew from 10,000 in 1948 to 215,000 in 1962 as a result of recruiting the lower grades of the local government and the National Health Service. Between 1934 and 1962, the NUPE was led by its general secretary, Bryn Roberts, a strong supporter of **industrial unionism**. In 1982, the NUPE had 710,450 members, of whom 65 percent were **women**; membership declined to 658,000 in 1986 and to 551,000 in 1992, of whom 70 percent were women. In 1993, the NUPE amalgamated with the **National and Local Government Officers' Association** to created UNISON. *See also* PUBLIC/PRIVATE SECTOR.

NEPAL. Organized labor in Nepal effectively dates from 1950, but no union organization was legally permitted until 1964, when the Nepal Labour Organization was formed; by 1975 it had been admitted to membership of the **International Confederation of Free Trade Unions** (ICFTU) and claimed a **membership** of 50,000, but it was not an affiliate in the 1980s. In 1992, the government enacted a labor union law that prohibited antiunion discrimination, but the law has not been followed in practice and the right to **strike** is restrictive. In 1993, the Nepal Trade Union Congress joined the ICFTU and claimed a membership of 140,000. In 2001-2002, the ICFTU reported that the government did not really recognize labor unions as valid representatives of workers, and **police** violence against unions continued. It noted that 200 labor union members had been murdered by Maoist guerillas during 2002, along with hundreds of other Nepalese.

NETHERLANDS. Organized labor in the Netherlands began in 1866 when printers and diamond cutters formed unions. A nonreligious labor federation was established in 1871 and a Protestant labor federation in 1877. Organized labor was divided by **politics** as well as religion. In 1893, a social democratic labor union center, the National Labor Secretariat, was created, which claimed to represent

16,000 members. The secretariat came to be infiltrated by **anarchists**, which caused its alienation from mainstream labor supporters. Union growth was slow; by the early 1900s there were only about 19,000 union members. Nevertheless, there were major **labor disputes** organized by longshoremen and railroad employees in 1903. These failures led to the formation of a new national labor federation in 1905. In 1909, a combined **Catholic** and Protestant labor federation was created, but the Catholics withdrew on orders from their bishop.

As in other countries, there was considerable growth in union **membership** in the Netherlands between 1913 and 1920, rising from 234,000 to 684,000. This growth took place along deep religious and political divisions, not just because these divisions were present in Dutch society but also because many unions were created by **socialists** or clergy in the absence of large-scale concentrations of manufacturing employment. In 1920, 23 percent of Dutch union members belonged to Catholic unions, 12 percent to Protestant unions, 37 percent to socialist unions, 7 percent to **syndicalist** or **communist** unions, and 21 percent to some other category. Although these proportions changed over time, the fundamental divisions remained part of the Dutch labor movement despite the formation of a nondenominational association of labor federations in 1929. During the Nazi occupation, organized labor was banned.

In 1943, secret meetings between the leaders of the employers and the unions led to a new understanding about the conduct of industrial relations after the war. This agreement produced a permanent employer-union body, the Foundation of Labor, in May 1945, which received recognition by government as the leading policymaker in socioeconomic matters. By 1950 there were nearly 1.2 million union members covering 42 percent of all employees, but since that time the proportion of employees enrolled by unions has steadily declined. In 1976, a new national labor federation, the *Federatie Nederlandse Vakbeweging* (Netherlands Federation of Labor Unions), sought to merge the social democratic and Catholic divisions of organized labor; the merger was completed in 1981. The Dutch labor movement was significantly reduced by the recession of the early 1980s, which cut the proportion of employees in unions from 32 percent in 1980, to 23 percent in 1989, to 19 percent in 2001.

NEW CALEDONIA. Still a territory of **France**, nine labor unions existed in New Caledonia by 1975. New Caledonia has only been an affiliate of the **International Confederation of Free Trade Unions** (ICFTU) since 1993, when it claimed to represent 3,600 members.

NEW ZEALAND. New Zealand has an importance in the history of organized labor belied by its small size and location in the southwest Pacific Ocean. It was first settled by Maoris in the mid-14th century and by Europeans from 1840. Exploiting shortages of skilled labor, the first unions emerged in the building trades from 1842. Sustained British **immigration** brought union members as well as the example of labor unions. Printers (1862) and tailors (1865) formed unions, and the British international unions, the **Amalgamated Society of Engineers** (1864) and the **Amalgamated Society of Carpenters and Joiners** (1875), set up New Zealand branches. The first urban trades council was formed in Auckland in 1876, an example followed by other cities and towns in the early 1880s. In 1879, following the successful election of S. P. Andrews, a plasterer, to parliament, a Working Men's Political Association was formed that was concerned with land tax, tariff protection for local industries, and the prohibition of Chinese immigration.

The most powerful influences on organized labor in New Zealand were **Australia** and the **United Kingdom**. In 1878, New Zealand followed the British example and legalized labor unions. In January 1885 the first New Zealand Trades Union Congress was held in Dunedin following the example set by Australian labor unions from 1879. As in other countries, there was a surge of union growth between 1886 and 1890. In 1886, for example, the Amalgamated Shearers' Union of Australia set up a New Zealand branch and made a special effort to recruit Maoris; in the same year, Christopher Leek founded a mass railroad union and called it after the union he had belonged to in England, the Amalgamated Society of Railway Servants. Between 1885 and mid-1890, the number of union members rose from 3,000 to 63,000.

The participation of New Zealand labor in the great Australian Maritime Strike of 1890 (August-November) and the economic depression that set in after it largely destroyed the unions' growth of the late 1880s. It was at this time that New Zealand embarked on a series of social experiments, which attracted international attention in the early 1900s. In 1894, New Zealand became the first country in the world to introduce a compulsory **conciliation and arbitration** system for **labor disputes**. Amending legislation was passed in 1898 which, although it encouraged union formation and growth through official registration, denied unions the right to **strike** once an award of the arbitration court was in force. The New Zealand experiment attracted interest and visits from **France** (F. Challye in 1903), the **United Kingdom** (Beatrice and Sidney Webb in 1898, Ramsay Macdonald in 1906, and Ernest Aves in 1907), and the **United States** (Henry Demarest Lloyd in 1900, V. S. Clark in 1906, and Colonel H. Weinstock in 1909).

The use of compulsion in conciliation and arbitration in labor disputes was adopted by Australia but remained unusual in the rest of the world. The constraints of the arbitration system led to labor disputes particularly as radical unions found they could legally strike if they were not registered organizations under the conciliation and arbitration legislation. There was a disastrous waterfront strike in 1913 which, despite Australian support, depleted the finances of the unions for four years. Radical ideas, particularly for the **One Big Union** (OBU), came though the **Industrial Workers of the World** (IWW), which formed a branch in New Zealand in 1912. A gold miners' strike at Waihi and Reefton in 1912 was marked by police and employer violence, which led to the death of a picketer.

In July 1916, the New Zealand Labour Party was formed and claimed 10,000 members. Yet compared to Australia, organized labor was weak; in 1920 only 26 percent of employees were union members, compared to 42 percent in Australia. In 1928, a coalition government abolished compulsory arbitration to enable wage reductions. In 1935, the Labour Party won a landslide victory and enacted legislation that established a strong regulatory role for government in economic and social management. In 1936, the Industrial Conciliation and Arbitration Act was amended to make union **membership** compulsory for any employee subject to a registered award of industrial agreement, a change that naturally led to a substantial growth in union membership. In 1937, the New Zealand Federation of Labour was formed and joined the **International Federation of Trade Unions** (IFTU) in 1938 and the **International Confederation of Free Trade Unions** (ICFTU) in 1951. Another feature of the period was the growth of **industrial unionism** in engineering and printing. With the exception of the 1951 waterfront strike, developments among organized labor were not especially noteworthy again until the late 1960s, when the **white-collar unions** formed a federation; it amalgamated with the New Zealand Federation of Labour in October 1987 to form the New Zealand Council of Trade Unions.

In the mid-1980s, in response to New Zealand's severe economic difficulties, a series of radical reforms were introduced that again made New Zealand a social laboratory, this time for economic deregulation and the free exercise of market forces. In 1984, the government made the first move to abolish compulsory arbitration in interest disputes (a distinction between rights and interest disputes was first introduced into New Zealand legislation in 1973) except in "essential" industries. Yet much of the system first created in 1894 remained in place up to 1991, when the Employment Contracts Act was enacted. The act abolished the arbitration system and its awards and changed the basis of the industrial relations system to the law of contract. It also ended the system of compulsory union membership, which had been introduced into bargaining arrangements in 1936.

Largely because of the economic problems faced by the New Zealand economy, but also because of the removal of the protection of compulsory membership, organized labor has fared poorly since 1991. In 1985, there were 683,000 union members in New Zealand covering 44 percent of employees but, by December 1994, there were only 375,900, covering 23 percent of full-time employees. The reelection of the Labour Party in November 1999 led to the replacement of the Employment Contracts Act by the Employment Relations Act, which made the legal environment fairer for organized labor. In 2000, there were 318,500 union members, covering about 17.5 percent of employees.

NICARAGUA. Although organized labor had emerged in Nicaragua by 1924, any progress was stifled by the dictatorship of the Somoza family, which was in power from 1936 to 1979. Organized labor reemerged briefly between 1945 and 1949 and again from 1956, with political struggle against the government taking priority. By 1965, Nicaragua had been admitted to membership of the **International Confederation of Free Trade Unions** (ICFTU) and has remained represented in the ICFTU despite a brutal civil war between 1981 and 1990. After the transition to democratic government, Nicaragua opened its first **export processing zone** in 1993. In

1996, the government promulgated a new labor code that removed many of the previous restrictions on forming labor unions, but the right to **strike** remains difficult to exercise in practice. In 2002, the ICFTU was particularly critical of working conditions in the 23 export processing zones, describing them as "close to **slavery**." Official intimidation of organized labor remains common in Nicaragua.

NIGER. Independent from **France** since August 1960, organized labor developed under French rule after World War II, but after independence was effectively placed under government control. Since 1992, Niger has moved towards democratic rule. In 1993, it was admitted to membership of the **International Confederation of Free Trade Unions** (ICFTU); its affiliate, the *Union des Syndicats des Travailleurs du Niger* (Union of Workers' Unions of Niger), claimed to represent 38,000 members. Since the strikes of 1994, Niger has been relatively peaceful, and in 2002 Niger was one of the few African countries not to be mentioned in the ICFTU's survey of **violations of trade union rights**.

NIGERIA. Independent from the **United Kingdom** since October 1960, organized labor in Nigeria began in 1912 with the formation of the Nigerian Civil Servants' Union; other unions were formed by teachers, miners, and railroad workers in the 1930s. In 1938, the British administration passed a trade union ordinance. The first national union federation was formed in 1943, and by 1957 Nigeria was represented by three affiliates in the **International Confederation of Free Trade Unions** (ICFTU). At independence in 1960, Nigeria had 631 labor unions representing 520,164 members. Organized labor in Nigeria was large but politically divided and therefore vulnerable to government efforts to place it under control, a process assisted by civil war between 1966 and 1970. Nigeria ceased to be represented in the ICFTU between 1975 and 1990 and was not readmitted until 2000, largely because promises made to an ICFTU delegation in 1993 that organized labor should be free of government control were not kept. In 1992, the government established **export processing zones** where organized labor was, in practice, excluded. In 2002, the ICFTU remained critical of the restrictions on the right to organize unions and the right to strike in Nigeria. On February 1, 2002, there was a national strike by **police** over wages arrears, which resulted in the sacking of 153 policemen and the laying of charges against 2,000 others. In July 2003 there was police violence during a general strike over oil price rises.

NIGHT WORK. Night work is an integral feature of industrial economies, particularly in certain industries, such as transportation, storage, and communication, and in some parts of **manufacturing**, such as baking. The problem of night work was recognized in an English law of 1802 designed to protect the health and morals of pauper children taken on as **apprentices**; it forebade any apprentice to work between 9 P.M. and 6 A.M. from June 1, 1803. Night work has long been held to be harmful to young employees and **women**, hence the efforts made by the **International Labour Organisation** to limit night work to adult males by Conventions No. 4 and No. 6 in 1919. These conventions were revised in 1948 to remove exceptions in the earlier conventions. *See also* WORKING HOURS.

NIHON RODOKUMIAI SORENGOKAI. See RENGO.

NORRIS-LAGUARDIA ACT. The Anti-Injunction (Norris-LaGuardia) Act was a fundamental piece of U.S. federal labor law, which was passed in 1932 and designed to give organized labor full freedom of association. It outlawed yellow dog contracts and prohibited federal courts from issuing injunctions (court orders restraining union activity on the grounds of the prevention of injury to property or other rights) during **labor disputes** except under particular circumstances. The effect of the Norris-LaGuardia Act was weakened by a series of Supreme Court decisions in the 1970s concerning the issuing of injunctions during disputes where there were contracts or **arbitration** machinery. *See also* NATIONAL INDUSTRIAL RECOVERY ACT.

NORTH KOREA. An independent state since 1948, having been a colony of **Japan** from 1910 to 1945, North Korea is run on essentially Stalinist principles. There has been no independent labor movement permitted in North Korea since 1925, when the Japanese administration outlawed trade unions. Since 1948, the government-controlled General Federation of Trade Unions is the only national labor organization allowed. Wages are set by the government and there is no right to **strike** or to engage in **collective bargaining**.

NORWAY. Organized labor in Norway began to emerge from the 1860s. As in other European countries, mutual aid or friendly societies preceded the formation of unions. The first union was founded by printers in Oslo in 1872. Labor federations were formed in the cities from 1882. In 1887, a political Labor Party was formed. Two pivotal events in Norwegian labor were the establishment of the *Landsorganisasjonen i Norge* (LO), the Labor Union Federation of Norway, in 1899, and a parallel national organization by employers in 1900. In 1902, the LO and the employers' organization signed their first agreement. A lockout in 1911 gave rise to a law on **labor disputes** passed in 1915 and revised in 1927, which introduced the concepts of rights and interests in disputes in an attempt to control **strikes**. In 1919, another law brought in the eight-hour work day. There was a failed **general strike** in 1921 and other major labor disputes in 1924 and 1931. In 1935, the Labor Party, which had become Norway's largest political party in 1927, won government. In the more cooperative political climate that followed, the first Basic Agreement (1935) was concluded between the LO and the employers' organization, thereby founding a tradition of **collective bargaining** characterized by a mixture of national and industry bargaining. The proportion of employees who were union members in Norway declined from a peak of 63 percent in 1960 to 55 percent in 1994 and to 39 percent in 2001. *See also* DENMARK; SWEDEN.

NOVEMBER PACT (STINNES-LEGIEN AGREEMENT). The November Pact (also known as the Stinnes-Legien Agreement) was signed in **Germany** between the largest **employers' organizations** and the Free (or Social Democratic labor unions), the **Hirsch-Duncker Trade Associations**, and the **Catholic** unions in November 1918. Designed to stabilize the revolutionary political climate that prevailed in Germany following its defeat in World War I, the agreement recognized the legitimacy of unions to engage in **collective bargaining**, granted the eight-hour work day, and provided for workers' committees in enterprises employing more than 50 employees to ensure that the conditions of employment of collective agreements were carried out. The November Pact led to the formation of the *Zentralarbeitsgemeinschaft* or Central Labor Association, an organization designed to implement the pact, but it was not effective after 1924 because of hostility by employers. *See also* LEGIEN, CARL; *MITBESTIMMUNG*.

-O-

OCCUPATIONAL HEALTH AND SAFETY. The term occupational health and safety covers all aspects of health at work, from the hazards that can cause injury or death to ways of improving the working environment. Knowledge about the risks of particular occupations and from handling certain materials dates from antiquity; the Roman architectural writer Vitruvius (c. 25 B.C.) was aware that lead smelting and lead pipes were harmful to producers and consumers. Over the past two centuries, occupational health and safety has grown as an area of concern for organized labor, particularly in occupations with a high risk of injury or death, such as **coal mining.** The **International Labour Organisation** (ILO) published its first encyclopedia on occupational health and safety in 1930. Since the 1930s, there has been a growth in joint management-union committees with responsibilities for occupational health and safety. General support for occupational health and safety in the workplace has been a standard feature of organized labor, particularly since the 1960s, and has increased as knowledge about hazards has grown. The leaking of toxic gas from the Union Carbide plant in Bhopal, **India,** on December 2-3, 1984, which led to the deaths of 2,600 people and injuries to 200,000 others, was a landmark in general awareness of occupational health and safety; organized labor at the plant had been demanding improved safety conditions for its workers since 1976. The incident raised the profile of occupational health and safety in the **International Confederation of Free Trade Unions** (ICFTU). On April 28, 1996, international labor unions inaugurated the International Commemoration Day for Dead and Injured Workers to focus attention on occupational health and safety.

OMAN. The labor law of 1973 does not provide for the existence of labor unions or **collective bargaining** in Oman. **Strikes** are illegal. About half of the labor force are expatriates. Committees of management and workers in enterprises where 50 or more are employed are provided for in law, but not always implemented. The Labor Welfare Board handles individual workers' grievances. In 1993, Oman joined the **International Labour Organisation** (ILO). In 2002, the **International Confederation of Free Trade Unions**

(ICFTU) described the outlook for organized labor in Oman as "bleak."

ONE BIG UNION (OBU). The one big union refers to the idea of organizing all employees into a single union, in contrast to both **craft unions** and **industrial unions**. It originated in the **United Kingdom** in 1834 when Robert Owen (1771-1858) and John Doherty (c. 1798-1854) organized the Grand United Consolidated Trades Union, which briefly attracted a membership of 16,000. In the **United States**, the International Labor Union made the first determined effort to recruit unskilled as well as skilled labor in the late 1870s, an idea followed by the **Knights of Labor** in the 1880s. In the United Kingdom, the idea of an OBU was revived by the **National Labour Federation** in 1886 and by unions such as the **Workers' Union** in 1898 and through federations of existing unions, such as the **General Federation of Trade Unions** in 1899, organizations both created following the defeat of the **Amalgamated Society of Engineers** in the lockout of 1897. The idea of the OBU was revived by the **Industrial Workers of the World** and was an important topic of debate internationally up to the early 1920s. In a limited way, the OBU has found practical expression in union **amalgamations**.

ORGANIZACIÓN REGIONAL INTERAMERICANA DE TRABAJADORES **(ORIT).** The ORIT, or Inter-American Regional Organization of Workers, was formed out of the *Confederación Interamericana de Trabajadores* or Inter-American Confederation of Workers in Mexico City in January 1951 by the representatives of 21 countries. The **United States** delegation was led by **George Meany** of the **American Federation of Labor**, and the **International Confederation of Free Trade Unions** (ICFTU) was represented by Sir Vincent Tewson, the general secretary of the British **Trades Union Congress** (TUC).

Originally based in **Mexico**, the ORIT has been based in Caracas, **Venezuela**, since the late 1990s. It was created within the framework of Cold War politics with the aim of resisting **communist** influence in Latin America. Despite its promotion of strong, democratic labor unions, the ORIT came under suspicion of being too close to the U.S. Department of State. The ORIT also faced competition from rival inter-American labor federations, the Marxist *Confederación de Trabajadores de America Latina* (Confederation of Latin American Workers) up to 1962, a **Catholic** labor federation formed in 1954, and the radical *Congreso Permanente de Unidad Sindical de los Trabajadores de America Latina* (Permanent Unity Congress of Labor Unions of Latin American Workers) from 1964 to the 1990s. The ORIT is the undisputed primary body for representing the Americas in the ICFTU. In 2001, the ORIT represented 32.4 million union members within the ICFTU or 21 percent of its total **membership**.

ORGANIZATION OF AFRICAN TRADE UNION UNITY (OATUU). The OATUU was formed in 1973 from the merger of the All-African Trade Union Federation (AATUF), the African Trade Union Confederation (ATUC), and the Pan-African Workers' Congress. The AATUF was formed in Casablanca in May 1961. It was the first international trade union federation designed to represent African countries only and was formed to exclude influence of both the **International Confederation of Free Trade Unions** (ICFTU) and the **World Confederation of Labor** (WCL), which were regarded as too conservative. Those national organizations that did not accept this view formed the ATUC in January 1962 as a rival organization. The merger of the AATUF and the ATUC to form the OATUU was made at the behest of the Organization of African Unity. The affiliation of African labor organizations with international labor bodies created discord within the OATUU, with both the ICFTU and the WCL claiming affiliates among bodies affiliated with the OATUU. In 1988, the OATUU and the WCL signed a formal statement of cooperation. In 2001, the OATUU claimed to represent 53 countries with a combined **membership** of 30 million; in contrast, the ICFTU claimed only 12.9 million members in Africa in 2001.

-P-

PACIFIC TRADE UNION COMMUNITY (PTUC). Originally called the Pacific Trade Union Forum, the PTUC was set up in 1980 to improve cooperation between organized labor in **Australia** and **New Zealand** and the South West Pacific countries, as well as to campaign against the testing of nuclear weapons in the region. In 1992, the PTUC had 14 country members representing about 3.2 million union members, with the bulk of these members living in

Australia, New Zealand, and **Papua New Guinea**. The **Australian Council of Trade Unions** provided the secretariat for the PTUC. In 1995, the PTUC was superseded by the **Asian and Pacific Regional Organization** (APRO).

PAKISTAN. Independent of the **United Kingdom** since 1947, organized labor inherited the labor law framework of British **India**, which dated from 1926, when unions were legalized, and played an active role in the independence movement. The All-Pakistan Trade Union Federation was formed in 1950 to represent unions in both Pakistan (then West Pakistan) and East Pakistan (**Bangladesh**). Between 1951 and 1968, the number of unions in Pakistan rose from 309 to 1,041 and their reported **membership** rose from 393,100 to 522,900, despite restrictions on organized labor imposed by military governments. In 1971, Bangladesh seceded from Pakistan. Pakistan has been represented in the **International Confederation of Free Trade Unions** (ICFTU) since 1951. In 1980, the government established **export processing zones** from which organized labor is effectively prohibited and there is no right to **strike**. In 2001, the ICFTU reported that although Pakistan had about 1.1 million union members, organized labor faced considerable hostility from the military government of General Pervez Musharraf, characterized by the arrest of union leaders; the torture of Nadeem Dar (president of the Leatherfield Labour Union) by the owner of the Leatherfield company; **police** intimidation; and coercion for employees to sign individual, nonunion employment contracts. Despite the release of a new labor policy in September 2002, the ICFTU noted that there were greater, not fewer, restrictions on organized labor.

PANAMA. Independent from **Colombia** since 1903, organized labor was introduced by the **American Federation of Labor** (AFL) in 1917 when it formed a section in the canal zone to cater to U.S. employees, but the American example did not really take hold among Panamanian workers until the 1930s, as shown by the formation of the first labor federation in 1939. Panama has been represented in the **International Confederation of Free Trade Unions** (ICFTU) since 1951, but Panamanian organized labor has been weakened by the usual political and religious divisions of Latin America. In 2001, the ICFTU was critical of the Panamanian government's restrictions on trade union rights for the **public sector**

and the layoff by the Chiquita Brands International Inc. of 400 banana workers in a dispute. In 2002, the ICFTU advised that conditions for organized labor in Panama had not improved.

PAN-AMERICAN FEDERATION OF LABOR (PAFL). The PAFL was the first international labor federation formed in the Americas; it operated between 1918 and 1940. It was formed at Laredo, Texas, on November 13, 1918, primarily through the efforts of Santiago Iglesias, the president of the labor federation of **Puerto Rico**, and John Murray of the International Typographical Union in California, working in conjunction with **Samuel Gompers**. The original members of the PAFL were **Colombia, Costa Rica, El Salvador, Guatemala, Mexico**, the **United States**, and Puerto Rico. Iglesias had been lobbying the **American Federation of Labor** (AFL) for the creation of a Pan-American labor federation since 1900, but his efforts did not begin to bear fruit until 1915. The value of good relations between organized labor in the United States and Mexico was shown in 1916 when Gompers secured the release of Americans taken prisoner during an illegal military raid in Mexico to capture Pancho Villa. The PAFL worked for peace between the United States and Mexico, concerned itself with the international migration of labor in the Americas, and opposed American intervention in the internal affairs of Central American and Caribbean countries. Although the Dominican Republic, **Nicaragua**, and **Peru** joined the PAFL, its effectiveness was reduced by the deaths of its key personnel: Murray in 1919, Gompers in 1924, and Iglesias in 1939. The last conference of the PAFL was held in New Orleans in 1940. *See also CONFEDERACIÓN INTERAMERICANA DE TRABAJADORES.*

PAPUA NEW GUINEA. Independent of **Australia** since September 1975, organized labor in Papua New Guinea developed under Australian influence, with the first unions being confined to European employees. However, the Australian presence was small until World War II, when the country was invaded by the Japanese and was the scene of fierce fighting. The colonial administration was opposed to the formation of labor unions by indigenous employees and it was not until the late 1950s that they began to be formed. The Papua New Guinea Trades Union Congress was formed in 1970 and has been an affiliate of the **International Confederation of Free Trade Unions** (ICFTU) since 1975. By 1973, there 41 registered labor unions with a total **membership** of 35,000. In 2001, Papua New Guinea had about 70,000 union members, compared to 60,000 in 1995.

PARAGUAY. Unions in Paraguay formed a federation in 1917 but were able to make little progress because of the lack of economic development, war with **Bolivia** from 1932 to 1935, and political oscillations; in 1936, organized labor was favored by the government, but a year later unions were restricted. The government sought to interfere with and manipulate organized labor in the 1940s and 1950s. A strike over the **minimum wage** in 1958 was widely supported, but repressed. Paraguay has been represented in the **International Confederation of Free Trade Unions** (ICFTU) from 1957 to 1975 and again since 1993. The 1993 labor code protected union leaders from dismissal but not union members or workers. Although the constitution guarantees unions and **collective bargaining**, these rights are restricted in practice, according to the ICFTU's survey of **violations of trade union rights** in 2002.

PART-TIME EMPLOYMENT. *See* FULL-TIME/PART-TIME EMPLOYMENT.

PERMANENT CONGRESS OF TRADE UNION UNITY OF LATIN AMERICAN WORKERS. *See CONGRESO PERMANENTE DE UNIDAD SINDICAL DE LOS TRABAJADORES DE AMERICA LATINA.*

PERU. Organized labor in Peru developed in the late 19th century; the first national labor federation was formed in 1919 and a second, under Marxist leadership, in 1929. There were about 25,000 union members by 1930. Because of its association with leftwing politics and support for land nationalization, organized labor was repressed by the military governments that ruled Peru in the 1930s and 1940s. The *Confederación de Trabajadores del Perú* (Confederation of Workers of Peru) was formed in May 1994 and was an affiliate of the **International Confederation of Free Trade Unions** (ICFTU) by 1951. Since the 1950s, organized labor in Peru has been caught up in the country's political divisions and by internal divisions based on religion. In 2000, organized labor played an active part in the campaign to get rid of the corrupt and autocratic president, Alberto Fujimori. By 2001, there were three Peruvian labor federations affiliated with the ICFTU claiming a combined **membership** of 265,000. Despite the return to democratic government after the repressive regime of Fujimori, the ICFTU remained critical of Peru's record of trade union rights during 2002, noting the use of the military to put down demonstrations against **privatization**.

PHILIPPINES. Although labor unions were not legalized in the Philippines until 1908, **craft unions** were formed after 1899; these unions set up a national federation of labor, *Union Obrera Democratica Filipina*, (Democratic Union of Philippine Workers), in 1902. Tolerated by the U.S. administration rather than encouraged, union growth was slow; by 1930, there were estimated to be only 67,000 union members. The labor movement was also divided between **communists** and noncommunists; the communists were more successful in enlisting union support for independence. After independence from the **United States** in 1946, Cipriano Cid, an official of the **Congress of Industrial Organizations** (CIO), set up the Philippines Association of Free Labor Unions. A **Catholic** labor federation, the Federation of Free Workers, was formed in 1950. In 1953, the Philippines was admitted to membership of the **International Confederation of Free Trade Unions** (ICFTU) and has remained represented there ever since.

In 1954, the Republic Act 875 gave labor unions legal protection and the right to engage in **collective bargaining**. Because of deep internal divisions, hostile management, legal complexities, and lack of public support, organized labor was unable to utilize fully the advantages of this law. In 1950, there were only 150,000 union members out of two million nonagricultural employees. In 1963, organized labor engaged directly in **politics** by creating the Workers' Party, but it fared poorly in the Manila elections of that year. In 1965, a new national labor federation, the Philippines Labor Center, was formed, but it did not result in a unified labor movement. From the early 1970s, industrial and political protests in the Philippines became intertwined.

President Ferdinand Marcos declared a state of emergency in September 1972, which was used to suspend the right to **strike** and to arrest labor leaders. In 1974, a new labor code aimed at reorganizing the unions along industrial lines. In 1975, the Trade Union Congress of the Philippines was established; it claimed a million members and remains the largest labor federation in the country. After the overthrow of Marcos in 1986, a new constitution was adopted in February 1987, which promised full legal protection for labor, organized and unorganized. Despite an improvement in the political and legal climate for organized labor, the ICFTU complained to the Philippine government about restrictions on the right to **collective bargaining** and discrimination against unions in 1991-1992. It has also noted the continuation of violence against labor officials and striking employees. In 2002, it noted restrictions on the right to strike, particularly in the **public sector**, and the discouragement of unions in the country's **export processing zones**.

Despite the country's political and economic problems, membership of labor unions in the Philippines grew from 1.9 to 3.8 million between 1980 and 2000, according to government figures. Like **Japan**, there are many unions in the Philippines. Between 1980 and 2000, the number of labor unions rose from 1,747 to 10,296.

PICKETING. Picketing refers to labor union members demonstrating outside a workplace, often with placards, in support of the union's claims against the workplace employer during **labor disputes**. The group carrying out the picketing (the "picket line") will also try to encourage employees not engaged in the dispute to stay away from the workplace. They can do this verbally or, on occasion, by violence. Picketing in this sense had entered English usage by 1867. Picketing was outlawed in the **United Kingdom** in 1825, but "peaceful picketing" was legalized in 1859. Violence during picketing was legally prohibited in 1875. The **Employment Act** of 1980 limited legal picketing to employees engaged in a labor dispute. *See also* "WINTER OF DISCONTENT."

POLAND. Organized labor in what is now Poland emerged during the late 19th century in Galicia, then part of the Austro-Hungarian Empire. Other unions were formed in German-controlled Poland but not in the Russian Partition, where unions were illegal before 1906. Organized labor and the Polish Socialist Party (formed in 1892) were closely linked. A national labor federation was created in 1918. Despite the difficult conditions for organizing and the heavily rural nature of the Polish economy, union growth was impressive. In 1920, there were 947,000 union members, who were mostly organized by industry groups. Political pressure by the Socialist Party gained exclusive rights for unions in **collective bargaining** in the 1920s, but the economic difficulties of the period reduced union membership from its peak of one million in 1921 to 539,100 by

1924. In 1926, the government forced employees of government-owned enterprises to belong to a government-sponsored union. Nevertheless, union **membership** reached 979,000 by 1930 and, despite the Depression, there were still claimed to be 738,900 members in 1933. This growth was to some extent a reflection of the increase in **manufacturing** employment, which nearly doubled from 1.3 to 2.5 million between 1921 and 1931. With the imposition of **communist** rule in 1948, an independent labor movement ceased to exist in Poland, although the trend towards an industrialized economy continued. Between 1950 and 1969, the number employed in manufacturing rose from 2.8 to 4 million.

In the 1970s, the first sustained popular challenge to the communist-dominated labor movement and society in Eastern Europe occurred in Poland. From December 1970 to January 1971, there was a wave of **labor disputes** in the Baltic cities that resulted in 44 deaths. Poland's continued economic problems—particularly its high inflation and large overseas debts—depressed living standards and maintained discontent. In September 1976, the Workers' Defense Committee (*Komitet Obrony Robotnikow* or KOR) was set up to help those who had lost their jobs in labor disputes. In May 1976, a committee of free labor unions was formed in the Baltic cities. The visit to Poland of the newly elected first Polish pope, John Paul II, in June 1979, provided a focus for economic grievances as well as nationalist, political, and religious feelings. A round of government-decreed price rises in the 1980s led to rolling **strikes** at the Lenin shipyard in Gdansk (the former German city of Danzig), which was the catalyst for the government conceding on August 31, 1980, the right not only to form independent labor unions but also to strike and broadcast religious programs, as well as the right to more civil liberties. It was from these origins that "Solidarity"— *"Solidarnosc" Niezalezny Samorzadny Zwaiazek Zawodowy* or Independent, Self-Governing Trade Union Solidarity NSZZ—was formed on September 22, 1980, with an unemployed former electrician, Lech Walesa, as its chairman. By December 1980, 40 independent labor unions had been formed and there was a growing movement to create a rural version of Solidarity. On January 1, 1981, the communist labor federation was disbanded, but these gains proved short-lived. The pace of change raised the threat of Russian intervention, a threat that had hung over Poland since the first Partition in 1772.

The government declared martial law in December 1981. In October 1982, Solidarity was driven underground by labor laws that dissolved all labor unions. It survived, but its membership fell from 10 to 1.3 million by 1995. There was much debate about Solidarity's goals, and a splinter organization, Solidarity 80, was formed.

In 1987, Solidarity was admitted to membership of the **International Confederation of Free Trade Unions** (ICFTU), the first labor organization to be admitted to the ICFTU from Eastern Europe that was not an organization in exile. In November 1984, the former communist labor federation reformed itself as the *Ogolnópolskie Porozumienie Zwiazków Zawodowych* (OPZZ) or All-Poland Alliance of Labor Unions, a nonauthoritarian body that recognized the independence of labor unions. The OPZZ derived its strength from its control of the assets of Solidarity, which enabled it to offer members benefits such as the use of holiday homes. In 1992, the OPZZ had 3 million members and another 1.5 million members who were **retired employees**.

Despite these national divisions, organized labor in Poland cooperates closely through joint councils at the enterprise level, which has enabled it to conduct many labor disputes since the end of communist rule in early 1990 and to obtain the election of Walesa as the new republic's first president. Since 1990, Solidarity has struggled with the consequences of Poland's conversion from a state-run to a capitalist economy and from a communist to a democratic society. Both Solidarity and the OPZZ are highly politicized organizations, and from 1992 both bodies have been represented along with representatives from government and **employers' organizations** on a tripartite commission that monitors the economy. In 2001, Solidarity declared a membership of 1.1 million to the ICFTU. In 2002, the ICFTU reported that changes to the labor code reduced the rights of Polish organized labor.

POLICE UNIONISM. Although the police usually appear as the historical enemies of labor unions, they have formed their own unions and have sometimes engaged in **labor disputes**. The inflation of World War I and the failure of police pay to be increased accordingly was the background to police strikes in a number of countries. In the **United Kingdom,** a Police Union was formed in 1918; it engaged in strikes in 1918 and 1919, incidents that led to the legal suppression of police unionism. Legislation in 1964 and 1972 allowed the formation of Police Federations but forbade their affiliation with the **Trades Union Congress** (TUC), a ban that has continued to the present. Police unions were formed in the states of **Australia** between 1915 and 1921 and a police strike was held in Melbourne in 1923. Unlike the United Kingdom, however, police unions have been able to affiliate with the national peak labor organization; the Police Federation of Australia was an affiliate of the **Australian Council of Trade Unions** (ACTU) in 2002.

Police unions were also formed in the **United States** in the 1910s. A police strike took place in Boston (1919). The Boston **strike** was the result of the suspension of some of the police, who had joined a new union sponsored by the **American Federation of Labor** (AFL). The governor of Massachusetts, Calvin Coolidge, strongly opposed the strike, thereby gaining a greatly enhanced standing with the public that assisted his election as president. Since the 1920s, other police labor disputes have occurred, such as the dispute in New York City in January 1971. During the 1970s, 245 illegal police strikes occurred in the **United States**. In February 1979, the International Union of Police Associations (formed in 1954) became the first independent law enforcement union to hold an **American Federation of Labor-Congress of Industrial Organizations** (AFL-CIO) charter, based partly on a successful police strike in Memphis, Tennessee. By 1997, this U.S. union had more than 80,000 members. Police unionism has also emerged in **Nigeria**.

POLITICAL ACTION COMMITTEES (PAC). PACs were set up by organized labor in the **United States** in the 1940s to circumvent federal legal restrictions on the amount of money organizations, businesses, or individuals could contribute to election campaigns. Since the 1940s, other organizations have set up their own PACs. The importance of PACs was increased by 1971 federal legislation. In 2000, there were 316 PACs run by organized labor, which contributed a total of $51.6 million to candidates. Of the $7.5 million contributed by labor PACs to congressional campaigns in 2000, $7 million went to Democrats and $0.5 million to Republicans. *See also* POLITICS.

POLITICS. By their very nature, labor unions are political institutions, offering a permanent challenge to the economic, political, and social order. In the last half of the 19th century, organized labor in the **United Kingdom** lobbied the Liberal Party to achieve its objectives, particularly legal protection. As labor unions banded together to form national and industry federations, they either worked with the established political order, or where they could not, formed their own political parties, as in **Australia, Austria, Finland, New Zealand, Norway, Sweden,** and the **United Kingdom**. The United **States** and **Canada** were unusual among Western nations in their lack of significant political parties based on organized labor, although the **National Labor Union** (NLU) was an exception.

Tensions could, and did, arise between organized labor and their political parties. For example, in 1906, organized labor in **France** and **Germany** declared its independence from control by political parties. In Third World countries, organized labor almost always played an active role in independence movements. Since 1945, organized labor has supported the efforts of social democratic parties in the Western nations to create welfare states to enhance **social security** and has been an active participant in **union-government agreements**. In both the United Kingdom and Australia, the respective parliamentary labor parties have sought to reduce the influence of organized labor within their parties in response to the decline of union **membership** during the 1990s. *See also* POLITICAL ACTION COMMITTEES; SOCIAL DEMOCRATIC, SOCIALIST, AND LABOR PARTIES.

PORTUGAL. Unions and leftwing political groups developed in parallel in Portugal after 1870, a response to Portugal's poverty and its political conservatism. A Socialist Party was set up in 1875 and **syndicalism** attracted much support. There was considerable labor unrest from the 1880s to the revolution of 1910, which caused the fall of the monarchy and the creation of a republic. By 1913, there were claimed to be 90,000 union members, and a national labor federation, named the *Confederaçao Geral de Trabalho* (General Confederation of Labor) from 1913, was created. The next 15 years were chaotic, with **general strikes** being declared in 1919, 1920, and 1921. **Collective bargaining** was legalized in 1924. In 1926, a fascist military-backed dictator, Antonio de Oliveira Salazar, took power and dissolved the *Confederaçao Geral de Trabalho*. Using the examples of fascist Italy and the Nazi *Deutsche Arbeitsfront*, Salazar established a corporate network of government-controlled unions that required compulsory **membership** in 1933. A general strike called by the left wing of organized labor in 1934 only led to more repression. An independent labor movement did not begin to emerge once more until 1970, when the present *Confederaço Geral dos Trabalhadores Portugueses-Intersindical Nacional* (General Confederation of Portuguese Workers-National Labor Unions) was formed illegally. After the revolution in 1974, conditions for organized labor began to improve. The right to **strike** was conditionally granted in 1974 and the right was extended in 1977. A rival **socialist** labor federation, the *União Geral de Trabalhadores* (UGT) (General Workers' Union), was formed in 1978 and was admitted to membership of the **International Confederation of Free Trade Unions** (ICFTU) in 1987 with 983,700 members; it has remained Portugal's representative in the ICFTU. In December 1996, the UGT, the government, and representatives of the **employers' organizations** signed a social pact aimed at creating employment and improving training in return for cooperation on improving economic performance. In 2001, the UGT had 251,000 members.

POSTAL, TELEGRAPH, AND TELEPHONE INTERNATIONAL (PTTI). The PTTI was founded in Milan, Italy, in 1920, although the first international conference of postal, telegraph, and telephone employees had been held in Paris in 1911. As with other **international trade secretariats**, the PTTI was a European body up to 1950, after which time it began to expand globally. Membership of the Geneva-based PTTI was 3.2 million in 1975 and four million in 1994. In August 1997, the PTTI renamed itself **Communication International**. *See also* COMMUNICATION WORKERS' UNION OF AMERICA.

PRINTING. Printing has an important place in the history of organized labor up to the 1970s. Printing was an unusual trade in that it demanded not just superior technical skills but also a high level of literacy. It was this combination that often placed printers at the forefront of employees both in terms of power at the workplace and as leaders within organized labor. Printing was also a leading industry in technological change, a fact that created problems as well as opportunities for its employees. **Labor disputes** in printing occurred as early as the 16th century in **Italy, France,** and **Switzerland.**

Printers were among the first to form formal unions in many countries, although they had been informally organized long before; for instance, in 1829, printers conducted one of **Australia's** first **strikes**. In **Germany**, printers formed the first national labor union, the *Nationaler Buchdrucker-Verein* (National Printers' Association), in 1848. The printing industry was often a pacesetter for other industries. The first collective agreement made in France in 1843 set wage rates for printers. The first international labor organization among printers was formed in 1889.

Philadelphia printers carried out the first strike of employees in a single trade in the **United States** in 1786, and a short-lived union existed among New York printers in the late 1770s. In 1804, the New York printers formed a union that lasted until 1815. Ely Moore, the first president of the National Trades' Union, the first U.S. labor federation in 1834, was a printer. In 1852, the National Typographical Association was formed which, after the affiliation of printing unions in **Canada**, renamed itself the International Typographical Union (ITU) in 1869. As a strong **craft union**, the ITU played an influential role in the creation of the Federation of Organized Trades and Labor Unions of the United States and Canada in 1881 and the **American Federation of Labor** in 1886.

Hierarchical occupational divisions were an important feature of the organization of printing work, with compositors being the highest group; their dominance of the ITU led to the creation of separate unions by other printing employees such as stereotypers and electroplaters, photoengravers, bookbinders, and journalists in the last decades of the 19th century. Ethnicity also played a role in the history of the ITU. In 1873, printers employed by the German-language press formed their own union, the German-American *Typographia*, but in 1894 this body merged with the ITU. In 1906, the ITU conducted a successful campaign in book and job-printing firms for the eight-hour work day, laying the foundation for its adoption elsewhere in the printing industry. In 1911, the ITU and other unions formed a printing industry body, the International Allied Printing Trades Association.

Until the 1960s, the printing industry unions throughout the world enjoyed considerable power but, with the coming of new technology, that power waned as many of the older mechanical skills were replaced by electronic machines and, more recently, by computers. Symptomatic of the decline of their power was the defeat of London printing unions over the introduction of new technology at Rupert Murdoch's Wapping plant in London in 1986. *See also* INTERNATIONAL GRAPHICAL ASSOCIATION.

PRIVATIZATION. Privatization refers to the sale or partial sale of a government-owned enterprise or agency, either to a private sector company or through the sale of shares offered to the general public. Privatization was adopted by the Conservative governments in the **United Kingdom** starting in 1979 as a means of improving the efficiency and productivity of the economy. It was based on the ideas of two economists, Friedrich von Hayek and Milton Friedman.

The economic effects of privatization have been much debated, but privatized concerns can achieve higher productivity at least in the short term if they are able to significantly reduce the number of employees. Generally, organized labor has opposed privatization because of the job losses it usually brings. From the early 1980s, a number of Western countries have used privatization to varying degrees as a means of improving their economic performance (for example, **Australia** and **New Zealand**).

Since the late 1980s the former communist countries of Eastern Europe have used privatization as part of the transition from planned to market economies. In Asia, privatization has been used both in noncommunist countries (for example, **Indonesia** and **Thailand**) and communist countries such as **Vietnam** and **China**. Privatization has produced major **labor disputes** in countries as different as China (October 1997), **India** (April 2002), and **South Africa** (October 2002). *See also* PUBLIC SECTOR.

PUBLIC SECTOR. In most Western countries one of the most significant trends in the structure of union membership over recent decades has been the large increase in the proportion of union members employed by the public sector (that is, by government or government agencies) compared to the private sector. Precise measurement of this trend is difficult because the statistics have not always been collected in a convenient form or because frequent changes of national policy (such as over the nationalization of industries in the **United Kingdom** since 1945) drain the meaning from longer term comparisons even if the data are available.

Nevertheless, the distribution of labor union **membership** for the United Kingdom (taking the public sector to be a combination of union membership employed by national government, local government and education, gas, electricity, water, postal, and telecommunications) suggests that 10 percent of union members were employed by the public sector by 1920, 20 percent by 1940, and 22 percent by 1960. In 1960, only 6 percent of union members in the **United States** were public sector employees. The growth of government employment after 1960 and structural changes in the private sector in the 1970s and 1980s (specifically the decline in large-scale **manufacturing** employment and the growth of the **service sector**) combined to raise the proportion of union members employed by the public sector to a historic high. In the United States the proportion of union members employed by the public sector rose from 11 percent in 1970 to 32 percent in 1983, and to 44 percent by 2001.

In 2001, the level of union membership among employees in the public sector remained far higher than in the private sector: 48 percent in Australia, 59 percent in the United Kingdom, and 37 in the United States. *See also* PRIVATIZATION; PUBLIC SERVICES INTERNATIONAL; WHITE-COLLAR UNIONISM; WOMEN.

PUBLIC SERVICES INTERNATIONAL (PSI). The PSI is one of the largest **international trade secretariats** in the world. It was formed in 1935 with the merger of the International Federation of Workers in Public Administration and Utilities (IFWPAU) and the Civil Servants' International. The IFWPAU was founded by representatives of local government unions from **Denmark, Germany, Hungary**, the **Netherlands, Sweden**, and **Switzerland** in 1907 at the suggestion of the Dutch. The Civil Servants' Association was created in 1925 in the Netherlands and represented employees of central governments. The activities of the PSI were severely restricted first by the disaffiliation of the British civil servants in 1927 (which was forced by legislation passed after the **General Strike** in 1926) and then by the suppression of organized labor by the Nazis in Germany in 1933. After World War II the PSI was re-established in London and its membership broadened to take in countries outside Europe. In 1957, persistent lobbying of the **International Labour Organisation** (ILO) by the PSI resulted in the formation of a committee for public services, although it was not until the early 1970s that the **public sector** was given greater attention by the ILO. Between 1976 and 1994, the **membership** of the PSI rose from 4.8 to 16 million. In 2001, the PSI claimed to represent 20 million members in 560 union affiliates in 140 countries. *See also* WHITE-COLLAR UNIONISM.

PUERTO RICO. An autonomous commonwealth of the **United States** since 1952, organized labor in Puerto Rico emerged after 1872 but was outlawed by the Spanish administration in 1888. From 1898 to 1952 Puerto Rico was under U.S. administration and the first unions date from 1898. Links with the **American Federation of Labor** (AFL) began in 1900. Organized labor effectively opted out of **collective bargaining** and sought a political role. In 1934, there was a large-scale sugar workers' **strike**. In March 1940 a new labor federation was formed. By 1951 Puerto Rico had joined the **International Confederation of Free Trade Unions** (ICFTU) and has remained a member. Between the 1960s and the mid-1970s, the proportion of union membership in Puerto Rico who belonged to U.S. unions fell from about 75 to 43 percent. In 1957, two labor federations merged to form the *Federación del Trabajo de Puerto Rico* (AFL-CIO) or Federation of the Workers of Puerto Rico (AFL-CIO), which was the country's ICFTU affiliate in 2001, with a claimed membership of 30,000.

-Q-

QATAR. There is no organized labor in Qatar and **collective bargaining** is illegal. About 75 percent of the labor force is expatriate. Joint consultative committees of management and workers' representatives are possible under the law, but they do not discuss wages. In theory, **labor disputes** are possible once they have been reported to a **conciliation** board, but in practice they do not occur. In 2002, the **International Confederation of Free Trade Unions** (ICFTU) noted that labor unions continued to be banned.

-R-

RACE AND ETHNICITY. Racial divisions have been both a unifier and divider in the history of organized labor. There were many instances of the use of different ethnic groups to break **strikes** in the 19th century. In the **United Kingdom**, Welsh, Irish, and Cornish miners were brought in by employers to break strikes. In the **United States**, immigrants were used as strikebreakers in the steel industry. In the 1870s and 1880s, violent anti-Chinese feelings, particularly in the mining industry, helped to promote labor unions in the western United States and southeastern **Australia**. In the United States, one of the objectives of the **National Labor Union** (NLU), a labor organization that operated between 1866 and 1876, was the restriction of Chinese **immigration**. It was the refusal of the NLU to accept racial integration that led to the operation of the Colored National Labor Union between 1869 and 1871. In the United States, and later in **South Africa**, organized labor tended to be the preserve of European males, although cooperation could occur, as was shown by the successful biracial strike of 1893 in New Orleans. The **Knights of Labor** were unusual in the mid-1880s in their practice of racial integration.

Attempts at racial integration in the United States for much of the 20th century floundered on the racism of many labor unions. In 1924, the Central Trades and Labor Council of Greater New York supported the creation of the Trade Union Committee for Organizing Negro Workers, but this body was defunct by 1927. In 1935, the Negro Labor Committee was formed in New York State and organized a march on Washington in 1941, which led to the setting up of the Fair Employment Practices Commission in 1943, which was designed to eliminate discrimination in employment in war industries or government on the grounds of "race, creed, color, or national origin." In 1960, A. Philip Randolph and other black leaders set up the Negro American Labor Council (NALC) to fight racial discrimination in unions affiliated with the **American Federation of Labor-Congress of Industrial Organizations** (AFL-CIO); the council operated throughout the 1960s and its relations with the AFL-CIO were often difficult. In the late 1960s, more radical black union groups came into being that challenged the leadership of the NALC within organized labor.

At its inaugural conference in November 1949, the **International Confederation of Free Trade Unions** (ICFTU) declared its intention to work together to "eliminate throughout the world every kind of discrimination or domination based upon race, creed, color, or sex." However, in practice it was not until the 1960s that the ICFTU was able to devote serious attention to the racial aspect of this resolution, mainly with respect to **South Africa**. It actively participated in the events of 1997, the European Year against Racism. Since the 1980s, organized labor has made more efforts to combat racism in its own ranks and in the labor force generally. In 1981, the British **Trades Union Congress** (TUC) released a major policy statement, *Black Workers: A TUC Charter for Equal Opportunity*. In 1996, *IG Metall* published a handbook concerning racial discrimination at the workplace.

In the United States, 15 percent of American labor union members were Afro-Americans in 2002, compared to 14 percent in 1983. The percentage of Hispanics among union members rose from 6 percent in 1983 to nearly 10 percent in 2001. African-Americans were more likely to be union members than white or Hispanic Americans; in 2002, 17 percent of African-American employees were union members, compared to 13 percent of white and 11 percent of Hispanic employees.

In the United Kingdom, an official household survey of labor union members also found that there was a significant lessening of variations in the proportions of employees by race who were union members; in 2001, 29 percent of white employees were union members, compared to 30 percent for blacks and 25 percent for Asians.

RAILROADS. The railroads were among the main battle grounds of organized labor between 1870 and 1920. Railway employment was characterized by long hours, dangerous working conditions, and management devices to control employees such as company towns (for instance, Pullman in Illinois and Crewe in England). Management attitudes and organization were based on the army. Occupations were divided horizontally as well as vertically. Despite these drawbacks, the railroads were attractive because they usually offered relatively secure employment and the prospect of promotion with experience and length of service. Under these conditions, unions were slow to emerge although a friendly society was set up by English locomotive engine drivers and firemen as early as 1839 and may have had some features of a labor union; locomotive enginemen are known to have formed unions in 1848 and 1860.

In 1865, an attempt to form a provident society by the guards of the Great Western Railway Company was crushed by the sacking of its leaders. In 1866, locomotive engine drivers and firemen formed a union that demanded the 10-hour work day. The other unions present within the railroad industry before 1870 were those of tradesmen working in the repair workshops. In 1871, the Amalgamated Society of Railway Servants of England, Ireland, Scotland, and Wales was formed and became the largest railroad union in

Britain; this union was the subject of the **Taff Vale Case** in 1901, which cast doubt on the legal status of labor unions. It amalgamated with two other unions in 1913 to become a genuine **industrial union** and changed its name to the National Union of Railwaymen. In the **United States**, the Brotherhood of Locomotive Firemen and Enginemen was formed in New York in 1873 with the original aim of providing sickness and funeral benefits for members but soon became a labor union. In 1883, the formation of the Brotherhood of Railroad Trainmen represented the first attempt to create an industrial union in the railroad industry.

In **Australia**, a locomotive engine drivers' union was formed in Victoria in 1870, and general railway unions, based on the Amalgamated Society of Railway Servants of England, Ireland, Scotland, and Wales, were formed in the various colonies between 1884 and 1899, and in **New Zealand** in 1886.

The railroad industry was the focus of some major **labor disputes** between management and employees. In the United States, there were three national clashes before 1900: 1877, the Burlington railroad strike of 1888-1889, and the Pullman strike and boycott of 1894. There was a national railroad strike in **France** in 1898. The first national railroad strike in Britain was in 1911 and lasted two days; it was followed by another one in 1919. One of Australia's largest strikes, from August to September 1917, was centered on the railroads.

REAGAN, RONALD (1911-). Reagan was the first U.S. president to have also been an executive officer in a national labor union; between 1959 and 1960 he was president of the Screen Actors' Guild (formed in 1933). Despite this background, his presidency (1981-1989) was hostile to organized labor, as shown by his crushing of the strike by the Professional Air Traffic Controllers' Organization (PATCO) in August 1981 by firing over 11,000 strikers and replacing them with military controllers and civilian controllers who returned to work.

RENGO. *Rengo,* an abbreviation for *Nihon Rodokumiai Sorengokai* (Japanese Trade Union Confederation), is the largest labor union federation in **Japan**. It is the product of a series of **amalgamations** with other labor federations. The largest part of *Rengo* began as *Sodomei* (Japanese Federation of Trade Unions) in 1946, which became *Domei* (Japanese Confederation of Labor) in 1964, by which time it had 2.1 million members. In 1987, *Domei* joined with *Sorengo* (National Federation of Trade Unions of Japan; formed in 1979) and *Shinsanbetsu* (National Federation of Industrial Organizations; formed in 1952) to form *Zenmin Roren* (Japanese Private Sector Trade Union Federation, now referred to as old *Rengo*). The second part of *Rengo* was the **public sector** labor federation *Sohyo* (General Council of Trade Unions of Japan), which was formed in 1950 when the noncommunist unions split from the **communist**-dominated *Sanbetsu-Kaigi* (Congress of Industrial Unions of Japan), which had been formed in 1946. Left-leaning and militant, *Sohyo* was largely responsible for beginning the **Shunto** or Spring Offensive for wage increases in 1956. In November 1989, *Zenmin Roren* and *Sohyo* merged to form *Rengo*. In 2001, *Rengo* represented 7.5 million union members or 65 percent of all Japan's labor union members.

RETIRED EMPLOYEES. Retired employees who were formerly labor union members are a neglected group in analysis or discussions of organized labor but have assumed greater importance since the 1970s with the layoff of older workers in **manufacturing** and the ageing of the labor force in most Western economies. In **Germany**, the **United Kingdom**, and the **United States**, union members often retain their membership after retirement. In 1986, it was estimated that retired employees on pensions made up less than 10 percent of union members in Germany and the United Kingdom, but about 18 percent in **Norway**.

Italy is one of the few countries in the world where organized labor has set up strong organizations of retired employees as autonomous associations within the main labor federations. Between 1951 and 1973, the number of pensioner union members was stable at about 600,000, but thereafter has grown steadily, to 1.7 million by 1980 and to 5.1 million by 1996. Between 1970 and 2001, the proportion of total union members in Italy who were retired employees rose from about 8 to 18 percent.

In 2002, the **United Auto Workers' Union** (UAW) had 710,000 active members and over 500,000 retired members in the United States and **Canada**. In addition to its 1.4 million employed members in 2001, the U.S. **Service Employees International Union** (SEIU) had 120,000 members who were retired. Retired members of the SEIU assist in the election of politicians favorable to organized labor.

In the late 1990s, concern over maintaining pensions became an area of interest for European organized labor. By 2002, the European Federation of Retired and Elderly Persons operated under the auspices of the **European Trade Union Confederation** (ETUC). National statistics on the numbers of retired employees who retain their **membership** of labor unions are generally not available. In **Australia**, the United Kingdom, and the United States, the labor force surveys of households that are used to generate statistics on labor union membership all exclude retired employees.

RÉUNION. A territory of **France**, organized labor on Réunion had emerged by the 1970s and conducted **general strikes** over inflation in May 1973 and February 1974. In 2000 Réunion was admitted to membership of the **International Confederation of Free Trade Unions** (ICFTU) with 15,100 members.

REUTHER, WALTER PHILIP (1907-1970). Reuther was one of the chief labor leaders in the **United States** in the post-1945 period through his presidency of the **United Auto Workers** (UAW), which he held from 1946 until his death. Born in Wheeling, West Virginia, he completed three years of secondary education before entering a tool and die maker **apprenticeship** with the Wheeling Steel Corporation. Fired for union activities by the corporation, he moved to Detroit in 1926. In 1931, he was fired by Ford, again for union activities. Unemployed, he took a world tour during 1933 to 1935 that included Europe, the Soviet Union, **China**, and **Japan**. On his return, he became an organizer and then an official of the UAW in Detroit. He was elected to the executive board of the UAW in 1936 and was one of the leaders of the UAW's campaign of sit-down **strikes** during 1937 against General Motors and Chrysler. The UAW's campaign for recognition against Ford was met with violence in which Reuther and Richard Frankensteen were beaten up by Ford's private **police**, an infamous incident dubbed the **"battle of the overpass."** During World War II, Reuther served on a number of federal government boards.

In 1946, his moderate faction won control of the UAW and Reuther became its president. The UAW's strike campaign for better pay and conditions in the motor industry culminated in a contract with General Motors in 1948, which included pay increases based on the official cost of living index. In the same year, Reuther was wounded by a shotgun in an attempted assassination. He became president of the **Congress of Industrial Organizations** (CIO) in 1952 and supported its merger with the **American Federation of Labor** (AFL) in 1955. He served as a vice president but led the UAW out of the AFL-CIO in 1968 following disagreements with its conservative president, **George Meany**. Before his death in a plane crash, Reuther's last major activity was his leadership of the Alliance for Labor Action.

RIGHT-TO-WORK LAWS. Under the federal **Taft-Hartley Act** of 1947, U.S. states were given the right to ban the union (or closed) shop within their borders. Under most union shop agreements, new employees typically had 30 days in which to join the union. Right-to-work laws make it possible for employees in unionized workplaces to remain nonunionists and have the general effect of inhibiting union **membership** growth. By 1999, 21 U.S. states had such laws; they included all of the South and most of the Midwest of the **United States**.

ROMANIA. Organized labor first emerged in what is now Romania among printers who formed mutual benefit societies, beginning at Brasov in 1846. During the 1860s, other employees formed associations, which were much influenced by **socialism**. In 1872, a general union was formed that was open to all employees without regard to occupation, sex, or religion. In 1893, the Romanian Social Democratic Party was formed and a national labor federation was set up in 1906. The unions supported the peasant uprisings in 1907. The labor federation was an affiliate of the **International Federation of Trade Unions** (IFTU) from 1909 to 1918 and from 1923 to 1938.

Between 1914 and 1920 union **membership** rose from 40,000 to 300,000, divided among 350 unions. In 1921, the Communist Party was constituted from the former Socialist Party and competed for the leadership of organized labor. Both parties sponsored their own labor federations. After a short period of cooperation, the Communist Party broke away from the united labor federation and was banned by the government in 1923; in 1929, its labor federation was banned too. There were many **labor disputes** in Romania in the late 1920s and early 1930s, a reflection of not just the deterioration in economic conditions but also the rise in **manufacturing** employment from 318,000 in 1913 to 953,000 in 1930. In 1936, a new labor federation was formed, with 310 individual unions representing 80,000 members, but when the fascist government came to power two years later, unions and **strikes** were outlawed. During World War II, the Romanian government was an ally of the Nazis until its overthrow in 1944. With the establishment of a communist republic in 1947, organized labor became part of the machinery of government.

An attempted formation of an independent union was made in 1979 but was harshly suppressed. A second clandestine effort was made in 1988 but was suppressed also. Communist rule in Romania was ended by a violent popular uprising between December 1989 and January 1990. In December 1989, *Fratia* ("Fraternity"), a broadly based independent labor union, was formed. The former communist labor federation (UGSR) was dissolved early in 1990 and replaced by what became the *Confederatia Nationala a Sindicatelator Libere din România* (CNSLR) or National Free Trade Union Confederation of Romania. A third independent labor body, *Alfa-Cartel*, was formed by 1991. In the same year, the government legalized the formation of independent labor unions.

As in **Bulgaria** and **Poland**, there have been conflicts between the independent labor organizations over the control of the assets of the former communist labor federations, but in Romania these have been minimized by a high degree of cooperation. In 1993, the CNSLR and *Fratia* joined forces to become the Romanian member of the **International Confederation of Free Trade Unions** (ICFTU), with a claimed membership of 3.2 million, which represented 39 percent of employees. In 2001, the two Romanian affiliates of the ICFTU claimed a total membership of 400,000. The ICFTU described the general legal framework of trade union rights in Romania in 2002 as "fairly well protected" but noted abuses, mainly from foreign firms.

ROOKES V. BARNARD. Rookes v. Barnard was an important legal case concerning the operation of labor unions in the **United Kingdom**. In 1955, Douglas Rookes, an employee of the British Overseas Airways Corporation, resigned from his union, the Association of Engineering and Shipbuilding Draftsmen. The union, wanting to maintain a closed shop, instigated his dismissal. Rookes sued the union and was awarded substantial damages; the association appealed to the House of Lords, but it upheld the original decision in 1964. The case, which reflected poorly on the attitude of a union towards an individual, opened up a loophole in the Trades Disputes

Act (1906) by making union officials liable for damages for threatening to **strike** in breach of contracts of employment. This loophole was closed by the Trades Disputes Act (1965). The legal issue raised by *Rookes v. Barnard* was one of the forces behind the appointment of the **Donovan Commission**.

RUSSIA. Before March 1906, unions were illegal throughout the Russian Empire. Their brief legalization produced a surge of **membership** growth to 123,000 by 1907 in the wake of the 1905 Revolution, but this development was wrecked by a government crackdown. There was some revival by organized labor between 1911 and 1914, but it was able to achieve little beyond conducting protest strikes. The revolutionary period between mid-1917 and 1920 saw an explosion of union membership from 1.5 to 5.2 million. The main division in the Russian labor movement was between those who supported the autonomy of organized labor from the political arm of labor (led by the Mensheviks) and the Bolsheviks, who held that the function of the unions was to help overthrow the government and transfer power to industrial wage earners, the proletariat. During 1919 and 1920, the Bolsheviks achieved control of the Russian labor movement. At first, the unions played an important role in the program of economic reconstruction known as the New Economic Plan, but from 1922 under Lenin, and then Stalin, the unions operated as agents of centralized **communist** rule whose main role was to increase economic output.

In 1978, some dissidents tried to form an independent union for professional employees, but it was suppressed by the Soviet government and its leaders imprisoned. The first sign of a mass independent labor movement came in mid-1989 with a wave of **strikes** in northern Russia, the **Ukraine**, and the Urals, which gave rise to Workers' Committees and the formation of an independent miners' union, which joined an independent Confederation of Labor when it was set up in May 1990. In October 1990, the All-Union Central Council of Trade Unions, the central communist body formed in November 1924, transformed itself into the General Confederation of Unions of the USSR; it recognized the rights of the newly independent nations within the former Soviet Union and pledged itself to protect union rights.

After the creation of the Commonwealth of Independent States on December 8, 1991, the General Confederation of Unions again reshaped itself to become the Federation of Independent Trade Unions of Russia, made up of seven of the new states (excluding the Ukraine) in April 1992. The organizational continuity of these moves was important for maintaining control of the assets of the former communist labor organization, a vexed issue in most other East European countries. Aside from the emergence of the independent labor organizations in the former Soviet republics, the main independent Russian labor organization is *Sotsprof*, a federation of social democratic and **socialist** unions formed in about 1990.

An official crackdown on independent organized labor began in August 1992 when there was a strike by air traffic controllers. In the same year the Boris Yeltsin government began a program of economic reform marked by **privatization** of state-run enterprises. A **collective bargaining** law was introduced in 1993 but changed little in the way the labor code worked, with its many restrictions on the right to strike and the banning of strikes on railroads, public transport, civil aviation, communications, energy, and defense. In 1994, trade union efforts to monitor or influence privatization of enterprises to ensure the protection of workers' rights was met with official violence and intimidation.

From the early 1990s, the **International Confederation of Free Trade Unions** (ICFTU) was able to take a growing role in the well-being of Russian organized labor. Beginning with trade union education, the ICFTU campaigned for the payment of wage arrears due to Russian workers, which culminated in the All-Russian Trade Union Day of Action in April 1998. The ICFTU also secured the participation of the **International Labour Organisation** (ILO) in the Russian wages campaign. During the economic turmoil of 1998, the ICFTU organized meetings between the leaders of Russian organized labor and the International Monetary Fund and the World Bank. The ICFTU successfully promoted cooperation between Russia's three labor federations. An ICFTU mission to Russia reported favorably on the country's organized labor.

In November 2000, the ICFTU took the historic decision to admit as affiliates the Federation of Independent Trade Unions of Russia, the All-Russian Confederation of Labor (formed in 1995), and the Confederation of Labor of Russia (also formed in 1995). This was the first time that Russia had ever been represented in an international labor organization that was independent of government control. In 2001, these three federations had a combined membership of 30.5 million. In 2002, the ICFTU noted that although Russian workers had the right to form unions, **collective bargaining** for smaller unions was difficult in practice and that generally, the political environment for organized labor had worsened since 2001. It also considered that the labor code that came into force on February 1, 2003, weakened the rights of labor unions, particularly smaller ones.

RWANDA. Independent from **Belgium** since July 1962, the first labor unions were branches of Belgian unions. Since independence, the history of Rwanda has been one of political turmoil and massive ethnic violence, culminating in a genocidal civil war in 1994. In 1993, the *Centrale des Syndicats des Travailleurs du Rwanda* (Central Union of the Workers of Uganda) was admitted to the **International Confederation of Free Trade Unions** (ICFTU) with 70,000 members. In 2002, the ICFTU reported that labor unions in Rwanda operated in a climate of fear, government interference, antiunion employers, and lack of effective legal protection.

RYDER, GUY (1957-). General secretary of the **International Confederation of Free Trade Unions** (ICFTU) since January 2002, Ryder was born in Liverpool, England. He worked as an assistant in the international department of the **Trades Union Congress** (TUC) between 1981 and 1985 before serving as secretary of the industry trade section of the *Fédération internationale des employés, techniciens et cadres* (International Federation of Commercial, Clerical, Professional, and Technical Employees) in Geneva from 1985 to 1988. In 1988, he joined the staff of the ICFTU in Geneva and rose to be the director of its office there. He was also secretary of the Workers' Group of the Governing Body of the **International Labour Office** (ILO) in 1993 to 1998 and other positions with the ILO before becoming general secretary of the ICFTU. In 2002, he listed his priorities as ICFTU general secretary in an interview as responding better to the challenge of **globalization**, increasing the effectiveness of the ICFTU, creating greater opportunities for **women**, and boosting recruitment to combat the ageing of the **membership** of organized labor.

-S-

SAINT CHRISTOPHER AND NEVIS. Independent from the **United Kingdom** since September 1983, labor unions on St. Christopher and Nevis have been legally recognized since 1940. The islands have been represented in the **International Confederation of Free Trade Unions** (ICFTU) since 1951. In 2001, there were about 400 labor union members on St. Christopher and Nevis.

SAINT HELENA. A territory of the **United Kingdom**, the St. Helena General Workers' Union has been the sole labor union on the island since its formation in 1958; it had about 700 members in 2001 and has been represented in the **International Confederation of Free Trade Unions** (ICFTU) since 1965.

SAINT LUCIA. Independent from the **United Kingdom** since February 1979, organized labor developed after the establishment of **collective bargaining** arrangements in 1938. The St. Lucia Workers' Union was formed in 1939 and was followed by the St. Lucia Waterfront Worker's Trade Union in 1945. Both unions have been affiliates of the **International Confederation of Free Trade Unions** (ICFTU) since 1953; in 2001, they had about 2,200 members.

SAINT VINCENT AND THE GRENADINES. Independent from the **United Kingdom** since October 1979, organized labor on St. Vincent and the Grenadines emerged after World War II. By 1957, the United Workers, Peasants, and Ratepayers' Union had become affiliated with the **International Confederation of Free Trade Unions** (ICFTU) and the islands have continued their affiliation ever since. In 2001, their ICFTU affiliate was the Commercial, Technical, and Allied Workers' Union, with 1,600 members.

SAN MARINO. The oldest republic in the world (dating from 1600), San Marino has been represented in the **International Confederation of Free Trade Unions** (ICFTU) since 1959 by the *Confederazione Democratica Lavoratori Sammarinesi* (Democratic Confederation of San Marino Workers). Since 1996, it has been joined by a second affiliated union; together, they claimed 7,600 members in 2001.

SAUDI ARABIA. Organized labor first made its presence felt in Saudi Arabia in 1953 when 13,000 Saudi nationals successfully went on **strike** in the oil industry to demand equality of conditions with U.S. workers. The government was subsequently presented with petitions asking for permission to form labor unions. Some temporary concessions were made, but these were withdrawn by 1959. About half the labor force in the 1990s were expatriates. **Collective bargaining** and labor unions are forbidden. In 1994, the government advised the **International Confederation of Free Trade Unions** (ICFTU) that trade union rights were considered to violate the principles of Islam. Although in theory workers have access to labor courts, in practice it is virtually impossible for expatriate workers to legally enforce their rights. In April 2002, amendments to the labor law allowed for the establishment of workers' committees made up of Saudis and expatriates in firms employing 100 or more as a way of improving work performance.

SENEGAL. Independent from **France** since April 1960, organized labor began in Senegal in 1937 in the form of branches of French labor unions; by 1956, total **membership** had risen to 50,000. The *Confédération Nationale des Travailleurs du Sénégal* (National Confederation of Workers of Senegal) was formed in 1969 and in 1993 was admitted to membership of the **International Confederation of Free Trade Unions** (ICFTU) with a claimed membership of 60,000. Despite challenges, Senegal has managed to retain a pluralist political system since independence. The ICFTU reported that although the 2001 constitution recognized the right to **collective bargaining**, the right to **strike** was curtailed. Similarly, the labor code recognized the right to form labor unions, but these unions had to be approved by the Ministry of the Interior. In 2001, Senegal was represented by two union federations with a combined membership of 132,400 members. The ICFTU reported that the government continued to retain the right to grant or withhold approval to form a labor union and that the constitution adopted in January 2001 undermined the right to strike, but admitted that the right to collective bargaining was recognized. Conditions for organized labor in Senegal did not improve during 2002.

SERBIA AND MONTENEGRO. *See* YUGOSLAVIA (FEDERAL REPUBLIC).

SERVICE EMPLOYEES INTERNATIONAL UNION (SEIU).
The SEIU is a leading U.S. labor union that recruits nurses, doctors, health technicians, workers in local government, state employees, security officers, janitors, and building service workers. It was formed in 1921 as the Building Service Employees International Union and was chartered by the **American Federation of Labor** (AFL). It adopted its present name in 1968. Between 1980 and 2001, the **membership** of the SEIU rose from 625,000 to 1.4 million, one of the few unions to successfully exploit the recruitment opportunities presented by the employment growth of the **service sector**; in addition, the SEIU has 120,000 members who are **retired employees**. In 2001, more than half its members were **women** and 20 percent were African-American. The SEIU claims to represent more immigrant workers than any other union in the **United States**. From the early 1980s to 1995, the president of the SEIU was **John Joseph Sweeney**. The SEIU operates a strong, grassroots political program.

SERVICE SECTOR. The service (or tertiary) sector is that part of the economy that provides consumer or producer goods (usually intangible) for immediate consumption, in contrast to the primary sector (**agriculture**, forestry, and fishing) and the secondary sector (**manufacturing**). Since World War II, the service sector has become the largest and fastest-growing sector in industrialized economies, both in terms of employment and value of economic output. In the **United States**, the proportion employed in the service sector rose from 51 percent in 1950 to 83 percent in 2001.

Within the service sector, the traditionally strong areas of labor union **membership** have been in the **railroads** (up to the 1920s), construction, and since World War II, **education** and communications. Outside of the **public sector**, the service sector, because of its diversity and part-time employment, has traditionally been a difficult recruiting area for organized labor. For example, in 2001 only 5 percent of employees in wholesale and retail trade in the United States were union members, compared to 24 percent of employees in transportation and public utilities.

SEYCHELLES. Independent from the **United Kingdom** since June 1976, organized labor in the Seychelles emerged in the 1960s. It has been represented in the **International Confederation of Free**

Trade Unions (ICFTU) since 1989 by its National Workers' Union, which was formed in 1978; it claimed 5,000 members in 2001.

SHORTER WORKING HOURS. From as early as the 16th century, unions have attempted to reduce **working hours**, or at least resist them being lengthened. There were two disputes in the **printing** industry in **France** in 1539 and 1572 over long working hours. In both the **United Kingdom** and the **United States**, there were moves by organized labor to gain a maximum working day of 10 hours in the 1830s. In the 1880s, there was an international movement by organized labor to reduce the work day to eight hours, but for most employees this was not achieved until the 20th century. Since 1945, metal workers' unions have generally been the vanguard for the reduction of working hours in the United Kingdom, **Germany**, **Italy**, and **Australia**. Since the 1980s, the target working week for organized labor has been the 35-hour week, but outside of France, which introduced the 35-hour working week in 2000 at the behest of organized labor, shorter working hours remain a desired not an attained goal in Western Europe. Indeed, in December 2002, the French parliament agreed to dilute the 35-hour week labor law. Further, statistics collected by the **International Labor Organisation** (ILO) indicate a worldwide rise in working hours since the early 1980s.

SHUNTO. Shunto is a Japanese term meaning "Spring Offensive" and refers to the national process of bargaining over wages, conditions of employment, and other issues between unions, employers, and the government. The *Shunto* was begun in **Japan** in February 1956 by *Sohyo* (General Council of Trade Unions of Japan) as a way of strengthening the power of the unions and of reducing earning differentials between enterprises and the thousands of unions based on them. As it has developed, the *Shunto* begins with an agreement by the unions about the amount of the pay increase they want and a corresponding decision by the **employers' organization** (*Nikkeiren*) about the size of the unions' demand that they are prepared to accept; the unions then formally present their demands. The *Shunto* next proceeds by industry groups in the private sector beginning with the iron and steel, shipbuilding, electrical equipment, and automobile industries. Later the *Shunto* moves on to industries such as textiles, petroleum, and food. Gains made in the larger enterprises are then applied to medium and smaller enterprises. The

Shunto reaches its climax in April. The outcome of increases gained by the *Shunto* in the private sector form the basis for the increase for government employees and employees in national enterprises. The *Shunto* has been responsible for gaining wage increases higher than the consumer price index. In 1975, the *Shunto* delivered a pay increase of 32.9 percent, but since 1976 these increases have been less than 10 percent; in 1995, the *Shunto* pay increase was 2.8 percent, its lowest level. Since 1995, the *Shunto* has declined in importance in response to the depressed state of the Japanese economy. *See also RENGO.*

SIERRA LEONE. Independent from the **United Kingdom** since April 1961, organized labor in Sierra Leone effectively dates from the 1920s, although the first attempts to form unions began in 1884. In 1942, there were 11 registered unions with a total **membership** of 800. In 1955, the unions conducted a **general strike.** The Sierra Leone Labour Congress came into being in 1976 from the merger of two labor federations formed in 1942 and 1958. It has been the country's affiliate with the **International Confederation of Free Trade Unions** (ICFTU) and claimed 20,200 members in 2001. Although there have been some tensions between organized labor and the government, conditions for organized labor have been relatively free. On May 8, 2000, a demonstration for peace by 2,000 union members resulted in the deaths of 19 and the wounding of 50 people by rebel insurgents; three bystanders were also killed. In 2002, Sierra Leone was one of only a few African countries not to be mentioned in the annual survey of **violations of trade union rights** conducted by the ICFTU.

SINGAPORE. Labor unions emerged in Singapore from 1946 and soon became part of the struggle against British rule. In the early 1950s Singapore's high level of **labor disputes** was a reflection of the political militancy of organized labor. In 1955, **strikes** were forbidden in essential services. The National Trade Union Congress was officially registered in 1964 but had its origins in a body formed in the 1950s, the Singapore Trade Union Congress. Between 1946 and 1962, the number of labor union members in Singapore grew from 18,700 to 189,000. In 1953, Singapore was admitted to membership of the **International Confederation of Free Trade Unions** (ICFTU). In 1965, Singapore left the Federation of Malayasia and has been sovereign since that time. With the defeat of political leftists in the early 1960s, organized labor in Singapore was increasingly brought under government control. Despite its lack of freedom, the National Trade Union Congress claimed 225,000 members, which represented about 14 percent of employees in 2001. In 2002, the ICFTU called for the Singapore government to update its labor legislation. *See also* MALAYSIA.

SLAVERY. The most extreme form of **forced labor**, slavery is often assumed to be a feature of the past, an institution that died out in the 19th century, but there is much evidence of a resurgence of slavery since the 1980s. In 1994, the Committee against Modern Slavery was established in Paris and between 1997 and 1998 investigated 135 cases, mainly involving Third World immigrant workers in Western Europe. Slavery reemerged in southwest Sudan in 1989 as part of the civil war waged by the Islamic fundamentalist regime in northern Sudan. There have also been incidents of trafficking in children as slaves in West and Central Africa from 1995 to 2001. In 1999, the **International Labour Organisation** (ILO) adopted the Worst Forms of Child Labour Convention (No. 182) in an effort to combat the practice. In 2000, Anti-Slavery International, a nongovernmental organization based in London, estimated that there were about 27 million people who were slaves—that is, they were forced to work through the threat of violence or punishment—in the world. *See also* CHILD LABOR; *SYNDICATS SANS FRONTIÈRES.*

SLOVAKIA. Formed from the eastern part of **Czechoslovakia** on January 1, 1993, Slovakia was represented in the **International Confederation of Free Trade Unions** (ICFTU) by the Confederation of Trade Unions of the Slovak Republic from 1993; it claimed 702,000 members in 2001. The ICFTU reported in 2001 that there had been a significant improvement in trade union rights in Slovakia, specifically removing the requirement that lists of names of striking workers be provided to the employer. A labor code was introduced in April 2002 that provided for **collective bargaining**, but no protection for labor unions that go on strike if a part of a collective bargain has not been honored by the employer.

SLOVENIA. Independent from the former **Yugoslavia** since 1991, Slovenia has enjoyed political stability and has made considerable strides from a state-run to a capitalist economy. A centralized system of **collective bargaining** has been in place since 1989. In 1993, independent labor unions were legalized and a codetermination system based on *Mitbestimmung* in **Germany** was introduced to enable unions to influence **privatization**. In 1994, organized labor was a participant in a **union-government agreement** on incomes policy. By 1994, there were four main labor federations, of which the largest was the reformed ex-communist organization. Although not a member of the **International Confederation of Free Trade Unions** (ICFTU), Slovenia had about 385,000 union members in 1998 or about 43 percent of the labor force.

SOCIAL-DEMOCRATIC, SOCIALIST, AND LABOR PAR-TIES. Social-democratic, socialist, and labor political parties grew out of the recognition that labor unions alone were not sufficient to improve the economic and social condition of working-class people. Usually composed of diverse groups and opinions, these parties developed their own characteristics depending upon their country of origin, but they were united by their vision of themselves as the political arm of the working class. Despite the formation of socialist groups in the 1880s, such as the Social Democratic Federation, the Socialist League, and the Fabians, it was the relative success of the political alliance of labor unions with the Liberal Party in the **United Kingdom** that delayed the formation of an independent political party based on unions. It was not until 1893 that the Independent Labour Party was formed; it cooperated with the **Trades Union Congress** (TUC) to form the Labour Representation Committee in 1900; it was renamed the British **Labour Party** in 1906. In **Norway**, a Labor Party was formed in 1887. In **Australia**, the Labor Party was established separately in the colonies of New South Wales and South Australia in 1891. Labor parties were formed in **South Africa** in 1909 and in **New Zealand** in 1916.

In continental Europe, the generally authoritarian political climate encouraged political parties with labor connections to be far more radical, even revolutionary. They drew the bulk of their political ideas from Marxism. This tendency was reinforced by the relative weakness of labor unions for most of the 19th century. The first European social-democratic party was formed in **Germany** in 1863 by Ferdinand Lassalle (1825-1864), as the German Workingmen's Association, and the second, also in Germany, by Wilhelm Liebknecht (1826-1900) and August Bebel (1840-1913) as the Social Democratic Party of Germany in 1866. In 1875, these two parties fused to form the Social Democratic Party. Socialist parties soon emerged in other Western European countries: **Denmark** (1871), **Czechoslavakia** (1872), **Portugal** (1875), **Spain** (1879), **France** (1880), **Belgium** (1885), **Austria** and **Switzerland** (1888), **Sweden** (1889), **Italy** (1892), **Romania** (1893), the **Netherlands** (1894), and **Finland** (1899).

Socialist parties were formed in Eastern Europe too: **Armenia** (1890), **Poland** (1892), **Bulgaria** (1893), **Hungary** (1894), **Lithuania** (1896), **Russia** (1898), and **Georgia** (1899); a social democratic party was formed in **Latvia** in 1904, and in the **Ukraine** in 1905. In the **United States**, a socialist labor party was formed in 1876, a Greenback-Labor Party in 1878, and a Socialist Party in 1901. A Socialist Party was formed in **Argentina** in 1892.

The Second International Workingmen's Association, which was set up in 1889, was the international forum for many of these parties. Although there was agreement about the need for change, there was much disagreement about the methods for achieving it. By the late 19th century, there were two main tendencies at work in these parties both within their national borders and internationally: those who wanted change by gradual reform within the political order and those who wanted change by full-scale social revolution. The second strand was incorporated into **communism** from 1917.

Electorally successful labor parties, that is, political parties built solely on organized labor, have been relatively rare since 1900 outside of Australia, the United Kingdom, and Scandinavia. Conflict can, and does, arise between the political and industrial wings of organized labor. One early instance of this occurred in Germany in 1906; it was resolved by the Mannheim Agreement, which declared the equality between the Social Democratic Party and the unions in providing the leadership for the working class. In France, the trade unions declared their independence from all political parties in the Charter of Amiens, also in 1906.

SOCIALISM. As a political ideology socialism took shape during the 19th century; as a word, it came from the Latin "socius" meaning friend or ally. Although the term "socialism" was applied to a wide range of beliefs, a shared concern was the need to assume some kind of collective control over the means of production, distribution, and exchange and to use this control for the greatest good of the members of society. Despite great interest in socialist ideas in organized labor, there was often little understanding of how to translate socialist theories into practice. In many countries, from about 1910, socialists within labor unions began to divide between reformists and revolutionaries, giving rise to **communism**. **Social-democratic, socialist, and labor parties** have been the means for introducing socialist policies into mainstream democratic politics, with organized labor being careful to preserve its independence from political parties. The inflationary effects of World War I caused a heightened sense of economic injustice among the working class and led to the incorporation of explicit socialist objectives into the platforms of the **British Labour Party** (1918) and the **Australian Labor Party** (1919). By and large, social-democratic, socialist, and labor parties saw parliament and legislation as the way to implement socialism before the 1950s, with organized labor playing a secondary role as a means of bringing about incremental improvements in pay and working conditions. However, there have been some important exceptions to the limited role assigned to organized labor within socialism. In the **United Kingdom**, guild socialists in the 1920s envisaged labor unions as the basis for a future socialist state. In Germany, organized labor gave formal support to the principle of economic democracy, an idea that became *Mitbestimmung* (codetermination) after 1945.

SOCIAL SECURITY. Social security has been defined by the **International Labour Organisation** (ILO) as embracing social insurance schemes (for occupational injury, health, pensions, and unemployment), public health, family allowances, war benefits, and special transfers to government employees. The growth of social security systems in Western economies during the 20th century was sought by organized labor not just to improve the conditions of employees generally but also as a means of reducing the competition for positions in the paid labor force from dependent groups such as children, mothers, and the aged. Of special importance was the introduction of unemployment benefits because the unemployed were the pool from which strikebreakers were traditionally drawn by employers. In 1950, the **International Confederation of Free Trade Unions** (ICFTU) issued a manifesto in favor of social security and old age and sickness insurance in the context of wider support for political and economic democracy.

In 1952, the ILO adopted Convention Number 102 on Social Security (Minimum Standards), which covered the following forms of benefits: medical, sickness, unemployment, old age, occupational injury and disease, family, maternity, and invalidity. Since the 1980s, there has been growing concern by governments about the adverse economic effects of spending on social security. Regardless of their political complexions, Western European governments have tried to reduce social security benefits based on the recognition that their maintenance in the long term is unsustainable because of the ageing of their populations. Their efforts have produced **strikes** in 2003 in France and Austria and conflict within the German Social Democratic Party. Nevertheless, social security systems are the main means for the redistribution of income from the better-off to the less well-off in Western societies. In February 2002, the ICFTU complained that only 40 countries had signed ILO Convention Number 102 on Social Security and that half the world's population had no access to social security benefits. *See also* MINIMUM WAGE.

SOMALIA. Formed from a merger of colonial territories of the **United Kingdom** and **Italy** in July 1960, labor unions in Somalia emerged in the 1940s and formed a labor federation in 1949, which was represented in the **International Confederation of Free Trade Unions** (ICFTU) by 1959, and Somalia continued to be represented in the ICFTU until 1969. Plagued by clan rivalries and prolonged civil strife since the late 1970s, organized labor effectively ceased to exist. Somalia has not been represented in the ICFTU since 1969.

SOUTH AFRICA. The first labor union in South Africa was the **Amalgamated Society of Carpenters and Joiners**, which was established by Europeans in Cape Town in 1881. Miners in the Kimberley set up a union in 1884, and the **Amalgamated Society of Engineers** formed a branch in Cape Town in 1891. A Federation of Unions was created in 1911. One remarkable feature of this development was the very low **membership** of organized labor in South Africa compared to similar societies such as **Australia** and **New Zealand**. There were only 3,800 union members in 1900 and only 11,900 by 1914, of whom 2,800 were members of the Amalgamated Society of Engineers. As in other countries, the following six years saw a large increase in union membership, to 135,100 by 1920, but this represented only about 12 percent of nonagricultural employees.

A second feature of European organization, though not one confined to South Africa, was its hostility to other racial groups. The South African Industrial Federation, which was formed in 1914, was aimed at protecting skilled Europeans and maintaining racial divisions. The South African branch of the **Industrial Workers of the World** (IWW) was unique in setting up a multiracial body, but it could not survive in such a racially divided society. The first black union was formed in 1917, but the largest body, the Industrial and Commercial Workers' Union, was set up in 1919; it claimed 100,000 members by 1925 but was made defunct by 1930. Gandhi also helped to form unions among Indian workers, but the growth of non-European unionism alarmed the Europeans, who went on **strike** in 1922; in the ensuing conflict, 230 strikers were killed by the army. The incident led to moves by European organized labor to reduce economic opportunities for non-Europeans, a policy that greatly harmed non-European unionism. Membership of all South African unions grew from 118,300 in 1930 to 272,500 in 1940 and to 408,600 in 1950. In 1941, some black unions formed the Council of Non-European Trade Unions; it claimed 158,000 members by 1945.

With the victory of the National Party in the 1948 elections, full apartheid became government policy, and this also entailed a hostile attitude towards non-European unions, which led to their politicization. In 1954, the Trade Union Council of South Africa was formed with unions from all the country's racial groups. In 1955, the South African Congress of Trade Unions was formed from the merger of some independent black unions and the Council of Non-European Trade Unions, but it was crushed by the government between 1962 and 1965 because of its radicalism. After strikes by black workers in Durban in 1972-1973, the government arrested the leaders and tried to suppress black unionism. The government reaction led to concerted support for black unions by international unionism through bodies such as the **International Metalworkers' Federation** (IMF) and through pressure from the union representatives on the boards of Swedish and German multinational companies operating in South Africa.

In 1979, the government appointed the Wiehahn Commission to investigate trade unionism; the commission successfully recommended that black labor unions be legally recognized and the system of racial reservation of occupations be abandoned. The recommendations did not mean complete freedom for black organized labor. Rural and domestic workers and state employees were denied access to **collective bargaining** and unions could not affiliate to a political party or support illegal strikes. Nevertheless, black unionism grew despite continued violence; in April 1987, for instance, seven strikers were killed during a railroad strike. In December 1985 the Congress of South African Unions, a mainly black labor federation, was formed; nonracial by policy, it claimed 1.3 million members by 1991. A radical black labor federation, the National Council of Trade Unions, was formed in 1986 and claimed 327,000 members in 1994, when it became affiliated with the **International Confederation of Free Trade Unions** (ICFTU), the first South African labor federation to be admitted because of apartheid and the restrictions on trade union rights.

The ICFTU had been lobbying hard against South Africa's policies since 1954 and had been actively supporting black organized labor since 1980. Although the apartheid system ended with multiracial elections in 1994, and the legal rights of organized labor were recognized by the 1995 Labour Relations Act and strengthened in March 2002, the ICFTU complained that they are often ignored in practice. In 2001, South Africa was represented by three labor federations in the ICFTU with a combined membership of nearly 2.7 million. *See also* RACE AND ETHNICITY.

SOUTH KOREA. The first **labor disputes** on the Korean peninsula date from the 1890s, and the first labor union was formed by longshoremen in 1898. Korea was a colony of **Japan** from 1910 to 1945. Following the suppression of a revolt for independence in 1919, Japanese policy was one of toleration until 1925. In this period three labor federations were formed (1920, 1922, and 1924). In 1925, the Japanese repressed organized labor by their Public Peace law; at this time there were about 123,000 union members in Korea. With Japan's defeat in 1945, organized labor revived and set up a large, broad-based, **communist** labor federation. It was challenged by an anticommunist, nationalist labor federation, the General Federation of Korean Trade Unions, in March 1946. After it led two **general strikes**, the communist federation was outlawed in 1947.

Although in theory labor was able to organize, **collectively bargain**, and strike under the constitution of 1948, in practice it was controlled by the government. In 1958, an independent labor federation was formed, but after a military coup in 1961, all labor unions were broken up and reorganized by the military into 14 industrial unions based on organized labor in **Germany**. Under the labor laws of 1953 (and subsequent years), most public sector employees were denied the right to strike. In 1963, unions were legally forbidden from participation in **politics**. Following the promise of constitutional reforms in June 1987, there was an outburst of independent activity among white- and **blue-collar** employees; it is estimated that 400,000 employees joined these unions by August 1987. An independent labor federation, the National Council of Labor Unions, was set up in January 1990 from a body originally formed in March 1984; it claimed about 200,000 members in 1992. Despite the lack of freedom of organized labor in South Korea since 1953, its labor federation has been a continuous member of the **International Confederation of Free Trade Unions** (ICFTU) since 1949. Since the late 1980s, South Korea has had a high level of labor disputes, a reflection of the abrasive nature of its labor relations. The ICFTU has been highly critical of the violent way in which the government has responded to strikes by organized labor. During 2002, 147 labor members were detained by the government and 55 remained detained at the end of the year. *See also* NORTH KOREA.

SOVIET UNION. *See* RUSSIA.

SPAIN. Organized labor developed slowly in 19th-century Spain, a reflection of the country's economic and political backwardness. In 1871, printers formed a union in Madrid, but unions were not legalized until 1881, an event that led to the formation of the first labor federation, the *Federación de Trabajadores de la Región Española* (Federation of Workers of the Region of Spain), which claimed to represent 58,000 members. This body was replaced in 1888 by the *Unión General de Trabajadores* (General Union of Workers) (UGT), which has continued to be Spain's largest labor federation; it was dominated by the **socialists**. In 1902, the UGT affiliated with the **International Federation of Trade Unions** (IFTU).

    Anarchism was one of the distinguishing characteristics of Spanish labor. It found particular appeal in rural areas and envisaged the overthrow of the state by a **general strike** and its replacement by democratically run cooperative groups covering the whole economy. In 1910, the anarchists formed their own federation, the *Confederación Nacional del Trabajo* (National Labor Federation), which continues to the present. Unions and union growth were relatively weak. Between the early 1900s and 1913 the number of union members rose from 26,000 to 128,000. Violence was also a feature of Spanish labor. During "Tragic Week" (July 1909), over 175 people were shot in riots led by revolutionary **syndicalists** in Catalonia after the calling up of reservists for the war in **Morocco**. The rioters' attacks on churches and convents led to the execution of anarchist leader Francisco Ferrer despite international protests. After World War I, unions grew significantly; between 1920 and 1930 the number of union members increased from 220,000 to 946,000, and by 1936 the UGT claimed two million members.

The Civil War (1936-1939) and the repression that followed under General Francisco Franco eliminated independent organized labor from political life officially in 1940. The UGT continued as an organization in exile in France. It was a founding organization of the **International Confederation of Free Trade Unions** (ICFTU) and maintained the ICFTU's hostility to Franco's regime; for example, in 1952, the ICFTU protested vehemently over the admission of Spain to the United Nations Educational, Scientific, and Cultural Organization. During the 1960s, the communists organized employees at the workplace and even led illegal **strikes**.

With the restoration of democracy following Franco's death in 1975, labor unions were legalized in 1977, although full legalization was not granted until 1985. As well as the UGT, the communists organized their own federation from the workplace groups they formed under Franco, the *Confederación Sindical de Comisiones Obreras* (Union Confederation of Workers' Commissions) (CCOO), and the anarchists reemerged, but with only a shadow of their pre-1936 strength. In 1984, the government and the *Unión General de Trabajadores* agreed to a social and economic pact to control wage claims as an antiinflationary measure. The pact, which was opposed by the CCOO, broke down after 1986. In 1980, Spain had about 1.7 million union members, but this figure had declined to about 1.2 million by 1990. In 2001, the four labor federations in Spain affiliated with the ICFTU claimed a total **membership** of nearly 1.4 million. *See also* BASQUE COUNTRY.

SPRING OFFENSIVE. *See SHUNTO.*

SRI LANKA. Independent from the **United Kingdom** since February 1948, and formerly known as Ceylon, organized labor developed at the end of the 19th century, beginning with the Ceylon Printers' Union in 1893. In 1926, the unions formed the All-Ceylon Trades Union Congress; by 1930, Ceylon had about 114,000 union members. In 1935, labor unions were legalized by the colonial administration. In 1940, the Ceylon Indian Congress Labour Union was formed for the Indian Tamils; it was reformed as the Ceylon Workers' Congress in 1950. Although organized labor in Sri Lanka claimed a large **membership**, it was characterized by fragmentation based on ethnic, political, language, and religious divisions. At independence, there were 1,592 registered unions; of these 412 unions that reported their membership totaled 398,400. By 1973, 590 unions reported that their total membership was 1.2 million. Sri Lanka has been represented in the **International Confederation of Free Trade Unions** (ICFTU) since 1951. Sri Lanka's political stability has been severely challenged by the Tamil insurgency since 1983, which led to emergency regulations and created the opportunity to restrict organized labor as well. The ICFTU has been highly critical of the **violation of trade union rights** in Sri Lanka's **export processing zones** in 2000 and 2001, but noted improvements in 2002. *See also* INDIA.

STEELWORKERS. *See* UNITED STEELWORKERS OF AMERICA.

STRIKE. A strike is a **labor dispute** initiated by a labor union or a group of unions, in contrast to a lockout or a labor dispute initiated by an employer or group of employers. In a strike, labor unions generally withdraw their labor from the employer. This meaning of "strike" in contrast to "lockout" has been established in English since about 1850. The origin of the word "strike" is unclear, but it does not seem to have a nautical origin as has been suggested. It was used in its modern sense in a hiring bond in 1763 between coal owners and miners at Newcastle in northern England and in connection with London tailors in 1764. Although labor disputes are often called "strikes" by the media, in practice the initiator can be difficult to determine, particularly as strikes are often called by labor unions in response to the actions of employers, such as reductions in wages and entitlements or adverse changes to working hours or conditions at work. Strikes in the sense of a broad offensive by labor unions are comparatively rare events and mainly occur in periods of prosperity combined with price inflation; examples include strikes by metal workers' unions in the early 1970s for higher pay. Strikes can take a variety of forms. Although most strikes typically have the extension or defense of wages and conditions as their objectives, they may have purely political objectives (as in **Venezuela** in 2002-2003) or may be in support of strikes by other labor unions, the so-called sympathetic strikes. Another variety is the unofficial or wildcat strike, in which a local or regional branch of a labor union engages in a strike without the approval of, or even in opposition to, the head office of the union. *See also* GENERAL STRIKES; LABOR DISPUTES; "WINTER OF DISCONTENT."

SUDAN. Independent from the **United Kingdom** and **Egypt** since January 1956, organized labor in the Sudan developed after World War II. In 1959, the 4,000-strong anticommunist Central Sudan Government Workers' Trade Unions' Federation, which formed in 1955, joined the **International Confederation of Free Trade Unions** (ICFTU) but was not represented subsequently. In the 1960s organized labor continued to grow but in a fragmented way. In 1971, the government dissolved Sudan's 562 separate labor unions and independent organized labor ceased to exist. There was some reemergence of organized labor in the 1970s and 1980s, but in 1989 the military government again dissolved the labor unions. In 1992, the government established its own organization to run labor unions. In 2000, a new labor code was introduced, but the ICFTU reported that it had not led to an improvement in Sudan's labor relations and that independent organized labor had been forced underground. The ICFTU reported that no improvement in conditions for organized labor had occurred in 2002.

SURINAM. Independent from the **Netherlands** since November 1975, organized labor in Surinam began effectively in the late 1940s, with the first labor federation being formed in 1947. By 1964, there were six national labor federations with a combined **membership** of 30,000. Organized labor was divided along political and religious lines. Surinam has been represented continuously in the **International Confederation of Free Trade Unions** (ICFTU) since 1951. Surinam was one of the few Latin American countries not to be reported in the ICFTU's survey of **violations of trade union rights** in 2002.

SWAZILAND. Independent from the **United Kingdom** since September 1968, organized labor has faced a difficult challenge to become established. Beginning as a large number of small bodies, the unions could make little headway in a country ruled by a king and a cabinet. A state of emergency has been in force since 1973 and political parties are banned. The Swaziland Federation of Trade Unions was registered in 1973 and became an affiliate of the **International Confederation of Free Trade Unions** (ICFTU) by 1989 with 26,000 members. In 1980, the government prohibited **strikes** by postal, radio, and **education** workers. In its survey of **violations of trade union rights** for 2002, the ICFTU was particularly critical of the government of Swaziland, noting its fiercely antiunion policies and its placing on trial of six union leaders who tried to present a petition to the government.

SWEDEN. The first true labor unions in Sweden were formed in the 1880s by skilled men, some of whom had contact with trade unionism in the **United Kingdom** and **Germany**. In 1886, the first of what became regular conferences was held between labor leaders of Sweden, **Denmark**, and **Norway**. In 1889, the unions formed the Social Democratic Party. But union membership growth was very slow; there were only 9,000 members or about 1 percent of nonagricultural employees by 1890. Thereafter, union **membership** grew steadily to 67,000 or 5 percent of employees by 1900. In 1898, a labor federation for **blue-collar** employees, the *Landsorganisationen i Sverge* (LO) or Labor Union Federation of Sweden, was formed, but the union movement faced a difficult political environment. In 1899, the government enacted a law that prevented strikes; it remained law until 1938.

Yet the unions demonstrated their power by conducting a **general strike** in 1902 for universal suffrage, which led to the formation of the *Svenska Arbetsgivaresöforreningen* (SAF) or Swedish Employers' Confederation. In 1906, the SAF and the LO signed their first agreement which, although it recognized the unions' right to organize and engage in **collective bargaining**, forced the unions to accept the employers' right to hire and fire employees and to make working arrangements. A massive but unsuccessful general strike in 1909 (the number of working days lost per thousand employees was 12,677, making it one of the biggest disputes in Sweden's history) hurt organized labor although union membership after 1910 continued to grow. Between 1913 and 1920, the number of union members rose from 134,000 to 403,000 and the proportion of employees in unions rose from 8 to 28 percent. Despite large-scale protests, the government enacted laws in 1928 that regulated collective bargaining contracts and set up a labor court to settle disputes. In 1931, **white-collar** employees in the private sector formed their own labor federation.

In 1932, the political climate for labor changed for the better with the election of the first **social-democratic** government. In 1936, the government passed a second major labor law which provided for the recognition of unions and the opening of negotiations by either employers or unions and outlawed the victimization of union members for taking part in legal union activities. National government employees formed a labor federation in 1937 and were granted the right to bargain in that year; the benefit was extended to employees of local government in 1940. Of particular significance was the Saltsjobaden Agreement in 1938 between the LO and the SAF; it specified dispute settlement procedures, the avoidance of disputes and, by implication, the avoidance of government intervention. This agreement is generally credited with securing a high degree of industrial peace until the economic problems of the 1970s. By 1940 there were 971,000 union members, covering 54 percent of employees. Since 1950, Sweden has had one of the highest levels of union membership in the world. In 2001, Swedish unions covered 90 percent of employees. *See also* COUNCIL OF NORDIC TRADE UNIONS.

SWEENEY, JOHN JOSEPH (1934-). Sweeney was elected president of the **American Federation of Labor-Congress of Industrial Organizations** (AFL-CIO) in October 1995 to replace **Joseph Lane Kirkland** and has been reelected twice since then. He was born in the Bronx, New York City. His trade union career began as a research assistant with the **International Ladies' Garment Workers' Union**. In 1960, he joined the **Service Employees International Union** (SEIU) as a contract director for New York City Local 32B. He went on to become union president and to lead two citywide **strikes** of apartment maintenance workers. At the time of his election as president of the AFL-CIO, he was serving his fourth four-year term as president of the SEIU, which grew from 625,000 to 1.1 million members under his leadership. He was elected as an AFL-CIO vice president in 1980. He is the author of *America Needs a Raise: Fighting for Economic Security and Social Justice* and has supported grassroots organizations and campaigns to achieve the objectives of organized labor.

SWITZERLAND. Organized labor in Switzerland began effectively in the late 1860s through contact with German **socialist** labor bodies. In 1873, an unsuccessful attempt was made to form a national federation but, in 1880, the socialist labor unions created the *Schweizerischer Gewerkschaftsbund* (Swiss Trade Union Confederation or SGB). In 1890, the Canton of Geneva passed a law that recognized agreements between unions and employers; it seems to have been the first legislation of its kind in Europe to legalize **collective bargaining**. In 1900, when the SGB declared its political neutrality, Switzerland had about 90,000 union members, covering about 10 percent of its nonagricultural employees. Switzerland was affiliated with the **International Federation of Trade Unions** (IFTU) from 1902 to 1945. A **white-collar** labor federation was established in 1903 and a **Catholic** labor federation in 1907. A **general strike** in 1918 was crushed by the army.

By 1920, there were 313,000 union members representing about 26 percent of nonagricultural employees. Swiss organized labor developed and grew in a tolerant political climate and in a relatively prosperous economy. In 1937, a peace **accord** was made in the engineering industry that became the basis for a national social partnership between unions and employers from the 1950s. It provided for bargaining in good faith and avoiding strikes or lockouts during the life of agreements. The consensus approach adopted so successfully in industrial relations reflected a wider respect for Switzerland's diversity of people, language, and religion. Spared the ravages of World War II, the Swiss labor movement continues to be formally divided by religion, unlike those of **Germany** and **Austria**. Switzerland has always been represented in the **International Confederation of Free Trade Unions** (ICFTU). In 2001, there were about 492,600 union members representing about 14 percent of employees. Since 2000, the right to strike in the **public sector** has been permitted in federal employment but had not been extended to all cantons and communes in 2002. *See also SYNDICATS SANS FRONTIÈRES.*

SYNDICALISM. Syndicalism was a set of practices and ideologies developed by French organized labor in the 1890s and 1900s. It derived from the French "syndical," meaning simply trade union but, as an ideology, syndicalism (or revolutionary syndicalism) meant the aggressive use of unions to gain political and social change. The class war was central to syndicalist thought, which saw governments and political parties, including **socialist** parties, as instruments of working-class oppression. Syndicalist thought stressed direct action, particularly the **general strike**, as the means to gain its objectives. It owed as much, if not more, to work experience as to ideas.

Syndicalism grew out of conditions peculiar to **France**, namely, its revolutionary tradition (1789, 1830, 1848, and 1871), the self-reliant attitude of its working class, the relatively slow growth of industrialization, and the importance of small enterprises in the economy. The French Charter of Amiens (1906), which was adopted by the national organization of French labor, the *Confédération Générale du Travail* (General Confederation of Labor), called for wage increases and **shorter hours** to be won by the taking over of the capitalist class and the general strike. In the **United States**, the **Knights of Labor** have been described as a U.S. version of syndicalism. In **Italy**, syndicalism began to emerge after 1902 as a reaction to reformism in the Italian Socialist Party and developed into an unstable combination of Marxism and populism. Some of the Italian syndicalists became fascists. For example, Edmondo Rossini (1884-1965), the head of the fascist labor union federation from 1922 to 1928, had been a revolutionary syndicalist labor organizer in Italy and New York before 1914. In **Spain**, syndicalism remained important until the late 1930s. *See also* INDUSTRIAL WORKERS OF THE WORLD; ONE BIG UNION.

SYNDICATS SANS FRONTIÈRES **(SSF).** SSF or Trade Unions without Borders is an affiliate of the *Schweizerischer Gewerkschaftsbund* (Swiss Trade Union Confederation) (SGB), which emerged in the late 1990s to fight for the rights of Third World workers treated as virtual slaves in Europe. SSF seeks the payment of wages for the workers concerned through the courts. *See also* SLAVERY; SWITZERLAND.

SYRIA. Independent organized labor does not exist in Syria. The sole national labor organization, the General Federation of Labor Unions, is run by the ruling Ba'th party government, which has a long history of repression. For example, in 1980 some engineers and medical doctors who went on **strike** were arrested; 15 years later, their fate was still unknown, according to the **International Confederation of Free Trade Unions** (ICFTU). In 2002, the ICFTU noted that although some legal restrictions on organized labor had been lifted, there were no free or independent labor unions or the right to freely engage in **collective bargaining**.

-T-

TAFF VALE CASE. The Taff Vale Case was a pivotal legal case in the history of organized labor in the **United Kingdom**. It arose from **picketing** by the Amalgamated Society of Railway Servants to prevent the use of nonunion labor during a **strike** in August 1900 on the Taff Vale railroad in South Wales. The general manager of the railroad, Ammon Beasley, sued the officials of the society for damages to the property of the railroad. The strike was settled through mediation after 11 days, but the company continued to press its claim through the courts. The company won the first round but lost in the court of appeal, after which it went to the House of Lords, which decided against the society in July 1901 and, in a consequent case, declared that the society would have to pay the company £23,000 plus its legal costs of £19,000 (about $100,000 in total), which were huge sums for the time. The Taff Vale Case was immediately followed by two other antiunion decisions by the House of Lords over **picketing** and boycotting (*Lyons v. Wilkins* and *Quinn v. Leathem*). The Taff Vale Case had three major results. First, it cast doubt on the legal status of labor union activity not just in Britain but in all countries that used British law, particularly **Canada, Australia,** and **New Zealand**. Second, it swung opinion within British organized labor round to the idea that it needed its own political party. The Labour Representation Committee, which had been formed in 1900, was upgraded; in 1903, a compulsory levy was made of unions to pay for Labour members of parliament and the committee itself was renamed the Labour Party in 1906. Third, pressure from organized labor on the Liberal government led to the Trade Disputes Act (1906), which granted the unions immunity from actions such as happened in the Taff Vale Case. *See also* BRITISH LABOUR PARTY; *ROOKES V. BARNARD.*

TAFT-HARTLEY ACT. The Taft-Hartley Act, known formally as the Labor-Management Relations Act, was a piece of U.S. federal law passed in 1947 to redress the imbalance in the law alleged to have been caused by the **Wagner Act** of 1935. Conservative politicians and employer groups claimed that the Wagner Act only dealt with coercive actions by employers and ignored such acts by unions. The legislation was passed at a time of increasing **labor disputes** generally and in **coal mining** and steel production in particular. Although the Taft-Hartley Act maintained the fundamental freedoms of unions, it imposed a number of important restrictions on them; it outlawed the union or closed shop and allowed the states to pass their own anti-closed shop or **right-to-work laws**. Unions were also made liable to be sued in the federal courts for breaches of contract and had to give at least 60 days' notice of the ending or amending of an agreement. Finally, unions were forbidden to spend any of their funds on political campaigns. The Taft-Hartley Act was used by President George W. Bush in October 2002 to end a lockout by maritime employers on the west coast, the first time the law had been used since 1978. *See also* POLITICAL ACTION COMMITTEES; UNITED MINE WORKERS OF AMERICA; UNITED STEELWORKERS OF AMERICA.

TAHITI. *See* FRENCH POLYNESIA.

TAIWAN. Following the imposition of martial law in 1949, **strikes** on Taiwan were outlawed and unions controlled by the Kuomintang Party encouraged. Between 1955 and 1989 the number of members in government-controlled unions rose from 198,000 to 2.4 million. The continuance of martial law was justified by the government on the grounds that Taiwan was still at war with mainland **China**; it was only lifted in 1987, a step that led to a pent-up wave of **labor disputes**. Strikes were permitted by the Arbitration Dispute Law, that allowed employees to strike after mediation but required them to return to work. Nevertheless, striking union members were jailed for striking in 1988 and 1989. In November 1987 a Labor Party was formed and there was significant growth in the membership of independent labor unions. Taiwan has been represented in the **International Confederation of Free Trade Unions** (ICFTU) since 1951 by the Chinese Federation of Labor, which claimed one million members in 2001. The ICFTU reported negatively about the legal system for organized labor in Taiwan in 2002, but noted an improved attitude towards labor unions by the government since 2000. On September 28, 2002, 60,000 teachers demonstrated for the right to form labor unions.

TAJIKISTAN. Independent from the former **Soviet Union** since September 9, 1991, there is no history of organized labor in Tajikistan. The labor code is ambiguous about the right to form unions, bargain collectively, and conduct strikes. Although **collective bargaining** is known to occur, civil war and ethnic conflict have exhausted the society. Tajikistan was not a member of the **International Confederation of Free Trade Unions** (ICFTU) in 2001. In 2002, the ICFTU noted that there were ambiguities in the labor law of Tajikistan, mainly in the freedom given to government to restrict the rights of organized labor. The **International Labour Organisation** (ILO) has repeatedly asked for clarification of the law.

TANZANIA. Tanzania was formed in December 1961 from the British territory of Tanganyika and the islands of Zanzibar and Pemba. Unlike most colonies, labor unions were legalized before there were any actual unions; a Trade Union Ordinance was passed in 1932 covering Tanganyika, but there were no unions formed until 1949. The Tanganyika Federation of Labour was formed in 1955 and was admitted to the **International Confederation of Free Trade Unions** (ICFTU) in 1957; it was abolished by the government in 1964, which sought to dominate organized labor. The one-party political system of Julius Nyerere that ran Tanzania gave way to a pluralistic system after 1992. In 1991, the government formed the Organisation of Tanzania Trade Unions, which was admitted to **membership** of the ICFTU in 1994 with a declared membership of 359,900. In 1995, the unions formed the Tanzania Federation of Free Trade Unions as a successor organization, but it was denied legal recognition and was dissolved by the government on July 1, 2000. In 2002, the ICFTU reported that there was considerable government interference in the affairs of organized labor.

TEAMSTERS. Officially known as the International Brotherhood of Teamsters, Chauffeurs, Warehousemen, and Helpers of America, the Teamsters was the largest labor union in the **United States** from the mid-1950s to 1987, when it was overtaken by the **National Educational Association**. The Teamsters began as the Team

Drivers' International Union in January 1899 with a **membership** of 1,700 based on drivers of horse teams. In 1902, part of the Chicago membership formed a rival body, the Teamsters' National Union but, in 1903, the two organizations agreed to merge as the International Brotherhood of Teamsters. In its early years, the Teamsters was a sprawling confederation of local unions controlled by powerful bosses rather than a unified national organization. It owed much of its organizational success to Daniel J. Tobin, who was its president from 1907 to 1952. In 1910, Tobin gained jurisdiction over truck drivers from the **American Federation of Labor** (AFL), a move that enabled it to grow with the fastest parts of the American economy and placed it in a strong bargaining position in many related industries. Even so, membership growth was slow between 1912 and 1930 (from only 84,000 to 98,800) but, after 1935, it grew quickly, reaching 441,600 in 1939 and 644,500 by 1945.

In 1955, the Teamsters had 1,291,100 members, the largest membership of any American labor union. Under presidents **Dave Beck** (1952-1957) and **James R. Hoffa** (1957-1971), the Teamsters continued to expand into employment sectors that were related to transportation, such as cold storage, warehousing, baking, laundry work, and canning, despite the convictions of Beck and then Hoffa for corruption and other offenses. In 1957, the Teamsters were expelled from the **American Federation of Labor-Congress of Industrial Organizations** (AFL-CIO) but were readmitted in November 1987. During the 1980s, the leadership of the Teamsters backed **Ronald Reagan** for president, but the reformed leadership that gained power in the late 1980s backed Bill Clinton's presidential campaign. The Teamsters claimed 1.4 million members in 1992. In 1997, the Teamsters successfully conducted a 16-day strike against United Parcel Services that attracted popular and international support. In 1999, James R. Hoffa's son, **John P. Hoffa**, was elected general president on a reform platform.

THAILAND. Unofficial organizations among Thai employees existed from the early 1880s. They conducted a number of **strikes** to gain formal recognition, but this was not granted until 1932 and then only lasted until 1934. Legal recognition of unions was not restored until after the Japanese were expelled in 1944; it was withdrawn in 1948, restored in 1955, and revoked in 1958. Unions were again legally recognized between 1972 and 1976, but the military government that took power in October 1976 once again withdrew recognition. Many union members in Thailand work in state-owned enterprises that have been vulnerable to changes in government policy, particularly **privatization**. Following a campaign by the unions, the right to strike was restored in January 1981 but was withdrawn for those employees working in state-owned enterprises in April 1991 following the military coup on February 23, 1991. In June 1991, the president of the Labor Congress of Thailand (formed in 1978), Thanong Po-arn, disappeared and was presumed murdered. Between 1989 and 1991 the number of union members in Thailand dropped from 309,000 to 160,000. In 1993, there were 800 unions and 26 labor federations in Thailand.

Thailand has been represented in the **International Confederation of Free Trade Unions** (ICFTU) since 1951. In 2001, it was represented by two affiliates with a combined membership of 243,000. The ICFTU has been critical of the lack of **collective bargaining** in Thailand and unchecked employer violence towards organized labor, both in 2002 and for earlier years.

THOMAS, ALBERT (1878-1932). French labor scholar, newspaper editor, and politician, Thomas was the first director of the **International Labour Organisation** (ILO) between 1920 and 1932. During the early 1900s he carried out research in **Germany, Russia,** and the eastern Mediterranean into **socialism, syndicalism,** and consumer cooperatives, which he published in 1903. In 1904, he was made assistant editor of the **socialist** newspaper *L'Humanité*. In 1910 he was elected to the Chamber of Deputies for the Socialist Party, a position he held until 1921. In 1915, he became under-secretary of state for artillery and munitions and minister for munitions in 1916. In 1917, he was ambassador to Alexander Kerensky's government in Russia. As ILO director, he worked tirelessly for the adoption of its conventions by member countries in a very difficult political climate.

TOGO. Independent from **France** from April 1960, the first unions in Togo were branches of French ones. All of Togo's unions were brought under government control in 1972-1973. Togo did not move to a pluralistic political system until the early 1990s. In 1992, two Togo labor federations, with a combined **membership** of 67,300, were admitted to the **International Confederation of Free Trade Unions** (ICFTU). In 2002, the ICFTU was critical of the weak protection afforded to Togo's unions by its laws, even though the right to join unions and to **strike** was legal. It was also critical of the lack of legal protection given to workers in the country's **export processing zones**.

TONGA. Independent from the **United Kingdom** since June 1970, organized labor began effectively in the 1970s with the Tonga Teachers' Association, with 222 members in 1976. Later merging with the Nurses' Association, the union became an affiliate of the **International Confederation of Free Trade Unions** (ICFTU) in 1990.

TRADE UNION ADVISORY COMMITTEE TO THE ORGANIZATION FOR ECONOMIC COOPERATION AND DEVELOPMENT (TUAC). The TUAC was formed in 1948 to represent the interests of organized labor within the Organization for Economic Cooperation and Development (OECD). The TUAC has consultative status with the OECD and is able to make its views known on multinational corporations, labor market reform, **privatization**, **globalization**, and unemployment.

TRADE UNION CONFEDERATION OF ARAB MAGHREB WORKERS (TUCAMW). The TUCAMW is an international labor organization formed in 1991 by the labor federations of **Algeria**, **Libya**, **Mauritania**, **Morocco**, and **Tunisia** to lobby for the inclusion of social objectives in the Arab Maghreb Union (formed in 1989) to promote greater cooperation among the governments of North Africa. These labor federations had a combined **membership** of 2.2 million in 2001. In November 2001, the TUCAMW signed a joint declaration with the **International Confederation of Free Trade Unions** (ICFTU) to strengthen cooperation between the two organizations. *See also* AFRICAN REGIONAL ORGANIZATION.

TRADES UNION CONGRESS (TUC). The TUC has been the largest national labor union organization in the **United Kingdom** since its formation in Manchester on June 2-6, 1868. Its constitution provided the model for the Federation of Organized Trades and Labor Unions of the **United States** and **Canada** in 1881, the organization that was the forerunner to the **American Federation of Labor** (AFL). In 1894, **Samuel Gompers** initiated an annual exchange of fraternal delegates between the AFL and the TUC. The TUC played only a minor role in international labor unionism before 1913; this role was taken by the **General Federation of Trade Unions**. Between 1868 and 1898, the number of members in unions affiliated with the TUC rose from 118,400 to 1.1 millon. By 1914, most British unions were affiliated with the TUC. The TUC is essentially a policy-making body for its affiliates; it has no power to direct them although it acts as the national voice of organized labor in Britain. From 1871, it operated through its parliamentary committee as a lobby to government in the interests of labor. It also provided a national forum for delegates to debate policy matters at its annual congresses. In 1892, Keir Hardie persuaded the TUC to pass a motion calling on its parliamentary committee to draw up a scheme for a fund to pay for the direct representation of labor members of parliament. Nothing came of the proposal and it was not until a conference of the parliamentary committee (representing less than half of the TUC) in 1900 that Hardie succeeded in setting up the Labour Representation Committee, the body that became the **British Labour Party**.

As organized labor grew, the TUC was drawn into adjudicating in disputes between its affiliates over which union had the right to recruit particular employees. In 1924, it drew up formal rules for the transfer of members between unions to avoid jurisdictional or demarcation conflicts. In 1939, these rules were codified into six principles known as the Bridlington Agreement. The operation of these procedures has been criticized as favoring larger over smaller unions. Under section 14 of the Trade Union Reform and Employment Rights Act 1993, the unions' power to exclude or expel employees was curtailed, thus giving individuals greater choice about which union to join and so substantially reducing the power of the TUC in deciding on jurisdictional disputes between affiliates. In 1981, the **membership** of affiliates with the TUC reached its highest point of 12.2 million, but by 1992 this membership had fallen to 7.8 million or the level it had in 1950. Over the same period, the number of affiliated unions fell from 109 to 72.

In 2001, the number of British unions affiliated with the TUC was 73 and they represented 6.7 million members. At its 2001 Brighton conference, delegates debated resolutions relating to rights at work, employment legislation and trade union rights, promoting equality and diversity, **equal pay for equal work**, racism, promoting trade unionism and work with young people, the public profile of trade unions in Britain, **manufacturing**, professional pay

organizations to achieve improved productivity, higher growth, and a range of other objectives. In September 1979, the **American Federation of Labor-Congress of Industrial Organizations** (AFL-CIO) and the Jimmy Carter administration reached a national accord under which the unions agreed to restrain wage claims in return for a package of economic and social measures, but the accord lapsed with Carter's defeat by **Ronald Reagan**.

One of the most successful union-government agreements was made in **Australia**. Named the Accord, it was formally agreed to between the **Australian Labor Party** (ALP) and the **Australian Council of Trade Unions** (ACTU) regarding economic and social policy in February 1983. The Accord set out details of policies to be implemented when the ALP was elected to the federal government. It covered prices, wages and working conditions, nonwage incomes (for instance, earnings from dividends and interest), taxation, government expenditure, **social security**, and health. The Accord grew out of conferences between the ALP and the ACTU in 1979 over new approaches to economic management. The Accord was renegotiated seven times but ceased with the defeat of the Labor Party in the national elections of March 1996. The Accord has been credited with modest general increases in wages and lower levels of **labor disputes** since 1983.

In **Spain**, a social and economic pact between the government and the noncommunist federation of unions (*Unión General de Trabajadores*) was agreed on in October 1984 but broke down after 1986. An accord between unions, the government, and the employers was signed in **Portugal** in 1990 and was judged to have been a success in helping to modernize the economy and introduce social reforms; a new accord was signed in January 1996.

Ireland has also experimented with union-government agreements. In 1987, the Irish Congress of Trade Unions suggested to the government that there should be a conference to produce a national plan for economic growth, including pay and a range of social issues. Such a plan was produced; it was called the Programme for National Recovery. It operated for three years (1988-1990) and was generally judged to have been a considerable success. It was replaced by a second and broader Programme, the Programme for Economic and Social Progress, in April 1991. The third Programme, the Programme for Competitiveness and Work, was negotiated in April 1994 and was intended to run until 1997. Unlike the

Australian Accord, these Programmes have included employers and
have been negotiated with conservative governments.

In **Germany**, the federal Social-Democratic/Green coalition
government set up the Alliance for Jobs, Training, and Competitiveness, a national forum of labor unions, employers, and government in 1999. The effectiveness of the forum has been debated, but
it continued with the return of the coalition government in the September 2002 elections.

UNION NETWORK INTERNATIONAL (UNI). The UNI was
formed on January 1, 2000, in response to the challenge of **globalization** to labor unions. It was founded by **Communications International**, the *Fédération internationale des employés, techniciens et cadres* or the International Federation of Commercial,
Clerical, Professional, and Technical Employees (FIET), the **International Graphical Federation**, and **Media Entertainment International**. Negotiations between these organizations for the formation of the UNI began in 1998. A prime goal of the UNI is to
lobby the **International Labour Organisation** (ILO) and international trade unions in discussions on reforming the global economy,
specifically improving the distribution of wealth. The UNI is organized around 12 sectors: commerce; electricity; finance; graphical;
hair and beauty; **white-collar**, professional, and information technology staff; media, entertainment, and the arts; post; property services; social insurance and private health care; telecommunications;
and tourism. Three groups cut across these sectors: **women, youth**,
and professional and managerial staff. UNI has its global headquarters at Nyon, near Geneva, Switzerland. In 2002, the UNI claimed a
membership of nearly 800 unions with 15.5 million members.

UNION WAGE DIFFERENTIAL. The union wage differential refers to the generally higher earnings of union members compared to
employees who are not union members. This differential is one way
of directly measuring the economic effects of unions. In the **United
States**, H. G. Lewis estimated that union members earned on average between 10 to 15 percent more than nonunion members between 1923 and 1929; this figure rose to about 25 percent for the
period 1931-1933 and fell to between 10 and 20 percent during
1939-1941. Between 1945 and 1949, union members were estimated to earn only about 5 percent more than nonunion members.

This gap widened to between 10 to 15 percent in 1957-1958 and has continued to exist. By 2002, the median earnings of **full-time** male employees who were union members were 16 percent higher than nonunion employees; for female full-time employees, the gap was 24 percent. In 1998, full-time union members in **Canada** earned 22 percent more than full-time nonunion members. In contrast, in **Australia**, a country with a higher level of unionization than the United States, the union wage differential was much less, though it has widened in recent years. In 2002, Australian union members employed full-time earned 10 percent more than nonunion employees.

The reasons why union members earn more than employees who are not union members include their tendency to work in larger enterprises (which usually pay higher wages than smaller ones) and in **manufacturing** or **public sector** industries. It has been suggested that the high union differential in the United States in the 1980s has contributed to the decline in the proportion of employees who were union members. *See also* Table 15, Appendix F.

UNISON. UNISON was formed in the **United Kingdom** on July 1, 1993, from the merger of three **white-collar** unions, the **Confederation of Health Service Employees**, the **National Union of Public Employees**, and the **National and Local Government Officers' Association**. Its full title is UNISON-The Public Service Union. Negotiations for the merger began in 1978 but took on greater urgency with declining **membership** in the late 1980s. In 1994, UNISON claimed 1,369,000 members, of whom 71 percent were **women**. It is the largest labor union in Britain and the largest **public sector** union in Western Europe. In 2002, Unison claimed 1.3 million members. The membership of UNISON is diverse and includes frontline staff and managers working full or part-time in local authorities, the National Heath Service, **police**, colleges and schools, electricity, gas and water utilities, and public transportation.

UNITED ARAB EMIRATES. Labor unions, **collective bargaining**, and **strikes** are not permitted in the United Arab Emirates. In 2001, 91 percent of the labor force were expatriates and liable for deportation if they form unions or engage in collective bargaining. In recent years, the Ministry of Labor and Social Affairs has taken some action with regard to complaints of unpaid wages to expatriate workers. In 2002, the **International Confederation of Free Trade Unions** (ICFTU) noted that organized labor had no rights in the United Arab Emirates.

UNITED AUTO WORKERS (UAW). The UAW—the general name for the United Automobile, Aerospace, and Agricultural Implement Workers of America International Union—has been one of the leading unions in the **United States** since the 1930s. The UAW grew out of the Carriage and Wagon Workers' International Union, which was formed in the early 1900s. Because of the metalworking nature of the industry, the union became party to many jurisdictional disputes with other unions, which led to the suspension of its charter by the **American Federation of Labor** (AFL) in 1918. The union was renamed the Automobile, Aircraft, and Vehicle Workers' Union of America; although its **membership** reached 40,000 in 1920, it collapsed during the 1920s.

Its revival in the 1930s occurred through the passage of the **National Industrial Recovery Act** in 1933 and the campaign by the AFL to recruit members in the auto industry. These efforts led to the formation of the National Council of Automobile Workers' Unions in 1934, but this did not satisfy the employees' demands for the AFL to charter an **industrial union** for the industry. The AFL issued a limited charter for the UAW in 1935. As before 1918, the UAW became embroiled in jurisdictional disputes with other unions. In 1936, it joined the Committee for Industrial Organizations, the forerunner of the **Congress of Industrial Organizations** (CIO), a move that led to the revocation of its charter by the AFL in 1938. The UAW was boosted by the militancy of the employees in the auto industry and, during 1937, led successful campaigns for recognition by General Motors and Chrysler, campaigns that raised membership to 478,500 by 1939. Recognition by Ford came after violence against union organizers in the **"battle of the overpass"** (1937) and pressure from the federal government in 1941. In 1946, the moderate leader **Walter Reuther** emerged as the winner from a long factional battle within the UAW and dominated the union until his death in 1970. In 1945, the UAW had 891,800 members, making it briefly the largest union in the United States. Thereafter its membership reflected the fortunes of the automobile industry; membership reached a peak of 1.3 million in 1955, but declined slowly after that time. In 2001, the UAW had about 710,000 employed members and over 500,000 members who were **retired employees** in the United States, **Canada**, and **Puerto Rico**.

UNITED FOOD AND COMMERCIAL WORKERS' INTERNATIONAL UNION (UFCW). The UFCW is the second largest union in the **United States** along with the **American Federation of State, County and Municipal Employees** (AFSCME). The UFCW was created in 1979 from the **amalgamation** of the Retail Clerks National Protective Association (formed in 1890) and the Amalgamated Meat Cutters (formed in 1897), with a combined **membership** of 1.1 million. The UFCW has maintained its membership largely through amalgamation. The UFCW absorbed the Retail, Wholesale Department Store Union (formed in the late 1930s) in 1993, the United Garment Workers of America (formed in 1891) in 1994, the United Textile Workers (formed in the late 1890s) in 1995, the Distillery Workers (formed in the mid-1940s) in 1995, and the International Chemical Workers Union (formed in 1944) in 1996. As a result of these mergers, the UFCW now covers a diverse range of industries and is particularly strong in food processing, which accounts for 70 percent of its members. The remaining 30 percent of members work in health care, insurance, department stores, garment **manufacturing**, distillery and wine making, chemical, and textiles. In 2001, the UFCW had 1.4 million members, of whom 53 percent were **women**.

UNITED KINGDOM. Although covert organizations among employees are known to have existed throughout history, it was in 18th-century England that organized labor in the form that it is most familiar today began to emerge. Between 1717 and 1800, 383 **labor disputes** are known to have occurred despite legal prohibitions on unions (called "combinations") and **strikes**. Most of the strikes and unions were organized by journeymen tailors and weavers. These actions led to the first efforts at large-scale industrial relations legislation (as opposed simply to the repression of unions and strikes). For instance, the Spitalfields Act (1773) provided for the statutory setting of wages and piece-rates; the level of wages could be proposed by a joint board of masters and journeymen.

From the late 18th century onwards, organized labor was shaped by two great forces: the Industrial Revolution and the gradual growth of democracy in Britain. These two forces, particularly the indigenous development of the Industrial Revolution in Britain, meant that its organized labor assumed a different character from that of organized labor in other parts of Western Europe. Because of their outlawing by the Combination Acts of 1799 and 1800, unions often disguised their activities as those of friendly societies. Although these acts were repealed in 1824, they were followed by amending legislation in 1825 that reintroduced the common law of conspiracy for certain union actions such as **picketing**.

Nevertheless, unions survived; indeed, the modern use of the word "union" was current in the ship and shipbuilding trades by the mid-1820s. In 1826, a union formed by Manchester engineers became the ancestor of the **Amalgamated Society of Engineers**. In 1827, carpenters and joiners formed a union. Better communications, especially the introduction of a national postal service and the expansion of the **railroads**, assisted with the creation of national labor bodies. In 1842, the Miners' Association of Great Britain and Ireland was formed; it claimed 70,000 members but had collapsed by 1848. In his investigations into the social condition of London in the 1850s, Henry Mayhew estimated that only about 10 percent of employees in skilled trades were members of unions (which he called "societies"). Significantly, he noted that the union men were paid for their work on the basis of custom and that the nonunion men were paid by market rates. According to the first directory of British labor unions, there were 290 unions in London in 1861.

Organized labor had also begun to play some role in the political system even though the restrictive franchise and the absence of payment of members of parliament limited its activities to lobbying and supporting occasional union officials as parliamentary candidates. In 1859, the National Association of United Trades for the Protection of Labour secured the Molestation of Workmen Act, which freed "peaceful" picketing from common law actions. In 1851 the Amalgamated Society of Engineers was formed; it was followed by the formation of the **Amalgamated Society of Carpenters and Joiners** in 1860. Both unions were distinctive in founding branches in other countries. Another important development was the creation of federations of unions (trades councils) in the cities and large towns; the London Trades Council was formed in 1860.

The 1860s were a formative period in shaping British unionism. Its relative success and moderate behavior attracted favorable interest and comment from French and German visitors. In 1867, the Second Reform Act gave the vote to the better-off urban working class, who made up the bulk of union members at the time. In June 1868, the **Trades Union Congress** (TUC) was formed in Manchester; it became the largest labor federation in Britain and was used as the model for the **American Federation of Labor** (AFL) in the **United States** and **Canada** in 1881.

Before 1870, union **membership** was largely confined to skilled urban workers and to industries that relied for their labor on large, long-established working-class communities such as **coal mining** and textiles. In the comparatively prosperous early 1870s other groups of employees formed unions: railroad employees (1871), gas workers, agricultural laborers, longshoremen, and builders' laborers (1872). The depression of the late 1870s reduced union numbers, but they rose again with the return of better conditions in the 1880s. The number of union members affiliated with the TUC rose from 289,000 in 1870 to 464,000 in 1880 and to 581,000 by 1886. As not all unions were affiliated with the TUC, these figures underestimate the real level of union membership. During the 1890s the number of union members doubled from one to two million. The 1890s also saw the rise of a regional consciousness within Britain, as shown by the formation of the Irish Trades Union Congress in 1894 and the Scottish Trades Union Congress in 1897.

The ability of British organized labor to work within the political system through the Liberal Party reduced the imperative for it to form a separate political party despite pressure from its left wing, led by James Keir Hardie. It took the **Taff Vale Case** in 1901 to transform the Labour Representation Committee into the **British Labour Party** in 1906. Despite the legal uncertainties created by the Taff Vale Case and the Osbourne Judgement in 1906, the number of union members grew from 2 to 4.1 million between 1900 and 1913. As well, the Labour Party increased in support and political experience. During World War I the demands of total war led to governments co-opting the support of organized labor, as also occurred in **France**, the **United States**, and **Germany**. In Britain, members of the Labour Party were included in the cabinet for the first time in 1915. In 1917, Whitley councils, made up of representatives from unions and management, were set up in a number of industries. One unintended consequence of the Whitley councils was the promotion of unionism among employees of the national government. Between 1913 and 1920, the number of union members who were national government employees rose from 20,800 to 136,200.

In 1920, largely as a result of official encouragement of organized labor during World War I, union membership reached 8.3 million or 48 percent of employees. Other aspects of this growth were an increase in **white-collar** unionists (who made up 15 percent of total union members by 1920) and the growth in the proportion of **women** labor union members (from 11 to 16 percent between 1913 and 1920). These changes reflected the rise in the number of **public sector** union members (whose numbers rose from 394,100 in 1913 to 854,900 in 1920).

The generally depressed economic conditions of the 1920s gave rise to high levels of unemployment, which sapped union strength. There was a lockout by engineering employers in 1922, the first since 1897-1898, which forced a wage cut on the industry. The return to the gold standard increased the price of British exports and encouraged employers to reduce wages in order to compete, steps that added to labor unrest and erupted in the disastrous **British General Strike** of 1926. Persistent high unemployment for the rest of the 1920s cut union membership to 4.8 million by 1930 and lowered its coverage rate to 26 percent of employees. The main positive developments of the 1920s among the unions were the formation of the **Transport and General Workers' Union** in 1922 and the decision of the Amalgamated Engineering Union to admit lesser-skilled employees as members in 1926. After the severe depression of the early 1930s union membership began to grow again, to reach 6.6 million by 1940.

During World War II, as in World War I, there was a resurgence of organized labor with the co-opting of both the Labour Party and the unions into the government and in the management of the economy. At the end of the war in 1945, union membership had grown to 7.8 million. As in other Western countries, organized labor in Britain had to expend some of its energy on resisting **communist** influence in a number of key unions. The **World Federation of Trade Unions** (WFTU) was set up in London in 1945, but its promise of a united global labor movement was dashed by its infiltration by the **Soviet Union**, a development that led organized labor in Britain, the United States, and other countries to form the **International Confederation of Free Trade Unions** (ICFTU) in 1949.

Within Britain, union membership in the 1950s was stable: in 1960, 44 percent of employees were union members (the same level as in 1950) and 74 percent worked in blue-collar jobs. The importance of organized labor in the management of the postwar economy was recognized by governments, but their experiments with wage restraint schemes from 1948 to 1950 and from 1951 to 1964 did not attract general union cooperation. The Wilson (Labour) government, which was elected in 1964, was able to secure the participation of the unions in the Prices and Incomes Board, but its efforts to raise productivity were disappointing.

In the mid-1960s the unions were the subject of close scrutiny by the **Donovan Commission**, which presented its report in 1968. But the voluntary approach advocated by the Donovan Commission was swept aside by official concern over Britain's poor economic performance and by frustration over unofficial labor disputes. Both the Conservatives (1968) and the Labour Party (1969) published policy papers that suggested ballots before unions could conduct strikes.

In 1979, organized labor in Britain claimed its highest ever membership—13.4 million—but this high-water mark was not maintained for long. The **"winter of discontent"** wave of strikes in 1978-1979 made organized labor unpopular and enabled the Conservative Party under Margaret Thatcher to easily win the May 1979 national elections and introduce a raft of measures, such as the **Employment Acts** and **privatization**, which brought about a radical change for the worse in the political and legal climate for organized labor. The process of consultation between the national government and the TUC that had begun during World War I and had accelerated during and after World War II was abruptly brought to a halt. The Employment Acts aim at restricting closed shops, picketing, and strikes without a ballot of members. The government also showed a determination to win confrontations with unions, a policy that was made plain by its defeat of the 12-month-long coal miners' strike in 1984-1985.

Since 1980, the British labor movement has been a case study of the "decline of labor," caused by a mixture of economic and political forces. The recession of the early 1980s drastically cut employment in the older parts of manufacturing such as steelmaking and shipbuilding, industries that were strongholds of organized labor. Union membership figures from the Certification Office of Trade Unions and Employers' Associations show a fall of 3.7 million between 1980 and 1991, of which nearly 2.5 million occurred between 1980 and 1985. When considered annually, these falls corresponded closely to falls in **manufacturing** employment. The decline was not offset by the growth in employment in the **services sector** because of the diversity of this employment and its often **part-time** or casual nature, which made union recruitment difficult. Neither did the unions show an understanding of the need for recruiting drives in these new areas of employment.

Considered by region, the percentage distribution of union members has been relatively stable between 1984 and 2002, but there have been substantial general declines in the proportion of employees who were union members. In London, the proportion of employees who were union members fell from 47 to 25 percent. In the North West, the fall was from 71 to 34 percent. Over this period, the national proportion of employees who were union members fell from 58 to 29 percent. At the same time, the level of unionization remained higher in Scotland, Wales, Northern Ireland, and the north of England than in southern England.

The 1980s saw the continued decline in the number of small unions, which were usually absorbed by larger ones. From a peak of 1,384 unions in 1920, the number of unions fell to 453 by 1979, to 254 by 1993, and to 226 by 2001. The most important union **amalgamations** since 1992 were those between the Amalgamated Engineering Union and the Electrical Electronic Telecommunication and Plumbing Union in 1992, and the mergers that created **UNISON** in 1993 and **Amicus** in 2002.

Ironically, it was under the Thatcher government that the quality of statistics about labor union members improved markedly, with the introduction of an annual labor force survey based on households beginning in 1989. The survey showed that between 1989 and 1997, the number of union members fell from 8.9 to 7.2 million and that the proportion of employees who were union members fell from 39 to 30 percent.

Although Thatcher was replaced as Conservative leader by John Major in 1990, the antiunion policies she had begun continued. On May 1, 1997, the Labour Party (now called "New Labour") under Tony Blair won a landslide victory at the national elections and maintained his majority with a second large win in June 2001. However, the change of government made little change to organized labor. The Employment Acts were not repealed and the government, mindful of public resentment over the strikes during the **"winter of discontent,"** was careful to keep its distance from organized labor. In turn, the left wing of organized labor has been critical of the New Labour of being too close to big business and ignoring the concerns of Labour voters.

Certainly the return of a Labour government has done nothing to halt the long-term decline in labor union membership. Between 1997 and 2002, the number of union members actually rose from 7.2 to 7.3 million, but this increase failed to match employment growth over the same period. As a result, the proportion of employees who were union members fell from 30 to 29 percent, with the main factor being a fall of union membership among males in full-time employment.

UNITED MINE WORKERS OF AMERICA (UMWA). From about 1905 to 1939, the UMWA was the largest labor union in the **United States**. As in the **United Kingdom**, the home of many of the first generation of U.S. coal miners, organization among miners began at a regional level. A Miners' Association was formed in St. Clair County, Illinois, in 1861; it became the American Miners' Association in 1863, by which time it had spread to the coalfields of Missouri, Ohio, and Pennsylvania. Its success proved short-lived; although it claimed 20,000 members, it had largely collapsed by 1866. Unionism was revived in the late 1870s by the miners of the Hocking Valley, Ohio, who formed a new union in 1882. In 1883, the Amalgamated Association of Miners of the United States was formed based largely on the coalfields of Ohio and Pennsylvania. A new body, the National Federation of Miners and Mine Laborers, was formed in Indianapolis in 1885. In 1886, the **Knights of Labor** formed a second national miners' union, the Miner and Mine Laborers' National District Assembly No. 135. To avoid competition between the two bodies, a joint conference agreed to the organization of the National Progressive Union of Miners and Mine Laborers, but the Knights of Labor body continued to operate more or less independently.

Finally, in January 1890, the National Progressive Union of Miners and Mine Laborers was reformed as the United Mine Workers of America and was recognized by the **American Federation of Labor** (AFL). Major defeats in **strikes** and the economic depression of the 1890s reduced the UMWA to only 10,000 members in the mid-1890s, but an unexpectedly successful **general strike** in the bituminous **coal mining** industry in 1898 (which gained its participants a standard wage and the eight-hour work day) boosted **membership** from 97,000 in 1898 to 250,100 by

1904. The UMWA's leader, John Mitchell, used the victory to organize the miners on the anthracite coalfields of western Pennsylvania. In 1902, the UMWA won a famous victory in its strike on the anthracite coalfields after the personal intervention of President Theodore Roosevelt.

Despite the failure to organize the miners of West Virginia and elsewhere, the membership of the UMWA grew to nearly four million by 1920, when the controversial **John L. Lewis** became its president, an office he held until 1960. Under Lewis, the UMWA became a far more centralized body and played a notable role in labor **politics**, notably through the formation of the **Congress of Industrial Organizations** (CIO). When it withdrew from the AFL in 1947, it followed an independent path. Lewis's leadership and the diminished importance of coal as an energy source reduced the membership of the UMWA to 213,100 by 1973, compared to its peak of 500,000 in 1945. In 1989, the UMWA claimed a membership of 150,000. In 2002, there were only 39,000 union members employed in mining (compared to 66,000 in 2001) or 9 percent of mining employees. *See also* MINEWORKERS' FEDERATION OF GREAT BRITAIN.

UNITED STATES OF AMERICA. Organized labor in the United States emerged in the late 18th century but was largely confined to Philadelphia and New York. British **immigration** injected journeymen and their working habits and attitudes into the colonial economy. A register of emigrants to North America compiled between 1773 and 1776 showed that, of the 6,190 emigrants whose occupations were known, 49 percent were artisans, mechanics, or craftsmen. During the 1780s, journeymen and their employers in Philadelphia began to meet annually to negotiate their wages. The first **strike** in a single trade (**printing**, 1786) and in the building trade (1791) also occurred in Philadelphia. The first formal labor union likewise was formed in Philadelphia in 1794 by shoemakers. The union lasted until 1806, when it was made defunct by an adverse court decision. What little union growth there was after 1806 was destroyed by the depression of 1819. Unions began to reappear in 1822. In 1827, the first citywide federation of unions was formed at Philadelphia. This federation, along with other federations, was the basis of the 12 Workingmen's political parties, which operated in the late 1820s and early 1830s. The General Trades Union was formed in New York in 1833. Despite these activities, union **mem-**

bership was small; there were only about 44,000 in 1835 and in the financial crash of 1837 organized labor collapsed.

By 1864, there were 270 unions with a total membership of about 200,000. The growth of industrialization after the Civil War accentuated the worst features of the capitalist economy that had been previously evident, namely long hours and low wages. Old skills became obsolete and the general trend of economic development reduced opportunities for selfemployment and independence. **Agriculture** no longer offered the escape valve it had before the Civil War. In addition, mass immigration kept the wages of the unskilled low in the major cities. In 1869, the **National Labor Union** was formed but was unable to provide leadership for labor either politically or industrially. In any case, organized labor suffered greatly following the financial crisis of 1873, which reduced the number of national unions from 30 to nine by 1877 and the number of union members from 300,000 to about 50,000. Although organized labor was weak in the late 1870s, there was no shortage of discontent, as proved by the massive violent national railroad strikes in 1877, or of labor activity, as shown by the conversion of the **Knights of Labor** into a national body and the formation of the International Labor Union in 1878.

The 1880s saw the emergence of mass unionism in the United States for the first time; there were over a million union members by 1886, of whom 70 percent were members of the Knights of Labor, but this success disguised serious weaknesses. What advances labor achieved were through the cooperation of **craft union** members in skilled occupations; without this support, the unskilled union members could achieve little. Moreover, much of the membership was new to unionism and its discontent over wages and hours of work applied to immigrants in the large cities. This, and the association of labor with violent protests, made it possible for organized labor to be portrayed as something foreign and outside of mainstream American society, which still had strong agricultural roots.

The demise of the Knights of Labor in the 1890s and the relative success of the better-paid employees represented by the craft unions of the **American Federation of Labor** (AFL) also reinforced, as well as reflected, the far wider dispersal in earnings between the skilled and unskilled compared to the **United Kingdom**. The barriers to organized labor achieving the fairly high coverage of nonagricultural employees that prevailed in Western Europe and

Australasia by 1913 were formidable. They included enormous racial and ethnic divisions, a generally hostile legal environment, and
strong, well-organized employers. The AFL added to these barriers
by its unwillingness to build a mass union movement among the
unskilled, leaving the task to alternative bodies such as the **Industrial Workers of the World** (IWW) and the **Congress of Industrial Organizations** (CIO) in the 1930s.

But it was in its attitude to politics that American organized
labor showed its greatest distinctiveness from the labor movements
of other Western nations. In Western Europe and Australasia, labor
unions by 1900 were closely associated with **social-democrat, socialist, and labor political parties**. In the United States, this kind
of permanent relationship did not exist (though this is not to say
that the AFL did not participate in **politics**). The AFL's leadership
regarded these relationships with intense suspicion and developed
its own peculiar conservative ideology of **voluntarism**, which put it
at odds with bodies such as the **International Federation of Trade
Unions** (IFTU). By 1930, only 9 percent of American employees
were union members, or the same level that had been reached in
1913.

The election of the Franklin D. Roosevelt administration in
1933 and its prolabor stance, as shown by its **National Labor Relations Act**, enabled the emergence of the **Congress of Industrial
Organizations** (CIO) and its recruitment of millions of semiskilled employees into the ranks of organized labor. It was the main
reason for raising the proportion of employees in unions to 28 percent by 1950, a good result for American labor, but a low figure by
Western European and Australasian standards. The proportion of
American employees who were union members peaked at 32 percent in 1953 but declined steadily thereafter. The public reputation
of organized labor suffered in the 1950s and 1960s with well-
publicized inquiries into corruption within certain unions, notably
the **Teamsters**. As in other Western economies, the impact of technological change whittled away at the parts of the labor force where
labor was traditionally strong such as **coal mining**, steel, **printing**,
and the **railroads**. At the same time, the labor force saw a general
shift towards **white-collar** employment and a rising number of
women employees. Union recruitment of new members was also
hampered by **right-to-work laws** in many states. The United States
is one of the very few industrialized countries that has not ratified
the **International Labour Organisation** Conventions 87 (Freedom

of Association and the Right to Organize, 1948) and 98 (Right to Organize and Collective Bargaining, 1949).

Politically, organized labor was just one interest group among many and although since 1936 it has been allied with the Democratic Party, this alliance has not protected it from antilabor forces within the party. Among reformers organized labor also suffered from its conservative posture, particularly its slowness in dealing with racial discrimination. From 1980, organized labor in the United States, as in other countries, entered a prolonged crisis, which was epitomized by severe slumps in steelmaking and automobile manufacturing, industries characterized by outmoded production methods. It also faced a hostile political climate under the Republican presidencies of **Ronald Reagan** (1981-1989) and George Bush (1989-1993). Between 1983 and 1993, the proportion of employees who were union members fell from 20 to 16 percent. Bill Clinton's election to the presidency in 1993—the first Democrat administration since 1981—brought some benefits to organized labor; for example, an antiunion presidential order concerning federal contractors was rescinded. However, in November 1994 the Democrats lost control of both the House of Representatives and the Senate to the Republicans, which limited Clinton's ability to introduce prounion policies for the rest of his administration. In the same year, Clinton successfully extended the North American Free Trade Agreement to Mexico, a move opposed by organized labor, even though it included a subagreement on workers' rights. Also in 1994, the Commission on the Future of Worker-Management Relations drew attention to the continued prevalence of concerted employer hostility to organized labor, as shown by practices such as "union busting," the illegal firing of union supporters trying to form unions in nonunionized workplaces, and a general lack of acceptance of the legitimacy of unions in democratic society, in contrast to Western Europe.

During the Clinton administration (1993-2000), the number of U.S. union members fell slightly from 16.6 to 16.3 million, despite substantial economic growth between 1994 and 2000. By 2002, the number of U.S. unions had fallen to 16.1 million or to only 13 percent of all employees. The highest proportions of union members by state in 2002 were among employees in New York (25 percent) and the lowest in North Carolina (3 percent). Although the presidency of George W. Bush (2001-) has been predictably antiunion in its policies, U.S. organized labor continues to suffer from long-term problems, some of which are of its own making. Notable among these is a poor public image and an association with racketeering and violence based on events from the 1930s into the 1970s. Under **John Sweeney**, the AFL-CIO has begun to address this problem by broadening the scope of organized labor to include social issues such as education, health, and pensions and by greater participation in grassroots campaigns.

In 2003, the International Confederation of Free Trade Unions (ICFTU) continued to feature the United States in its annual survey of **violations of trade union rights** on the grounds that there were legal restrictions that excluded 32 million employees from **collective bargaining** and that private companies harassed labor union members and actively discouraged attempts to form unions. It claimed that at least 10 percent of union supporters trying to form a union were illegally fired. It was also critical about legal restrictions on the right to strike and collective bargaining in the **public sector**.

UNITED STEELWORKERS OF AMERICA (USWA). Despite promising beginnings, the steel industry of the **United States** was a mainly nonunion industry until 1936. The first union was formed by skilled British puddlers in Pittsburgh in 1857. They were joined by the formation of a union among skilled workers in the furnaces and rolling mills in 1861. A united industry union of skilled workers, the Amalgamated Association of Iron and Steel Workers of the United States, was formed in Pittsburgh in 1876. By 1891, this union claimed 24,000 members, but in 1892 it suffered a crushing defeat in a **strike** to resist wage cuts by the Carnegie Steel Company at Homestead, Pennsylvania. In the following years, the Amalgamated proved incapable of meeting the enormous managerial and technological changes that came into steelmaking in the 1890s and 1900s. In particular, the unions faced a general deskilling of jobs, which greatly reduced their bargaining power. Lesser skilled jobs meant that wages could be kept low and that immigrants could be easily recruited. In 1909, the largest steel company, the United States Steel Company, refused to recognize the association and defeated it in a strike. The company was able to maintain a union-free labor force until 1937. By 1912, the United States steelmaking industry was a byword for high productivity but with low wages and long working hours. Discontent among its employees led to the great strike of 1919, which was organized by the **American Fed-**

eration of Labor (AFL) through its Iron and Steel Organizing Committee. Despite 300,000 taking part, the strike ended after three and a half months on January 8, 1920, in the utter defeat of the strikers.

The **National Industrial Recovery Act** of 1933 laid the foundation for a revival of unionism in the steel industry. In 1934, the AFL began a campaign to recruit union members in the steel industry, but these efforts were frustrated by the leadership of the Amalgamated, which wanted its almost defunct union to lead the campaign; it was then swept aside in 1936 by the **Congress of Industrial Organizations** (CIO), which launched its own campaign to unionize the industry. Led by **Philip Murray** on behalf of **John L. Lewis**, the aim of the campaign was to build an **industrial union** for the steel industry and to increase the bargaining power of the **United Mine Workers of America** in negotiating with steel companies that owned coal mines. The CIO recruited 200,000 steelworkers for the Steel Workers' Organizing Committee and in secret discussions Lewis secured not only recognition for the Committee from U.S. Steel in March 1937 but also a 10 percent wage increase, an eight-hour work day, and a 40-hour work week. However, the CIO's campaign against the independent steel producers was defeated by violence and a downturn in the demand for steel. Ten strikers were killed and 80 wounded by **police** at the steelworks of the Republic Steel Company in South Chicago in May 1937.

In 1942, the Steel Workers' Organizing Committee was reorganized as the United Steelworkers of America and was forced to use the National War Labor Board to compel the independent steel producers to engage in collective bargaining. Murray led the USWA from its formation to his death in 1952. In 1946, the USWA conducted a month-long strike throughout the industry, which yielded it a large pay increase. Through strikes in 1949 and 1952 and bargaining, the USWA gained the closed or union shop and a pension scheme for members. Defeat in the strike of 1959 against management's attempt to change work rules and a downturn in the national economy caused the USWA's **membership** to fall from 1.2 million in 1956 to 876,000 in 1965. By 1975, membership had recovered to the one million mark, but the worldwide crisis in the steel industry in 1982-1983 caused membership to fall to 572,000 by 1985 and to 459,000 by 1992. In 2001-2002, the USWA successfully lobbied the federal government to impose tariffs on imported steel from certain countries.

UNIVERSAL ALLIANCE OF DIAMOND WORKERS (UADW). The UADW **international trade secretariat** (ITS) was formed in Antwerp in 1905, although international conferences among diamond employees began in 1889. By 1913, the UADW had 22,700 members. Between 1975 and 1992, **membership** of the UADW was stationary at about 10,000. The UADW was one of 16 international trade secretariats associated with the **International Confederation of Free Trade Unions** (ICFTU) in 1995. In November 2000, the UADW merged with the **International Federation of Chemical, Energy, Mine, And General Workers' Unions.** At the time of its merger, the UADW had about 100,000 members. One of its last acts was to accuse the diamond industry of financing wars in **Angola, Democratic Republic of the Congo, Liberia,** and **Sierra Leone.**

URUGUAY. Organized labor in Uruguay was imported by European **immigration; strikes** were recorded by 1884 and the first union congress was held in 1896 to campaign for the eight-hour day. By 1930, there were 28,000 union members in Uruguay. Organized labor was politically divided, mainly between **socialists** and **communists.** Uruguay was represented in the **International Confederation of Free Trade Unions** (ICFTU) between 1951 and 1975. Its representative in 1975 was the *Confederación General de Trabajadores del Uruguay* (General Confederation of Uruguay Workers); with 40,000 members, it had existed in various forms since 1951. In June 1973, organized labor conducted a **general strike** against the military government's economic program that was defeated and ushered in a highly repressive response. Uruguay's government became one of the world's worst offenders of **human rights** abuses, and the country has not been represented in the ICFTU since the 1970s. In 2001, there were about 120,000 union members in Uruguay.

UZBEKISTAN. Independent of the former **Soviet Union** since August 1991, organized labor has failed to emerge in Uzbekistan because of the country's lack of economic and social development. In 2002, Uzbekistan was not mentioned by the **International Con-**

federation of Free Trade Unions (ICFTU) in its survey of **violations of trade union rights**.

-V-

VANUATU. Independent of the **United Kingdom** and **France** since July 1980 and formerly known as the New Hebrides, organized labor in Vanuatu has developed since the 1970s. In 1988, the Vanuatu Trade Union Congress with 1,500 members joined the **International Confederation of Free Trade Unions** (ICFTU).

VATICAN. Independent from **Italy** since February 1929, the Vatican was represented in the **International Confederation of Free Trade Unions** (ICFTU) by 1987 by the Associazione Dipendenti Laici Vaticani (Vatican Association of Dependent Laity) which had about 700 members in 1996.

VENEZUELA. Organized labor developed in secret during the dictatorship of General Juan Vincente Gómez between 1908 and 1935. After Gomez's death in 1935, Venezuela began to move gradually towards democracy, aided by organized labor in alliance with peasants and students. The *Confederación des Trabajadores de Venezuela* (Confederation of Workers of Venezuela) (CTV) was formed in December 1936. Also in 1936, organized labor formed a **socialist** political party, *Acción Democrática* (Democratic Action), to work for democracy and social change. The CTV was weakened by divisions between supporters of Democratic Action and **communists**. In 1941, organized labor was legalized, and in 1945 a military coup brought in a democratic government. Democratic Action won the 1947 elections, but a military counter coup on November 24, 1948, ousted the government and repressed organized labor. The CTV was formally dissolved by the government on February 25, 1949. Democratic rule was not restored until January 1958 following a **general strike**. The CTV was a member in exile of the **International Confederation of Free Trade Unions** (ICFTU) from 1951 (when it claimed 200,000 members) and was a full member from 1959. In 2001, it claimed 750,700 members. Although both the Employment Law of 1990 and the 1999 constitution promote **freedom of association**, the ICFTU noted continued government interference in the affairs of organized labor in its global reports for

2000, 2001, and 2002, particularly the efforts of the Hugo Chávez government to replace organized labor with government-run puppet organizations. Between December 2, 2002, and February 3, 2003, there was an unsuccessful general strike in Venezuela led by oil workers against the Chávez government.

VER.DI. *Ver.di*, the shortened version of *Vereinte Dienstleistungsgewerkschaft* (United Services Labor Union), is the largest labor union in the world with just under three million members. It was formed in **Germany** on March 21, 2001, by the **amalgamation** of five labor unions: *Gewerkschaft Öffentliche Dienste, Transport und Verkehr* (Public Service, Transportation, and Traffic Labor Union or ÖTV) with 1.5 million members, the *Deutsche Angestellten-Gewerkschaft* (German **Private Sector** White-Collar Labor Union) with 450,000 members, the *Gewerkschaft Handel, Banken und Versicherungen* (Commerce, Banking, and Insurance Labor Union) with 440,600 members, the *Deutsche Postgewerkschaft* (German Postal Labor Union) with 446,000 members, and the *Industriegewerkschaft Medien* (Media Industrial Labor Union) with 175,000 members. Negotiations for the creation of *Ver.di* began in November 1998. The purpose of the merger was to arrest the decline in the **membership** of the unions (the four constituent unions had 3.4 million members in 1996) and to enable them to compete with large employers. In his inaugural address in Berlin, the president of *Ver.di*, Frank Bsirske, formerly of the ÖTV, stressed the need to recruit new members among **youth** (those under 30) and in the former East Germany. Almost two-thirds of the members of *Ver.di* are private sector **white-collar** employees and one-quarter work in the state of North Rhine-Westphalia.

VIETNAM. Organized labor in Vietnam originated in the participation by some Vietnamese intellectuals in labor affairs in **France** during World War I. Using this experience, they set up some unions in Vietnam (then French Indochina), beginning in Hanoi in 1920. Most labor organizing thereafter was carried out by **communists**. In 1929, the communists formed a labor federation as part of the struggle for independence from French rule. By 1930, the federation claimed 6,000 members, but it was crushed in 1930-1931 during a major peasant uprising against the French. Despite a new labor code and more toleration of labor organizations in the Popular Front period (1936-1939), these initiatives proved short-lived in the face of widespread discontent in Vietnam, the fall of the Léon Blum government in France, and the start of World War II. During the war, Vietnam was occupied by the Japanese. In 1946, the North Vietnamese government set up the Vietnam General Confederation of Labor on the Soviet model. In what was South Vietnam, the French **Catholic** labor federation, the *Confédération Française des Travailleurs Chrétiens*, was instrumental in forming the *Confédération Vietnamienne du Travail* (Vietnamese Confederation of Labor), which was based on unions among rice growers and employees in river transportation and later claimed 500,000 members. Two other labor federations were formed in 1952 and 1953, but they never had more than 70,000 members between them. In 1959, Vietnam was represented in the **International Confederation of Free Trade Unions** (ICFTU) by the *Union Ouvrière du Viet-nam* (Union of Vietnamese Workers), but this body had ceased to be affiliated by 1965. After the military reunification of Vietnam, the Vietnam General Federation of Labor Unions was created in June 1975, which subsumed the labor organizations of the South.

With the opening up of the Vietnamese economy to foreign investment and enterprises in the late 1980s, there was widespread exploitation manifested in long hours, low pay, and physical abuse. The federation, with assistance provided by the Australian chapter of the **International Labour Organisation** (ILO), persuaded the National Assembly at the end of June 1994 to approve a new labor code. The code obliged every foreign joint venture to establish a trade union within six months of beginning operations, allowed the employees of such enterprises the right to **strike**, set up independent courts of **conciliation and arbitration**, protected these employees from wrongful dismissal, and required retrenched employees to be paid severance pay. The first legal strike under the code occurred in August 1994. In 2002, the ICFTU reported that although labor unions were controlled by the Vietnam General Confederation of Labor, some strike action was tolerated and there were indications of independent activity among sections of the labor force, for example, among taxi drivers, market porters, and cooks. It also reported that there had been violence towards employees at some foreign-owned firms.

VIOLATIONS OF TRADE UNION RIGHTS. An annual survey conducted since 1984 by the **International Confederation of Free**

Trade Unions (ICFTU). The survey documents the condition of organized labor according to the relevant conventions of the **International Labour Organisation** (ILO). The survey includes information on labor union members murdered or assassinated, injured, arrested, or dismissed, by continent. The survey is one of the main ways in which the ICFTU reports on the effectiveness of the ILO's **international standard-setting** and is a prime source of information on the state of organized labor in the world.

VOLUNTARISM. Voluntarism is a term with two different meanings. In the **United States**, it referred to a doctrine subscribed to by the **American Federation of Labor** (AFL) and promoted by **Samuel Gompers** from the late 1890s to the early 1930s that stressed the need for organized labor to rely on its own resources for gaining improvement of pay and conditions and not on **politics** or political parties. Voluntarism saw a separation between the political process and organized labor, though the doctrine did not exclude lobbying political parties for favors. Voluntarism was strengthened within the AFL after its crushing failure to organize the steel industry in 1919. The doctrine suited workers in skilled unions that could provide welfare benefits to members but ignored the lesser skilled employees.

In the **United Kingdom**, the term voluntarism usually refers to the abstaining by the state from intervention in labor relations, particularly **labor disputes**, except to support or extend **collective bargaining**. For example, the Advisory Conciliation and Arbitration Service, the British government agency that was established in 1974 to resolve labor disputes, can only operate if the parties to the dispute agree to its participation. Since 1980, British governments have shown a greater willingness to intervene in labor relations and have passed laws to regulate their internal management and behavior. *See also* EMPLOYMENT ACTS.

-W-

WAGES. Wages, together with working hours, have traditionally been central topics for organized labor in **collective bargaining** with employers. Although the amount of wages was usually of most concern, the method and timing of payment also figured as issues in the 19th century. Payment in goods instead of money (or "truck") was widespread in the **United Kingdom** in the early 19th century even though it was outlawed as early as 1411. Similarly, the common practice of monthly payment of wages imposed undue hardship on employees and forced them into debt to meet day-to-day living costs.

The ability of organized labor to raise wages largely depends on the condition of the trade cycle. One area of wages where organized labor has been traditionally most active is in maintaining the differentials between wages in occupations by means of margins such as for skill or seniority. With the generally higher level of union strength between 1940 and 1980 in most Western countries, organized labor has sought to use economic growth to extend wages claims to cover holidays, severance, and redundancy. It has also tried to use increased productivity as a means of raising wages. The importance of unions in economic management, particularly to control inflation, was recognized by government through various experiments in prices and incomes policies in the United Kingdom and the **United States** in the 1970s; they attempted to limit general increases in wages. *See also* SHORTER WORKING HOURS; UNION-GOVERNMENT AGREEMENTS.

WAGNER ACT. Officially known as the National Labor Relations Act, this U.S. federal law, named for its promoter, Senator Robert F. Wagner, was passed by the Senate 11 days before the **National Industrial Recovery Act** (1933) was declared unconstitutional by the Supreme Court. The Wagner Act reaffirmed the legal right of organized labor to recruit and represent employees in **collective bargaining** without interference from employers. A National Labor Relations Board was created to administer the act. The scope of the act was amended by the **Taft-Hartley Act** in 1947.

WESTERN LABOR UNION. *See* AMERICAN LABOR UNION.

WESTERN SAMOA. Independent of **New Zealand** since January 1962, an association of school teachers existed by 1973, but no labor unions as such. The Public Service Association was the country's affiliate of the **International Confederation of Free Trade Unions** (ICFTU) by 1988, with 2,200 members.

"WINTER OF DISCONTENT." This phrase from the opening of William Shakespeare's *Richard III* has been commonly applied to a wave of **strikes** in the **United Kingdom** during the winter of 1978-1979. The number of working days lost per thousand employees was 1,270 in 1979, compared to 410 in 1978. The strikes occurred mainly in transportation, garbage collection, hospitals, cemeteries, and the **public sector**. 1979 was the worst year for working days lost per thousand employees in **labor disputes** since the **British General Strike** in 1926. Many of the strikes were accompanied by violence during **picketing**. The "winter of discontent" ended the **union-government agreement** between the British **Labour Party** and the Trades Union Congress (TUC) begun in 1974 that had tried to limit voluntarily union wage claims to 5 percent. The strike wave lost organized labor much public support and was a main reason why the Labour government of Jim Callaghan was defeated in the national elections in May 1979 by the Conservative Party led by Margaret Thatcher. Between 1980 and 1993 the Conservative governments passed a series of **Employment Acts** to reduce the power of organized labor.

WHITE-COLLAR UNIONISM. Up to the 1940s white-collar employees were a minor part of organized labor in most Western countries, with unions of **blue-collar** employees being the dominant force. Blue-collar unions tended to regard white-collar unions poorly because their members did not perform "real" work. Typically, white-collar occupations included teachers, salaried government workers, and clerks in all industries. For most of history, distinctions of social class underlay blue- and white-collar work. Blue-collar workers were, by general definition, the working class, whereas white-collar employees came from the middle class and often saw themselves as socially superior. In **Germany**, federal laws from 1911 even recognized a "collar line" that treated white-collar workers better than blue-collar workers. As members of the middle class, white-collar employees were less likely to join unions, particularly if they enjoyed advantageous conditions from their employers.

Although lacking the stature of blue-collar unions within organized labor, unions of white-collar employees have a long history. In the **United States**, the first white-collar unions emerged among retail clerks in the 1830s who wanted employers to adopt a standard early closing time; in 1864, dry goods employees in New York went on **strike** to prevent the imposition of longer hours. In the **United Kingdom**, the first white-collar unions were formed among teachers in the 1860s as a result of school managers being given the right to appoint and dismiss teachers. Yet it was not until the 1880s that sustained growth in the number of white-collar unions occurred. In the United States, the first national white-collar union, the Retail Clerks' National Protective Association, joined the **American Federation of Labor** (AFL) in 1888. In the United Kingdom, white-collar unions were formed among national government clerks (1890) and postal workers (1891).

As the economies of Western nations matured, the **service sector** grew, and, with it, so did the number of white-collar employees. Between about 1910 and 1930, the proportion of white-collar employees in the labor forces of the United States, Germany, and Britain rose from about 13 to about 20 percent. Within organized labor in Britain, **Denmark**, and Germany, a fifth of labor union members were white-collar employees by 1930.

After 1950, white-collar unions grew with the growth in **public sector** employment, particularly as government was more likely to concede recognition to unions than the private sector. At the same time, blue-collar occupations grew relatively slowly and their share of the labor force declined. During the 1960s white-collar employees became more willing to join unions, and their labor federations joined with the traditional labor bodies based on blue-collar employees. In 2001, 45 percent of union members in **Australia** and 48 percent in the United States were white-collar employees. *See also* BLUE-COLLAR/WHITE-COLLAR; EDUCATION; FEDERA-TION OF INTERNATIONAL CIVIL SERVANTS' ASSOCIA-TIONS; NATIONAL EDUCATION ASSOCIATION; UNISON; WOMEN.

WOMEN. One of the biggest changes in the post-1950 structure of union **membership** has been the rising proportion of women. In 1913, women made up only 11 percent of labor union members in the **United Kingdom**, 8 percent in **Germany**, and 4 percent in **Australia** and the **United States**. By 1950, women made up 18 percent of labor union members in Britain and Germany, 19 percent in Australia, and 23 percent in **Japan**.

The entry of women into the labor force gathered pace after 1960 both in numbers and in the proportion of women working, making them more likely to be recruited by the largely male-dominated labor unions. Increasingly, women moved into the expanding **white-collar** occupations and were no longer just to be found in low-paid **manufacturing** occupations such as in the clothing industry. The **International Confederation of Free Trade Unions** (ICFTU) estimated that between 1949 and 1970, the proportion of women among its affiliates rose from 7 to 22 percent and to 36 percent by 1996. In 1956, the ICFTU set up a Women's Committee, and a secretariat in 1957. In 1962, it introduced specialized training programs for women in Third World countries. In 1992, the ICFTU launched its Positive Action Program for Women in Development Cooperation with the objective of setting a minimum target of 30 percent for women's participation in all labor union activities.

In 2001, the proportion of women in labor unions was 47 percent in the United Kingdom, 43 percent in Australia, and 42 percent in the United States, double what it had been in 1960. In contrast, the proportion of women in labor unions in Germany and Japan has changed little over this period. In December 2002, the ICFTU admitted its first woman into a leadership position: Mamounta Cissé, an African, was appointed as the second assistant secretary-general of the ICFTU. *See also* WHITE-COLLAR UNIONISM; table 12, appendix F.

WORKERS' UNION (WU). The WU was one of the largest general unions in the **United Kingdom** in the early 20th century. Formed in May 1898, it set out to recruit all employees whether skilled or unskilled and, through militancy, work towards the creation of a **socialist** society. The WU was formed in the wake of the major defeat suffered by the **Amalgamated Society of Engineers** in London in 1897 by the leading labor left wing leader Tom Mann (1856-1941). The new union barely survived its first few years: **membership** reached 2,000 by the end of 1898, and 4,170 by 1899, but fell to 1,000 by 1902. With the recovery in the economy after 1906, membership rose to 91,000 in 1913 and to 140,000 by 1914. Much of this growth was achieved through the recruitment of poorly paid employees, particularly in engineering and **agriculture**. By 1918, membership reached a peak of 379,000, a quarter of them **women**. Although the WU affiliated with the **Trades Union Congress** (TUC) in 1917 (after two failed attempts), it was disliked by a number of other unions such as the Agricultural Labourers' Union and especially by the Amalgamated Engineers as a competitor for members.

In 1916, the WU began negotiations for **amalgamation** with the National Amalgamated Union of Labour and the Municipal Employees' Association, which resulted in the formation of a new, but only partly amalgamated, organization, the National Amalgamated Workers' Union, in January 1919; this body claimed 500,000 members in 1920. Thereafter, membership of the WU plummeted to 140,000 in 1923 through economic depression, high turnover of members, and hostility from other unions. The WU never recovered and, in 1929, was absorbed into the **Transport and General Workers' Union** (TGWU), but the WU gave the TGWU an organizational foothold in a number of industries whose employment growth helped it to become Britain's largest union by the late 1930s.

WORKING HOURS. Although there are few statistics on working hours before the Industrial Revolution, there is an impression that working hours, although long, were more varied before it than after it. Where work was monotonous, customs like "Saint Monday" were observed by the 18th century. Figures for the **Amalgamated Society of Engineers** in the **United Kingdom** show that the number of hours its members worked in a week varied from 57 to 63 in 1851 and from 56 to 60 by 1869. In **Germany**, the typical work week in manufacturing was 78 hours in the 1860s, 66 hours in the 1870s, and between 58 and 60 hours between 1911 and 1914. The long, monotonous week brought by the Industrial Revolution made the reduction of work hours an important issue for organized labor in Europe and North America.

The Ten Hours movement began with textile employees in England in the 1830s, and the short-lived radical body, the National Regeneration Society (1833-1834), advocated an eight-hour work day. In **Australia**, James Stephens (1821-1889), an English Chartist, played an important role in winning the eight-hour work day in a number of skilled trades in the colony of Victoria in the mid-1850s. In 1869, the **National Labor Union** succeeded in gaining the eight-hour work day for U.S. federal employees. In 1871-1872 engineering and building employees in northeast England won the nine-hour work day through **labor disputes**.

Most governments before 1900 avoided legislating for maximum work hours. The English Factory Act of 1875 laid down a maximum work week of 56.5 hours for **women** and teenagers but ignored men. In the 1880s and early 1890s, there was international agitation for the eight-hour work day by organized labor. British railroad employees did not get the eight-hour work day until 1920 and then only after a national **strike** in 1919. Since 1945, metal unions have been at the forefront of reducing work hours in **Australia**, Germany, and the United Kingdom. For example, the first debates about the 35-hour week in Western Europe were conducted within *IG Metall* in 1977. Despite the efforts of organized labor, declining membership of labor unions has coincided with increases in working hours in most industrialized countries since the 1980s. In 1999, the **International Labour Organisation** (ILO) reported that the number of working hours worked per person per year was 1,966 in the **United States,** 1,889 in **Japan,** 1,866 in **Australia,** 1,656 in **France,** 1,731 in the **United Kingdom,** and 1,399 in **Norway.** *See also* FULL-TIME/PART-TIME EMPLOYMENT; SHORTER WORKING HOURS.

WORLD CONFEDERATION OF LABOR (WCL). The WCL began as the International Federation of Christian Trade Unions (IFCTU), which was formed in The Hague in 1920 and traced its origins to the Ghent Anti-Socialist League, which had been organized in 1878. The IFCTU represented labor unions that objected to the anticlericalism of the **socialist** and **anarchist** labor unions that dominated European organized labor. The entry of the IFCTU into the **International Confederation of Free Trade Unions** (ICFTU) was opposed by **socialist** labor unions in Western Europe, and the IFCTU turned its attention to the Third World and recruiting affiliates from Muslim and Buddhist countries, with the main criterion for membership being belief in a religion rather than adherence to Christianity. In 1968, the IFCTU changed its name to the World Confederation of Labor. In 2001, the WCL claimed 26 million members (compared to 19 million in 1992 and 14.5 million in 1973), mainly in Latin America or countries where **Catholicism** was strong. On May 28, 2003, the **International Confederation of Free Trade Unions** issued a call to the WCL to join with it to better meet the challenge of **globalization.**

WORLD CONFEDERATION OF ORGANIZATIONS OF THE TEACHING PROFESSION (WCOPT). The WCOPT was made up of two federations, the International Federation of Teachers' Associations and the International Federation of Secondary Teachers, from its foundation in 1952 until February 1993, when it agreed to merge with the **International Federation of Free Teaching Unions** to form the **Education International**. An independent, nonpolitical body, the WCOPT had 13 million members in 191 countries at the announcement of its merger. *See also* EDUCATION.

WORLD FEDERATION OF TRADE UNIONS (WFTU). The WFTU was formed in Paris on September 25, 1945 at an international conference of labor organizations to replace the **International Federation of Trade Unions**. The WFTU was ruptured by the Cold War and communist opposition to the Marshall Plan. In December 1949 the noncommunist countries withdrew from the WFTU and set up their own international labor organization, the **International Confederation of Free Trade Unions** (ICFTU). The WFTU continued as a communist-dominated organization, but since the collapse of the Soviet Union in 1989 has lost much of its support. Its membership is largely confined to countries where independent organized labor is not permitted. At its 2000 conference, the WFTU claimed to represent 120 million members, compared to 214 million in 1991.

-Y-

YEMEN. Part of the Ottoman Empire until 1918, Yemen had a precarious independence until the late 1940s. Poverty, the lack of democratic tradition, and conflict between royalist and extreme **socialist** ideologies made for political instability and warfare that resulted in the splitting of the country in 1967. North and South Yemen were not reunited until May 1990, and the first general election was not held until April 1993. Despite this unpromising political and economic background, Yemeni civil society gave rise to **human rights** and **women's** groups, cooperatives, and labor unions. In 1990, the General Federation of Workers' Trade Unions (GFWTU) was created, uniting Yemeni labor unions just before the country's reunification and claimed a **membership** of 350,000. Since 1990, the GFWTU has been an active player in promoting democracy in Yemen and became an affiliate of the **International Confederation of Free Trade Unions** (ICFTU) in 2002, with a declared membership of 300,000. In late 2002, a new labor law came into force that met most of the **International Labour Or-**

ganisation (ILO) standards, but with some restrictions such as banning **strikes** at ports, airports, and hospitals.

YOUTH. Youth traditionally became union members in most Western countries through the completion of an **apprenticeship**, a system of trade training and employment. Since the 1960s, apprenticeship has declined and this, along with other changes in the labor market, has made it harder for organized labor to recruit youth. By the 1970s, it was noted that youth often had broken work experience (whether through choice or necessity) and that their relatively high labor mobility contributed to their low **membership of organized labor**. Also, youth are often employed in relatively low-skilled jobs in wholesale and retail trade, an industry where union membership is low and labor turnover high. Youth also suffer from disproportionately high levels of unemployment even in periods of prosperity.

In 1999, the **International Confederation of Free Trade Unions** (ICFTU) recognized the need for organized labor to make a greater effort to recruit youth into organized labor. In 2001, labor force surveys in the **United Kingdom** and the **United States** both showed low levels of union membership among youth: 5 percent for the United Kingdom for those aged under 20 and 5 percent also for the United States for those aged 16 to 24. *See also* CHILD LABOR.

YUGOSLAVIA. The former federal republic of Yugoslavia was created in 1918 from part of the Austro-Hungarian Empire; it lasted until 1991 when it was torn apart by a murderous civil war. Within the borders of the former republic, organized labor first emerged in the form of mutual aid societies in the 1870s. The first labor unions were formed in 1894 in **Slovenia**, in 1904 in **Croatia** and Serbia, and in 1905 in **Bosnia-Herzegovina**, **Macedonia**, and Montenegro. In 1904, when it became affiliated with the **International Federation of Trade Unions** (IFTU), Serbia had about 5,100 union members; Croatia became an affiliate in 1907 and Bosnia in 1910. By 1913, the number of union members in these countries was 10,000 in Serbia, 7,000 in Croatia, and 5,000 in Bosnia.

After the creation of Yugoslavia, a Communist Party and a national labor federation were formed in 1919. By 1920, there were 25,000 union members, but following a number of **strikes**, the Communist Party and the labor federation were banned by the government. A new labor federation was formed by the **communists** and those unions not affiliated with any political party. In 1922, the Social Democrats set up a labor federation called the United Federation of Workers' Unions of Yugoslavia, which was an affiliate of the IFTU until 1939. From 1934, the United Federation of Workers' Unions of Yugoslavia became more militant through communist influence; in 1935, the government challenged its power by setting up a labor federation modeled on the fascist example of **Italy** and **Germany**. Before its suppression in 1940 the federation claimed 100,000 members.

After the Nazi withdrawal in December 1944, a new labor federation was established in 1945, which adopted its present title, *Savez Sindikata Jugoslaviji*, in 1948. Reflecting Yugoslavia's independence from Soviet control, it withdrew from the **World Federation of Trade Unions** (WFTU) in 1950 although relations improved after 1969. Organized labor in Yugoslavia was given greater freedom than elsewhere in Eastern Europe between 1948 and 1988 (for example, in being able to conduct local strikes). In late 1988, the first independent demonstrations occurred among Yugoslav employees. Independent labor unions were formed during 1989 by railroad engineers and airline pilots. Of the four separate republics created by the breakup of Yugoslavia, only two have been admitted to membership of the **International Confederation of Free Trade Unions** (ICFTU): **Croatia** (in 1997) and **Yugoslavia (Federal Republic** (in 2000).

YUGOSLAVIA (FEDERAL REPUBLIC). A remnant nation created from the federal republic of **Yugoslavia** by the breakaway of **Croatia, Slovenia**, and **Bosnia-Herzogovina** in 1991, Yugoslavia (Federal Republic) has been represented in the **International Confederation of Free Trade Unions** (ICFTU) since 2000 by two labor federations in Serbia and Montenegro with a combined membership of 243,700. The ICFTU has reported that procedure for the registration of unions is difficult, requiring the consent of the employer. It also reported harassment of union officials and members in 2002. On February 3, 2003, the name of the country was officially changed to Serbia and Montenegro.

-Z-

ZAIRE. *See* CONGO (DEMOCRATIC REPUBLIC).

ZAMBIA. Independent from the **United Kingdom** since October 1964, organized labor in Zambia dates from the early 1930s when there were tensions between European and African miners. Labor unions were legalized in 1949. The Northern Rhodesia Trades Union Congress was an affiliate of the **International Confederation of Free Trade Unions** (ICFTU) by 1957 and claimed 9,300 members. After independence, the government disapproved of union federations or individual unions joining international labor bodies. The Zambia Congress of Trade Unions (formed in 1965) did not affiliate with the ICFTU until 1990 and claimed 299,000 members by 2001. Zambia's dependence upon copper exports made its economy vulnerable to the fall in the world price of copper since 1975 and was the underlying cause of economic malaise and social unrest. Although the laws of Zambia tolerate organized labor, the ICFTU noted that the government has been increasingly antiunion since 1999 in response to **strikes** over falling pay and living standards, particularly among government employees. In 2002, it noted that there had not been a single legal strike in Zambia since 1994.

ZIMBABWE. Independent from the **United Kingdom** since April 1980, although ruled by a minority European government that declared its independence in 1965, the first unions were formed by Europeans in the early 20th century. The first African union, the Industrial and Commercial Workers' Union, was formed in 1927. As in other African countries, organized labor was closely associated with the independence movement. Although some biracial unions developed, notably among miners and steelworkers, most unions were of one race only. The Zimbabwe Congress of Trade Unions affiliated with the **International Confederation of Free Trade Unions** (ICFTU) in 1991 and claimed a **membership** of 361,000. Since the late 1990s, organized labor has been caught up in the tyranny and violence of the Robert Mugabe government and economic decline. In its survey of **violations of trade union rights** for 2002 the ICFTU noted the use of workers' committees (begun in 1985) to undermine labor unions, the exemption of the **export processing zones** from labor regulation, and a general climate of heightened violence, harassment, and intimidation by the government against the leaders of organized labor as well as other opponents of the Mugabe government.

.

BIBLIOGRAPHY

INTRODUCTION

Labor unions have always attracted interest from different disciplines, each offering its own insights. As well as historians, labor unions are regularly studied by economists, political scientists, sociologists, and lawyers. As the literature on this subject is vast, the bibliography is restricted mainly to scholarly books with their own bibliographies. Preference has been given to works published since 1980; earlier works are listed where they have become sources in their own right or where they have attained the status of classics in the field or simply because there was no obvious later work.

Because the study of organized labor is often controversial, the inclusion of a work in the bibliography does not necessarily imply recommendation; it is simply to note its importance and possible interest to the reader. It should be noted too that this bibliography makes no claim to be complete, particularly for the topics not expressly about organized labor, but rather to indicate what works are available and might be consulted with profit.

The bibliography contains a comprehensive listing of international comparative studies of industrial relations because these works, both old and new, are convenient starting points for investigating countries as well as being useful sources of information on organized labor. Although they typically stress contemporary developments, they usually contain a summary of past historical developments.

Given that this dictionary is part of a series about religions, philosophies, and movements, it is also important not to overlook the more general guides to reference material. Of special importance is Alan Day and Joan M. Harvey (eds.), *Walford's Guide to Reference Material Volume 2: Social and Historical Sciences, Philosophy and Religion* (5th ed. London: The Library Association, 1990).

Scarecrow Press publishes a series of historical dictionaries on most countries, some of which have special relevance for the history of organized labor. Volumes of special note are James C. Docherty, *Historical Dictionary of Australia* (1999); Paula S. Fichtner, *Historical Dictionary of Austria* (1999); Mark F. Gilbert and K. Robert Nilsson, *Historical Dictionary of Modern Italy* (1999); Arend H. Huussen, *Historical Dictionary of the Netherlands* (1998); George Maude, *Historical Dictionary of Finland* (1995); Kenneth J. Panton and Keith A. Cowlard, *Historical Dictionary of the United Kingdom* (2 vols., 1997, 1998); Irene Scobbie, *Historical Dictionary of Sweden* (1995); Angel Smith, *Historical Dictionary of Spain* (1996); Robert Stallaerts, *Historical Dictionary of Belgium* (1999); Alastair H. Thomas and Stewart P. Oakley, *Historical Dictionary of Denmark* (1998); and Wayne C. Thompson, Susan S. Thompson, and Juliet S. Thompson, *Historical Dictionary of Germany* (1994).

Current information and references can be found in the journals which are listed in section A.7 of the bibliography and in works such as National Labor Relations Board, *New Books and Current Labor Articles* (Washington, D.C.). In addition, since the late 1980s, the U.S. Department of Labor has published a series on all the major countries in the world called *Foreign Labor Trends.* John Harper Publishing, *Trade Unions of the World* (London: John Harper, 2001) is the best current guide to global organized labor, with detailed entries for every country. In recent years, the Internet has become an indispensable source of information. Details of relevant websites are given in appendix A.

The Study of Organized Labor

For anyone just beginning to study organized labor, the best place to start is by gaining a general appreciation of economic history, specifically the Industrial Revolution and the economic, social, and intellectual ferment it created. Useful starting points are *The Fontana Economic History of Europe*, edited by Carlo M. Cipolla (6 vols. Glasgow: Collins/Fontana Books, 1972-1976); Fernand Braudel, *Civilization and Capitalism: 15th-18th Centuries* (3 vols. London: Fontana Press, 1981-1984), Sidney Pollard, *Peaceful Conquest: The Industrialization of Europe, 1760-1970* (Oxford: Oxford University Press, 1981), M. Teich and R Porter (eds.), *The Industrial Revolution in National Context: Europe and the U.S.A.* (Cambridge: Cambridge University Press, 1996), and Derek H. Aldcroft and Steven Morewood, *The European Economy, 1914-2000* (4th ed., London: Routledge, 2001). For the United States, see Robert Heilbroner and

Aaron Singer, *The Economic Transformation of America: 1600 to the Present* (Fort Worth, Texas: 3rd ed., Harcourt Brace, 1994). Charles P. Kindleberger, *World Economic Primacy, 1500-1990* (New York: Oxford University Press, 1996), provides an up-to-date account of global economic history in a single volume. There is a wealth of ideas, as well as scholarship, in David Hackett Fischer, *The Great Wave: Price Revolutions and the Rhythm of History* (New York: Oxford University Press, 1996).

For economic history in the 20th century, the five-volume *Pelican History of the World Economy in the Twentieth Century* under the general editorship of Wolfram Fischer, published between 1977 and 1987, is also recommended. The last work in this series, Herman Van Der Wee, *Prosperity and Upheaval: The World Economy, 1945-1980* (1987), is most relevant as a backdrop to modern organized labor.

On the crowded developments in world economic history and economic thought since 1980, easily the best single work is Daniel Yergin and Joseph Stanislaw, *The Commanding Heights: The Battle for the World Economy* (New York: Simon and Schuster, 2002). It provides not only a readable account of difficult issues but also a good bibliography. For anyone who wants to gain a good understanding of the economic problems that have beset organized labor in Western economies since 1980, it is indispensable.

For the social and economic ferment of 19th-century Europe, two good introductions from different points of view are given in the opening chapters of Philip Taylor, *The Distant Magnet: European Emigration to the U.S.A.* (New York: Harper Torchbooks, 1971) and in Dick Geary, *European Labour Protest, 1848-1939* (London: Methuen, 1984). Although not about organized labor as such, John Carey, *The Intellectuals and the Masses, 1800-1939: Pride and Prejudice among the Literary Intelligentsia* (London: Faber, 1992) gives a valuable, if chilling, alternative perspective on one level of response to population growth and the rise of the modern working class. On social class, Arthur Marwick, *Class: Image and Reality in Britain, France, and the USA since 1930* (Glasgow: Fontana/Collins, 1980) provides stimulating reading. Works like these are important for helping to place the study of organized labor in a wider historical perspective, a perspective that can all too easily become lost in the forest of specialist studies.

For economic thought, Robert L. Heilbroner, *The Worldly Philosophers* (6th ed., New York: Touchstone, 1986), provides a masterly introduction to the world of economic ideas written with a wit and humor seldom found in such works. For economic issues generally, the major reference work is John Eastwell, Murray Milgate, and Peter Newman (eds.), *The New Palgrave: A Dictionary of Economics* (4 vols. London: Macmillan, 1987), which has bibliographies after each entry; the entries on arbitration, collective bargaining, strikes, and trade unions are of particular interest. Also worth noting as a background reference work is Carl Heyel (ed.), *The Encyclopedia of Management* (3rd ed., New York: Van Nostrand Reinhold, 1982).

Although organized labor has never lacked students since Adam Smith's famous reference to it in the *Wealth of Nations* (1776) as "combinations," it mainly attracted attention from economists and lawyers or from political theorists such as Karl Marx. By 1920, pioneers like Sidney and Beatrice Webb in Britain and John R. Commons and Selig Perlman in the United States established organized labor as an academically respectable field of study. Under their influence, organized labor tended to be studied from the viewpoint of its institutions; this was a "top down" approach with a strong emphasis on leaders.

Modern labor history dates from about 1960 with the works of American scholars like Irving Bernstein and David Brody and Eric Hobsbawm and E. P. Thompson in Britain. The publication of E. P. Thompson, *The Making of the English Working Class* (London: Victor Gollancz, 1963 and Penguin Books, 1968) was an inspirational milestone in labor history and a foundation work of modern social history.

What united the British and American works was their concern with the social and political setting of employees and to show the diversity of the experiences of particular groups. Over the past 30 years the output of social histories has been huge, although their quality has often been variable.

At this point, a word of warning is needed for the beginner. The study of organized labor is intimately bound up with the study of the Industrial Revolution, whose effects have been hotly disputed by generations of participants and scholars. The older optimistic view of the Industrial Revolution, which E. P. Thompson rightly attacked, was that it represented general material progress. He was able to show that for many groups in the labor force conditions deteriorated.

Like any revolution, the Industrial Revolution had its good and bad sides, but all too often only the bad is presented. Many of the sources are fiercely polemical, and the secondary works have been similarly influenced. Studies often focus on the negative aspects of industrialization, on what went wrong rather than on what succeeded. It has often been more appealing to write about dramatic, noble failures, or the distressed condition of particular groups of workers than the slow, if duller process of general material improvement. Consider, for instance, the general absence of modern scholarly works about the cooperative movement compared to the abundance of books on the left wing of labor.

The debate about the Industrial Revolution continues to the present, though in different forms. This is particularly evident in the attitudes of the various disciplines. The works of many of the economic writers, for example, tend to take a far more positive view of the Industrial Revolution than those of social historians. For these reasons, it is vital to keep an open mind about the subject and to be mindful of the political ideologies which often still color much of the writing about organized labor.

Despite the maturing of labor history, there is a relative lack of studies of its historiography. An important exception is the U.S. study by Melvyn Dubofsky, *Hard Work: The Making of Labor History* (Urbana: University of Illinois Press, 2000). In this work, Dubofsky argued that labor history is no longer the cutting edge in historical research because it has been largely successful in entering the historical mainstream. This may be true for the United States and the United Kingdom, but this should not be taken to mean that labor history generally is a problem "solved" and that there are no more worlds for the researcher to conquer.

Finding Out about Organized Labor

After gaining a broad appreciation of the Industrial Revolution, the following works provide a sound introduction to the study of labor unions. W. E. J. McCarthy (ed.), *Trade Unions: Selected Readings* (2nd ed., Harmondsworth: Penguin, 1985) contains a valuable selection of important readings, some of which are hard to locate in their original form. The political side of labor is approached in an interesting way by Walter Korpi in his *The Democratic Class Struggle* (London: Routledge Kegan Paul, 1983). There is an excellent view of the topic by Jelle Visser, "Trade Unions from a Comparative

Perspective," in Joris Van Ruysseveldt et al. (eds.), *Comparative Industrial and Employment Relations* (London: Sage, 1995), pp. 37-67.

For critical labor union functions and collective bargaining, see Allan Flanders (ed.), *Collective Bargaining: Selected Readings* (Harmondsworth: Penguin, 1969), and H. Katz and T. Kochan, *An Introduction to Collective Bargaining and Industrial Relations* (New York: McGraw-Hill, 1992). For labor economics, a useful introductory text is Lloyd G. Reynolds et al., *Labor Economics and Labor Relations* (9th ed., Englewood Cliffs, N.J: Prentice-Hall, 1986).

There are numerous ways of approaching the many topics within the study of organized labor. For American studies, there are excellent bibliographical essays in Foster R. Dulles and Melvyn Dubofsky, *Labor in America: A History* (4th ed., Arlington Heights, Il.: Harlan Davidson, 1984), Bruce Laurie, *Artisans into Workers: Labor in Nineteenth-Century America* (New York: Hill and Wang, 1989), and Robert H. Zieger, *American Workers, American Unions, 1920-1985* (2nd ed., Baltimore, Md.: Johns Hopkins University Press, 1994). For British works, there are bibliographic guides in Henry Pelling, *A History of British Trade Unionism* (5th ed., London: Macmillan, 1992) and Dick Geary, *European Labour Protest, 1848-1939* (London: Methuen, 1984).

Students of American and British labor are blessed with comprehensive and high-quality bibliographies which were published in the early 1980s, particularly those by Maurice F. Neufeld for the United States and Arthur Marsh for Britain. These can be readily supplemented by recourse to book reviews and book notices in journals like *Labor History*, the *Monthly Labor Review*, and the *British Journal of Industrial Relations*. *Labor History*, for instance, has published an annual bibliography of labor journal articles and other scholarly work since 1965. There is also important bibliographical information in the *International Review of Social History*.

The *Journal of Economic Literature* (Pittsburgh) contains a useful annotated listing of new books. For sheer convenience as well as breadth, there is an outstanding bibliography organized by country in Marcel van der Linden and Jürgen Rojahn (eds.), *The Formation of Labour Movements, 1870-1914: An International Perspective* (Leiden: E.J. Brill, 1990), Vol. II, pp. 701-81.

Another important bibliographical source is the International Labour Office, *International Labour Documentation*, which has been issued monthly since 1965. This source covers all topics pertaining to labor and is international in coverage. The 200,000 records it contains can be accessed at www.ilo.org/labordoc.

Specific Topics

Because the study of organized labor is often about the details of work, it is essential to gain some familiarity with industrial archaeology, which is concerned with the study of the physical remains and processes of the Industrial Revolution. As well as being important for its own sake, industrial archaeology gives many insights into the organization and conditions of work and living in past times. There is a useful encyclopedia devoted to this subject, Barrie Trinder (ed.), *The Blackwell Encyclopedia of Industrial Archaeology* (Oxford: Basil Blackwell, 1992), which is international in scope and contains an excellent bibliography. In addition, Shire, a British publisher, specialized in this field, and their Shire Album series of over 100 booklets written by experts covers topics from chain making to woodworking tools. Several of these are listed in the bibliography.

Since the late 1970s, students of organized labor have some excellent labor-saving reference works at their disposal. There are historical directories of labor unions for Britain and the United States. The British series compiled by Arthur Marsh and Victoria Ryan consists of four volumes, *Historical Directory of Trade Unions* (Westmead: Gower Press, 1980-1994). This remarkable series covers about 6,000 unions.

American unions are well covered by Gary M. Fink (ed.), *Labor Unions* (Westport, Conn.: Greenwood Press, 1977), which has entries on over 200 U.S. unions, each entry with its own bibliography. The work also contains national union affiliation details, a chronology, union genealogies, union executive lists, membership statistics, and a glossary.

No comparable work is currently available for Australia, but in 1982, Michael Quinlan and Margaret Gardner at the School of Industrial Relations, Griffith University, Queensland, began to prepare a computer database covering Australian unions and labor disputes between 1825 and 1925. This database contains reasonably full entries on 1,506 unions which operated between 1825 and 1900.

One of the most welcome developments of the past 20 years has been the appearance of biographical dictionaries of labor leaders. The labor movement is often ignored in many national biographical dictionaries, and it is often hard to find even the most elementary background information about its leaders let alone its rank-and-file. For Britain, the leading work is the nine volumes edited by Joyce Bellamy and John Saville, *Dictionary of Labour Biography* (London: Macmillan, 1972-1993). For the United States, there is a one-volume work edited by Gary M. Fink, *Biographical Dictionary of American Labor* (rev. ed., Westport, Conn.: Greenwood Press, 1985) that has entries on about 750 individuals.

A biographical register of Australian labor since 1788 is being prepared by Andrew Moore and John Shields at the University of Western Sydney. The finished work may not be published in printed form, but might be made available on the Internet.

With the exception of Britain, all these efforts seem small compared to what is available for French labor. Jean Maitron (ed.), *Dictionnaire Biographique du Mouvement Ouvrier Français* (Paris: Les Editions Ouvriers, 1964-1997) consists of 44 volumes and covers the period from 1789 to 1939. It includes leaders as well as rank-and-file members of the labor movement. A new series has begun to cover the period from 1940 to 1968. Jean Maitron was also general editor of another series, *Dictionnaire Biographique du Mouvement Ouvrier International*, which consists of dictionaries for Austria, China, and Japan (two volumes) and Germany. Section A.3 lists labor biographical dictionaries.

Most studies of organized labor are of Britain, the United States, and Western Europe. Henry Pelling, *A History of British Trade Unionism* (5th ed., London: Macmillan, 1992) remains the best known survey work. It can be supplemented by Chris Wrigley, *British Trade Unions since 1933* (Cambridge: Cambridge University Press, 2002). Keith Laybourn, *A History of British Trade Unionism, c. 1770-1990* (Wolfeboro Falls, N.H.: Allan Sutton, 1992), is a good guide to the academic debates of recent years. Hugh A. Clegg, *A History of British Trade Unions since 1889* (3 vols. Oxford: Oxford University Press, 1964-1994) is the standard scholarly work; the first volume was written with Alan Fox and A. F. Thompson. Although often heavy going, it covers the period up to 1951. It is invaluable as a reference work.

For the United States, good, comprehensive single-volume surveys are available in Foster Rhea Dulles and Melvy Dubofsky, *Labor in America* (4th ed., Arlington Heights, Ill.: Harlan Davidson, 1984) and Ronald L. Filippelli, *Labor in the USA: A History* (New York: Knopf, 1984). For Germany, John A. Moses, *Trade Unionism in Germany from Bismarck to Hitler, 1869 to 1933* (2 vols. London: George Prior Publishers, 1982) provides a valuable survey with translations of some key documents. Moses's history can be profitably supplemented with the more recent work by Michael Schneider, *A Brief History of the German Trade Unions* (trans. Barrie Selman, Bonn: J. H. W. Dietz Nachf., 1991), which covers the whole period up to the present and is good for biographical details and statistics.

C. R. Dobson, *Masters and Journeymen: A Prehistory of Industrial Relations, 1717-1800* (London: Croom Helm, 1980) is a short but valuable work largely devoted to labor disputes in the 18th century. It is a reminder that labor unions and labor disputes were evident *before* the Industrial Revolution and, therefore, may presumably still be in existence in the often predicted postindustrial world.

For the ideas that have influenced organized labor and its general development, see James C. Docherty, *Historical Dictionary of Socialism* (Lanham, Md.: Scarecrow Press, 1997), which provides a general global survey. Michael Poole, *Theories of Trade Unionism* (rev. ed., London: Routledge and Kegan Paul, 1984), offers a sociological approach to labor unions.

Because of the variable coverage they give to organized labor, the bibliography does not include a separate section on histories of particular industries, although this is not to say they are unimportant; on the contrary, they must be investigated by serious students. That said, an exception needs to be made for John Hatcher and others, *The History of the British Coal Industry* (5 vols. Oxford: Clarendon Press, 1984-1993), which deals with an industry which played a central role in British organized labor up to the 1950s.

Structure of the Bibliography
The organization of this bibliography is as follows:

A   *Research Guides, Sources, and Journals*

A.1   Bibliographies and Finding Aids

E.   Labor and Society

F.   Labor and the economy

G.   Organized Labor and the Future

A. RESEARCH GUIDES, SOURCES, AND JOURNALS

A.1 Bibliographies and Finding Aids

ABC-Clio Information Services. *Labor in America: A Historical Bibliography.* Santa Barbara, Calif.: ABC-Clio, 1985. [Annotated bibliography of journal articles only.]

Allen, V. L. (ed.). *International Bibliography of Trade Unionism.* London: Merlin Maspero, 1968.

Allison, Peter B. *Labor, Worklife and Industrial Relations: Sources of Information.* New York: Haworth Press, 1984.

Bain, George S., and John Bennett (eds.). *Bibliography of British Industrial Relations, 1971-1979.* Cambridge: Cambridge University Press, 1985.

Bain, George S., and Gillian B. Woolven (eds.). *Bibliography of British Industrial Relations.* Cambridge: Cambridge University Press, 1979. [Contains 15,000 works covering the period from 1880 to 1970.]

Bennett, John, and Julian Fawcett (eds.). *Industrial Relations: An International and Comparative Bibliography.* London: Mansell, 1985.

Bishoff, Ros, Richard Mitchell, and Andrea Steer (eds.). *Australian Labour Law: A Selected Bibliography.* Melbourne: Labour Studies Programme, University of Melbourne, 1985.

Burnett, John, David Vincent, and David Mayall (eds.). *The Autobiography of the Working Class: A Critical and Annotated Bibliography.* 2 vols. Brighton, Sussex, England: The Harvester Press/New York: New York University Press, 1984, 1987. [Covers the period from 1790 to 1945.]

Campbell, Anne et al. (eds.). *Industrial Relations: A Select Annotated Bibliography.* London: Commonwealth Secretariat, c. 1978.

Carrington, Arthur V. (ed.). *Human Rights: A Bibliography.* Huntington, N.Y.: Nova Science Books, 2000.

Chan, Ming K. (ed.). *Historiography of the Chinese Labor Movement, 1895-1949: A Critical Survey and Bibliography of Selected Chinese Source Materials at the Hoover Institution.* Stanford, Calif.: Hoover Institution Press, 1981.

Chester, A. E. *Aspects of Australian Industrial Relations: A Select Bibliography.* Adelaide: South Australian Institute of Technology, 1980.

Dowe, Dieter (ed.). *Führer zu den Archiven, Bibliotheken und Forschungseinrichtungen zur Geschichte der europäischen Arbeiterbewegung.* Bonn: Verlag Neue Gesellschaft, 1984. [A guide to the holdings of labor movement materials in European archives and libraries.]

Feldman, Shelley, and Eveline Ferretti (eds.). *Informal Work and Social Change: A Bibliographic Survey.* Ithaca, N.Y.: ILR Press, 1998. [Contains over 800 entries beginning from 1970.]

Fowler, Simon (ed.). *Sources for Labour History.* London: Public Record Office, 1995.

Fox, M. J., and P. C. Howard. *Labor Relations and Collective Bargaining: A Bibliographical Guide to Doctoral Research.* Metuchen, N.J: Scarecrow Press, 1983.

Gibbney, H. J. (comp.). *Labor in Print: A Guide to the People who Created a Labor Press in Australia between 1850 and 1939.* Canberra: History Department, Research School of Social Sciences, Australian National University, 1975. [Lists 488 labor newspapers and publications.]

Harrison, Royden, Gillian Woolven, and Robert Duncan (eds.). *The Warwick Guide to British Labour Periodicals, 1790-1970: A Check List.* Atlantic Highlands, N..J.: Harvester Press, 1977. [Lists 4,125 periodicals.]

Harzig, Christiane, and Dirk Hoerder (eds.). *The Immigrant Labor Press in North America, 1840s-1970s: An Annotated Bibliography.* New York: Greenwood Press, 1987.

Hessisches Hauptstaatsarchiv. Volker Eicherler (ed.). *Inventar zur Geschichte der deutschen Arbeitwegung in den staatlichen Archiven der Bundesrepublik Deutschland.* Berlin: Colloquium Verlag, 1996.

Hill, John. *Strikes in Australia: A Select Bibliography.* Canberra: Canberra College of Advanced Education Library, 1983.

Houkes, John M. *Industrial Relations Theses and Dissertations, 1949-1969: A Cumulative Bibliography.* Ann Arbor, Mich.: Xerox University Microfilms, 1973.

Huls, Mary E. (ed.). *United States Government Documents on Women, 1800-1900: A Comprehensive Bibliography. Vol. II: Labor.* Westport, Conn.: Greenwood, 1993.

International Labour Office. *Annotated Bibliography on Child Labour.* Geneva: International Labour Office, 1986.

————. *International Labour Documentation.* Geneva: International Labour Office, 1965 to date.

————. *Women Workers: An Annotated Bibliography, 1983-94.* Geneva: International Labour Office, 1995.

Jadeja, Raj. *Parties to the Award: A Guide to the Pedigrees and Archival Resources of Federally Registered Trade Unions, Employers' Associations and Their Peak Councils in Australia.* Canberra: Noel Butlin Archives Centre, Research School of Social Sciences, Australian National University, 1994. [An extremely important research tool which includes a historical introduction and a comprehensive bilbliography.]

Jones, Gregory P. *A Guide to Sources of Information on Australian Industrial Relations.* Sydney: Pergamon Press, 1988.

Lily, Terry Ann et al. (eds.). *Work-Family Research: An Annoatated Bibliography.* Westport, Conn.: Greenwood Press, 1997.

Magnaghi, Russell M. (ed.). *Indian Slavery, Labor, Evangelization, and Captivity in the Americas: An Annotated Bibliography.* Lanham, Md.: Scarecrow Press, 1998.

Maley, Barry et al. (eds.). *Industrial Democracy and Worker Participation.* Sydney: Department of Organizational Behaviour, University of New South Wales, 1979. [An annotated bibliography consisting of 560 works in English covering Australia and other countries covering the period 1960-1976.]

March, Arthur (ed.). *Employees Relations Bibliography and Abstracts.* Oxford: Employees Relations Bibliography and Abstracts, 1985. [A major bibliography with a concentration on British material.]

Marsh, Arthur (ed.). *Employee Relations Bibliography & Abstract Journal.* Oxford: Employee Relations Bibliography and Abstracts, 1989 to date. [Issued four times a year, this work supplements the same editor's 1985 *Employees Relations Bibliography and Abstracts.*]

Martens, G. R. (ed.). *African Trade Unionism: A Bibliography with a Guide to Trade Union Organizations and Publications.* Boston, Mass.: G. K. Hall, 1977. [Contains 946 references with over half in English.]

McBrearty, James (ed.). *American Labor History and Comparative Labor Movements: A Selected Bibliography.* Tucson: University of Arizona Press, 1973.

Neufeld, Maurice F., Daniel J. Leab, and Dorothy Swanson (eds.). *American Working Class History: A Representative Bibliography.* New York: R. R. Bowker, 1983. [A major work with about 7,200 entries including doctoral theses.]

Pettman, Barrie O. (ed.). *Industrial Democracy: A Selected Bibliography.* Bradford, West Yorkshire: MCB, 1978.

———. (ed.). *Strikes: A Selected Bibliography.* Bradford, England: MCB Books, 1976. [Contains 1,230 references to books, reports, articles, and theses published 1950-1975 and covers 32 countries.]

Roth, Herbert O. (ed.). *New Zealand Trade Unions: A Bibliography.* 2nd ed. Wellington: Oxford University Press, 1977.

Russell, Thyra K. (ed.). *Job Sharing: An Annotated Bibliography.* Lanham, Md.: Scarecrow Press, 1994. [Provides a guide to over 825 books, articles, and other publications relating to job sharing in the United States, United Kingdom, Canada, and Australia.]

Shimakoa, H. R. *Selected Bibliographies on Labor and Industrial Relations in Australia, India, Japan, New Zealand and the Philippines.* Honolulu: University of Hawaii Industrial Relations Center, 1961.

Smart, John (ed.). *Records of the Department of Labour.* Ottawa: National Archives of Canada, 1988.

Smethurst, John B. (ed.). *A Bibliography of Co-operative Societies' Histories.* Manchester: Co-operative Union, n.d. [A comprehensive bibliography of British histories published in about 1971.]

Smith, Harold (ed.). *The British Labour Movement to 1970: A Bibliography.* London: Mansell, 1981. [Contains 3,838 references.]

Sri Lanka. Ministry of Labour. *Bibliography of Labour Relations.* 2 vols. Colombo, Sri Lanka: Ministry of Labour, 1981.

Staatsarchiv Bremen, Werner Garbas, and Margo Müller (eds.). *Inventar zur Geschichte der deutschen Arbeitbewegung in den staatlichen Archiven der Bundesrepublik Deutschland.* Berlin: Colloquium Verlag, 1991. [This is the major series of archival listings for the German labor movement by state.]

Staatsarchiv Hamburg, Klaus Weinhauer, et al. (eds.). *Inventar zur Geschichte der deutschen Arbeitbewegung in den staatlichesn Archiven der Bundesrepublik Deutschland.* Berlin: Colloquium Verlag, 1992.

Stern, Robert, and Daniel B. Cornfield (eds.). *The U.S. Labor Movement: References and Resources.* New York: G. K. Hall,

1996. [An annotated bibliography of 1,549 items.]

Switzer, Teri R. (ed.). *Telecommuters: The Workforce of the 21st Century*. Lanham, Md.: Scarecrow Press, 1996.

Tuskan, Erhan (ed.). *Inventory of the Archives of the International Confederation of Free Trade Unions (ICFTU), 1949-1993*. Amsterdam: Stichting beheer IISG, 1997.

University of the Philippines, Asian Labor Education Center, Research Section. *An Annotated Bibliography on Philippine Labor*. Quezon City: National Book Store, 1979.

Vaisey, G. Douglas (ed.). *The Labour Companion: A Bibliography of Canadian Labour History Based on Materials Printed from 1950 to 1975*. Halifax, Nova Scotia: Committee on Canadian Labour History, 1980.

Vocino, Michael C., and Lucille W. Cameron (eds.). *Labor and Industrial Relations Journals and Serials: An Analytical Guide*. New York: Greenwood Press, 1989.

Walsh, Kenneth. *Industrial Disputes: Methods and Measurement in the European Community*. Luxembourg, Office for the Official Publications of the European Communities: Eurostat, 1982.

Whitaker, Marian, and Ian Miles (eds.). *Bibliography of Information Technology: An Annotated Critical Bibliography of English Language Sources since 1980*. London: Edward Elgar (Gower), 1989.

Wilson, Joseph (comp. and ed.). *Black Labor in America, 1865-1983: A Selected Annotated Bibliography*. Westport, Conn.: Greenwood Press, 1986.

Zaniello, Tom. *Working Stiffs, Union Maids, Reds, and Riffraff: An Organized Guide to Films about Organized Labor*. Ithaca, N.Y.: Cornell University Press, 1996. [Provides an analytical guide to 150 films.]

Zappala, Jon. *Workplace Industrial Relations in Australia: An Annotated and Selected Bibliography*. Sydney: Centre for Industrial Relations Research, University of Sydney and Business Council of Australia, 1988.

A.2 Directories and Reference Works

Arrowsmith, J. D. *Canada's Trade Unions: An Information Manual*. Kingston, Ontario: Queen's University Industrial Relations Centre Press, 1992.

Blanpain, Roger (ed.). *International Encyclopaedia for Labour Law and Industrial Relations.* 10 vols. Deventer, Netherlands: Kluwer, 1977 to date.   [This work is in loose-leaf form and regularly updated.]

Bottomore, Tom (ed.). *A Dictionary of Marxist Thought.* 2nd ed. Oxford: Blackwell, 1991. [First published in 1983, this comprehensive work has references at the end of entries.]

Buhle, Mari Jo, Paul Buhle, and Dan Georgakas (eds.). *Encyclopedia of the American Left.* New York: Garland, 1990. [An outstanding reference work, thorough, comprehensive, cross-referenced, references after entries, and an index.]

Campbell, Joan (ed.). *European Labor Unions.* Westport, Conn.: Greenwood Press, 1993. [A major work dealing with both Eastern and Western Europe; it includes an appendix giving chronologies for the countries studied.]

Coldrick, A. P., and Philip Jones. *The International Directory of the Trade Union Movement.* London: Macmillan, 1979.

Craft, Donna, and Terrance W. Peck (eds.). *Profiles of American Labor Unions.* 2nd ed. Farmington Hills, Mich.: Gale, 1998.

Ebbinghaus, Bernard, and Jelle Visser. *Trade Unions in Western Europe since 1945.* London: Macmillan Reference, 2000. [Contains data on 15 countries and includes a CD-ROM with statistics.]

European Communities. *Glossary of Labour and the Trade Union Movement.* Luxembourg: European Communities, 1984. [English, French, Spanish, German, Italian, Dutch, Greek, Danish, Swedish, and Norwegian.]

Filippelli, Ronald L. (ed.). *Labor Conflict in the United States: An Encyclopedia.* New York: Garland, 1990.

Fink, Gary M. (ed.). *Labor Unions.* Westport, Conn.: Greenwood Press, 1977. [A historical directory of over 200 U.S. unions. Each entry has a bibliography. The work also contains national union affiliation details, a chronology, union genealogies, union executive lists, membership statistics, and a glossary.]

Gabaglio, E., and R. Hoffman (eds.). *European Trade Union Yearbook, 1995.* Brussels: European Trade Union Institute, 1996.

Garlock, Jonathan. *Guide to the Local Assemblies of the Knights of Labor.* Westport, Conn.: Greenwood Press, 1982.

Gifford, Courtney D. (ed.). *Directory of U.S. Labor Organizations. 1988-89 Edition.* 4th ed. Washington, D.C.: Bureau of National Affairs, 1988.

Greenfield, Gerald M., and Maram, Sheldon, M. (eds.). *Latin American Labor Organizations.* Westport, Conn.: Greenwood Press, 1987.

Harbridge, Raymond, and Kevin Hince. *A Sourcebook of New Zealand Trade Unions and Employee Organisations.* Wellington: Industrial Relations Centre, Victoria University of Wellington, 1994.

Huntley, Pat. *Australia's Super Unions.* Northbridge, New South Wales: Huntley, 1993. [A loose-leaf subscription work which supersedes the author's *Australian Trade Union Monitor.*]

Industrial Relations Center, University of Hawaii. *Robert's Dictionary of Industrial Relations.* 4th ed. Washington, D.C.: Bureau of National Affairs/University of Hawaii Industrial Relations Center, 1994.

Information Australia. *Industrial Relations Index: A Guide to Unions, Employer Groups and the Industrial Relations Industry.* Melbourne: Information Australia, 1985 to date.

John Harper Publishing. *Trade Unions of the World.* London: John Harper, 2001. [An updated version of a work first published in 1987 which includes comprehensive information on Internet addresses and contact addresses.]

Jones, J., and M. Morris (eds.). *A-Z of Trade Unionism and Industrial Relations.* London: Heinemann, 1982.

Kittner, Michael (ed.). *Gewerkschafts Jahrbuch 1991.* Cologne: Bund-Verlag, 1991. [This German work includes a chronology for 1990.]

Lawson, Edward (comp.). *Encyclopedia of Human Rights.* 2nd ed. Washington, D.C.: Taylor and Francis, 1996.

Lecher, W. (ed.). *Trade Unions in the European Union: A Handbook.* London: Lawrence and Wishart, 1994.

Marsh, Arthur. *Concise Encyclopedia of Industrial Relations.* Westmead: Gower Press, 1979. [An excellent work with internal references and a separate bibliography.]

——— (ed.). *Trade Union Handbook.* 5th ed. Aldershot, England: Gower, 1991. [An excellent, historically informed guide to British organized labor in the early 1990s.]

Marsh, Arthur, and Victoria Ryan (eds.). *Historical Directory of Trade Unions.* 4 vols. Westmead, England: Gower Press, 1980,

1984, 1987, and 1994 (with John B. Smethurst, Scolar Press, Aldershot).

Paradis, Adrian A. *The Labor Reference Book.* Philadelphia: Chilton, 1972. [A dictionary about American labor with a bibliography; it is still useful as a work for first resort.]

Peters, Lawrence H., et al. (eds.). *The Blackwell Encyclopedic Dictionary of Human Resource Management.* Oxford: Blackwell, 1998.

Rifkin, Bernard, and Susan Rifkin, (eds.). *American Labor Sourcebook.* New York: McGraw-Hill, 1979. [Although mainly about labor in the late 1970s, this excellent work includes a detailed chronology and glossary of terms.]

Russell, Spomer C., and J. M Nixon. *American Directory of Organized Labor: Unions, Locals, Agreements, and Employers.* Detroit, Mich.: Gale Research , 1992.

Schneider, Dorothy, and Carl J. Schneider (eds.). *The ABC-CLIO Companion to Women in the Workplace.* Santa Barbara, Calif.: ABC-Clio, 1993.

Stearns, Peter N., and John H. Hinshaw (eds.). *The ABC-CLIO World History Companion to the Industrial Revolution.* Santa Barbara, Calif.: ABC-Clio, 1996.

Sutcliffe, Paul, and Ron Callus (eds.). *Glossary of Australian Industrial Relations Terms.* Sydney: Australian Centre for Industrial Relations Research and Teaching, University of Sydney, and Australian Centre in Strategic Management, Queensland University of Technology, 1994.

Trinder, Barrie (ed.). *The Blackwell Encyclopedia of Industrial Archaeology.* Oxford: Basil Blackwell, 1992. [A major reference work with international coverage and a large bibliography.]

Yerbury, Di, and Maria Karlsson (eds.). *The CCH Macquarie Dictionary of Employment and Industrial Relations.* Sydney: CCH Australia and Macquarie Library, 1992.

A.3 Biographical Dictionaries

Andreucci, Franco, and Detti Tommasco (eds.). *Il movimento operaio italiano: Dizionario biografico, 1853-1943.* 5 vols. Rome: Riuniti, 1975-1978.

Bellamy, Joyce, and John Saville (eds.). *Dictionary of Labour Biography.* 9 vols. London: Macmillan, 1972-1993.

Bianco, L., and V. Chevrier. (eds.). *Dictionnaire Biographique du Mouvement Ouvrier International: La Chine.* Paris: Editions Ouvrières, 1985. [An important reference work on the Chinese labor movement.]

Bourdet, Y., et al. (eds.). *Dictionnaire Biographique du Mouvement Ouvrier International: Autriche.* Paris: Editions Ouvrières, 1982.

Droz, Jacques (ed.). *Dictionnaire Biographique du Mouvement Ouvrier International: L'Allemagne.* Paris: Editions Ouvrières, 1990. [Covers the German labor movement up to the 1930s.]

Fink, Gary M. (ed.). *Biographical Dictionary of American Labor.* rev. ed. Westport, Conn.: Greenwood Press, 1985. [Contains entries on about 750 individuals. First published 1974.]

Gupte, V., et al. (eds.). *Profiles: Short Biographies of 101 Trade Union Leaders in India Based on Their Memoirs.* Bombay: Mumbai, 1996.

Knox, William (ed.). *Scottish Labour Leaders, 1918-39: A Biographical Dictionary.* Edinburgh: Mainstream, 1984.

Lane, A. Thomas (ed.). *Biographical Dictionary of European Labor Leaders.* 2 vols. Westport: Conn.: Greenwood Press, 1995. [Contains over 1,500 entries on labor leaders past and present.]

Maitron, Jean (ed.). *Dictionnaire Biographique du Mouvement Ouvrier Français.* 44 vols. Paris: Editions Ouvrières, 1964-1997. [The largest work of its kind for any country, this monumental study covers the period from 1789 to 1939. A new series has begun to cover the period from 1940 to 1968.]

Meertens, van P. J., et al. (eds.). *Biografisch woordenboek van het socialisme en de arbeidersbeweging in Nederland.* 5 vols. Amsterdam: Sicting beheer IISG, 1986-1992. [A biographical dictionary of about 400 Dutch socialists and labor leaders from 1840 to 1940.]

Nyathi, Pathisa (ed.). *Masotsha Ndlovu.* Edinburgh: Longman, 1998. [Biographies of trade union officials and employees in Zimbabwe.]

Shiota, S. (ed.). *Dictionnaire Biographique du Mouvement Ouvrier International: Japon.* 2 vols. Paris: Editions Ouvrières, 1982.

Zimmermann, Rüdiger (ed.). *100 Jahre ÖTV: Biographien. Die Geschichte einer Gewerkschaft und ihrer Vorläuferorganisationen.* Frankfurt: Union-Druckerei und Verlagsanstalt, 1996. [The second volume of the official history of the German *Gewerkschaft Öffentliche Dienste, Transport and Verkehr* (ÖTV), or Public Service, Transportation, and Traffic

Labor Union, to mark its centenary. Suppressed by the Nazis in 1933, it was refounded in January 1949. This volume contains biographical details of its leaders and officials.]

A.4 Statistics

Australian Bureau of Statistics. *A Guide to Labour Statistics.* Canberra: Australian Bureau of Statistics, 1986. [ABS Catalogue No. 6102.0.]

Bain, G. S., and R. Price. *Profiles of Union Growth: A Comparative Statistical Portrait of Eight Countries.* Oxford: Basil Blackwell, 1980. [The countries were Britain, United States, Australia, Canada, Germany, Sweden, Denmark, and Norway.]

Bairoch, Paul, et al. *The Working Population and Its Structure.* Brussels: Free University of Brussels, 1968. [Contains census data on the industry structure of the labor force from the last half of the 19th century to the present for every country.]

Bean, R. (ed.). *International Labour Statistics: A Handbook, Guide, and Recent Trends.* London: Routledge, 1989. [Includes data on labor union membership as well as labor disputes.]

Conk, Margo. *The United States Census and Labor Force Change: A History of Occupational Statistics,1870-1940.* Ann Arbor, Mich.: UMI Research Press, 1980.

Flora, Peter, Franz Kraus, and Winfried Pfenning (eds.). *State, Economy, and Society in Western Europe, 1815-1975: A Data Handbook.* 2 vols. Chicago: St. James Press, 1983, 1987. [Chapter 10, pp. 679-753 of Vol. II contains valuable annual time series on the labor force and labor disputes.]

Hirsh, Barry T., and David A. Macpherson (eds.). *Union Membership and Earnings Data Book: Compilations from the Current Population Survey.* Washington, D.C.: Bureau of National Affairs, 1994 to date.

India, Labour Bureau. *Indian Labour Year Book.* Simla: Labour Bureau, 1947 to date.

International Labour Office. *Sources and Methods: Labour Statistics, Volume 7, Strikes and Lockouts.* Geneva: International Labour Office, 1993. [Explains the methods used for collecting labor dispute data for each ILO member as well as giving the titles of national publications.]

————. *Year Book of Labour Statistics*. Geneva: International Labour Office, 1935-1936 to date. [From 1927 published as Vol. II of the ILO *Year Book*, this is the principal international source of labor force data; it includes statistics on labor disputes, hours worked, unemployment, occupational health and safety, consumer prices indices, household income and expenditure surveys, but not labor unions.]

————. *Year Book of Labour Statistics: Retrospective Edition on Population Censuses, 1945-1989*. Geneva: International Labour Office, 1990.

Jacobs, Eva E. (ed.). *Handbook of U. S. Labor Statistics: Employment, Earnings, Prices, Productivity, and Other Labor Data*. 3rd ed. Lanham, Md.: Bernan Press, 1999. [Covers the topics indicated in the title but no labor union membership statistics.]

Lacey, Michael, and Mary Fumer (eds.). *The State and Social Investigation in Britain and the United States*. Cambridge: Cambridge University Press, 1993.

Organisation for Economic Co-operation and Development. *Historical Statistics 1960-1990*. Paris: OECD, 1992.

Philippines, Department of Labor. *Yearbook of Labor Statistics*. Manila: Department of Labor, 1981 to date.

Plowman, D. H. *Australian Trade Union Statistics*. 2nd ed. Sydney: Industrial Relations Research Centre, University of New South Wales, 1981.

Prywes, Ruth W. *The United States Labor Force: A Descriptive Analysis*. Westport, Conn.: Quorum Books, 2000.

Rawson, D. W., and Sue Wrightson. *Australian Unions 1984*. Sydney: Croom Helm Australia, 1985. [First published in 1970.]

Ross, John M. *Employment/Unemployment and Earnings Statistics: A Guide to Locating Data in U.S. Documents*. Lanham, Md.: Scarecrow Press, 1990.

Routh, Guy. *Occupation and Pay in Great Britain, 1906-79*. 2nd ed. London: Macmillan, 1980. [First published in 1965.]

United States Department of Labor, Bureau of Labor Statistics. *Directory of National Unions and Employee Associations*. Washington, D.C.: Bureau of Labor Statistics, 1930-1980.

————. *Employment and Earnings*. Washington, D.C.: Department of Labor, Bureau of Labor Statistics, 1969 to date.

Visser, Jelle. *European Trade Unionism in Figures, 1913-1985*. Deventer, Netherlands, and Boston: Kluwer, 1989.

————. *In Search of Inclusive Unionism.* Special Issue, *Bulletin of Comparative Industrial Relations*, No. 18. Deventer, Netherlands: Kluwer Law and Taxation Publishers, 1990.

Walsh, Kenneth. *Trade Union Membership: Methods and Measurement in the European Community.* Brussels: EUROSTAT, 1985.

A.5 Sources

Auerbach, Jerold S. (ed.). *American Labor: The Twentieth Century.* Indianapolis: Bobbs-Merrill, 1969. [This is still a useful documenttary collection.]

Baxandall, Rosalyn, et al. (eds.). *America's Working Women: A Documentary History—1600 to the Present.* New York: Random House, 1976.

Bernhardt, Debra E., and Rachel Bernstein (eds.). *Ordinary People, Extraordinary Lives: A Pictorial History of Working People in New York City.* New York: New York University Press, 2000.

Blewett, Mary H. (ed.). *We Will Rise in Our Might: Working Women's Voices from Nineteenth-Century New England.* Ithaca, N.Y.: Cornell University Press, 1991.

Cole, G. D. H., and A .W. Filson (eds.). *British Working Class Movements: Select Documents, 1789-1875.* London: Macmillan, 1951. [A major collection of documents which was reprinted in 1965 and again in 1967.]

Commons, John R., et al. (eds.). *A Documentary History of American Industrial Society.* 10 vols. New York: Russell and Russell, 1910-1911.

Foner, Philip S., and Herbert Shapiro (eds.). *Northern Labor and Antislavery: A Documentary History.* Westport, Conn.: Greenwood Press, 1994.

Gorman, John. *To Build Jerusalem: A Photographic Remembrance of British Working Class Life, 1875-1950.* London: Scorpion, 1980.

Hagan, Jim (ed.). *Australian Trade Unionism in Documents.* Melbourne: Longman Cheshire, 1986.

Hurley, F. Jack. *Industry and the Photographic Image: 153 Great Prints from 1850 to the Present.* New York: Dover in Association with George Eastman House, 1980.

International Confederation of Free Trade Unions. *Annual Survey of Violations of Trade Union Rights.* Brussels: International

Confederation of Free Trade Unions, 1985 to date. [The first year to be surveyed was 1984.]

International Labour Office. *Legislative Series.* Geneva: International Labor Office, 1919-1989; continued as *Labour Law Documents,* 1990 to date.

———. *World Labour Report 2.* Geneva: International Labor Office, 1985. [Includes a report on organized labor.]

Lack, John, et al. (eds.). *'The Workers' Paradise?' Robert Schachner's Letters from Australia, 1906-07.* Melbourne: University of Melbourne, 1990.

McKinlay, Brian (ed.). *Australian Labor History in Documents.* 3 vols. Burwood, Victoria: Collins Dove, 1990. [A revised version of a work originally published in 1979.]

Morton, Desmond. *Working People: An Illustrated History of the Canadian Labour Movement.* 4th ed. Montreal, Ontario: McGill-Queen's University Press, 1998.

O'Farrell, Brigid, and Joyce L. Cornbluh (eds.). *Rocking the Boat: Women's Voices, 1915-1975.* New Brunswick, N.J.: Rutgers University Press, 1996.

Rock, Howard B. (ed.). *The New York Artisan, 1789-1825: A Documentary History.* Albany: State University of New York Press, 1989.

Traugott, Mark (ed.). *The French Worker: Autobiographies from the Early Industrial Era.* Berkeley: University of California Press, 1993.

Troy, Leo, and Neil Sheflin. *Union Sourcebook—Membership, Structure, Finance, Directory.* West Orange, N.J: Industrial Relations Data and Information Services, 1985.

Walker, Charles R. *Steel: The Diary of a Furnace Worker.* Annotated and edited by Kenneth J. Kobus. Warrendale, Pa.: Iron and Steel Society, 1999.

Ward, J. T., and W. Hamish Fraser (eds.). *Workers and Employers: Documents on Trade Unions and Industrial Relations in Britain since the Eighteenth Century.* London: Macmillan, 1980.

Wrigley, Chris (eds.). *British Trade Unions, 1945-1995.* Manchester: Manchester University Press, 1997. [A documentary history with extracts from over 150 documents.]

A.6 Selected Classic Labor Studies

Bell, Lady Florence. *At the Works: A Study of a Manufacturing Town.* London: Virago Press, 1985. [Reproduction of the first edition published by Edward Arnold, London, in 1907; it was a study of Middlesborough, Yorkshire.]

Chile, Vere G. *How Labour Governs: A Study of Workers' Representation in Australia.* Melbourne: Melbourne University Press, 1964. [First published in 1923.]

Coghlan, Timothy A. *Labour and Industry in Australia from the First Settlement in 1788 to the Establishment of the Commonwealth in 1901.* 4 vols. Oxford: Oxford University Press, 1918. [Reissued by Macmillan, Melbourne, in 1968.]

Commons, John R., et al. *History of Labor in the United States.* 4 vols. New York: Macmillan, 1918-1935.

Coombes, B. L. *These Poor Hands: The Autobiography of a Miner Working in South Wales.* London: Victor Gollancz, 1939.

Drake, Barbara. *Women in Trade Unions.* London: Virago Press, 1984. [First published in 1920.]

Engels, Frederick. *The Condition of the Working Class in England.* London: Panther Books, 1969.

Fynes, Richard. *The Miners of Northumberland and Durham: A History of Their Social and Political Progress.* Sunderland, England: Thos. Summerbell, 1963. [First published in 1873.]

Mayhew, Henry. *London Labour and the London Poor.* 4 vols. New York: Dover, 1968, [Reproduction of the edition of 1861-1862.]

Orwell, George. *The Road to Wigan Pier.* Harmondsworth, England: Penguin Books, 1962, reprinted many times thereafter. [First published in 1937.]

Paris, Le Comte de. *The Trade Unions of England.* Trans. Nassau J. Senior. London: Smith Elder, 1869.

Roberts, Peter. *Anthracite Coal Communities: A Study of the Demography, the Social, Educational and Moral Life of the Anthracite Regions.* New York: Macmillan, 1904.

Thompson, E. P., and Eileen Yeo (eds.). *The Unknown Mayhew: Selections from the Morning Chronicle, 1849-50.* London: Merlin Press, 1971.

Tressell, Robert [pen-name of Robert Noonan]. *The Ragged Trousered Philanthropists.* London: Panther Books, 1965. [A novel set in the building trade in Hastings, England, in about 1906.

It was originally published in an incomplete and misleading form by his daughter in 1914, and a full version based on the complete manuscript was not published until 1955.]

Webb, Sidney, and Beatrice Webb. *History of Trade Unionism.* rev. ed. 2 vols. London: Longmans, Green, 1907. [First published in 1894.]

———. *Trade Union Democracy.* London: Longmans, Green, 1898.

Wilkinson, Ellen. *The Town That Was Murdered: The Life-Story of Jarrow.* London: Victor Gollancz, 1939.

Wilson, John. *A History of the Durham Miners' Association, 1870-1904.* Durham: J. H. Veitch & Sons, 1907.

Zola, Émile. *Germinal.* Harmondsworth, England: Penguin Books, 1963. [First published in 1885.]

A.7 Journals

Asian Labour Update (Kowloon), 1980 to date.

British Journal of Industrial Relations (London School of Economics), 1963 to date.

Bulletin of Comparative Labour Relations (Deventer), 1968 to date.

Conditions of Work Digest (International Labour Office, Geneva), 1986 to date.

Economic and Industrial Democracy (Industrial Relations Services, London), 1980 to date.

Employee Relations (Bradford), 1978 to date.

Euromarch News (St. Helens), 1997 to date.

European Industrial Relations Review (London), 1974 to date.

European Journal of Industrial Relations (London), 1995 to date.

Free Labour World (International Confederation of Free Trade Unions, Brussels), 1950-1997. [Replaced by *Trade Union World*, October 1997.]

Government Employee Relations Report (Bureau of National Affairs, Washington, D.C), 1952 to date. [A detailed, indexed, weekly report on federal, state, and local government industrial relations in the United States.]

Historical Abstracts (New York), 1955 to date.

Historical Studies in Industrial Relations (Keele), 1996 to date.

IDS European Report (Income Data Services, London), 1984 to date.

Indian Journal of Industrial Relations (New Delhi), 1965 to date.

Industrial and Labor Relations Review (Ithaca, N.Y.), 1946 to date.

Industrial Law Journal (London/Oxford), 1971 to date.

Industrial Relations (Berkeley), 1961 to date.

Industrial Relations Journal (Oxford), 1970 to date.

Industrial Relations Review and Report (Industrial Relations Services, London), 1975 to date.

International Journal of Comparative Labour Law and Industrial Relations (Deventer), 1977 to date.

International Journal of Human Resource Management (London), 1990 to date.

International Labor and Working Class History (Los Angeles), 1976 to date.

International Labour Review (International Labour Office, Geneva), 1923 to date.

International Review of Social History (Assen, Netherlands), 1956 to date.

International Transport (London: International Transport Workers' Federation), 2000 to date.

Japan Labor Bulletin (Tokyo), 1961 to date.

Japanese Unionism Information (Australia-Japan Exchange Centre, University of New South Wales), 1991 to date.

Journal of Communist Studies (London), 1985 to date.

Journal of Economic Literature (Pittsburgh), 1962 to date. [Particularly useful for its annotated lists of new books which cover labor and economic history topics.]

Journal of Industrial Relations (Sydney), 1959 to date.

Journal of Labor Economics (Chicago), 1983 to date.

Journal of Labour Research (Fairfax), 1980 to date.

Journal of Management Studies (Oxford), 1964 to date.

Journal of Social History (Berkeley, Calif.), 1967 to date.

Labor Developments Abroad (U.S. Department of Labor, Bureau of Labor Statistics), 1956-1972. [A useful compendium of international labor events and developments for this period.]

Labor History (New York), 1960 to date.

Labor Law Journal (Chicago), 1949 to date.

Labor Studies Journal (Rutgers University, N.J), 1975 to date.

Labour: Review of Labour Economics and Industrial Relations (Oxford), 1986 to date.

Labour & Industry (Brisbane/Geelong), 1987 to date.

Labour and Society (Geneva), 1977 to date.

Labour Market Trends [present title: the original title was *The Labour Gazette*] (Department of Employment; formerly the Department of Labour, London), 1893 to date.

Labour/Le Travail (Halifax), 1976 to date.

Labour, Capital and Society (Montreal), 1979 to date.

Labour History (Canberra/ Sydney), 1962 to date.

Labour Research (London), 1980 to date.

Labour: Review of Labour Economics and Industrial Relations (Rome), 1987 to date.

Monthly Labor Review (U.S. Bureau of Labor Statistics, Washington D.C.), 1915 to date.

New Zealand Journal of Industrial Relations (Dunedin), 1976 to date.

Policy Studies (London), 1979 to date.

Regional Labor Review (New York), 1999 to date.

Socialist Register (London), 1964 to date.

South-East Europe Review for Labour and Social Affairs (Düsseldorf), 1998 to date.

Trade Union World (International Confederation of Free Trade Unions, Brussels), 1997 to July-August 2002. A continuation of *Free Labour World* in a magazine format; particularly useful for Third World information.

Transfer (Brussels), 1995 to date.

Work, Employment and Society (Durham, England), 1987 to date.

B. INTERNATIONAL STUDIES

B.1 International Unionism

Barnouin, Barbara. *The European Labor Movement and European Integration.* London: Frances Pinter, 1986.

Bartolomei de la Cruz, Héctor, et al. *The International Labor Organization: The International Standards System and Basic Human Rights.* Boulder, Colo. and Oxford: Westview Press and HarperCollins, 1996.

Bendiner, Barton. *International Labour Affairs: The World Trade Unions and the Multinational Companies.* Oxford: Oxford University Press, 1987.

Busch, Gary K. *Political Currents in the International Trade Movement.* 2 vols. London: The Economist Intelligence Unit, 1980.

———. *The Political Role of International Trade Unions.* London: Macmillan, 1983.

Carew, Andrew, et al. (ed.). *The International Confederation of Free Trade Unions.* Bern, Switzerland: P. Lang, 2000.

Ghebali, Victor-Yves. *The International Labour Organisation: A Case Study on the Evolution of U.N. Specialised Agencies.* Dordrecht: Kluwer Academic Publishers, 1989.

Gordon, Michael E., and Lowell Turner (eds.). *Transnational Cooperation among Labor Unions.* Ithaca, N.Y.: ILR Press, 2000.

Holthoon, F. van, and Marcel van der Linden (eds.). *Internationalism in the Labour Movement, 1830-1940.* Leiden: E.J. Brill, 1990.

Horne, John N. *Labour at War: France and Britain, 1914-1918.* Oxford: Clarendon Press, 1991.

International Confederation of Free Trade Unions. *The Challenge of Change: Report to the 14th ICFTU World Congress on the Tasks Ahead for the International Free Trade Union Movement.* Brussels: International Confederation of Free Trade Unions, 1988.

International Labour Office. *World Labour Report.* Geneva: International Labour Office, 1984 to date. [*Reports* 2 and 6 contain chapters on the state of labor unions in the world.]

International Labour Organization. *Industrial Relations, Democracy, and Social Stability.* Geneva: International Labour Organization, 1997. [An examination of international organized labor in the mid-1990s.]

International Metalworkers' Federation. *World of the IMF—IMF and the World: An Introduction to the International Metalworkers' Federation.* Geneva: International Metalworkers' Federation, 1996.

International Transport Workers' Federation. *Solidarity: The First 100 Years of the International Transport Workers' Federation.* London: Pluto Press, 1996.

Johansson, Knut, and Jan-Erik Norling. *Building the Future.* Geneva: International Federation of Building and Wood Workers, 1997.

Linden, Marcel van der, and Jürgen Rojahn (eds.). *The Formation of Labour Movements: An International Perspective, 1870-1914.* 2 vols. Leiden: E. J. Brill, 1990.

Lis, Katharina, Jan Lucassen, and Hugo Soly (eds.). *Before the*

Unions: Wage Earners and Collective Action in Europe, 1300-1850. Cambridge: Cambridge University Press, 1995. [An important study of preindustrial labor organizations, particularly in agriculture, mining, seafaring, and printing.]

MacShane, Denis. *International Labour and the Origins of the Cold War.* Oxford: Clarendon Press, 1992.

Milner, Susan. *The Dilemmas of Internationalism: French Syndicalism and the International Labor Movement, 1900-1914.* New York: Berg, 1990.

Newton, Douglas J. *British Labour, European Socialism and the Struggle for Peace, 1889-1914.* Oxford: Clarendon Press, 1985.

Pasture, Patrick, and Johan Verberckmoes (eds.). *Working-Class Internationalism and the Appeal of National Identity: Historical Debates and Current Perspectives.* Oxford: Berg, 1998.

Prochaska, Alice. *History of the General Federation of Trade Unions.* London: Allen & Unwin, 1982. [A useful work on this neglected body which represented British labor internationally before 1914.]

Reinalda, Bob (ed.). *The International Transport Workers' Federation, 1914-1945: The Edo Fimmen Era.* Amsterdam: Stichting beheer IISG, 1997. [Edo Fimmen (1881-1942) was an important chairman of the Federation.]

Schevenels, Walther. *Forty-Five Years: International Federation of Trade Unions.* Brussels: Board of Trustees of the International Federation of Trade Unions, 1956. [An important source work written by a leading participant.]

Southall, Roger. *Imperialism or Solidarity: International Labour and South African Trade Unions.* Rondebosch, South Africa: UCT Press, 1995. [A study based on events since about 1970.]

Teague, Paul, and John Gahl. *Industrial Relations and European Integration.* London: Lawrence & Wishart, 1992.

Thorpe, W. *The Workers Themselves: Revolutionary Syndicalism and International Labour.* Dordrecht, Netherlands: Kluwer, 1990.

Wallerstein, I. (ed.). *Labor in the World Social Structure.* London: Sage, 1983.

Western, Bruce. *Between Class and Market: Postwar Unionization in the Capitalist Democracies.* Princeton, N.J.: Princeton University Press, 1999.

Windmuller, J. P. *The International Trade Union Movement.* Deventer: Kluwer, 1980.

World Federation of Trade Unions. *The World Federation of Trade Unions, 1945-1985.* Prague: World Federation of Trade Unions, 1985.

B.2 International Comparative Studies

. Adams, R. A. (ed.). *Comparative Industrial Relations: Contemporary Research and Theory.* London: HarperCollins, 1991.
———— (ed.). *Industrial Relations under Liberal Democracy: North America in Comparative Perspective.* Columbia: University of South Carolina Press, 1995.

Ananaba, Wogu. *The Trade Union Movement in Africa: Promise and Performance.* London: Hurst, 1979.

Baglioni, Guido, and Colin Crouch (eds.). *European Industrial Relations: The Challenge of Flexibility.* London: Sage, 1990.

Ballot, M., et al. *Labor-Management Relations in a Changing Environment.* New York: John Wiley, 1992.

Bamber, Greg J., et al. (eds.). *Employment Relations in Asia-Pacific: Changing Approaches.* Sydney: Allen and Unwin, 2000. [Contains contributions on Australia, China, Indonesia, Japan, South Korea, New Zealand and Taiwan.]

Bamber, Greg J., and Russell D. Lansbury (eds.). *International and Comparative Industrial Relations: A Study of Industrialised Market Economies.* Sydney: Allen & Unwin, 1993.

Barbash, Jack, and Kate Barbash (eds.). *Theories and Concepts in Comparative Industrial Relations.* Columbia: University of South Carolina Press, 1989.

Bean, R. *Comparative Industrial Relations: An Introduction to Cross-National Perspectives.* London: Croom Helm, 1985.

Berger, Stefan, and David Broughton (eds.). *The Force of Labour: The Western European Labour Movement and the Working Class in the Twentieth Century.* Oxford: Berg Publishers, 1995. [An excellent textbook with bibliographies and a statistical appendix.]

Bergquist, Charles. *Labor in Latin America: Comparative Essays on Chile, Argentina, Venezuela, and Colombia.* Stanford, Calif.: Stanford University Press, 1986.

Beyme, Klaus von. *Challenge to Power: Trade Unions and Industrial Relations in Capitalist Countries.* London: Sage, 1980.

Boyd, Rosalind E., Robert Cohen, and Peter C. Gutkind (eds.). *International Labour and the Third World: The Making of a New*

Working Class. Aldershot, England: Avebury, 1987. [Contains an extensive bibliography.]

Brandell, I. (ed.). *Workers in Third World Industrialization.* London: Macmillan, 1991.

Córdova, Efren (ed.). *Industrial Relations in Latin America.* New York: Praeger, 1984.

Crouch, Colin. *Industrial Relations and the European State Traditions.* Oxford: Clarendon Press, 1992.

Damachi, Ukandi G., H. Dieter Seibel, and Lester Trachtman (eds.). *Industrial Relations in Africa.* New York: St. Martin's Press, 1979.

Ferner, Anthony, and Richard Hyman (eds.). *Changing Industrial Relations in Europe.* Oxford: Blackwell, 1998. [A revised version of a work first published in 1992.]

————. *New Frontiers in European Industrial Relations.* Cambridge, Mass.: Blackwell, 1994.

Frenkel, Stephen J. (ed.). *Organized Labor in the Asia-Pacific Region: A Comparative Study of Trade Unionism in Nine Countries.* Ithaca, N.Y.: ILR Press, 1993. [Studies Australia, China, Malaysia, New Zealand, Hong Kong, Singapore, South Korea, and Taiwan.]

Frenkel, Stephen J., and Jeffrey Harrod (eds.). *Industrialization and Labor Relations: Contemporary Research in Seven Countries.* Ithaca, N.Y.: ILR Press, 1995. [A study of South Korea, Malaysia, Hong Kong, Singapore, South Africa, Thailand, and Taiwan.]

Frenkel, Stephen J., et al. *Organization of Work in the Information Economy.* Ithaca, N.Y.: ILR Press, 1999.

Galenson, Walter. *Labor and Economic Growth in Five Asian Countries: South Korea, Malaysia, Taiwan and the Philippines.* New York: Praeger, 1992.

Geary, Dick (ed.). *Labour and Socialist Movements in Europe before 1914.* Oxford: Berg, 1989. [Deals with the United Kingdom, France, Germany, Russia, Italy, and Spain.]

Hanson, Charles, Sheila Jackson, and Douglas Miller. *The Closed Shop: A Comparative Study in Public Policy and Trade Union Security in Britain, the USA and West Germany.* New York: St. Martin's Press, 1982.

Martin, Ross M. *Trade Unionism: Purposes and Forms.* Oxford: Clarendon Press, 1989. [Concentrates on the political aspects of trade unions; it also contains a comprehensive and well-organized bibliography.]

Maurice, M., F. Sellier, and J. Silvestre. *The Social Foundations of Industrial Power: A Comparison of France and Germany*. Cambridge, Mass.: M.I.T. Press, 1986.

Mommsen, Wolfgang, J., and Hans-Gerhard Husung (eds.). *The Development of Trade Unionism in Great Britain and Germany, 1880-1914*. London: George Allen and Unwin, 1986.

Peetz, David, Alison Preston, and Jim Docherty (eds.). *Workplace Bargaining in the International Context: First Report of the Workplace Bargaining Research Project*. Canberra: Department of Industrial Relations, 1993. [Studies Australia, Germany, Sweden, Britain, Japan, Canada, United States, and New Zealand.]

Poole, Michael. *Industrial Relations: Origins and Patterns of National Diversity*. London: Routledge & Kegan Paul, 1986.

Pravada, A., and B. A. Ruble (eds.). *Trade Unions in Communist States*. London: Allen & Unwin, 1987.

Rigby, Mike, Roger Smith, and Teresa Lawlor (eds.). *European Trade Unions: Change and Response*. London: Routledge, 1999.

Rothman, M., et al. (eds.). *Industrial Relations around the World: Labor Relations for Multinational Companies*. Berlin: De Gruyter, 1992.

Ruysseveldt, J. van, and Jelle Visser. *Industrial Relations in Europe: Tradition and Transformations*. London: Sage, 1996.

Sisson, K. *The Management of Collective Bargaining: An International Comparison*. Oxford: Basil Blackwell, 1987.

Smith, E. Owen (ed.). *Trade Unions in the Developed Economies*. London: Croom Helm, 1981.

Southall, Roger (ed.). *Trade Unions and the New Industrialisation of the Third World*. London: University of Ottawa Press, 1988.

Sraïeb, Noureddine, A. Ben Hamida, and J. Bessis (eds.). *Le mouvement ouvrier magrébin*. Paris: Editions du Centre National de la Recherche Scientifique, 1985.

Sturmthal, Adolf F. *Left of Center: European Labor since World War II*. Urbana: University of Illinois Press, 1983.

Thirkell, John et al. (eds.). *Labour Relations and Political Change in Eastern Europe: A Comparative Perspective*. London: UCL Press, 1995.

Valenzuela, J. Samuel, and Jeffrey Goodwin. *Labor Movements under Authoritarian Regimes*. Cambridge, Mass.: Center for European Studies, Harvard University, 1983.

Waddington, Jeremy, and Reiner Hoffman (eds.). *Trade Unions in*

Europe: Facing Challenges and Searching for Solutions. Brussels: European Trade Union Institute, 2001. [A study of 16 countries.]

Wilkinson, Barry. *Labour and Industry in the Asia-Pacific: Lessons for the Newly Industrialized Countries.* New York: Walter de Gruyter, 1994.

C. NATIONAL STUDIES

C.1 Histories of Peak National Organizations of Unions

Andrews, Gregg. *Shoulder to Shoulder? The American Federation of Labor, the United States and the Mexican Revolution, 1910-1924.* Berkeley: University of California Press, 1991.

Boudali, Nouri. *L'union génerale tunisienne du travail: souvenirs et récits.* Tunis: N. Boudali, 1998. [A history of the Tunisian General Union of Labor.]

Clark, Jon, H. Hartmann, C. Lau, and D. Winchester. *Trade Unions, National Politics and Economic Management: A Comparative Study of the TUC and the DGB.* London: Anglo-German Foundation for the Study of Industrial Society, 1980.

Dorfman, Gerald A. *British Trade Unionism against the Trades Union Congress.* Stanford, Calif.: Hoover Institution Press, 1983.

Draper, Alan. *A Rope of Sand: The AFL-CIO Committee on Political Education.* New York: Praeger, 1988.

Hagan, Jim. *The History of the A.C.T.U.* Melbourne: Longman Cheshire, 1981.

Levenstein, Nelson. *Communism, Anti-Communism and the CIO.* Westport, Conn.: Greenwood Press, 1981.

Lewis, Jon. *Industrialisation and Trade Union Organisation in South Africa, 1924-55: The Rise and Fall of the South African Trades and Labour Council.* Cambridge: Cambridge University Press, 1984.

Lichtenstein, Nelson N. *Labor's War at Home: The CIO in World War II.* New York: Cambridge University Press, 1982.

Martin, Ross M. *TUC: The Growth of a Pressure Group, 1868-1976.* Oxford: Oxford University Press, 1980.

Mort, Jo-Ann (ed.). *Not Your Father's Union Movement: Inside the AFL-CIO.* New York: Verso, 1998.

Nicholson, Marjorie. *The TUC Overseas: The Roots of Policy.* London: Allen & Unwin, 1986.

Prochaska, Alice. *History of the General Federation of Trade Unions.* London: Allen & Unwin, 1982.

Taylor, Robert. *The TUC: From the General Strike to New Unionism.* New York: St. Martin's Press, 2000.

Tine, Warren Van, et al. *In the Workers' Interest: A History of the Ohio AFL-CIO, 1958-1998.* Columbus: Ohio State University Center for Labor Research, 1998.

Tuckett, Angela. *The Scottish Trade Union Congress: The First 80 Years, 1897-1977.* Edinburgh: Mainstream, 1986.

C.2 Histories of Organized Labor in Individual Countries

C.2.1 Africa

Andr, Gunilla. *Union Power in the Nigerian Textile Industry: Labour Regime and Adjustment.* New Brunswick, N.J.: Transaction Publishers, 1999.

Asante, S. *The Democratization Process and the Trade Unions in Africa.* Brussels: Worldsolidarity, 1993.

Bauer, Gretchen. *Labor and Democracy in Namibia, 1971-1996.* Athens: Ohio University Press, 1998.

Bekko, Gregg J., and Geroge M. Muchai. *Protecting Workers in Micro and Small Enterprises: Can Trade Unions Make a Difference?: A Case Study of the Bakery and Confectionery Sub-Sector in Kenya.* Geneva: International Labour Organisation, 2002.

Du Toit, M. A. *South African Trade Unions.* Johannesburg: McGraw-Hill, 1976.

Hirson, B. *Yours for the Union: Class and Community Struggles in South Africa, 1930-1947.* London: Zed Books, 1989.

Kester, Gérard, and Ousmane Oumarou Sidibé (eds.). *Trade Unions and Sustainable Democracy in Africa.* Trans. Michael Cummingham. Aldershot, England: Ashgate, 1997. [A sub-Saharan study.]

Lewis, Jon. *Industrialisation and Trade Union Organization in South Africa 1924-1955: The Rise and Fall of the South African Trades and Labour Council.* Cambridge: Cambridge University Press, 1984.

Luckhardt, Ken, and Wall, B. *Organise or Starve! A History of the South African Congress of Trade Unions.* London: Lawrence and Wishart, 1980.

Odigie, S. A. *State Intervention in Industrial Relations in Nigeria, 1861-1989.* Benin City: [privately printed], 1993.

Otobo, D. *Trade Union Movement in Nigeria: Yesterday, Today, and Tomorrow.* Lagos: Malthouse Press, 1995.

Panford, Kwamina. *IMF-World Bank and Labor's Burdens in Africa: Ghana's Experience.* Westport, Conn.: Praeger, 2001.

C.2.2 British Isles

Boyle, John W. *The Irish Labor Movement in the Nineteenth Century.* Washington, D.C.: Catholic University of America Press, 1988.

Brown, Henry Phelps. *The Origins of Trade Union Power.* Oxford: Oxford University Press, 1986. [Although mainly about Britain, this work contains chapters on the United States, Canada, and Australia.]

Charlton, John. *The Chartists: The First National Workers' Movement.* London: Pluto Press, 1997.

Chase, Malcolm. *Early Trade Unionism: Fraternity, Skill, and the Politics of Labour.* Aldershot, England: Ashgate, 2000.

Clegg, Hugh A. *A History of British Trade Unions since 1889: Volume II, 1911-1933.* Oxford: Oxford University Press, 1985.

———. *A History of British Trade Unions since 1889: Volume III, 1934-1951.* Oxford: Oxford University Press, 1994.

Clegg, Hugh A., Alan Fox, and A. F. Thompson. *A History of British Trade Unions since 1889: Volume I, 1889-1910.* Oxford: Oxford University Press, 1964.

Coates, Ken, and Tony Topham. *Trade Unions in Britain.* Nottingham, England: Spokesman, 1980. [A comprehensive profile of British organized labor in the late 1970s.]

Dobson, C. R. *Masters and Journeymen: A Prehistory of Industrial Relations, 1717-1800.* London: Croom Helm, 1980.

Fraser, W. Hamish. *A History of British Trade Unionism, 1700-1998.* Basingstoke, England: Macmillan, 1999.

Kenefick, W., and A. McIvor. *Roots of Red Clydeside, 1910-1914? Labour Unrest and Industrial Relations in West Scotland.* Edinburgh: John Donald, 1996.

Laybourn, Keith. *History of British Trade Unionism, c. 1770-1990.* Wolfeboro Falls, N.H.: Allan Sutton, 1992.

Leeson, R. A. *Travelling Brothers: The Six Centuries' Road from Craft Fellowship to Trade Unionism.* London: George Allen & Unwin, 1979.

McCarthy, C. *Trade Unions in Ireland, 1894-1960.* Dublin: Institute of Public Administration, 1977.

Pelling, Henry. *A History of British Trade Unionism.* 5th ed. Basingstoke: Macmillan, 1992. [First published in 1963, this is still the main single volume survey work on the UK. It includes an annotated bibliography and statistical appendix.]

Price, Richard. *Labour in British History: An Interpretative History.* London: Routledge, 1990. [First published by Croom Helm in 1986.]

Wrigley, Chris. *British Trade Unions since 1933.* Cambridge: Cambridge University Press, 2002. [Covers the period from 1933 to 2000.]

C.2.3 Middle East and Asia

Chalmers, Norma. *Industrial Relations in Japan: The Peripheral Workforce.* London: Routledge, 1989.

Chen, P. K. *The Labour Movement in China.* Hong Kong: Swindon Books, 1985.

Choi, Jang J. *Labor and the Authoritarian State: Labor Unions in South Korean Manufacturing Industries, 1961-1980.* Seoul: Korea University Press, 1989.

Dejillas, Leopoldo J. *Trade Union Behavior in the Philippines, 1946-1990.* Manilla: Anteneo De Manila University Press, 1994.

Gibbs, Michael H. *Struggle and Purpose in Postwar Japanese Unionism.* Berkeley, Calif.: Institute of East Asian Studies, 2000.

Heller, Patrick. *The Labor of Development: Workers and the Transformation of Capitalism in Kerala, India.* Ithaca, N.Y.: Cornell University Press, 1999.

Hutchinson, Jane, and Andrew Brown (eds.). *Organising Labour in Globalising Asia.* London: Routledge: 2001.

Ingleson, John. *In Search of Justice: Workers and Unions in Colonial Java, 1908-1926.* Singapore: Oxford University Press, 1986.

Khan, B. A. *Trade Unionism and Industrial Relations in Pakistan.* Karachi: Royal, 1980.

Kim, S. J. *Trade Unionism in Korea.* Seoul: Federation of Korean Trade Unions, 1996.

Kume, Ikuo. *Disparaged Success: Labor Politics in Postwar Japan.* Ithaca, N.Y.: Cornell University Press, 1998.

Ladjevardi, Habib. *Labor Unions and Autocracy in Iran.* New York: Syracuse University Press, 1985.

Lambert, R. *Authoritarian State Unionism in New Order Indonesia.* Perth, Western Australia: Murdoch University, 1993.

Lee, Lai To. *Trade Unions in China, 1949 to the Present: The Organization and Leadership of the All-China Federation of Trade Unions.* Singapore: Singapore University Press, 1986.

Matsuzaki, H. *Japanese Business Unionism: The Historical Development of a Unique Labour Movement.* Sydney: University of New South Wales, 1992.

Mehta, B. L. *The Trade Union Movement in India.* New Delhi: Kanishka, 1991.

Ng, Hong Sek, and Malcolm Warner. *China's Trade Unions and Management.* New York: St. Martin's Press, 1998.

Ramachandran, Selvakumaran and Kris Arjunan. *Trade Unionism in the Malaysian Plantation Industry.* Sydney: University of New South Wales Studies in Human Resource Management and Industrial Relations in Asia, No. 2, 1993.

Ramasamy, P. *Plantation Labour, Unions, Capital, and the State in Peninsular Malaysia.* Kuala Lumpur: Oxford University Press, 1994.

Shalev, Michael. *Labour and the Political Economy in Israel.* New York: Oxford University Press, 1992.

Sheehan, Jackie. *Chinese Workers: A New History.* London: Routledge, 1998. [A timely study of efforts to form an independent labor movement in China.]

Song, Ho Keun. *Labour Unions in the Republic of Korea.* Geneva: International Institute for Labour Studies, 1999.

Verma, Pramod, and S. Mookherjee. *Trade Unions in India.* New Delhi: Oxford and IBA, 1982.

Warner, Malcolm (ed.). *Changing Workplace Relations in the Chinese Economy.* London: Macmillan, 2000.

Woodiwiss, Anthony. *Law, Labour and Society in Japan: From Repression to Reluctant Recognition.* London: Routledge, 1991.

C.2.4 Europe

Agóes, Sándor. *The Troubled Origins of the Italian Catholic Labor Movement, 1878-1914.* Detroit, Mich.: Wayne State University Press, 1988.

Ashwin, Sarah. *Russian Workers: The Anatomy of Patience.* Manchester: Manchester University Press, 1999.

Barkan, J. *Visions of Emancipation: The Italian Workers' Movement since 1945.* New York: Praeger, 1984.

Berghahn, V. R., and D. Karsten. *Industrial Relations in West Germany.* Oxford: Berg, 1987.

Borisov, V., et al. *The Workers' Movement in Russia.* Aldershot, England: Edward Elgar, 1995. [A study of three independent unions which developed between 1987 and 1995.]

Bridgford, Jeff. *The Politics of French Trade Unionism.* Leicester: Leicester University Press, 1991.

Davis, Sue. *Trade Unions in Russia and the Ukraine, 1985-95.* Basingstoke, UK: Palgrave, 2001.

Chapman, Herrick, Mark Kesselman, and Martin Schain (eds.). *A Century of Organized Labor in France: A Union Movement for the Twenty-first Century?* New York: St. Martin's Press, 1998.

Christiansen, Paul T. *Russian Workers in Transition: Labor, Management, and the State under Gorbachev and Yeltsin.* De Kalb: North Illinois University Press, 1999.

Dawen, Wolfgang Uellenberg-van. *Gewerkschaften in Deutschland von 1848 bis heute: Ein Überblick.* Munich: Olzog, 1997. [A general survey with a German bibliography.]

European Trade Union Institute. *Information Booklets on the Trade Union Movement: Great Britain, Sweden, Greece, Germany, Italy, Austria, Spain and Belgium.* Brussels, European Trade Union Institute, 1982-1987. [A handy and reliable source of up-to-date information.]

Galenson, Walter. *The World's Strongest Trade Unions: The Scandinavian Labor Movement.* Westport, Conn.: Quorum, 1998. [Mainly deals with the post-1985 years.]

Golden, Miriam. *Labor Divided: Austerity and Working-Class Politics in Contemporary Italy.* Ithaca, N.Y.: Cornell University Press, 1988.

Katzenstein, Peter J. *Corporatism and Change: Austria, Switzerland and the Politics of Industry*. Ithaca, N.Y.: Cornell University Press, 1984.

———— (ed.). *Industry and Politics in West Germany*. Ithaca, N.Y.: Cornell University Press, 1989.

Kauppinen, T., et al. *Labour Relations in Finland*. Helsinki: Ministry of Labour, 1990.

Kesselman, M. (ed.). *The French Workers' Movement: Economic Crisis and Political Change*. London: Allen & Unwin, 1984.

Lange, P., G. Ross, and M. Vannicelli (eds.). *Unions, Change and Crisis: French and Italian Union Strategy and the Political Economy, 1945-1980*. London: Allen & Unwin, 1982.

Lewis, Jill. *Fascism and the Working Class in Austria, 1918-1934: The Failure of Labour in the First Republic*. New York: Berg, 1991.

Macgraw, Roger. *A History of the French Working Class*. 2 vols. Oxford: Blackwell Publishers, 1992.

Markovits, Andrei S. *The Politics of the West German Trade Unions: Strategies of Class and Interest Representation in Growth and Crisis*. Cambridge: Cambridge University Press, 1986. [An impressive study of the post-1945 period; it contains chapters on *IG Metall*, the metal workers' union, and three other major unions as well as a glossary of German terms.]

Moses, John A. *Trade Unionism in Germany from Bismarck to Hitler, 1869 to 1933*. 2 vols. London: George Prior, 1982. [A good survey work with translations of key documents.]

Sassoon, Donald. *Contemporary Italy: Politics, Economy and Society since 1945*. London: Longman, 1986.

Schneider, Michael. *A Brief History of the German Trade Unions*. Trans. Barrie Selman. Bonn: J. H. W. Dietz Nachf., 1991. [First published in German in 1989, this is an excellent and detailed survey with statistics, a German bibliography, and a list of abbreviations.]

Shkliarevsky, Gennady. *Labor in the Russian Revolution: Factory Committees and Trade Unions, 1917-1918*. New York: St. Martin's Press, 1993.

Stefancic, D. R. *Robotnik: A Short History of the Struggle for Worker Self-Management and Free Trade Unions in Poland, 1944-1981*. New York: Columbia University Press, 1992.

Thelen, Kathleen A. *Union of Parts: Labor Politics in Postwar Germany.* Ithaca, N.Y.: Cornell University Press, 1992.

Torigian, Michael. *Every Factory a Fortress: The French Labor Movement in the Age of Ford and Hitler.* Athens: Ohio University Press, 1999.

Wrigley, Chris (ed.). *Challenges of Labour: Central and Western Europe, 1917-1920.* New York: Routledge, 1993.

C.2.5 Latin America and the Caribbean

Alexander, Robert J. *A History of Organized Labor in Brazil.* Westport, Conn.: Praeger, 2003.

———. *A History of Organized Labor in Cuba.* Westport, Conn.: Praeger, 2002.

Barros, Maurício Rands. *Labour Relations and the New Unionism in Contemporary Brazil.* London: Macmillan, 1999.

Decker, David R. *The Political, Economic, and Labor Climate of Argentina.* Philadelphia: University of Pennsylvania Press, 1983.

Drake, Paul W. *Labor Movements and Dictatorships in the Southern Cone in Comparative Perspective.* Baltimore, Md.: Johns Hopkins University Press, 1996.

Epstein, Edward C. *Labor Autonomy and the State in Latin America.* Boston: Unwin Hyman, 1989.

French, John D. *The Brazilian Workers' ABC: Class Conflict and Alliances in Modern São Paulo.* Chapel Hill: University of North Carolina Press, 1992.

Greenfield, Gerald M., and Sheldon L. Maram. *Latin American Labor Organizations.* New York: Greenwood Press, 1987.

Look Lai, Walton. *Indentured Labour, Caribbean Sugar: Chinese and Indian Migrants to the British West Indies, 1838-1918.* Baltimore, Md.: Johns Hopkins Studies in Atlantic History and Culture, Johns Hopkins University Press, 1993.

Middlebrook, K. J. *Paradox of Revolution: Labor, the State, and Authoritarianism in Mexico.* Baltimore, Md.: Johns Hopkins University Press, 1995. [Covers the period from the 1920s to the early 1990s.]

———. *Unions, Workers, and the State in Mexico.* San Diego: University of California Press, 1991.

Murillo, Maria V. *Labor Unions, Partisan Coalitions, and Market Reforms in Latin America* Cambridge: Cambridge University

Press, 2001.

Nurse, Lawrence A. *Trade Unionism and Industrial Relations in the Commonwealth Caribbean: History, Contemporary Practice and Prospect.* Westport, Conn.: Greenwood Press, 1992.

Ramdin, Ron. *From Chattel Slave to Wage Earner: A History of Trade Unionism in Trinidad and Tobago.* London: Martin Brian & O'Keefe, 1982.

Roberts, Kenneth M. *Deepening Democracy: The Modern Left and Social Movements in Chile and Peru.* Stanford, Calif.: Stanford University Press, 1998.

Rodney, Walter. *A History of Guyanese Working People, 1881-1905.* Baltimore, Md.: Johns Hopkins University Press, 1981.

C.2.6 North America

Brody, David. *Workers in Industrial America: Essays on the Twentieth Century Struggle.* New York: Oxford University Press, 1980.

Derber, Milton, et al. *Labor in Illinois: The Affluent Years, 1945-80.* Urbana: University of Illinois Press, 1989.

Dubofksy, Melvyn. *Industrialism and the American Worker, 1865-1920.* 3rd ed. Wheeling, Ill.: Harlan Davidson, 1996.

Dubofksy, Melvyn, and Foster Rhea Dulles. *Labor in America: A History.* 6th ed. Wheeling, Ill.: Harlan Davidson, 1999.

Dulles, Foster R., and Melvyn Dubofsky. *Labor in America: A History.* 4th ed. Arlington Heights, Ill.: Harlan Davidson, 1984.

Forsey, Eugene. *Trade Unions in Canada, 1812-1902.* Toronto: University of Toronto Press, 1982.

Galenson, Walter. *The American Labor Movement, 1955-1995.* Westport, Conn.: Greenwood Press, 1996.

Jacoby, Daniel. *Laboring for Freedom: A New Look at the History of Labor in America.* Armonk, N.Y.: M. E. Sharpe, 1998.

Kochan, T., H. Katz, and R. McKerzie. *The Transformation of American Industrial Relations.* New York: Basic Books, 1986.

McCartin, Joseph. *Labor's Great War: The Struggle for Industrial Democracy and the Origins of Modern American Labor Relations.* Chapel Hill: University of North Carolina Press, 1997.

Mendel, Ronald. *"A Broad and Ennobling Spirit": Workers and Their Unions in Late Gilded Age New York and Brooklyn, 1886-1898.* Westport, Conn.: Praeger, 2003.

Montgomery, David. *The Fall of the House of Labor: The Workplace, the State and American Labor Activism, 1860-1987.* Cambridge: Cambridge University Press, 1987.

Peirce, Jon. *Canadian Industrial Relations.* Scarborough, Ontario: Prentice Hall Canada, 2000.

Zieger, Robert H. *American Workers, American Unions, 1920-1994.* 2nd ed. Baltimore, Md.: Johns Hopkins University Press, 1994.

C.2.7 Oceania

Ford, Bill, and David Plowman (eds.). *Australian Unions: An Industrial Relations Perspective.* Melbourne: Macmillan, 1983.

Hess, Michael. *Unions under Economic Development: Private Sector Unions in Papua New Guinea.* Melbourne: Oxford University Press, 1992.

Markey, Ray. *In Case of Oppression: The Life and Times of the Labor Council of New South Wales.* Sydney: Pluto Press, 1994.

Martin, Ross M. *Trade Unions in Australia.* 2nd ed. Harmondsworth, England: Penguin, 1980. [A useful short survey but without a bibliography.]

Roth, H. *Trade Unions in New Zealand: Past and Present.* Wellington: A. H. and A. W. Reed, 1973.

C.3 Industrial Relations in Particular Countries

Adams, Roy J., and Noah M. Meltz (eds.). *Industrial Relations Theory: Its Nature, Scope, and Pedagogy.* Management and Labor Relations Series No. 4. Lanham, Md.: Scarecrow Press, 1993.

Alexander, R., and J. Lewer. *Understanding Australian Industrial Relations.* 4th ed. Sydney: Harcourt Brace, 1996.

Anderson, J., M. Gunderson, and A. Ponak. (eds.). *Union-Management Relations in Canada.* 2nd ed. Don Mills, Ontario: Addison-Wesley, 1989.

Brown, William (ed.). *The Changing Contours of British Industrial Relations.* Oxford: Blackwell, 1981. [Contains valuable survey findings.]

Chaykowski, R., and A. Verma (eds.). *Industrial Relations in Canadian Industry.* Toronto: Dryden, 1992.

Chelius, James, and James Dworkin (eds.). *Reflections on the Transformation of Industrial Relations.* Management and Labor Relations Series No. 1. Lanham, Md.: Scarecrow Press, 1990.

Deeks, John, Jane Parker, and Rose Ryan. *Labour and Employment Relations in New Zealand.* Auckland: Longman Paul, 1994. [Second edition of a text first published as *Labour Relations in New Zealand* in 1989.]

Deery, Stephen, and David Plowman. *Australian Industrial Relations.* 3rd ed. Sydney: McGraw-Hill, 1991.

Kessler, Sid, and Fred Bayliss. *Contemporary British Industrial Relations.* Basingstoke: Macmillan, 1992.

Lipsky, D., and C. Donn (eds.). *Collective Bargaining in American Industry.* Lexington, Mass.: Lexington Books, 1987.

Murphy, T., B. Hillery, and A. Kelly (eds.). *Industrial Relations in Ireland: Contemporary Issues and Developments.* Dublin: University College, Dublin, 1989.

Roomkin, Myron J. *Profit Sharing and Gain Sharing.* Management and Labor Relations Series No. 2. Lanham, Md.: Scarecrow Press, 1990.

Slomp, Hans. *Labor Relations in Europe: A History of Issues and Developments.* Westport, Conn.: Greenwood Press, 1990.

Thirkell, J. E. M., K. Petkov, and S. A. Vickerstaff. *The Transformation of Labour Relations: Restructuring and Privatization in Eastern Europe and Russia.* New York: Oxford University Press, 1998.

Wooden, Mark et al. *The Transformation of Australian Industrial Relations.* Leichhardt, New South Wales: Federation Press, 2000.

Wrigley, Chris (ed.). *A History of British Industrial Relations.* 2 vols. Brighton, Sussex: Harvester Press, 1982, 1987. [Covers the period from 1875 to 1939.]

D. FEATURES OF LABOR UNIONS

D.1 Histories of Particular Unions

Bagwell, P. S. *The Railwaymen: The History of the National Union of Railwaymen.* 2 vols. London: Allen & Unwin, 1963, 1982.

Beasley, Margo. *The Missos: A History of the Federated Miscellaneous Workers' Union.* Sydney: Allen and Unwin, 1996.

————. *Wharfies: A History of the Waterside Workers' Federation of Australia*. Sydney: Halstead Press in Association with the Australian National Maritime Museum, 1996.

Bowden, Badley. *Driving Force: The History of the Transport Workers' Union of Australia, 1883–1992*. Sydney: Allen and Unwin, 1993.

Bray, Mark, and Malcolm Rimmer. *Delivering the Goods: A History of the Transport Workers' Union in New South Wales 1886-1986*. Sydney: Allen & Unwin, 1987.

Carpenter, Mick. *They Still Go Marching On: A Celebration of the COHSE's First 75 Years*. Banstead, England: Confederation of Health Service Employees, 1985.

Clinton, Allen. *Post Office Workers: A Trade Union and Social History*. London: Allen & Unwin, 1984.

Coates, Ken, and Tony Topham. *The History of the Transport and General Workers' Union*. Oxford: Basil Blackwell, 1991. [Published as one volume in two parts.]

Croucher, Richard. *Engineers at War*. London: Merlin Press, 1982. [A study of the British engineering unions during World War II.]

Freeman, Joshua B. *In Transit: The Transport Workers' Union in New York City, 1933-1966*. New York: Oxford University Press, 1989.

Galenson, Walter. *The United Brotherhood of Carpenters*. Cambridge, Mass.: Harvard University Press, 1983.

Gennard, John. *A History of the National Graphical Association*. London: Unwin Hyman, 1990. [A history of a powerful British craft union.]

Halpern, Martin. *UAW Politics in the Cold War Era*. Albany: State University of New York Press, 1988. [Deals with the United Auto Workers.]

Hearn, Mark and Harry Knowles. *One Big Union: A History of the Australian Workers Union*. Melbourne: Cambridge University Press, 1996.

Laslett, John H. M. (ed.). *The United Mine Workers of America: A Model of Industrial Solidarity?* University Park: State University of Pennsylvania, 1996.

Maguire, Martin. *Servants to the Public: A History of the Local Government and Public Services Union, 1901-1990*. Dublin: Institute of Public Administration, 1998.

Marsh, Arthur, and Victoria Ryan. *The Clerks: A History of Apex, 1890-1989*. Oxford: Malthouse, 1997.

Mitchell, Glenn. *On Strong Foundations: The BWIU and Industrial Relations in the Australian Construction Industry, 1942-1992.* Sydney: Harcourt Brace, 1996.

Murray, Robert, and Kate White. *The Ironworkers: A History of the Federated Ironworkers' Association of Australia.* Sydney: Hale and Iremonger, 1982.

Nachmann, Walter. *100 Jahre ÖTV: Geschichte: Die Geschichte einer Gewerkschaft und ihrer Vorläuforganisationen.* Frankfurt: Union-Druckerei und Verlagsanstalt, 1996. [This is the official history of the German *Gewerksschaft Öffentliche Dienste, Transport und Verkehr (ÖTV)* or Public Service, Transportation, and Traffic Labor Union. Suppressed by the Nazis in 1933, it was refounded in January 1949. The book was issued as two volumes of which this is the first; the second is a biographical dictionary whose details are listed under Rüdiger Zimmerman in the earlier section (A.3) for biographical dictionaries.]

Schatz, Ronald. *The Electrical Workers: A History of Labor at General Electric and Westinghouse, 1923-1960.* Urbana: University of Illinois Press, 1983.

Spaull, Andrew. *Australian Education Union: From Federal Registration to National Reconciliation.* Sydney: ACER Press, 2000.

Strachan, Glenda. *Labour of Love: The History of the Nurses' Association in Queensland.* Sydney: Allen and Unwin, 1996.

Tyler, Gus. *Look for the Union Label: A History of the International Ladies' Garment Workers Union.* Armonk, N.Y.: M. E. Sharp, 1995.

Wellman, David. *The Union Makes Us Strong: Radical Unionism on the San Francisco Waterfront.* Cambridge: Cambridge University Press, 1995.

Yates, C. A. B. *From Plant to Politics: The Autoworkers' Union in Postwar Canada.* Philadelphia, Pa.: Temple University Press, 1993.

Zieger, Robert H. *Rebuilding the Pulp and Paper Workers' Union, 1933-1941.* Knoxville: University of Tennessee Press, 1984.

D.2 Unions in Particular Industries or Occupations

Aaron, B., J. Najita, and J. Stern. *Public-Sector Bargaining.* 2nd ed. Washington, D.C.: Bureau of National Affairs, 1988.

Andræ, Gunilla, and Björn Beckman. *Union Power in the Nigerian Textile Industry: Labour Regime and Adjustment.* New Brunswick, N.J.: Transaction Publication, 1999.

Arnold, Gordon B. *The Politics of Faculty Unionization: The Experience of Three New England Universities.* Westport, Conn.: Bergin and Garvey, 2000.

Bach, Stephen et al. (eds.). *Public Service Employment Relations in Europe: Transformation, Modernisation, or Inertia?* London: Routledge, 1999.

Bahl, V. *The Making of the Indian Working Class: A Case Study of the Tata Iron and Steel Company, 1880-1946.* New Delhi: Sage, 1995.

Baxter, Vern K. *Labor and Politics in the U. S. Postal Service.* New York: Plenum, 1994.

Benin, Leigh D. *The New Labor Radicalism and New York City's Garment Industry: Progressive Labor Insurgents in the 1960s.* New York: Garland, 2000.

Burgmann, Meredith and Verity Burgmann. *Green Bans, Red Union: Environmental Activism and the New South Wales Builders' Federation.* Sydney: University of New South Wales Press, 1998.

Cooper, Bruce S. (ed.). *Labor Relations in Education: An International Perspective.* Westport, Conn.: Greenwood Press, 1992.

Creese, Gillian L. *Contracting Masculinity: Gender, Class, and Race in a White-Collar Union, 1944-1994.* Toronto: Oxford University Press, 1999.

Daniel, Cletus E. *Bitter Harvest: A History of California Farmworkers, 1870-1941.* Ithaca, N.Y.: Cornell University Press, 1981.

Docherty, C. *Steel and Steelworkers: The Sons of Vulcan.* London: Heinemann Educational Books, 1983. [A British study.]

Edwards, C., and E. Heery. *Management Control and Union Power: A Study of Labour Relations in Coal-mining.* Oxford: Clarendon Press, 1989.

Ellem, Bradon. *In Women's Hands: A History of Clothing Trades Unionism in Australia.* Sydney: University of New South Wales Press, 1989.

Feldman, G. D., and K. Tenfelde (eds.). *Workers, Owners and Politics in Coal Mining: An International Comparison of Industrial Relations.* New York: Berg, 1990.

Freeman, Richard B., and Casey Ichniowksi. *When Public Sector Workers Unionize*. Chicago: University of Chicago Press, 1988.

Gavroglou, Stavros. *Labor's Power and Industrial Performance: Automotive Production Regimes in the U.S., Germany, and Japan*. New York: Garland Press, 1998.

Green, W. C., and E. J. Yanarella. *North American Auto Unions in Crisis: Lean Production as Contested Terrain*. Albany: State University of New York Press, 1996.

Griffin, Gerard. *White-Collar Militancy: The Australian Banking and Insurance Unions*. Sydney: Croom Helm, 1985.

Harris, Howell J. *Bloodless Victories: The Rise and Fall of the Open Shop in the Philadelphia Metal Trades, 1890-1940*. Cambridge: Cambridge University Press, 2000.

Hatcher, John, et al. *The History of the British Coal Industry*. 5 vols. Oxford: Clarendon Press, 1984-93.

Ironside, Mike. *Facing up to Thatcherism: The History of NALGO, 1979-1993*. Oxford: Oxford University Press, 2000.

Jaffe, James A. *The Struggle for Market Power: Industrial Relations in the British Coal Industry, 1800-1840*. Cambridge: Cambridge University Press, 2002.

Jowitt, J. A., and A. J. McIvor (eds.). *Employers and Labour in the English Textile Industries, 1850-1939*. New York: Routledge, Chapman & Hall, 1988.

Katz, H. C. (ed.). *Telecommunications: Restructuring Work and Employment Relations Worldwide*. Ithaca, N.Y.: ILR Press, 1997.

Kazin, Michael. *Barons of Labor: The San Francisco Building Trades and Union Power in the Progressive Era*. Urbana: University of Illinois Press, 1987.

Kimeldorf, Howard. *Reds or Rackets? The Making of Radical and Conservative Unions on the Waterfront*. Berkeley: University of California Press, 1988.

Langemann, Ellen C. (ed.). *Nursing History: New Perspectives, New Possibilities*. New York: Teachers College Press, 1983.

Lawn, Martin (ed.). *The Politics of Teacher Unionism: International Perspectives*. London: Croom Helm, 1985.

Levitan, Sar A., and Alexandra B Noden. *Working for the Sovereign: Employee Relations in the Federal Government*. Baltimore, Md.: Johns Hopkins University Press, 1983.

Licht, Walter. *Working for the Railroad: The Organization of Work in the Nineteenth Century.* Princeton, N.J.: Princeton University Press, 1983.

Mangum, Garth L., and John Walsh. *Union Resilience in Troubled Times, AFL-CIO, 1960-1993.* Armonk, N.Y.: M. E. Sharpe, 1994.

McKelvey, Jean T. (ed.). *Cleared for Takeoff: Airline Labor Relations Since Deregulation.* New York: ILR Press, 1988.

Murphy, Marjorie. *Blackboard Unions: The AFT and the NEA, 1900-1980.* Ithaca, N.Y.: Cornell University Press, 1990.

Palmer, David. *Organizing the Shipyards: Union Strategy in Three Northeast Ports, 1933-1945.* Ithaca, N.Y.: ILR Press, 1998.

Peirats, José. *The CNT in the Spanish Revolution.* Hastings, England: Meltzer Press, 2001.

Peterson, Joyce S. *American Automobile Workers, 1900-1933.* Albany: State University of New York Press, 1987.

Schact, John N. *The Making of Telephone Unionism, 1920-1947.* New Brunswick, N.J: Rutgers University Press, 1985.

Smith, David F. *White-Collar Unionism in New Zealand.* Wellington: New Zealand Institute of Industrial Relations Research, 1987.

Stein, Margot B. *The Social Origins of a Labor Elite: French Engine Drivers, 1837-1914.* New York: Garland, 1987. [Includes a comparison with U.S. engine drivers.]

Stomquist, Shelton. *A Generation of Boomers: The Pattern of Railroad Labor Conflict in Nineteenth Century America.* Champaign: University of Illinois Press, 1987.

Synott, John P. *Teacher Unions, Social Movements, and the Politics of Education in Asia.* Aldershot, England: Ashgate, 2002.

Turnbull, P., and V. Wass. *Reform and Structural Adjustment in the World's Ports: The Future for Labour and the Unions.* London: International Transport Workers' Federation, 1994.

Tyler, Gus. *Look for the Union Label: A History of the International Ladies' Garment Workers' Union.* Armonk, N.Y.: M. E. Sharpe, 1995.

Upham, Martin. *Tempered—Not Quenched: The History of the ISTC, 1851-1997.* London: Lawrence and Wishart, 1997. [A history of the Iron and Steel Industry Confederation.]

Vicary, Adrian. *In the Interests of Education: A History of Education Unionism in South Australia.* Sydney: Allen and Unwin, 1997.

Weir, Robert E. *Beyond Labor's Veil: The Culture of the Knights of Labor.* University Park: Pennsylvania State University Press, 1996.

Welch, Cliff. *The Seed was Planted: The São Paulo Roots of Brazil's Rural Labor Movement, 1924-1964*. University Park: Pennsylvania State University Press, 1999.

Wellman, David. *The Union Makes Us Strong: Radical Unionism on the San Francisco Waterfront*. Cambridge: Cambridge University Press, 1995.

D.3 Unions and the Workplace or in Particular Regions

Ackers, Peter, et al. (eds.). *The New Workplace and Trade Unionism: Critical Perspectives on Work and Organization*. London: Routledge, 1995.

Appelbaum, Eileen, and Rosemary Batt. *The New American Workplace: Transforming Work Systems in the United States*. Ithaca, N.Y.: Cornell University Press, 1994.

Callus, Ron, et al. *Industrial Relations at Work: The Australian Workplace Industrial Relations Survey*. Canberra: Australian Government Publishing Service, 1991. [This important survey was conducted in 1989-1990 and a second survey was held in 1995.]

Cully, Mark, et al. *Britain at Work: As Depicted by the 1998 Workplace Employee Relations Survey*. London: Routledge, 1999. [Previous studies were conducted in 1980, 1984, and 1990.]

Cully, Mark, and Richard Fraser. *The Australian Workplace Industrial Relations Survey (AWIRS): The State Dimension*. Canberra: Department of Industrial Relations, 1993. [A statistical study.]

Daniel, W. W., and Neil Millward. *Workplace Industrial Relations in Britain*. London: Heinemann, 1983.

Hershatter, Gail. *The Workers of Tianjin, 1900-1949*. Stanford, Calif.: Stanford University Press, 1986. [A case study of a Chinese city.]

Kulczycki, John. *The Polish Coal Miners' Union and the German Labor Movement in the Ruhr, 1902-1934: National and Social Solidarity*. Oxford: Berg, 1997.

Kumar, Pradeep. *Unions and Workplace Change in Canada*. Kingston, Ontario: IRC Press, 1995.

Lynd, Staughton (ed.). *"We Are All Leaders": The Alternative Unionism of the 1930s*. Urbana: University of Illinois Press, 1996. [Deals with community-based unionism.]

Martin, Ron, Peter Sunley, and Jane Willis. *Union Retreat and the Regions: The Shrinking Landscape of Organized Labour*. London: J. Kingsley Publishers, 1996.

Millward, Neil, Alex Bryson, and John Forth. *All Change? British Employment Relations, 1980-1998, as Portrayed by the Workplace Industrial Relations Survey.* London: Routledge, 2000.

Millward, Neil, and Mark Stevens. *British Workplace Industrial Relations.* Aldershot, England: Gower, 1986.

Morehead, Alison, et al. *Changes at Work: The 1995 Australian Workplace Industrial Relations Survey.* Melbourne: Longman, 1997.

Tillman, Ray M., and Michael S. Cummings (eds.). *The Transformation of U.S. Unions: Voices, Visions, and Strategies from the Grassroots.* Boulder, Colo.: Lynne Rienner, 1998.

D.4 Ideas, Movements, and Religion

Barrow, Logie. *Democratic Ideas and the British Labour Movement.* Cambridge: Cambridge University Press, 1996.

Buhle, Paul. *Marxism in the United States: Remapping the History of the American Left.* London: Verso, 1987.

Docherty, James C. *Historical Dictionary of Socialism.* Lanham, Md.: Scarecrow Press, 1997. [Provides a general global survey.]

Dubofsky, Melvyn. *We Shall Be All: A History of the Industrial Workers of the World.* 2nd ed. Urbana: University of Illinois Press, 1988.

Heineman, Kenneth J. *A Catholic New Deal: Religion and Reform in Depression Pittsburgh.* University Park: Pennsylvania State University Press, 1999.

Holton, Bob. *British Syndicalism, 1910-14: Myths and Realities.* London: Pluto Press, 1976.

Kimeldorf, Howard. *Battling for American Labor: Wobblies, Craft Workers, and the Making of the Union Movement.* Berkeley: University of California Press, 1999.

Lieberman, Sima. *Labor Movements and Labor Thought : Spain, France, Germany and the United States.* New York: Praeger, 1986.

Linden, Marcel van der, and Wayne Thorpe (eds.). *Revolutionary Syndicalism: An International Perspective.* Aldershot, England: Scolar Press, 1990.

Marshall, Peter. *Demanding the Impossible: A History of Anarchism.* London: HarperCollins, 1992.

Olssen, Erik. *The Red Feds: Revolutionary Industrial Unionism and the New Zealand Federation of Labour, 1908-14.* Auckland: Oxford University Press, 1988.

Roberts, David D. *The Syndicalist Tradition and Italian Fascism.* Chapel Hill: University of North Carolina Press, 1979.

Seaton, Douglas P. *Catholics and Radicals: The Association of Catholic Trade Unionists and the Labor Movement, from Depression to Cold War.* Lewisburg, Pa.: Bucknell University Press, 1981.

Strath, Bo. *The Organisation of Labour Markets: Modernity, Culture, and Governance in Germany, Britain, and Japan.* London: Routledge, 1996.

Stepan-Norris, Judith, and Maurice Zeitlin. *Left Out: Reds and America's Industrial Unions.* Cambridge: Cambridge University Press, 2002.

D.5 Autobiographies and Biographies of Labor Leaders

Bobumil, Walter. *A Biography of Florida Union Organizer—Frank E'Dalgo.* Lewiston, N.Y.: Edward Mellen Press, 2000.

Bull, Tas. *Life on the Waterfront: An Autobiography.* Melbourne: HarperCollins, 1998. [Tas Bull was an· important figure in Australian and international maritime unionism.]

Bussel, Robert. *From Harvard to the Ranks of Labor: Powers Hapgood and the American Working Class.* University Park: Pennsylvania State University Press, 1999.

Carlson, Peter. *Roughneck: The Life and Times of Big Bill Haywood.* New York: Norton, 1983.

Clark, Paul, et al. *Forging a Union of Steel: Philip Murray, SWOC, & the United Steelworkers.* Ithaca, N.Y.: Cornell ILR Press, 1987.

Cook, Alice H. *A Lifetime of Labor: The Autobiography of Alice H. Cook.* New York: Feminist Press at the City University of New York, 1998.

Day, David. *Ben Chifley.* London: HarperCollins, 2001.

Dickmyer, Elizabeth R. *Reuther: A Daughter Strikes.* Southfield, Mich.: Spelman Publishers Division, 1989.

Dubofsky, Melvyn, and Warren Van Tine. (eds.). *Labor Leaders in America.* Urbana: University of Illinois Press, 1986.

Fraser, Steven. *Labor Will Rule: Sidney Hillman and the Rise of American Labor.* New York: The Free Press, 1991.

Guy, Bill. *A Life on the Left: A Biography of Clyde Cameron.* Adelaide: Wakefield Press, 1999. [A biography of a prominent Australian labor union official and later politician from the 1950s to the 1970s.]

Jones, Jack. *Union Man: An Autobiography.* London: Collins, 1986.

Kirby, Diane. *Alice Henry—The Power of Pen and Voice: The Life of an Australian-American Labor Reformer.* New York: Cambridge University Press, 1991.

Lichtenstein, Nelson. *The Most Dangerous Man in Detroit: Walter Reuther and the Fate of American Labor.* New York: Basic Books, 1995.

Morgan, Kenneth O. *Labour People: Hardie to Kinnock.* 2nd ed. Oxford: Oxford University Press, 1992.

Mortimer, Jim W. *A Life on the Left.* Lewes, East Sussex, England: The Book Guild, 1998.

Norington, Brad. *Jennie George.* Sydney: Allen and Unwin, 1998. [Life of the first woman to become president of the Australian Council of Trade Unions.]

Phelan, Craig. *Divided Loyalties: The Public and Private Life of Labor Leader John Mitchell.* Albany: State University of New York Press, 1995.

————. *Grand Master Workman: Terence Powderly and the Knights of Labor.* Westport, Conn.: Greenwood Press, 2000.

Rickard, John. *H.B. Higgins: The Rebel as Judge.* Sydney: Allen & Unwin, 1985.

Robinson, Archie. *George Meany and His Times: A Biography.* New York: Simon & Schuster, 1981.

Salvatore, Nick. *Eugene V. Debs: Citizen and Socialist.* Urbana: University of Illinois Press, 1982.

Sloane, Arthur A. *Hoffa.* Cambridge, Mass.: MIT Press, 1991.

Tsuzuki, Chushichi. *Tom Mann, 1856-1941: The Challenge of Labour.* Oxford: Clarendon Press, 1991.

Ziegler, Robert H. *John L. Lewis, Labor Leader.* Boston: Twayne, 1988.

D.6 Women's Labor and Labor Unions

Blewett, Mary H. *Men, Women, and Work: Class, Gender and Protest in the New England Shoe Industry, 1780-1910.* Urbana: University of Illinois Press, 1988.

Briskin, Linda and Patricia McDermott (eds.). *Women Challenging Unions: Feminism, Democracy and Militancy.* Toronto: University of Toronto Press, 1994.

Chateauvert, Melinda. *Marching Together: Women of the Brotherhood of Sleeping Car Porters.* Champaign: University of Illinois Press, 1998.

Clark, Anna. *The Struggle for the Breeches: Gender and the Making of the British Working Class.* Berkeley: University of California Press, 1995.

Cobble, Dorothy S. (ed.). *Women and Unions: Forging a Partnership.* Ithaca, N.Y.: ILR Press, 1993.

Cook, Alice, et al. (eds.). *Women and Trade Unions in Eleven Industrialized Countries.* Philadelphia, Pa.: Temple University Press, 1984.

Cunnison, S., and J. Stageman. *Feminizing the Unions: Challenging the Culture of Masculinity.* Aldershot, England: Avebury, 1995.

D'Aprano, Zelda, and Kath Williams: *The Unions and the Fight for Equal Pay.* North Melbourne: Spinifex Press, 2001. [Account of the campaign for equal pay for women in Australia in the 1950s and 1960s.]

Downs, Laura L. *Manufacturing Inequality: Gender Division in the French and British Metalworking Industries, 1914-1939.* Ithaca, N.Y.: Cornell University Press, 1995.

Dye, Nancy S. *As Equals and as Sisters: Feminism, Unionism, and the Women's Trade Union League of New York.* Columbia: University of Missouri Press, 1980.

Foner, Philip S. *Women and the American Labor Movement.* 2 vols. New York: Free Press, 1979, 1980.

Franzway, Suzanne. *Sexual Politics and Greedy Institutions: Union Women, Commitments, and Conflicts in Public and Private.* Sydney: Pluto Press, 2001. [A contemporary Australian study.]

Gabin, Nancy F. *Feminism in the Labor Movement: Women and the United Auto Workers, 1935-1975.* Ithaca, N.Y.: Cornell University Press, 1990.

Gordon, Eleanor. *Women and the Labour Movement in Scotland, 1850-1914.* Oxford: Clarendon Press, 1991.

Gronman, Carol, and Mary B. Norton (eds.). *"To Toil the Livelong Day": America's Women at Work, 1780-1980.* Ithaca, N.Y.: Cornell University Press, 1987.

Groote, Gertjan de, and Marlon Schrover (eds.). *Women Workers and Technological Change in the Nineteenth and Twentieth Centuries.* London: Taylor and Francis, 1995.

Kessler-Harris, Alice. *Out to Work: A History of Wage-Earning Women in the United States.* New York: Oxford University Press, 1982.

Lawrence, Elizabeth. *Gender and Trade Unions.* Bristol, Pa.: Taylor and Francis, 1994.

Lindsey, Charles, and Lorna Duffin (eds.). *Women and Work in Pre-industrial England.* London: Croom Helm, 1985.

Nash, June, and Maria P. Fernández-Kelly (eds.). *Women, Men, and the International Division of Labor.* Albany: State University of New York Press, 1983.

Norwood, Stephen H. *Labor's Flaming Youth: Telephone Operators and Workers' Militancy, 1878-1923.* Urbana: University of Illinois Press, 1990.

Pocock, Barbara (ed.). *Strife: Sex and Politics in Labour Unions.* Sydney: Allen and Unwin, 1997. [The countries covered are Australia, Canada, United States, and United Kingdom.]

Roberts, Ron E. *Mother Jones and Her Sisters: A Century of Women Activitists in the American Coal Fields.* Dubuque, Iowa: Kendall/Hunt, 1998.

Riccucci, Norma M. *Women, Minorities, and Unions in the Public Sector.* Westport, Conn.: Greenwood Press, 1990.

Ruiz, Vicki L. *Cannery Women/Cannery Lives: Mexican Women, Unionization and the Californian Food Processing Industry, 1930-1950.* Albuquerque: University of New Mexico Press, 1987.

Soldon, Norbert C. (ed.). *The World of Women's Trade Unionism: Comparative Historical Essays.* Westport, Conn.: Greenwood Press, 1985.

Steedman, Mercedes. *Angels of the Workplace: Women and the Construction of Gender Relations in the Canadian Clothing Industry, 1890-1949.* Don Mills, Ontario: Oxford University Press, 1997.

Summerfield, Penny. *Women Workers in the Second World War: Production and Patriarchy in Conflict.* London: Croom Helm, 1984.

Ward, Kathryn (ed.). *Women Workers and Global Restructuring.* Ithaca, N.Y.: ILR Press, Cornell University, 1990.

D.7 Democracy in Labor Unions and Rank-and-File Studies

Blanpain, Roger (ed.). *Trade Union Democracy and Industrial Relations.* Special Issue, *Bulletin of Comparative Industrial Relations*, No. 17. Deventer, Netherlands: Kluwer Law and Taxation Publishers, 1988.

Botz, Dan la. *Rank and File Rebellion: Teamsters for a Democratic Union.* London: Verso, 1990.

Clark, Paul F. *The Miners' Fight for Democracy: Arnold Miller and the Reform of the United Mine Workers.* Ithaca: New York State School of Industrial and Labor Relations, Cornell University, 1981.

Clinton, Allen. *The Trade Union Rank and File: Trades Councils in Britain, 1900-1940.* Manchester: Manchester University Press, 1977.

Davis, Edward M. *Democracy in Australian Trade Unions: A Comparative Study of Six Unions.* Sydney: Allen & Unwin, 1987.

Dickenson, Mary. *Democracy in Trade Unions: Studies in Membership Participation and Control.* St. Lucia: University of Queensland Press, 1982.

Elias, Patrick, and Keith Wing. *Trade Union Democracy, Members' Rights and the Law.* London: Mansell, 1987.

Estreicher, Samuel, et al. (eds.). *The Internal Governance and Organizational Effectiveness of Labor Unions: Essays in Honor of George Brooks.* New York : Kluwer Law International, 2001.

Fosh, Patricia, and Edmund Heery. *Trade Unions and Their Members: Studies in Union Democracy and Organisation.* London: Macmillan, 1990.

Gould, William. *Black Workers in White Unions: Job Discrimination in the United States.* Ithaca, N.Y.: Cornell University Press, 1977. [An important study which deals with the period from 1964 to 1973.]

Green, Max. *Epitaph for American Labor: How Union Leaders Lost Touch with America.* Washington, D.C.: AEI Press, 1996.

Kelly, John. *Working for the Union: British Trade Union Officers.* Cambridge: Cambridge University Press, 1994.

Lynd, Staughton, and Alice Lynd (eds.). *The New Rank and File.* Ithaca, N.Y.: Cornell University Press, 2000.

Nyden, Philip W. *Steelworkers' Rank-and-File: The Political Economy of a Union Reform Movement.* New York: Praeger, 1984.

Sisya, Frank D. *The Political Life of a Public Employee Labor Union: Regional Union Democracy.* Lewiston, N.Y.: Edwin Mellen, 2000.
Undy, R., and R. Martin. *Ballots and Trade Union Democracy.* Oxford: Basil Blackwell, 1984.

D.8 Industrial Democracy

Dickman, Howard. *Industrial Democracy in America.* La Salle, Ill.: Open Court, 1987.
European Trade Union Institute. *Workers' Representation and Rights in the Workplace in Western Europe.* Brussels: European Trade Union Institute, 1990.
Industrial Democracy in Europe, International Research Group. *Industrial Democracy in Europe Revisited.* Oxford: Oxford University Press, 1993.
Knudsen, H. *Employee Participation in Europe.* London: Sage, 1995. [A study covering the 1950s to 1993.]
Lammers, Cornelius J., and Széll, György (eds.). *International Handbook of Participation in Organizations: Vol. I— Organizational Democracy: Taking Stock.* Oxford: Oxford University Press, 1988.
Lichtenstein, Nelson, and John H. Howell. (eds.). *Industrial Democracy in America: The Ambiguous Promise.* New York: Woodrow Wilson Center Press and Cambridge University Press, 1993.
Rogers, Joel, and Wolfgang Streeck (eds.). *Works Councils: Consultation, Representation and Cooperation in Industrial Relations.* Chicago: University of Chicago Press, 1995.
Russell, R., and V. Rus (eds.). *International Handbook of Participation in Organizations for the Study of Organizational Democracy, Co-operation and Self-Management: Vol. II— Ownership and Participation.* Oxford: Oxford University Press, 1991.

D.9 Interunion Relations

Chaison, G. N. *Union Mergers in Hard Times: The View from Five Countries.* Ithaca, N. Y.: ILR Press, 1996.
Elgar, J., and R. Simpson. *The TUC's Bridlington Principles and Inter-Union Competition.* London: London School of Economics,

Centre for Economic Performance, Discussion Paper No. 160, 1993.

Waddington, Jeremy. *The Politics of Bargaining: The Merger Process and British Trade Union Structural Development, 1892-1987.* London: Mansell, 1995.

D.10 Labor Disputes

Aris, Rosemary. *Trade Unions and the Management of Industrial Conflict.* Basingstoke, England: Macmillan, 1998.

Brecher, Jeremy. *Strike.* rev. ed. Boston: South End Press, 1997. [A U.S. rank-and-file study.]

Charlesworth, Andrew, et al. *An Atlas of Industrial Protest in Britain, 1750-1990.* Basingstoke, England: Macmillan, 1996.

Cohn, Samuel. *When Strikes Make Sense—and Why: Lessons from the Third Republic of French Coal Miners.* New York: Plenum Books, 1993.

Connor, Walter D. *Tattered Banners: Labor, Conflict, and Corporatism in Postcommunist Russia.* Boulder, Colo.: Westview Press, 1996.

Dobson, C. R. *Masters and Journeymen: A Prehistory of Industrial Relations, 1717-1800.* London: Croom Helm, 1980. [Much of this work deals with labor disputes.]

Dubrovskii, Oleg. *Fighting Back in Ukraine: A Worker Who Took on the Bureaucrats and Bosses.* London: Index Books, 1997.

Edwards, P. K. *Strikes in the United States, 1881-1974.* Oxford: Basil Blackwell, 1981.

Filippelli, Ronald L. (ed.). *Labor Conflict in the United States: An Encyclopedia.* New York : Garland, 1990.

Franzosi, Roberto. *The Puzzle of Strikes: Class and State Strategies in Postwar Italy.* Cambridge: Cambridge University Press, 1995.

Haimson, L. H., and C. Tilley (eds.). *Strikes, Wars, and Revolutions in an International Perspective.* Cambridge: Cambridge University Press, 1989.

Hanami, Tadashi, and Roger Blanpain (eds.). *Industrial Conflict Resolution in Market Economies: A Study of Australia, the Federal Republic of Germany, Italy, Japan and the USA.* Deventer, Netherlands: Kluwer Law and Taxation Publishers, 1984.

Hyman, Richard. *Strikes.* 3rd ed. Aylesbury: Fontana, 1984.

Jackson, Michael P. *Strikes.* New York: St. Martin's Press, 1987. [An excellent study of strike trends in Britain, United States, and Australia.]

Jennings, Kenneth M. *Labor Relations at the New York Daily News: Peripheral Bargaining and the 1990 Strike.* Westport, Conn.: Praeger, 1993.

Juravich, Tom, and Kate Bronfenbrener. *Ravenswood: The Steelworkers' Victory and the Revival of American Labor.* Ithaca, N.Y.: Cornell University Press, 1999. [Case study of a 20-month labor dispute in the early 1990s.]

Kapsa, Michael. *Labor Strife and the Economy in the 1970s: A Decade of Discord.* New York: Garland, 1998.

Kawanishi, Hirosuke (ed.). *The Human Face of Industrial Conflict in Post-War Japan.* London: Kegan Paul International, 1999.

Loewenberg, J. J., et al. *Compulsory Arbitration: An International Comparison.* Lexington, Mass.: D. C. Heath, 1976.

Metcalf, David, and Simon Milner (eds.). *New Perspectives on Industrial Disputes.* London: LSE/Routledge, 1993.

Morris, Margaret. *The General Strike.* Harmondsworth, England: Penguin, 1976. [Deals with the British General Strike in 1926.]

Ness, Immanuel. *Trade Unions and the Betrayal of the Unemployed: Labor Conflicts during the 1990s.* New York: Garland Press, 1998.

Nordlund, Willis J. *Silent Skies: The Air Traffic Controllers' Strike.* Westport, Conn.: Praeger, 1998.

Rachleff, Peter. *Hard-Pressed in the Heartland: The Hormel Strike and the Future of the American Labor Movement.* Boston: South End Press, 1993.

Reddy, Y. R. K. *Trends, Patterns and Impact of Strikes: The Indian Case.* New Delhi, India: Society for Policy Analysis and Development, 1990.

Svensen, Stuart. *The Sinews of War: Hard Cash and the 1890 Maritime Strike.* Sydney: University of New South Wales Press, 1995.

Walsh, Kenneth. *Strikes in Europe and the United States: Management and Incidence.* London: Frances Pinter, 1983.

Waters, Malcolm. *Strikes in Australia: A Sociological Analysis of Industrial Conflict.* Sydney: George Allen & Unwin, 1982.

Winterton, Jonathan, and R. Winterton. *Coal, Crisis and Conflict: The 1984-5 Miners' Strike in Yorkshire.* Manchester: Manchester University Press, 1989.

Zetka, James R., Jr. *Militancy, Market Dynamics and Workplace Authority: The Struggle over Labor Process Outcomes in the U.S. Automobile Industry, 1946 to 1973.* Albany: State University of New York Press, 1995.

E. LABOR AND SOCIETY

E.1 The Experience and Study of Work

Applebaum. Herbert A. *The American Work Ethic and the Changing Work Force: An Historical Perspective.* Westport, Conn.: Greenwood Press, 1998.

Bermeo, Nancy (ed.). *Unemployment in the New Europe.* Cambridge: Cambridge University Press, 2001.

Biernacki, Richard. *The Fabrication of Labor: Germany and England, 1640-1914.* Berkeley: University of California Press, 1995.

Bina, Cyrus, Laurie Clements, and Chuck Davis (eds.). *Beyond Survival: Wage Labor in the Late Twentieth Century.* Armonk, N.Y.: M. E. Sharpe, 1996.

Blackwell, Trevor, and Jeremy Seabrook (eds.). *Talking Work: An Oral History.* London: Faber and Faber, 1996.

Blau, Joel. *Illusions of Prosperity: America's Working Families in an Age of Economic Insecurity.* New York: Oxford University Press, 1999.

Boris, Eileen. *Home to Work: Motherhood and the Politics of Industrial Housework in the United States.* New York: Cambridge University Press, 1994.

Brody, David. *In Labor's Cause: Main Themes on the History of the American Worker.* New York: Oxford University Press, 1993.

Burnett, John (ed.). *Useful Toil: Autobiographies of Working People from the 1820s to the 1920s.* London: Allen Lane, 1974. [A collection of documents.]

Chinoy, E. *Automobile Workers and the American Dream.* 2nd ed. Urbana: University of Illinois Press, 1992.

Cross, Gary. *A Quest for Time: The Reduction of Work in Britain and France, 1840-1940.* Berkeley: University of California Press, 1989.

Derickson, Alan. *Workers' Health, Workers' Democracy: The Western Miners' Struggle, 1891-1925.* Ithaca, N.Y.: Cornell University Press, 1989.

Dinerstein, Ana C., and Mike Neary. *The Labour Debate: An Investigation into the Theory and Reality of Capitalist Work.* Aldershot, England: Ashgate, 2002.

Edwards, R. *Contested Terrain: The Transformation of the Workplace in the Twentieth Century.* London: Heinemann, 1979.

Fraser, Ronald (ed.). *Work: Twenty Personal Accounts.* 2 vols. Harmondsworth: Penguin, 1968, 1969.

Gordon, D. M., R. Edwards, and M. Reich. *Segmented Work, Divided Workers: The Historical Transformation of Labor in the United States.* Cambridge: Cambridge University Press, 1982.

Gorz, André. *Reclaiming Work: Beyond the Wage-Based Society.* Cambridge: Polity Press, 1999.

Grint, Keith. *The Sociology of Work: An Introduction.* Oxford and Cambridge: Basil Blackwell and Polity Press, 1991.

Harrison, Royden, and Jonathan Zeitlin (eds.). *Divisions of Labour: Skilled Workers and Technological Change in 19th Century Britain.* Urbana: University of Illinois Press, 1985.

Hindman, Hugh D. *Child Labor: An American History.* Armonk, N.Y.: M. E. Sharpe, 2002.

Howard, Ann (ed.). *The Changing Nature of Work.* San Francisco, Calif.: Jossey-Bass, 1995.

Jacoby, Daniel. *Laboring for Freedom: A New Look at the History of Labor in America.* Armonk, N.Y.: M. E. Sharpe, 1998.

Jacoby, S. M. *Employing Bureaucracy: Managers, Unions and the Transformation of Work in American Industry, 1900-1945.* New York: Columbia University Press, 1985.

Jaffe, James A. *Striking a Bargain: Work and Industrial Relations in England, 1815-1865.* Manchester: Manchester University Press, 2000.

Jones, Jacqueline. *American Work Four Centuries of Black and White Labour.* New York: W. W. Norton, 1998.

Joyce, Patrick (ed.). *The Historical Meanings of Work.* Cambridge: Cambridge University Press, 1987.

Kamata, Satoshi. *Japan in the Passing Lane: An Insider's Account of Life in a Japanese Auto Factory.* New York: Pantheon, 1982.

Kent, George. *Children in the International Political Economy.* Basingstoke, England: Macmillan, 1995.

Lane, Joan. *Apprenticeship in England, 1600-1914.* London: UCL Press, 1996.

Lavalette, Michael (ed.). *A Thing of the Past? Child Labour in Britain, 1800 to the Present.* Liverpool: Liverpool University Press, 1999.

Lincoln, J. R., and A. L. Kalleberg. *Culture, Control and Commitment: A Study of Work Organization and Work Attitudes in the United States and Japan.* Cambridge: Cambridge University Press, 1990.

Lowenstein, Wendy. *Weevils at Work: What's Happening to Work in Australia—An Oral Record.* Sydney: Catalyst Press, 1997.

McCreery, David. *The Sweat of Their Brow: A History of Work in Latin America.* Armonk, N.Y.: M. E. Sharp, 2000.

McIntosh, Robert. *Boys in the Pits: Child Labor in Coal Mines.* Montreal, Quebec: McGill-Queen's University Press, 2000.

McIvor, Arthur. *A History of Work in Britain, 1880-1950.* Basingstoke, UK: Palgave, 2001.

Meldrum, Timothy. *Domestic Service and Gender, 1660-1750.* New York: Pearson Education, 2000.

Nobel, A. *Forces of Production: A Social History of Industrial Automation.* New York: Alfred A. Knopf, 1984.

Pahl, R. E. (ed.). *On Work: Historical, Comparative and Theoretical Perspectives.* Oxford: Basil Blackwell, 1988.

Pollert, Anna. *Transformation of Work in the New Market Economies of Central Eastern Europe.* London: Sage, 1999.

Ransome, Paul. *The Work Paradigm: A Theoretical Investigation of Concepts of Work.* Aldershot, England: Avebury, 1996.

Roediger, David R., and Philip S. Foner. *Our Own Time: A History of American Labor and the Working Day.* New York: Verso Paper, 1989.

Rule, J. *The Experience of Labour in Eighteenth Century England.* London: Croom Helm, 1981.

Shaiken, Harley. *Work Transformed.* New York: Holt, Rinehart and Winston, 1984.

Shields, John (ed.). *All Our Labours: Oral Histories of Working Life in Twentieth Century Sydney.* Sydney: University of New South Wales, 1992.

Silverman, Dan P. *Hitler's Economy: Nazi Work Creation Programs, 1933-1936.* Cambridge, Mass.: Harvard University Press, 1998.

Strom, Sharon H. *Beyond the Typewriter: Gender, Class and the Origins of Modern American Office Work, 1900-1930.* Urbana: University of Illinois Press, 1992.

Terkel, Studs. *Working.* New York: Pantheon Books, 1972. [Also available in paperback by Avon.] [A sourcebook of interviews.]

Tilly, Chris, and Charles Tilly. *Work under Capitalism.* Boulder, Colo.: Westview Press, 1998.

Thomas, Keith (ed.). *The Oxford Book of Work.* Oxford: Oxford University Press, 1999.

Whipp, Richard. *Patterns of Labour: Work and Social Change in the Pottery Industry.* London: Routledge, Chapman and Hall, 1990.

E.2 Forced or Involuntary Labor

Brass, Tom, and Marcel van der Linden (eds.). *Free and Unfree Labour: The Debate Continues.* Bern: Peter Lang, 1997.

Gillespie, Michele. *Free Labor in an Unfree World: White Artisans in Slaveholding Georgia, 1789-1860.* Athens: University of Georgia Press, 2000.

Lichtenstein, Alex. *Twice the Work of Free Labor: The Political Economy of Convict Labor in the New South.* London: Verso, 1996.

Nicholas, Stephen (ed.). *Convict Workers: Interpreting Australia's Past.* Sydney: Cambridge University Press, 1988.

Rodriguez, Junius P. (ed.). *The Historical Encyclopedia of Slavery.* 2 vols. Santa Barbara, Calif.: ABC-CLIO, 1997.

Shapiro, Karin. A. *A New South Rebellion: The Battle against Convict Labor in the Tennessee Coalfields, 1871–1896.* Chapel Hill: University of North Carolina Press, 1998.

E.3 Occupational Health and Safety

Aldrich, Mark. *Safety First: Technology, Labour, and Business in the Building of American Work Safety, 1870-1939.* Baltimore, Md.: Johns Hopkins University Press, 1997.

Bohle, Phil, and Michael Quinlan. *Managing Occupational Health and Safety: A Multidisciplinary Approach.* 2nd ed. Melbourne: Macmillan Education Australia, 2000.

Derickson, Alan. *Workers' Health, Workers' Democracy: The Western Miners' Struggle, 1891-1925.* Ithaca, N.Y.: Cornell University Press, 1988.

International Labour Office. *Encyclopaedia of Occupational Health and Safety.* 3rd ed. Geneva: International Labour Office, 1983. [First published in 1930.]

E.4 Industrial Archaeology and Iconography

Fogg, Charles. *Chains and Chainmaking.* Aylesbury, Buckinghamshire: Shire, 1981.

Gale, W. K. V. *Ironworking.* Aylesbury, Buckinghamshire: Shire, 1981.

Gorman, John. *Banner Bright: An Illustrated History of the British Trade Union Movement.* London: Allen Lane, 1974.

Gorman, John. *Images of Labour: Selected Memorabilia from the National Museum of Labour History.* London: Scorpion, 1985.

Griffin, A. R. *The Collier.* Aylesbury, Buckinghamshire: Shire, 1982.

Martin, Paul. *The Trade Union Badge: Material Culture in Action.* Aldershot, England: Ashgate, 2002.

Trinder, Barrie (ed.). *The Blackwell Encyclopedia of Industrial Archaeology.* Oxford: Basil Blackwell, 1992.

E.5 Unions and Politics (*see also* D.4)

Arnesen, Eric et al. *Labor Histories: Class, Politics, and the Working Class Experience.* Urbana: University of Illinois Press, 1998.

Asher, H., E. Ripley, and R. B. Snyde. *American Labor Unions in the Electoral Arena: People, Passions, and Power.* Lanham, Md.: Rowman & Littlefield, 2000.

Brennan, James P. *The Labor Wars in Córdoba, 1955-1976: Ideology, Work, and Labor Politics in an Argentine Industrial City.* Cambridge, Mass.: Harvard University Press, 1994.

Burwood, Stephen. *American Labor, France, and the Politics of Intervention, 1945-1952: Workers and the Cold War.* Lewiston, N.Y.: Mellen Press, 1998.

Campbell, Alan, et al. *British Trade Unions and Industrial Politics: The Post-War Compromise, 1945-64.* Aldershot, England: Ashgate, 1999.

Carsten, F. L. *The German Workers and the Nazis*. Aldershot, England: Scolar Press, 1995.

Chatterji, Rakhahari. *Unions, Politics and the State: A Study of Indian Labour Politics*. New Delhi: South Asian Publishers, 1980.

Conner, Valerie J. *The National War Labor Board: Stability, Social Justice and the Voluntary State in World War I*. Chapel Hill: University of North Carolina Press, 1983.

Dark, Taylor E. *The Unions and the Democrats: An Enduring Alliance*. Ithaca, N.Y.: ILR Press, 1999.

Davidson, Roger. *Whitehall and the Labour Problem in Late-Victorian and Edwardian Britain*. London: Croom Helm, 1985.

Davis, Mike. *Prisoners of the American Dream: Politics and Economy in the History of the U.S. Working Class*. London: Verso, 1986.

Dorey, Peter. *The Conservative Party and the Trade Unions*. London: Routledge, 1995.

Draper, Alan. *A Rope of Sand: The AFL-CIO Committee on Political Education, 1955-1967*. New York: Praeger, 1989.

Filippelli, Ronald L. *American Labor and Postwar Italy, 1943-1953: A Study of Cold War Politics*. Stanford, Calif.: Stanford University Press, 1989.

Fink, Leon. *Workingmen's Democracy: The Knights of Labor and American Politics*. Urbana: University of Illinois Press, 1983.

Form, William. *Segmented Labor, Fractured Politics: Labor Politics in American Life*. New York : Plenum Press, 1995.

Friedman, Gerald. *State Making and Labor Movements: France and the United States, 1876-1914*. Ithaca, N.Y.: Cornell University Press, 1998.

Fulcher, James. *Labour Movements, Employers and the State: Conflict and Co-operation in Britain and Sweden*. Oxford: Clarendon Press, 1991.

Gall, Gilbert. *The Politics of Right to Work: The Labor Federations as Special Interests, 1943-1979*. Westport, Conn.: Greenwood Press, 1988.

Gordon, Colin. *New Deals: Business, Labor, and Politics in America, 1920-1935*. New York: Cambridge University Press, 1994.

Greene, Julie. *Pure and Simple Politics: The American Federation of Labor and Political Activism, 1881-1917*. Cambridge: Cambridge University Press, 1998.

Gupta, Partha S. *Imperialism and the British Labour Movement, 1914-1964*. London: Macmillan, 1975.

Haydu, Jeffrey. *Between Craft and Class: Skilled Workers and Factory Politics in the US and Britain, 1890-1922.* Berkeley: University of California Press, 1988.

Katzenstein, Peter J. *Corporatist and Change: Austria, Switzerland and the Politics of Industry.* Ithaca, N.Y.: Cornell University Press, 1984.

Korpi, Walter. *The Democratic Class Struggle.* London: Routledge and Kegan Paul, 1983.

Kosciel, Frank. Divided *Loyalties: American Unions and the Vietnam War.* New York: Garland, 1999.

Kume, Ikuo. *Disparaged Success: Labor Politics in Postwar Japan.* Ithaca, N.Y.: Cornell University Press, 1998.

Large, Stephen S. *Organized Workers and Socialist Politics in Interwar Japan.* New York: Cambridge University Press, 1981.

Marks, Gary. *Unions in Politics: Britain, Germany, and the United States in the Nineteenth and Early Twentieth Centuries.* Princeton, N.J.: Princeton University Press, 1989.

McMullin, Ross. *The Light on the Hill: The Australian Labor Party, 1891-1991.* Melbourne: Oxford University Press, 1991.

Mink, Gwendolyn. *Old Labor and New Labor in American Political Development: Union, Party and State, 1875-1920.* Ithaca, N.Y.: Cornell University Press, 1986.

Minkun, Lewis. *The Contentious Alliance: Trade Unions and the Labour Party.* New York: Columbia University Press, 1993. [A study of the British Labour Party and organized labor.]

Montgomery, David. *The Fall of the House of Labor: The Workplace, the State, and American Radicalism, 1865-1925.* New York: Cambridge University Press, 1987.

Perusek, Glenn, and Kent Worcester (eds.). *Trade Union Politics: American Unions and Economic Change, 1960s–1990s.* Atlantic Highlands, N.J.: Humanities Press, 1995.

Pimlott, Ben, and Chris Cook (eds.). *Trade Unions in British Politics: The First 250 Years.* 2nd ed. New York: Longman, 1991.

Robertson, David B. *Capital, Labor, and State: The Battle for American Labor Markets from the Civil War to the New Deal.* Lanham, Md.: Rowman & Littlefield, 2000.

Roxborough, Ian. *Unions and Politics in Mexico: The Case of the Automobile Industry.* Cambridge: Cambridge University Press, 1984.

Singleton, Gwynnoth. *The Accord and the Australian Labour Movement.* Melbourne: Melbourne University Press, 1990.

Taylor, R. *The Trade Union Question in British Politics: Government and Unions since 1945.* Oxford: Blackwell, 1994.

Tolliday, S., and J. Zeitlin (eds.). *Shopfloor Bargaining and the State.* Cambridge: Cambridge University Press, 1985.

Turner, Lowell. *Fighting for Partnership: Labor and Politics in Unified Germany.* Ithaca, N.Y.: Cornell University Press, 1998.

Wilentz, Sean. *Chants Democratic: New York City and the Rise of the Working Class, 1788-1850.* New York: Oxford University Press, 1984.

E.6 Employers

Amerasinghe, E. F. G. *Employers' Federation of Ceylon, 1929-1994.* Colombo: Employers' Federation of Ceylon, 1994.

Chubb, B. *FIE: Federation of Irish Employers, 1942-1992.* Dublin: Gill and Macmillan, 1992.

Cohen, Isaac. *American Management and British Labor: A Comparative Study of the Cotton Spinning Industry.* Westport, Conn.: Greenwood Press, 1990.

Gillespie, Richard. *Manufacturing Knowledge: A History of the Hawthorne Experiments.* New York: Cambridge University Press, 1991.

Gospel, H. F., and C. R. Littler (eds.). *Managerial Strategies and Industrial Relations.* London: Heinemann, 1983.

Harris, Howell J. *The Right to Manage: Industrial Relations Politics of American Business in the 1940s.* Madison: University of Wisconsin Press, 1982.

Hattam, Victoria C. *Labor Visions and State Power: The Origins of Business Unionism in the United States.* Princeton, N.J.: Princeton University Press, 1993.

Jacoby, S. (ed.). *Masters to Managers: Historical and Comparative Perspectives on American Employers.* New York: Columbia University Press, 1991.

Jacques, Roy. *Manufacturing the Employee: Management Knowledge from the Nineteenth to Twenty–First Centuries.* London: Sage, 1996.

Jowitt, J. A., and A. J. McIvor (eds.). *Employers and Labour in the English Textile Industries, 1850-1939.* London: Routledge, Chapman & Hall, 1988.

McIvor, Arthur J. *Organised Capital: Employers' Associations and Industrial Relations in Northern England, 1880-1939.* Cambridge: Cambridge University Press, 1996.

Myer, Stephen. *The Five Dollar Day: Labor Management and Social Control in the Ford Motor Company, 1908-1921.* Albany: State University of New York Press, 1981.

Tolliday, S., and J. Zeitlin (eds.). *The Power to Manage? Employers and Industrial Relations in Comparative-Historical Perspective.* London: Routledge, 1991.

Windmuller, J. P., and A. Gladstone (eds.). *Employer Associations and Industrial Relations: A Comparative Study.* New York: Oxford University Press, 1984.

Wright, Christopher. *The Management of Labour: A History of Australian Employers.* Melbourne: Oxford University Press, 1995.

E.7 Social Histories and Immigration

Atkinson, Frank. *North-East England: People at Work, 1860-1960.* Ashbourne, Derbyshire, England: Moorland, 1980. [Contains a comprehensive collection of photographs.]

Babson, Steve. *Building the Union: Skilled Workers and Anglo-Gaelic Immigrants in the Rise of the UAW.* New Brunswick, N.J.: Rutgers University, 1991.

———. *Working Detroit: The Making of a Union Town.* Detroit, Mich.: Wayne State University Press, 1984.

Bahl, Vinay. *The Making of the Indian Working Class.* New Delhi: Sage, 1995.

Berlanstein, Lenard R. *Rethinking Labor History: Essays on Discourse and Class Analysis.* Champaign: University of Illinois Press, 1993.

Bodnar, John. *Workers' World: Kinship, Community, and Protest in an Industrial Society, 1900-1940.* Baltimore, Md.: Johns Hopkins University Press, 1982.

Briggs, Vernon M. *Immigration and American Unionism.* Ithaca, N.Y.: Cornell University Press, 2001.

Brody, David. *Workers in Industrial America: Essays on the Twentieth Century Struggle.* New York: Oxford University Press, 1980.

Cantor, Milton (ed.). *American Working-Class Culture: Explorations in American Labor and Social History.* Westport, Conn.: Greenwood Press, 1979.

Cherwinski, W., and G. Kealey (eds.). *Lectures in Canadian Labour and Working-Class History.* St. Johns, Newfoundland: Committee on Canadian Labour History, St. Johns, 1985.

Cornford, Daniel (ed.). *Working People of California.* Berkeley: University of California Press, 1995.

Crew, David. *Town in the Ruhr: A Social History of Bochum, 1860-1914.* New York: Columbia University Press, 1979.

Docherty, James C. *Newcastle: The Making of an Australian City.* Sydney: Hale & Iremonger, 1983.

Drummond, Diane K. *Crewe: Railway Town, Company and People, 1840-1914.* Aldershot, England: Scolar Press, 1995.

Dublin, Thomas. *Women at Work: The Transformation of Work and Community in Lowell, Mass., 1826-1860.* New York: Columbia University Press, 1979.

Ellis, P. Berresford. *A History of the Irish Working Class.* rev. ed. London: Pluto Press, 1996.

Emberson-Bain, 'Atu. *Labour and Gold in Fiji.* Melbourne: Cambridge University Press, 1994.

Fagge, Roger. *Power, Culture, and Conflict in the Coalfields: West Virginia and South Wales, 1900-1922.* Manchester: Manchester University Press, 1996.

Faue, Elizabeth. *Community of Suffering & Struggle: Women, Men and the Labor Movement in Minneapolis, 1915-1945.* Chapel Hill: University of North Carolina Press, 1991.

Frisch, Michael, and Daniel J. Walkowitz (eds.). *Working-Class America: Essays on Labor, Community and American Society.* Urbana: University of Illinois Press, 1983.

Fry, Eric (ed.). *Common Cause: Essays in Australian and New Zealand Labour History.* Wellington and Sydney: Allen & Unwin/Port Nicholson Press, 1986.

Gardner, James B., and George R. Adams (eds.). *Ordinary People and Everyday Life: Perspectives on the New Social History.* Nashville, Tenn.: American Association for State and Local History, 1983.

Gerstle, Gary. *Working-Class Americanism: The Politics of Labor in a Textile City, 1914-60.* New York: Cambridge University Press, 1989.

Guerin-Gonzales, Camile, and Carl Strikwerda (eds.). *The Politics of Immigrant Workers: Labor Activism and Migration in the World Economy since 1830.* New York : Holmes and Meier, 1993.

Hoerder, Dirk (ed.). *"Struggle a Hard Battle": Essays on Working-Class Immigrants.* De Kalb: North Illinois University Press, 1986.

Isaacman, Allen and Richart Roberts (ed.). *Cotton, Colonialism, and Social History in Sub-Saharan Africa.* Portsmouth, N.H.: Reed Elsevier, 1995.

Kealey, G., and G. Patmore. (eds.). *Canadian and Australian Labour History: Towards a Comparative Perspective.* Brisbane: Australian Society for the Study of Labour History, 1990.

Kleinberg, S. J. *The Shadow of the Mills: Working-Class Families in Pittsburgh, 1870-1907.* Pittsburgh: University of Pittsburgh Press, 1989.

Kornblum, William. *Blue-Collar Community.* Chicago: University of Chicago Press, 1974. [Deals with U.S steelworkers.]

Krause, Paul. *The Battle for Homestead, 1880-1892: Politics, Culture, and Steel.* Pittsburgh: Pittsburgh University Press, 1992.

Laslett, John H. M. *Nature's Noblemen: The Fortunes of the Independent Collier in Scotland and the American Midwest, 1855-1889.* Los Angeles: UCLA Institute of Industrial Relations Monograph and Research Series No. 34, 1983.

Lever-Tracy, Constance. *A Divided Working Class: Ethnic Segregation and Industrial Conflict in Australia.* London: Routledge & Kegan Paul, 1988.

Lichtenstein, Nelson, and Stephen Myer (eds.). *On the Line: Essays in the History of Auto Work.* Champaign: University of Illinois Press, 1989.

Littlefield, Alice, and Martha C. Knack (eds.). *Native Americans and Wage Labor: Ethnohistorical Perspectives.* Norman: University of Oklahoma Press, 1996.

Look Lai, Walton. *Indentured Labor, Caribbean Sugar: Chinese and Indian Migrants to the British West Indies, 1838-1918.* Baltimore, Md.: Johns Hopkins University Press, 1993.

Lummis, Trevor. *The Labour Aristocracy, 1850-1914.* Aldershot, England: Scolar Press, 1994.

Lynch, John. *A Tale of Three Cities: Comparative Studies in Working*

Class Life. Basingstoke, England: Macmillan, 1998.

MacRaild, Donald M. *Labour in British Society, 1830-1914*. New York: St. Martin's Press, 2000.

Mohl, Raymond A. and Neil Betten. *Steel City: Urban and Ethnic Patterns in Gary, Indiana, 1906-1950*. New York: Holmes and Meier, 1986.

Moody, J. Carroll, and Alice Kessler-Harris (eds.). *Perspectives on American Labor History: The Problems of Synthesis*. De Kalb: Northern Illinois University Press, 1989.

Norris, P., A. R. Townsend, and J. C. Dewdney. *Demographic and Social Change in the Durham Coalfield*. Working Papers 23, 24, 25. Durham: University of Durham, Department of Geography, Census Research Unit, 1983 and 1984. [An impressive study of 65,000 records of individuals from the population censuses of 1851, 1861, 1871, and 1881 covering occupational change, birthplace, and migration.]

O'Donnell, L. A. *Irish Voice and Organized Labor in America: A Biographical Study*. Westport, Conn.: Greenwood Press, 1997.

Oestreicher, Robert L. *Solidarity and Fragmentation: Working People and Class Consciousness in Detroit, 1875-1900*. Urbana: University of Illinois Press, 1986.

Penninx, Rinus, and Judith Roosblad (eds). *Trade Unions, Immigration, and Immigrants in Europe, 1960-1993*. New York: Berghahn Book, 2000.

Prude, Jonathan. *The Coming of Industrial Order: Town and Factory Life in Rural Massachusetts, 1800-1860*. New York: Cambridge University Press, 1983.

Rorabaugh, W. J. *The Craft Apprentice: From Franklin to the Machine Age in America*. New York: Oxford University Press, 1986.

Saunders, Kay (ed.). *Indentured Labour in the British Empire, 1834-1920*. London: Croom Helm, 1984.

Schultz, Ronald. *The Republic of Labor: Philadelphia Artisans and the Politics of Class, 1720-1830*. New York: Oxford University Press, 1993.

Shergold, Peter R. *Working-Class Life: The "American Standard" in Comparative Perspective, 1899-1913*. Pittsburgh: Pittsburgh University Press, 1982. [An important, and all too rare, comparative study of working-class living standards in Pittsburgh, Pennsylvania, and Birmingham, England.]

Zippay, Allison. *From Middle Income to Poor: Downward Mobility among Displaced Steelworkers.* New York: Praeger, 1991.

E.8 Labor and Race

Alexander, Peter. *Workers, War and the Origins of Apartheid: Labour and Politics in South Africa, 1939-48.* Oxford: James Currey, 2000.

Brown, Cliff. *Racial Conflict and Violence in the Labor Market: Roots in the 1919 Steel Strike.* New York: Garland Press, 1998.

Draper, Alan. *Conflict of Interests: Organized Labor and the Civil Rights Movement in the South, 1954-1968.* Ithaca, N.Y.: ILR Press, 1994.

Harris, William H. *The Harder We Run: Black Workers since the Civil War.* New York: Oxford University Press, 1982.

Honey, Michael K. *Southern Labor and Black Civil Rights: Organizing Memphis Workers.* Urbana: University of Illinois Press, 1993.

Iton, Richard. *Solidarity Blues: Race, Culture, and the American Left.* Chapel Hill: University of North Carolina Press, 2000.

Kent, Ronald C., et al. (eds.). *Culture, Gender, Race, and U.S. Labor Relations.* Westport, Conn. : Greenwood Press, 1993.

Letwin, Daniel. *The Challenge of Interracial Unionism: Alabama Coal Miners, 1878-1921.* Chapel Hill: University of North Carolina Press, 1998.

Minchin, Timothy J. *Hiring the Black Worker: The Racial Integration of the Southern Textile Industry, 1960-1980.* Chapel Hill: University of North Carolina Press, 1999.

Nelson, Bruce. *Divided We Stand: American Workers and the Struggle for Black Equality.* Princeton, N.J.: Princeton University Press, 2001.

Rachleff, Peter S. *Black Labor in the South: Richmond, Virginia, 1865-1890.* Philadelphia, Pa.: Temple University Press, 1984.

Ramdin, Ron. *The Making of the Black Working Class in Britain.* Aldershot, England: Gower, 1987.

Roediger, David R. *The Wages of Whiteness: Race and the Making of the American Working Class.* London: Verso, 1991.

E.9 Labor Sociology

Bruno, Robert. *Steelworker Alley: How Class Works in Youngstown.* Ithaca, N.Y.: Cornell University Press, 1999.

Due, Jesper, et al. *The Survival of the Danish Model: A Historical Sociological Analysis of the Danish System of Collective Bargaining.* Copenhagen: DJØF, 1994.

Halle, David. *America's Working Man: Work, Home, and Politics among Blue-Collar Property Owners.* Chicago: University of Chicago Press, 1984.

Kim, Hyunhee. *Working Class Stratification and the Demand for Unions in the United States.* New York: Garland, 1997.

Marwick, Arthur. *Class: Image and Reality in Britain, France and the USA since 1930.* Glasgow: Fontana/Collins, 1980.

Poole, Michael. *Theories of Trade Unionism.* rev. ed. London: Routledge & Kegan Paul, 1984. [A sociological approach to labor unions.]

Robertson, James E. *Japanese Working Lives.* London: Routledge, 1998.

E.10 Labor and the Law

Atleson, J. *Values and Assumptions in American Labor Law.* Amherst: University of Massachusetts Press, 1983.

Bennett, Laura. *Making Labour Law in Australia: Industrial Relations, Politics and Law.* Sydney: Law Book, 1994.

Betten, Lammy. *International Labor Law: Selected Issues.* Deventer, Netherlands and Boston: Kluwer, 1993.

Blanpain, Roger, and C. Engels (eds.). *Comparative Labour Law and Industrial Relations in Industrialized Market Economies.* 5th ed. Deventer, Netherlands: Kluwer Law and Taxation Publishers, 1993.

Blanpain, Roger. *Labour Law and Industrial Relations of the European Union: Maastricht and Beyond, from a Community to a Union.* Deventer, Netherlands: Kluwer Law and Taxation, 1992.

CCH Canada. *Canadian Master Labour Guide: A Guide to Canadian Labour Law.* 8th ed., Don Mills, Ontario: CCH Canada, 1993.

Creighton, Breen, and Andrew Stewart. *Labour Law: An Introduction.* 2nd ed. Sydney: Federation Press, 1994. [An introduction to Australian labor law.]

Deery, Stephen J., and J. Mitchell (eds.). *Labour Law and Industrial Relations in Asia: Eight Country Studies.* Melbourne: Longman Cheshire, 1993. [The countries covered are Hong Kong, Malaysia, Singapore, South Korea, Japan, Philippines, Thailand, and Taiwan.]

England, J., and J. Rear. *Industrial Relations and Law in Hong Kong.* Hong Kong: Oxford University Press, 1981.

Ewing, K. D. *Trade Unions, the Labour Party and the Law: A Study of the Trade Union Act, 1913.* Edinburgh: Edinburgh University Press, 1982.

Forbath, W. E. *Law and the Shaping of the American Labor Movement.* Cambridge, Mass.: Harvard University Press, 1991.

Hanson, Charles. *The Closed Shop: A Comparative Study of Public Policy and Trade Union Security in Britain, the USA and West Germany.* London: Gower, 1982.

Hepple, Bob (ed.). *The Making of Labour Law in Europe: A Comparative Study of Nine Countries up to 1945.* London: Mansell, 1986.

International Labour Office. *Freedom of Association: Digest of Decisions and Principles of the Freedom of Association Committee of the Governing Body of the ILO.* 3rd ed. Geneva: International Labour Office, 1985.

International Labour Office. *Freedom of Association and Collective Bargaining.* Geneva: International Labour Office, 1994.

Kahn-Freund, Otto, et al. *Labour Law and Politics in the Weimar Republic.* Oxford: Basil Blackwell, 1981.

Koniaris, T. B. *Labour Law and Industrial Relations in Greece.* Deventer, Netherlands: Kluwer and Taxation Publishers, 1990.

Linnick, Stuart et al. *The Developing Labor Law.* 2nd ed., 3rd supplement. Washington, D.C.: Bureau of National Affairs, 1988.

Prondzynski, Ferdinand von. *Freedom of Association and Industrial Relations.* London: Mansell, 1987.

Schmitt, M. N., et al. *Turkish Labor Law.* Irvington-on-Hudson, N.Y.: Transaction Publishers, 1996.

Sugeno, Kazuo. *Japanese Labor Law.* Seattle: University of Washington Press, 1992.

Tomlins, Christopher L. *Law, Labor and Ideology in the Early American Republic.* New York: Cambridge University Press, 1993. [Covers the period from 1790 to 1850.]

———. *The State and the Unions: Labor Relations, Law, and the Organized Labor Movement in America, 1880-1960.* New York: Cambridge University Press, 1985.

Undy, R., P. Fosh, H. Morris, and P. Smith. *Managing the Unions: The Impact of Legislation on Trade Unions' Behaviour.* Oxford: Clarendon Press, 1996. [Mainly concerned with British legislation since 1980.]

E.11 Labor, Films, Theater, and the Media

Booker, Keith. *Film and the American Left: A Research Guide.* Westport, Conn.: Greenwood Press, 1999.

Duffy, Susan (ed.). *The Political Left in the American Theatre of the 1930's: A Bibliographical Sourcebook.* Metuchen, N.J.: Scarecrow Press, 1992.

Filewod, Alan, and David Watt. *Workers' Playtime: Theatre and the Labour Movement since 1970.* Sydney: Currency Press, 2001. [An Australian study.]

Godfried, Nathan. *WCFL: Chicago's Voice of Labor, 1926-1978.* Champaign: University of Illinois Press, 1997.

Jones, Stephen G. *The British Labour Movement and Film, 1918-1939.* London: Routledge & Kegan Paul, 1988.

Manning, Paul. *Spinning for Labour: Trade Unions and the New Media Environment.* Aldershot, England: Ashgate, 1998.

Puette, W. J. *Through Jaundiced Eyes: How the Media View Organized Labor.* Ithaca, N.Y.: ILR Press, 1992. [Covers the period from 1930 to 1991 and includes film and television as well as the press.]

F. LABOR AND THE ECONOMY

F.1 General Works

Aldcroft, Derek H., and Michael Oliver. *Trade Unions and the Economy, 1870-2000.* Adershot, England: Ashgate: 2000.

Aldcroft, Derek H., and Steven Morewood, *The European Economy, 1914-2000.* 4th ed. London: Routledge, 2001.

Bishel, Lawrence, Jared Bernstein, and John Schmitt. *The State of Working America, 1996–97.* Armonk, N.Y.: M. E. Sharpe, 1997.

Bluestone, B., and B. Harrison. *The Great U-Turn: Corporate Restructuring and the Polarizing of America.* New York: Basic Books, 1985.

Booth, Alison L. (ed.). *The Economics of Trade Unions.* Cheltenham, England: Edward Elgar, 2002.

Brunetta, R., and C. Dell'Aringa (eds.). *Labour Relations and Economic Performance.* London: Macmillan, 1990.

Bruno, Michael, and Jeffrey D. Sachs. *The Economics of Worldwide Stagflation.* Cambridge, Mass.: Harvard University Press, 1985.

Burtless, G. (ed.). *A Future of Lousy Jobs? The Changing Structure of U.S. Wages.* Washington, D.C.: The Brookings Institution, 1990.

Clarke, Thomas (ed.). *International Privatisation: Strategies and Practices.* Berlin: Walter de Gruyter, 1994.

Ehrenberg, R. G., and R. S. Smith. *Modern Labour Economics: Theory and Public Policy.* 3rd ed. Glenview, Ill.: Scott Foresman, 1988.

Fallick, J., and R. Elliott (eds.). *Incomes Policies, Inflation and Relative Pay.* London: Allen & Unwin, 1981.

Flanagan, R. J., D. W. Soskice, and L. Ulman. *Unionism, Economic Stabilisation and Incomes Policies: European Experience.* Washington, D.C.: The Brookings Institution, 1983.

Handy, L .J. *Wages Policy in the British Coalmining Industry: A Study of National Wage Bargaining.* Cambridge: Cambridge University Press, 1981.

Hart, Vivien. *Bound by Our Constitution: Women, Workers, and the Minimum Wage.* Princeton, N.J: Princeton University Press, 1994. [A comparison of the minimum wage movements in the United States and Britain.]

Hirsch, Barry T. *Labor Unions and the Economic Performance of Firms.* Kalamazoo, Mich.: W. E. Upjohn Institute, 1991.

Hyman, R., and W. Streeck. *New Technology and Industrial Relations.* Oxford: Basil Blackwell, 1988.

Iversen, Torben et al. *Unions, Employers, and Central Banks: Macroeconomic Coordination and Institutional Change in Social Market Economies.* Cambridge: Cambridge University Press, 2000. [A study of northern European countries.]

Kaufman, Bruce E. *The Economics of Labor Markets and Labor Relations.* 2nd ed. Chicago: Dryden Press, 1989.

Kleinknecht, A., E. Mandel, and I. Wallerstein (eds.). *New Findings in Long Wave Research*. London: Macmillan, 1992.

Lane, Christel. *Management and Labour in Europe*. Aldershot, England: Edward Elgar, 1989.

Lewis, H. G. *Union Relative Wage Effects: A Survey*. Chicago: University of Chicago Press, 1986.

Lindberg, Leon N., and Charles S. Maier (eds.). *The Politics of Inflation and Economic Stagnation*. Washington, D.C.: The Brookings Institution, 1985.

Locke, Richard, et al. (eds.). *Employment Relations in a Changing World Economy*. Cambridge, Mass.: MIT Press, 1995.

Marshall, Ray. *Unheard Voices: Labor and Economic Policy in a Competitive World*. New York: Basic Books, 1987.

Mishels, Lawrence, and Paula Voos (eds.). *Unions and Economic Competitiveness*. Armonk, N.Y.: M. E. Sharpe, 1992.

Palokangas, Tapio. *Labour Unions, Public Policy and Economic Growth*. Cambridge: Cambridge University Press, 2000. [This work challenges the commonly held view that collective bargaining has a negative impact on economic welfare and argues that with the existence of market failure, collective bargaining can be welfare enhancing.]

Piore, Michael J., and Charles F. Sabel. *The Second Industrial Divide*. New York: Basic Books, 1984.

Posusney, Marshall P. *Labor and the State in Egypt: Workers, Unions, and Economic Restructuring*. New York: Columbia University Press, 1997.

Reynolds, Lloyd G., et al. *Labor Economics and Labor Relations*. 9th ed., Englewood Cliffs, N.J: Prentice-Hall, 1986. [A useful introductory text.]

Scholliers, Peter, and Vera Zamagni (eds.). *Labour's Reward: Real Wages and Economic Change in Nineteenth and Twentieth-Century Europe*. Aldershot, England: Elgar, 1995.

Sengenberger, Werner, and Duncan Campbell (eds.). *International Labour Standards and Economic Interdependence*. Geneva: International Institute for Labour Studies, 1994.

Slomp, H. *Labor Relations in Europe: A History of Issues and Developments*. Westport, Conn.: Greenwood Press, 1990.

Villa, Paola. *The Structuring of Labour Markets: An Analysis of the Italian Construction and Steel Industries*. Oxford: Oxford

University Press, 1987. [Contains an important introduction to the study of labor market structures.]

Western, Bruce. *Between Class and Market: Postwar Unionisation in Capitalist Democracies.* Princeton, N.J.: Princeton University Press, 1997. [A study of 18 OECD countries from 1950 to 1990.]

Wilson, Kenneth G. *The Impact of Unions on United States Economy-Wide Productivity.* New York: Garland, 1995.

F.2 Globalization and Work Practices since 1980

Aidt, Toke. *Unions and Collective Bargaining: Economic Effects in a Global Environment.* Washington, D.C.: World Bank, 2002.

Beaumont, P. B. *The Decline of Trade Union Organisation.* London: Croom Helm, 1987.

Brierley, William (ed.). *Trade Unions and the Economic Crisis of the 1980s.* London: Gower, 1987.

Clark, G. L. *Unions and Communities Under Siege: American Communities and the Crisis of Organized Labor.* Cambridge: Cambridge University Press, 1989.

Coates, D. *The Crisis of Labour: Industrial Relations and the State in Contemporary Britain.* Oxford: Philip Allan, 1989.

Craver, C. B. *Can Unions Survive? The Rejuvenation of the American Labor Movement.* New York: New York University Press, 1993.

Galenson, Walter. *Trade Union Growth and Decline: An International Study.* Westport, Conn.: Praeger, 1994.

Gereluk, Winston. *Sustainable Development of the Global Economy: A Trade Union Perspective.* Geneva: International Labour Organisation, 2002.

Goldfield, Michael. *The Decline of Organized Labor in the United States.* Chicago: University of Chicago Press, 1985.

Gourevitch, P., et al. *Unions and Economic Crisis: Britain, West Germany and Sweden.* London: George Allen & Unwin, 1984.

Grant, John. *Blood Brothers: The Division and Decline of British Trade Unions.* London: Weidenfeld & Nicholson, 1992.

Hammer, Michael. *Beyond Reengineering: How the Process-Centered Organization Is Changing Our Work and Lives.* New York: HarperBusiness, 1996. [Argues, among other things, that the changes to work practices in the past 20 years are largely attributable to the power of consumers to demand better products at lower prices.]

Heckscher, Charles C. *The New Unionism*. Ithaca, N.Y.: ILR Press, 1996. [A U.S. study.]

Hoerr, John P. *And the Wolf Finally Came: The Decline of the American Steel Industry*. Pittsburgh: University of Pittsburgh Press, 1988.

Hyman, Richard. *Understanding European Trade Unionism: Between Market, Class, and Society*. London: Sage, 2001.

International Confederation of Free Trade Unions. *A Trade Union Guide to Globalisation*. Brussels: International Confederation of Free Trade Unions, 2002.

Jacobs, David C. *Collective Bargaining as an Instrument of Social Change*. Westport, Conn.: Quorum Books, 1994.

Juris, H., et al. (eds.). *Industrial Relations in a Decade of Change*. Madison, Wis.: Industrial Relations Research Association Series, 1985.

Kochan, T. (ed.). *Challenges and Choices Facing American Unions*. Cambridge, Mass.: MIT Press, 1985.

Lash, Scott, and J. Urry. *The End of Organized Capitalism*. Madison: Wisconsin University Press, 1987.

Leisink, Peter, et al. (eds.). *The Challenge to Trade Unions in Europe: Innovation and Adaptation*. Aldershot, England: Edward Elgar, 1996.

Littek, W., and T. Charles (eds.). *The New Division of Labour*. Berlin: De Gruyter, 1994.

Martin, Andrew, et al. *The Brave New World of European Labor: European Trade Unions at the Millennium*. New York: Berghahn Books, 1999.

Masters, Marick F. *Unions at the Crossroads: Strategic Membership, Financial and Political Perspectives*. Westport Conn.: Quorum Books, 1997. [A well-received study of 28 U.S. unions.]

Meiksins, Ellen, et al. (eds.). *Rising from the Ashes? Labor in the Age of "Global Capitalism."* New York: Monthly Review Press, 1998. [Covers East Asia, Eastern Europe, Germany, Sweden, Mexico, the United States, and the United Kingdom.]

Moody, Kim. *An Injury to All: The Decline of American Unionism*. London: Verso, 1988.

Olney, Shauna. *Unions in a Changing World*. Washington, D.C.: International Labour Organisation, 1996. [A study of eight countries.]

Perrucci, C., et al. (eds.). *Plant Closings: International Context and Social Costs*. New York: Walter de Gruyter, 1988.

Roozendaal, Gerda van. *Trade Unions and Global Governance: The Debate on a Social Clause*. London: Continuum, 2002.

Sennett, Richard. *The Corrosion of Character: The Personal Consequences of Work in the New Capitalism*. New York: W. W. Norton, 1999.

Smith, Chris, et al. (eds.). *The New Workplace and Trade Unionism*. New York: Routledge, 1995. [A British study.]

Strauss, George, et al. (eds.). *The State of the Unions*. Madison, Wis.: Industrial Relations Research Association Series, 1991.

Thomas, H. *Globalization and the Third World Trade Unions: The Challenge of Rapid Economic Change*. London: Zed Books, 1995.

Waddington, Jeremy (ed.). *Globalization and the Patterns of Union Resistance*. New York: Mansell, 1999.

Willman, Paul, et al. *Union Business: Trade Union Organisation and Financial Reform in the Thatcher Years*. Cambridge: Cambridge University Press, 1993.

G. ORGANIZED LABOR AND THE FUTURE

Boeri, Tito, et al. (eds.). *The Role of Trade Unions in the Twenty-First Century: A Report for the Fondazione Rodolfo Debenedetti*. Oxford: Oxford University Press, 2001.

Crouch, C., and F. Traxler. *Organized Industrial Relations in Europe: What Future?* Aldershot, England: Avebury, 1995.

Evatt Foundation. *Unions 2001: A Blueprint for Trade Union Activism*. Sydney: Evatt Foundation, 1995. [Deals with Australian unions.]

Hannigan, Thomas A. *Managing Tomorrow's High-Performance Unions*. Westport, Conn.: Quorum Books, 1998. [A U.S. study.]

Harrod, Jeffrey, and Robert O'Brien. *Global Unions: Theories and Strategies of Organized Labor in the Global Political Economy*. New York: Routledge, 2002.

Heery, Ed, and John Kelly. *Union Revitalization in the United Kingdom*. Geneva : International Institute for Labour Studies, 2002.

Peetz, David. *Unions in a Contrary World: The Future of the Australian Trade Union Movement.* Cambridge: Cambridge University Press, 1998.

Shostak, Arthur B. *The Cyberunion Handbook: Transforming Labor through Technology.* Armonk, N.Y.: M. E. Sharpe, 2002.

Sverke, Magnus (ed.). *The Future of Trade Unionism: International Perspectives on Emerging Union Structures.* Aldershot, England: Ashgate, 1997.

Turner, Lowell, et al. (eds.). *Rekindling the Movement: Labor's Quest for Relevance in the Twenty-First Century.* Ithaca, N.Y.: ILR Press, 2001.

Weil, David. *Turning the Tide: Strategic Planning for Labor Unions.* New York: Lexington Books, 1994.

Wheeler, Hoyt N., and Lynn S. Williams. *The Future of the American Labor Movement.* Cambridge: Cambridge University Press, 2002.

APPENDIX A

INTERNET SITES: A SELECTED GUIDE

Whether for sending messages or accessing websites, the Internet has become an indispensable tool for researchers, making it possible for them to obtain directly the latest information about a subject or organization. Unlike a book, websites are ephemeral and there is no guarantee that they will be available for consultation at some future time. Labor unions began displaying their own websites on the Internet in about 1995 and by 1999 there were about 2,000 of these websites, a figure that can be expected to grow in the future. This guide is designed to complement and expand the works listed in the bibliography and in the appendixes. It provides a brief, selected guide to the main websites relating to organized labor in May 2003. It does not claim to be comprehensive, but it does provide starting points for research. It should be noted that these websites are extensively linked to other websites. For further information on specific organizations, see John Harper Publishing, *Trade Unions of the World* (London: John Harper Publishing, 2001), which contains websites and contact addresses.

The guide lists websites relating to:

A. International Guides
B. International Labor Organizations and Guides
C. National Councils of Labor Unions
D. British Labor Unions before 1900
E. Labor Unions with More Than One Million Members in 2002
F. Government Departments Concerned with Labor Issues
G. Academic Websites
H. Other Websites

A. International Guides

www.cf.ac.uk/socsi/union
The Cyber Picket Line; it contains links to about 2,000 websites relating to labor unions throughout the world.

www.ilo.org/labordoc
Provides access to the main library catalog of the International Labour Organisation.

www.labourstart.org
Has links to organized labor websites.

www.unions.org
Union Resource Network.
A directory of labor unions. Organized by state for United States, Canada, and Australia; by nation for other countries.

B. International Labor Organizations and Guides

www.commonwealthtuc.org
Commonwealth Trade Union Council.

www.etuc.org
European Trade Union Confederation.

www.eiro.eurofound.ie
European Industry Relations Observatory (EIRO).

www.global-unions.org
The website for the international trade union bodies based on particular industries.

www.icftu.org
International Confederation of Free Trade Unions.

www.ioe-emp.org
International Organisation of Employers.

www.wftu.cz
World Federation of Trade Unions.

www.tuac.org
TUAC—Trade Union Advisory Committee.
An advisory group within the Organization for Economic
Cooperation and Development to give advice on its policies and
programs and to the yearly Group of Eight country summits from the
perspective of labor unions in developed countries.

www.ifj.org
International Federation of Journalists.

www.ifbww.org
International Federation of Building and Wood Workers.

C. National Councils of Labor Unions

www.aflcio.org
American Federation of Labor-Congress of Industrial Organizations.

www.actu.asn.au
Australian Council of Trade Unions.

www.clc-ctc.ca
Canadian Labour Congress.

www.cosatu.org.za
Congress of South African Trade Unions.

www.ctu.org.nz
New Zealand Council of Trade Unions.

www.dgb.de
Deutscher Gewerkschaftsbund (German Confederation of Labor
Unions).

www.ictu.ie
Irish Congress of Trade Unions.

www.kctu.org
Korean Confederation of Trade Unions.

www.lo.se
Landsorganisationen I Sverige
(Swedish Labor Union Confederation).

www.tuc.org.uk
Trades Union Congress (United Kingdom).

D. British Labor Unions before 1900

dspace.dial.pipex.com/town/terrace/adw03/peel/tus.htm
Trade Unions 1830-1851.

dspace.dial.pipex.com/town/terrace/adw03/peel/tuchar.htm
Characteristics of Trade Unions 1830-1850.

dspace.dial.pipex.com/town/terrace/adw03/peel/gnctu.htm
Grand National Consolidated Trade Union.

www.bbc.co.uk/history/bytime/wales/trade_unionism.shtml
Deals with the rise of organized labor from 1830 to 1900.

E. Labor Unions with More Than One Million Members in 2002

www.afscme.org
American Federation of State, County, and Municipal Employees.
[A model website, skillfully organized with high quality past as well
as current material.]

www.aft.org
American Federation of Teachers.

www.igmetall.de
IG Metall (German Metal Workers' Union).

www.nea.org
National Education Association (U.S.).

www.seiu.org
Service Employees International Union.

www.teamster.org
Teamsters (U.S.).

www.ufcw.org
United Food and Commercial Workers' International Union (U.S.).

www.unison.org.uk
Unison (U.K.).

www.verdi.de
Ver.di (United Services Labor Union) (Germany).
The world's largest labor union, formed in March 2001.

F. Government Departments Concerned with Labor Issues

www.dti.gov.uk/employment/index.htm
Department of Trade and Industry.
Contains two vital sources on labor union statistics: *Labour Market Trends* (which contains the results of the annual labor force survey of labor union membership) and the *Annual Report of the Certification Officer* (which provides membership and financial information on individual labor unions). *Labour Market Trends* also publishes an annual survey of labor disputes in OECD countries. [Search first for "Trade Unions and Collective Rights" and then "Trade Union Statistics."] The website also contains research reports as well as legislative changes.

www.state.gov
Country Reports on Human Rights Practices.
U.S. State Department, Bureau of Democracy, Human Rights and Labor.

stats.bls.gov
U.S. Department of Labor, Bureau of Labor Statistics. [Search for "labor union."]

www.nlrb.gov
The National Labor Relations Board is the U.S. federal agency that administers the National Labor Relations Act.

G. Academic Websites

anulib.anu.edu.au/nbac
Noel Butlin Archives Centre–Australian National University Library.

www.kentlaw.edu/ilhs
Kent State University—Illinois Labor History Society.
Chicago-Kent College of Law posts news, academic information, and other resources on labor unions and their history. Has links to related sites.

www.lib.berkeley.edu/IIRL/iirlnet.html
University of California, Berkeley—Labor Links.
A directory of links compiled by the library to labor unions, history archives, international organizations, and government agencies.

www.pscw.uva.nl/sociosite/TOPICS/indrel.html
SocioSite—Industrial Relations and Trade Unions
Furnishes access to a wide assortment of study guides and research resources relating to industrial relations, trade unions, and general labor history.

H. Other Websites

flag.blackened.net/revolt/ws99/ws56_union.html
Anarchists and the Trade Unions.

oshweb.me.tut.fi/index.html
Oshweb.
Extensive index of occupational health and safety resources on the web. Searchable by keyword and category.

utopia.knoware.nl/users/modijk
Trade Unions and Homosexuality.
Report of a global conference of 1998 to discuss the role of trade unions in fighting for the rights of lesbians and gay men.

www.africanet.com/africanet/country/tanzania/history.htm
Tanzania—Africanet History.
Synopsis focuses on events after independence from Britain in 1961. Describes the formation of a regional trade union with Kenya and Uganda.

www.labornet.org
LaborNet.
Community of labor unions, activists, and organizations offers a network for the discussion of economic justice and rights issues.

www.llb.labournet.org.uk/links
Labour Left Briefing.
Offers a listing of links to international labor movement, trade union, socialist, communist, and related websites.

www.summersault.com/~agj/clr
Campaign for Labor Rights.
Features action alerts for the group's campaigns to halt labor abuse, and includes a newsletter archive and country reports.

www.thehistorynet.com/WomensHistory/articles/19967_text.htm
Women in the Workplace, Labor Unions.
Details the development of the Women's Trade Union League in 1903 and later advancements in women's rights in employment.

www.uniononline.com
UnionOnline.com.
Directory offers listings of unions in a wide array of fields.

APPENDIX B

GLOSSARY OF TERMS

Like any other movement, organized labor has its own specialized terms, which can appear in the primary sources or in the secondary literature. What follows is a sample of terms intended to provide a starting point for a reader; further information about some of them can be found in the specialized works listed in the bibliography. Cross-references to other terms in the glossary are in bold.

Agency shop.
U.S term referring to a collective agreement that excludes free-riders by forcing them to pay the equivalent of the union membership fee in order to retain employment at that workplace.

Angestellte.
German term for private sector white-collar employee, in contrast to **Beamte**.

Arbeiter.
German term for manual or blue-collar workers, in contrast to **Angestellte** and **Beamte**.

Beamte.
German term for public sector employees including civil servants and employees in state-run enterprises, such as postal services, railroads and schools, in contrast to **Angestellte**.

Betriebsräte.
German term for works' councils. They began in the late 19th century, were enacted in legislation in 1920, and were incorporated into co-determination (*Mitbestimmung*).

369

Brownfield site.
A workplace where there are established unions and a long-standing system of industrial relations characterized by customs and practices recognized by employers and unions, in contrast to a **greenfield** site.

Ca'canny.
Originally a Scottish term meaning to go carefully, it was first recorded in 1896 to refer to employees deliberately reducing the pace of their work or the quantity of their output. By 1918, "ca'canny" had entered standard English usage in Britain.

Candy men.
Term used in 19th-century England to describe the men employed by coal owners to evict miners from company-owned housing during labor disputes. The term originated in the English coal miners' strike of 1844, when some sellers of "dandy candy" in Newcastle-upon-Tyne were employed as bailiffs to evict miners from company-owned houses.

Checkoff.
A formal arrangement between an employer and a union whereby the employer deducts union fees and dues from their employees' pay and remits them to the union

Closed (or union) shop.
A workplace where union membership is a condition of employment; closed shop is British usage, union shop is American usage. There are two main forms of the closed shop: workplaces where an individual must be a member of a particular union before being employed and those where the individual must join a particular union after being employed at the workplace. The opposite term is **open shop**.

Company union.
A company union is one formed by the management of a company among its employees and run for the benefit of the employer. Such unions are also variously called house unions, yellow unions, and even employee representation plans. Although a company union was formed in France in 1899, company unions were largely a feature of American labor relations. They flourished in the 1920s and early 1930s but were effectively killed off by the National Labor Relations Act in 1935. Some observers regard the relatively docile unions of large Japanese companies as a form of company union.

Conseils de prud'hommes.
French labor tribunals that date from 1806.

Corporatism.
The organization of large interest groups in society into corporate bodies. The term specifically refers to industry groups, unions, and governments. The creation of such umbrella organizations was a feature of the fascist governments of Italy and Germany. Hence, the term "neocorporatism" has been coined to describe the close cooperation between government, business, and unions in Western European countries since the 1960s to develop and implement economic policies such as over wages or managing technological change.

Demarcation. *See* **Jurisdiction.**

Free-riders.
Employees who are not union members but who nevertheless benefit from the collective bargaining arrangements on pay and conditions achieved by organized labor at their place of work.

Gherao (plural **gheraos**).
Indian term for a labor dispute in which employees harass employers and prevent them from leaving the workplace until the employees' claims are granted.

Greenfield site.
A new workplace where there are no established unions or system of industrial relations. Often such sites are objects of competition between unions to recruit members and to gain exclusive recognition from management, in contrast to a **brownfield** site.

Industrial relations.
A general term for the interaction between management and its employees; it implies that both sides are organized. Industrial relations can also include governments and their representatives. As a term, industrial relations dates from the 1920s. Since 1945, the term labor-management relations—or just labor relations—has also come into use.

Industry.
A general description of the type of goods or services produced or provided by the various sectors of the economy. Industries can be classified in a number of ways. One approach is to divide the economy into three parts: primary (agriculture and mining), secondary (manufacturing), and tertiary (other industries, also called service industries). For statistical purposes, most countries use a variant of the United Nations' International Standard Industrial Classification. Generally, unions recruit their members by occupations rather than industries.

Inflation/deflation.
These terms refer to movements in the level of prices of goods and services in an economy. Inflation refers to rising prices and deflation refers to falling prices. If real wages do not match the changes of prices in an inflationary period, organized labor is more likely to engage in disputes for higher wages.

Internal labor market.
The labor market that operates in a large enterprise such as the railroads. In the past, it has often been characterized by clearly defined points of entry, vertical organization, bureaucratic rules, and promotion of employees within the organization.

Journeymen.
Term first recorded in England by the 14th century to describe an artisan or mechanic who had completed an apprenticeship and then worked as an employee. Journeymen were the main groups in the formation of early labor unions in 18th-century England and the United States.

Jurisdiction.
Jurisdiction refers to the work boundaries recognized by unions for recruiting members for a particular union. Unions can, and do, disagree over which union has the right to recruit members carrying out certain kinds of work, and this can lead to disputes. Work boundaries can also be altered by technological change. In British usage, jurisdiction is demarcation.

Kragenlinie.
German noun literally meaning "collar line" but really referring to the social distinction between blue- and white-collar employees.

"Labor Aristocracy."
The term "labor aristocracy" was used by Marx and Engels to describe the emergence of labor unions by skilled, relatively well-paid employees in Britain after 1850. Such employees included stonemasons, engineers, railroad engine drivers, carpenters, and printers. Because of their better-off condition, such unions were less likely to support radical social change and more likely to identify with middle-class ideas and values. The labor aristocracy made up about 15 percent of working-class employees in late 19th-century Britain.

Labor economics.
The branch of economics that studies the supply and demand for human beings. Theoretical advances and the availability of computerized data sets have enabled labor economics to advance greatly since the 1960s through the use of quantitative analysis or econometrics. One topic that has received attention from labor economists has been the economic effects of organized labor.

Labor force.
The economically active part of the population. It includes those who are employed (the employed labor force) and the unemployed.

Lockout.
A labor dispute initiated by an employer or group of employers in contrast to a strike (that is, a labor dispute initiated by employees). The word was first recorded in 1860 to describe a labor dispute in which the employees were literally locked out of their workplace. In practice, lockouts are difficult to measure because provocation by an employer can mean that the dispute takes the form of a strike. An example of a national lockout occurred in the United States in October 2002 when a lockout of the longshoremen resulted in the closure of 19 ports on the West Coast.

Luddism.
Luddism was the name given to a systematic if sporadic campaign of **machine breaking** by employees in the English textile industry between 1812 and 1818. Luddism drew its name from an imaginary leader, Ned Ludd, who was also referred to as Captain Ludd and General Ludd.

Machine breaking.
Machine breaking, that is, the wrecking of new machinery by employees, was a form of industrial protest dating from at least the late 17th century and a feature of industrial relations before the recognition of labor unions.

New economy.
A catchall term for a host of economic and labor market trends evident since about 1980. The new economy has been described as being based on information manipulation, transformation, and transfer and using computers. New economy or post-industrial economy trends are particularly evident in finance and banking.

Nominal wages.
The amount of wages received without taking account of inflation, in contrast to **real wages**.

Normative.
In economic and sociological literature, normative refers to what ought to be, that is, the outcome predicted by a theory in contrast to "positive" or what actually happens in reality.

Occupation.
The specific job an individual is paid to carry out. There are two main kinds of occupation: manual or blue-collar occupations and nonmanual or white-collar occupations. Unions generally base their recruitment of members on groups of occupations. Historically, unions drawn from manual occupations tend to be more militant than those drawn from white-collar occupations.

Occupational status.
Refers to the division of the employed labor force into employers, self-employed, employees, and unpaid helpers.

Open shop.
In contrast to a **closed shop**, an open shop is a place of employment where employees may not be union members, either by choice or by coercion by the employer.

Order 1305.
A British wartime regulatory measure issued in June 1940 to enforce compulsory arbitration as a final resort in labor disputes, but they

continued. Order 1305 was withdrawn in August 1951, although the tribunal it established survived until 1958.

Osbourne Judgement.
The Osbourne Judgement was a landmark decision by the British House of Lords in December 1909, which declared that it was illegal for labor unions to contribute funds to the British Labour Party. Organized labor was only able to get redress from the Osbourne Judgement after the Liberal Party, led by Lloyd George, was elected to government in 1911.

Outworker.
Literally, someone who works "out"—that is, outside a factory and from home. Outworkers are common in the textile industry. Outworkers typically work under poor conditions for very low pay. The word has been used in this sense since 1856.

Piece worker.
An employee paid on the basis of defined tangible results (literally the production of "pieces") as opposed to attendance time at work. The term piece worker was used by 1884, but piece work dates from 1795.

Primary labor market.
A labor market characterized by high or difficult entry qualifications, high pay, good working conditions, and good promotion prospects, in contrast to the **secondary labor market**.

Pull economy.
Refers to the tendency in Western economies since the 1970s for supply to exceed demand, thereby forcing businesses to compete harder for customers. Lower business profits and more difficult trading conditions have made it harder for labor unions to gain pay increases. The rise of the pull economy is a reflection of greater economic maturity and the growth of more demanding and knowledgeable consumers.

Push economy.
Refers to the tendency in Western economies from the end of World War II to the 1970s for demand to exceed supply. In these favorable economic conditions, business profits were good and labor unions were able to demand and receive pay increases relatively easily.

Real wages.

Real wages are **nominal wages** taking account of inflation or deflation. Changes in levels of real wages, particularly falls, have been a potent cause of labor unrest. An older term for real wages was effective wages.

Rights and interest.

A distinction sometimes made between types of labor disputes: "Rights" refers to the interpretation of the rights of unions and management in a contract or employment agreement, whereas "interest" refers to the making of those terms. For example, an interest dispute could be over the recognition of a union by management; rights disputes are usually about alleged violations of agreed conditions of employment by one of the parties to the agreement.

"Saint Monday."

A custom observed from about the mid-17th century by shoemakers, tailors, and other **journeymen** of taking Monday as a holiday and sometimes even Tuesday. The custom also seems to have been observed by French textile employees. By 1764, it was observed by bricklayers, painters, and hand loom employees. Work not performed on Monday was made up later in the week at night. The purpose of the custom was to create a period of leisure and to exert more control over when work was done. Its opponents claimed that "Saint Monday" was observed mainly in ale-houses and taverns. The custom was gradually eliminated by the factory system and replaced by a regulated system of hours.

Salting.

A U.S. term that refers to the placing of paid union organizers as employees in the workplace with the object of recruiting new union members. The term probably comes from the mining industry and the addition of outside ore to a mine to make it seem richer than it really is.

Scab.

Scab is a pejorative term used by organized labor in the United States and elsewhere to describe persons brought in by employers to replace employees on strike. In the United States, its use was first recorded in 1806 to describe employees who would not join a union of their occupation. Used as a term for strikebreaker, its usage was recorded in the United Kingdom by 1890.

Secondary labor market.
A labor market usually characterized by low entry qualifications, low pay, poor working conditions, and limited opportunities for promotion, in contrast to the **primary labor market**.

Segmented labor market.
A labor market that is dominated by one sex, race, or other group. Sex is a common characteristic of a segmented labor market; for example, most librarians are female and most engineers are male.

Shop stewards.
Also known as delegates, shop stewards are the representatives of a union at the workplace but are not officials of the union. Shop stewards have been very important in British labor unions since 1918.

Sliding scale.
A system of payment that linked wages directly to the price obtained for the good being produced by an **industry**. In 1795, agricultural laborers in Norfolk, England, suggested a sliding scale that would have tied their wage rate to the price of wheat. Sliding scales that linked wages to the price of coal were prevalent in the coal mining industry in the 1870s and 1880s in Britain and the United States. Although the system could yield higher wages when coal prices were high, it could have disastrous effects on miners' earnings if the coal price fell sharply.

Social dialogue.
A term that came into vogue in the 1980s to describe formal discussions between representatives of labor unions and employers, and/or governments on ways to achieve shared outcomes, such as economic growth and the reduction of unemployment. Social dialogue has been successful in Western Europe, but not so elsewhere, generally speaking.

Social dumping.
A term coined in Western Europe in the late 1980s to refer to the adverse effects on affluent countries of economic competition from poorer countries. These effects can take the form of unemployment caused by the displacement of relatively highly paid employees because of the import of goods produced by poorly paid employees, the relocation of centers of employment from countries of high pay to ones with low pay, and attempts to lower the pay and conditions of

employment in affluent societies by pitting them against workers in Third World countries. The term has also been applied to the migration of workers from low-wage countries to high-wage countries.

Structural adjustment.
A term that came into vogue in the 1980s to describe the economic changes that debtor Third World nations had to implement to receive economic assistance from organizations such as the International Monetary Fund and the World Bank. These changes typically include privatization and reductions in government expenditure.

"Tolpuddle Martyrs."
The "Tolpuddle Martyrs" were a group of six English agricultural laborers who were convicted of unlawful oaths and conspiracy at the village of Tolpuddle in Dorset. Led by George Loveless (1797-1874), who was also a lay Methodist preacher, the six men seemed to have used an initiation ceremony in the process of setting up a union to seek higher wages. Their union may have been part of the expansion of the Grand National Consolidated Trades Union. After a summary trial in March 1834, the six were convicted under conspiracy and mutiny laws of 1797 and 1819 and transported to New South Wales, Australia. They were not pardoned until 1838.

Tripartite.
Bodies made up of representatives of employers, unions, and government. Tripartite bodies of this kind are usually designed to address a problem of labor relations such as a dispute, training, or occupational health and safety. The International Labor Organisation has a tripartite structure.

Truck.
A term first recorded in England in 1665 to describe the payment of employees' wages in kind rather than money. The abuse arose from the goods often having a lesser value than the wages owed. Truck was first outlawed in 1701 but remained an abuse throughout the 19th century despite laws passed in 1831, 1887, and 1896. Truck was also an abuse in Germany and the United States. By the late 19th century the term was extended to refer to an employer's fines or unauthorized deductions from an employee's wages.

Unemployment rate.
The number of unemployed as a percentage of the total labor force. The level of unemployment is important for labor unions as a factor in determining their strength in negotiations with employers.

Union density.
Union members as a percentage of potential union members, usually defined as the number of employees in a particular industry or of all employees in a national economy.

Union shop. *See* **Closed shop**.

Warnstreik.
German term for "warning strike." A labor dispute of short duration in support of union claims for higher pay or better working conditions. The purpose of the strike is to indicate that the claims are serious and that longer strikes may occur.

Yellow dog contracts.
One of the means by which English employers defeated the Grand United Council of Trade Unions in 1834 was by requiring employees to sign "The Document" by which they would give an undertaking to leave a union and not join another one. In the United States, this tactic was known as a yellow dog contract, from "yellow dog" meaning a contemptible person. In the 1890s, yellow dog contracts that forbade union membership became more common and were not outlawed until 1932 by the Anti-Injunction (Norris-LaGuardia) Act.

APPENDIX C

INTERNATIONAL FEDERATION OF TRADE UNIONS: LEADERS, 1901-1945

Presidents/country of origin	Period of office
Carl LEGIEN/Germany*	**1901-1919**
James Henry THOMAS/United Kingdom	**1920-1924**
Albert Arthur William PURCELL/ United Kingdom	**1925-1928**
Walter McLennan CITRINE/ United Kingdom	**1928-1945**
Secretary/country of origin	
Carl LEGIEN/Germany*	**1901-1919**
Jan OUDEGESST/Netherlands [joint secretary]	**1919-1927**
Edo FIMMEN/Finland [joint secretary]	**1919-1927**
General Secretary/country of origin	
Johann SASSENBACH/Germany	**1927-1930 (interim)**
Walther SCHEVELS/Netherlands	**1930-1945**

*Entry in Dictionary.

Source: Walther Schevenels, *Forty-Five Years: International Federation of Trade Unions* (Brussels: Board of Trustees of the International Federation of Trade Unions, 1956), *passim*.

APPENDIX D

INTERNATIONAL CONFEDERATION OF FREE TRADE UNIONS: GENERAL SECRETARIES, 1949-2003

Name	Period of office
Jacobus Hendrik OLDENBROEK	1949-1960
Omer BECU	1960-1967
Harm G. BULTER	1967-1971
Otto KERSTEN	1972-1982
John VANDERVEKEN	1982-1992
Enzo FRISO	1992-1994
Bill JORDAN*	1995-2001
Guy RYDER*	2002-

*Entry in Dictionary.

Source: *Trade Union World*, September 1999, p. 36; December 2001-January 2002, p.30.

APPENDIX E

INTERNATIONAL CONFEDERATION OF FREE TRADE UNIONS: AFFILIATES, NOVEMBER 2001

Country	Affiliated organization	Members (thousands)
Region	**AFRICA**	
Algeria	*Union Générale des Travailleurs Algériens*	1,350.0
Angola	*Central Geral de Sindicatos Independentes e Livres de Angola*	51.0
Benin	*Union Nationale des Syndicats des Travailleurs du Bénin*	40.0
	Centrale des Syndicats Autonomes du Bénin	51.0
Botswana	Botswana Federation of Trade Unions	18.0
Burkina Faso	*Organisation Nationale des Syndicats Libres*	42.5
	Confédération Syndicale Burkinabé	17.0
Cameroon	*Confédération Syndicale des Travailleurs du Cameroun*	385.0
Cape Verde	*União Nacional dos Trabalhadores de Cabo Verde - Central Sindical*	15.0
Central African Republic	*Union Syndicale des Travailleurs de Centrafrique*	15.0

Country	Affiliated organization	Members (thousands)
Congo	*Confédération des Syndicats Libres Autonomes du Congo*	13.0
	Confédération Syndicale des Travailleurs du Congo	67.8
Democratic Republic of the Congo	*Confédération Démocratique du Travail*	200.0
Democratic Republic of the Congo	*Union Nationale des Travailleurs du Congo*	326.5
Côte d'Ivoire	*Union Générale des Travailleurs de Côte d'Ivoire*	120.0
Djibouti	*Union Djiboutienne du travail*	15.0
Eritrea	National Confederation of Eritrean Workers	18.0
Gabon	*Confédération Gabonaise des Syndicats Libres*	19.0
Gambia	Gambia Workers' Union	3.0
Ghana	Trades Union Congress	450.0
Guinea	*Organisation Nationale des Syndicats Libres de Guinée*	43.5
	Union Syndicale des Travailleurs de Guinée	40.2
Guinea-Bissau	*Union Nationale des Travailleurs de Guinée Bissau*	39.7
Kenya	Central Organisation of Trade Unions	233.5
Liberia	Liberia Federation of Labour Unions	10.0
Madagascar	*Fivondronamben'ny Mpiasa Malagasy*	18.5
Malawi	Malawi Congress of Trade Unions	45.0
Mali	*Union Nationale des Travailleurs du Mali*	122.0
	Confédération Syndicale des Travailleurs du Mali	15.0

Country	Affiliated organization	Members (thousands)
Mauritania	*Confédération Générale des Travailleurs de Mauritanie*	25.0
	Union des Travailleurs de Mauritanie	45.0
Mauritius	Mauritius Labour Congress	30.0
Morocco	*Union Marocaine du Travail*	305.1
Mozambique	*Organizaçâo dos Trabalhadores de Moçambique*	119.9
Namibia	National Union of Namibian Workers	65.0
Niger	*Union des Syndicats des Travailleurs du Niger*	38.0
Nigeria	Nigeria Labour Congress	4,000.0
Réunion	*Union Interprofessionelle de la Réunion*	15.1
Rwanda	*Centrale des Syndicats des Travailleurs du Rwanda*	72.0
Senegal	*Confédération Nationale des Travailleurs du Sénégal*	80.0
	Union Nationale des Syndicats Autonomes du Sénégal	52.4
Seychelles	Seychelles Federation of Workers' Unions	5.0
Sierra Leone	Sierra Leone Labour Congress	20.2
South Africa	National Council of Trade Unions	327.0
	Congress of South African Trade Unions	1,800.0
	Federation of Unions of South Africa	548.6
St. Helena	St. Helena General Workers' Union	0.7
Swaziland	Swaziland Federation of Trade Unions	25.0
Tanzania	Trade Unions' Congress of Tanzania	359.9

Country	Affiliated organization	Members (thousands)
Togo	*Confédération Nationale des Travailleurs du Togo*	35.0
	Union Nationale des Syndicats Indépendants du Togo	7.7
Tunisia	*Union Générale Tunisienne du Travail*	532.9
Uganda	National Organisation of Trade Unions	79.5
Zambia	Zambia Congress of Trade Unions	298.9
Zimbabwe	Zimbabwe Congress of Trade Unions	169.3
TOTAL AFRICA		**12,871.4**
Region	**ASIA**	
Bangladesh	Bangladesh *Mukto Sramik* Federation	191.4
Bangladesh	Bangladesh Free Trade Union Congress	157.1
	Bangladesh Jatyatabadi Sramik Dal	180.0
	Jatiya Sramik Party	110.0
	Jatio Sramik League	250.2
Hong Kong	Hong Kong and Kowloon Trades Union Council	28.5
	Hong Kong Confederation of Trade Unions	140.0
India	*Hind Mazdoor Sabha*	5,020.0
	Indian National Trade Union Congress	6,820.2
Indonesia	*Kongres Buruh Islam Merdeka*	130.0
	Gabungan Serikat Buruh Industri Indonesia	150.0
	Gerakan Organisasi Buruh Sjarikat Islam Indonesia	52.6
	Sarikat Buruh Muslimin Indonesia	100.0

Country	Affiliated organization	Members (thousands)
Malaysia	Malaysian Trades Union Congress	404.0
Mongolia	Confederation of Mongolian Trade Unions	450.0
Nepal	Nepal Trade Union Congress	140.0
Pakistan	Pakistan National Federation of Trade Unions	250.0
	All-Pakistan Federation of Labour	291.6
	All-Pakistan Federation of Trade Unions	598.7
Philippines	Trade Union Congress of the Philippines	475.0
Singapore	National Trades Union Congress	225.0
South Korea	Federation of Korean Trade Unions	988.5
	Korean Confederation of Trade Unions	418.2
Sri Lanka	Ceylon Workers' Congress	185.0
Taiwan	Chinese Federation of Labor	1,000.1
Thailand	Labour Congress of Thailand	120.0
	Thai Trade Union Congress	123.2
TOTAL ASIA		**26,499.3**
Region	**MIDDLE EAST**	
Azerbaijan	Azerbaijan Trade Union Confederation	735.0
Cyprus	Cyprus Workers' Confederation	63.0
	Cyprus Turkish Trade Unions Federation	3.0
Israel	General Federation of Labor in Israel (Histadrut)	450.0
Jordan	General Federation of Jordanian Trade Unions	200.0

Country	Affiliated organization	Members (thousands)
Lebanon	*Ligue des Syndicats des Employés et des Ouvriers dans la République Libanaise*	13.0
	Fédération des Syndicats-Unis des Employés et des Ouvriers au Liban	10.0
	Fédération Ouvrière des Offices Autonomes et des Entreprises Publiques et Privées au Liban	13.0
	Federation of Petroleum Labor Unions in Lebanon	1.0
	Fédération des Syndicats des Employés des Banques au Liban	5.0
	Federation of Insurance Sector Employees in Lebanon	1.0
	Federation of Health and Education Labor Unions in Lebanon	25.0
	Fédération des Syndicats des Employés du Commerce au Liban	1.0
	Federation of Airlines Companies Employees and Laborers of Lebanon	4.0
	Labor Unions Federation of Sea Transportation in Lebanon	8.0
	Fédération des Syndicats des Employés et Ouvriers des Offices Autonomes. et Services Publique au Liban.	9.0
	Fédération des Employés des Hôtels Restaurants et Lieux de Loisirs au Liban	2.8
	Fédération des Syndicats d'Ouvriers des Imprimeries et de l'Information au Liban	5.0

Country	Affiliated organization	Members (thousands)
Turkey	*Kamu Emekçileri Sendikalari Konfederasyonu*	404.5
	Confederation of Turkish Trade Unions (TÜRK-IS)	250.0
	Devrimci Isçi Sendikalari Konfederasyonu	250.0
	Confederation of Turkish Real Trade Unions (HAK-IS)	325.0
Yemen	General Federation of Workers' Trade Unions of Yemen	300.0
TOTAL MIDDLE EAST		**3,078.3**
Region	**OCEANIA**	
Australia	Australian Council of Trade Unions	2,000.0
Cook Islands	Cook Islands Workers' Association Inc.	0.7
Fiji	Fiji Trades Union Congress	42.0
French Polynesia	*A Tia I Mua*	1.3
Kiribati	Kiribati Trades Union Congress	2.6
New Caledonia	*Union des Syndicats des Ouvriers et Employés de Nouvelle Calédonie*	3.6
New Zealand	New Zealand Council of Trade Unions	100.0
Papua New Guinea	Papua New Guinea Trade Union Congress	70.0
Tonga	Friendly Islands Teachers' /Association Tonga Nurses' Association	0.6
Vanuatu	Vanuatu Council of Trade Unions	2.3
Western Samoa	Samoa Trade Union Congress	2.2
TOTAL OCEANIA		**2,225.3**

Country	Affiliated organization	Members (thousands)
Region	**WESTERN EUROPE**	
Austria	*Österreichischer Gewerkschaftsbund*	1,442.4
Belgium	*Fédération Générale du Travail de Belgique*	1,008.5
	Centrale générale des Syndicats libéraux de Belgique	220.0
Croatia	Union of Autonomous Trade Unions of Croatia	345.9
Denmark	*Landsorganisationen i Danmark*	1,454.4
	Funktionaerernes og Tjenestemaendenes Faellesrad	350.3
	Akademikernes Centralorganisation	226.0
Finland	*Suomen Ammattiliittojen Keskusjärjestö*	1,010.0
	Confederation of Unions for Academic Professionals in Finland	269.8
	The Finnish Confederation of Salaried Employees	452.0
France	*Confédération Générale du Travail - Force Ouvrière*	1,015.0
	Confédération Française Démocratique du Travail	830.6
Germany	*Deutscher Gewerkschaftsbund*	7,600.0
Greece	Greek General Confederation of Labour	300.0
Iceland	Icelandic Federation of Labor	66.2
	Bandalag Starfsmanna Rikis og Baeja	16.7
Ireland	Irish Congress of Trade Unions	758.8
Italy	*Confederazione Italiana Sindacati Lavoratori*	4,000.0
	Unione Italiana del Lavoro	1,776.9

Country	Affiliated organization	Members (thousands)
	Confederazione Generale Italiana del Lavoro	5,287.0
Luxembourg	*Confédération Générale du Travail du Luxembourg*	56.4
Malta	General Workers' Union	36.0
Netherlands	*Federatie Nederlandse Vakbeweging*	1,226.6
Norway	*Landsorganisasjonen i Norge*	817.7
Portugal	*Uniâo Geral de Trabalhadores*	251.0
San Marino	*Confederazione Democratica Lavoratori Sammarinesi*	3.9
	Confederazione Sammarinese del Lavoro	3.7
Spain	*Eusko Langileen Alkartasuna Solidaridad de Trabajadores Vascos* - Basque Country	110.0
	Unión General de Trabajadores	665.8
	Confederación Sindical de Comisiones Obreras	600.0
Sweden	*Landsorganisationen i Sverige*	1,753.8
	Tjänstemännens Centralorganisation	1,045.0
	Swedish Confederation of Professional Associations	478.7
Switzerland	*Schweizerischer Gewerkschaftsbund*	387.0
United Kingdom	Trades Union Congress	6,744.4
Vatican	*Associazione Dipendenti Laici Vaticani*	0.6
TOTAL WESTERN EUROPE		**42,611.1**
Region	**EASTERN EUROPE**	
Bulgaria	Confederation of Labor (PODKREPA)	155.3

Country	Affiliated organization	Members (thousands)
	Confederation of Independent Trade Unions in Bulgaria	400.0
Czech Republic	Czech-Moravian Confederation of Trade Unions (CMKOS)	883.0
Estonia	Confederation of Estonian Trade Unions (EAKL)	57.0
Georgia	Georgian Trade Union Amalgamation	650.0
Hungary	Democratic Confederation of Free Trade Unions (LIGA)	101.0
	National Confederation of Hungarian Trade Unions (MSZOSZ)	537.0
	Autonomous Trade Union Confederation	128.0
Latvia	Free Trade Union Confederation of Latvia (LBAS)	207.4
Lithuania	Lithuanian Trade Union Unification (LPSS)	39.6
	Lithuanian Workers' Union (LWU)	52.0
Moldova	Consiliul Confederatiei Sindicatelor din Republica Moldova	618.0
Poland	"Solidarnosc" [Solidarity]	1,100.0
Romania	National Confederation of Free Trade Unions of Romania (CNSLR-FRATIA)	250.0
	Blocul National Sindical	150.0
Russian Federation	All-Russian Confederation of Labor (VKT)	1,270.9
	Federation of Independent Trade Unions of Russia (FNPR)	28,000.0

Country	Affiliated organization	Members (thousands)
Slovakia	Confederation of Trade Unions of the Slovak Republic (KOZSR)	702.4
Yugoslavia	*Nezavisnost*	153.7
(Federal Republic)	Confederation of Independent Trade Unions of Montenegro	90.0
TOTAL EASTERN EUROPE		**36,795.3**
Region	**NORTH AMERICA**	
Canada	Canadian Labour Congress	1,500.0
	Confédération des Syndicats Nationaux	260.0
United States	American Federation of Labor and Congress of Industrial Organizations (AFL-CIO)	13,226.0
TOTAL NORTH AMERICA		**14,986.0**
Region	**LATIN AMERICA AND CARIBBEAN**	
Antigua and Barbuda	Antigua and Barbuda Workers' Union	4.0
	Antigua and Barbuda Public Service Association	0.4
Antilles (Netherlands)	*Sentral di Sindikatonan di Korsou*	5.1
Argentina	*Confederación General del Trabajo de la República Argentina*	4,401.0
Bahamas	Commonwealth of the Bahamas Trade Union Congress	2.5
Barbados	Barbados Workers' Union	15.0
Belize	National Trade Union Congress of Belize	2.4
Bermuda	Bermuda Industrial Union	5.0
Brazil	*Confederaçâo Geral dos Trabalhadores*	2,200.0
	Força Sindical	2,100.0

Country	Affiliated organization	Members (thousands)
	Central Única dos Trabalhadores	4,571.9
Chile	*Central Unitaria de Trabajadores*	400.0
Colombia	*Confederación de Trabajadores de Colombia*	120.0
Costa Rica	*Confederación de Trabajadores Rerum Novarum*	45.5
Dominica	Dominica Trade Union	0.8
	Waterfront and Allied Workers' Union	1.0
Dominican Republic	*Confederación Nacional de Trabajadores Dominicanos*	143.0
	Confederación de Trabajadores Unitaria	125.0
Ecuador	*Confederación Ecuatoriana de Organizaciones Sindicales Libres*	150.0
El Salvador	*Central de Trabajadores Democráticos de El Salvador*	85.5
	Federación Nacional Sindical de Trabajadores Salvadoreños	36.0
Falkland Islands	Falkland Islands General Employees' Union	0.2
Grenada	Grenada Trades' Union Council	7.5
Guatemala	*Confederación de Unidad Sindical de Guatemala*	50.0
Guyana	Guyana Trades Union Congress	15.0
Honduras	*Confederación de Trabajadores de Honduras*	35.0
Jamaica	Jamaica Confederation of Trade Unions	23.0
Mexico	*Confederación de Trabajadores de Mexico*	1,450.0
Montserrat	Montserrat Allied Workers' Union	0.2

Country	Affiliated organization	Members (thousands)
Nicaragua	*Confederación de Unificación Syndical*	32.0
	Central Sandinista de Trabajadores	40.0
Panama	*Confederación de Trabajadores de la República de Panamá*	40.0
	Convergencia Sindical	130.0
Paraguay	*Central Unitaria de Trabajadores*	34.4
Peru	*Confederación de Trabajadores del Perú*	120.0
	Confederación Nacional de Trabajadores	120.0
	Confederación Unitaria de Trabajadores del Perú	25.0
Puerto Rico	*Federación del Trabajo de Puerto Rico*	30.0
St. Kitts-Nevis	St. Kitts-Nevis Trades and Labour Union	0.4
St. Lucia	St. Lucia Workers' Union	1.0
	St. Lucia Seamen, Waterfront and General Workers' Trade Union	1.2
St. Vincent and Grenadines	Commercial, Technical and Allied Workers' Union	1.6
Surinam	*Algemeen Verbond van Vakverenigingen in Suriname "De Moederbond"*	5.0
	Progressive Federation of Trade Unions (C-47)	12.0
	Centrale van Landsdienaren Organisaties	17.5
Trinidad and Tobago	National Trade Union Centre of Trinidad and Tobago	45.0

Country	Affiliated organization	Members (thousands)
Venezuela	*Confederación de Trabajadores de Venezuela*	750.7
TOTAL LATIN AMERICA AND CARIBBEAN		**17,400.8**
WORLD TOTAL		**156,467.5**

Note: The membership shown is that declared by affiliates.

SOURCE: International Confederation of Free Trade Unions.

APPENDIX F

HISTORICAL STATISTICS OF LABOR UNION MEMBERSHIP

The Neglect of Labor Union Statistics

The tables in this appendix trace the growth and main features of labor union membership in the world since about 1870, with an emphasis on recent developments. The figures refer to labor unions able to engage in collective bargaining in a reasonably free political and legal environment and exclude countries whose unions were (or are) under the effective control of an authoritarian government such as under fascism or communism.

Although like any historical statistical series, they present problems, the absence of data on labor unions in the main readily available reference books on historical statistics is a powerful reason for their presentation here. For example, B. R. Mitchell, *International Historical Statistics: Europe, 1750-1988* (New York: Stockton Press, 1992), follows his earlier international statistical works and gives data on the negative side of organized labor, that is labor disputes, but ignores labor union membership despite the time series information available in George S. Bain and Robert Price, *Profiles of Union Growth: A Comparative Statistical Portrait of Eight Countries* (Oxford: Basil Blackwell, 1980). The second volume of the monumental data book by Peter Flora et al., *State, Economy, and Society in Western Europe, 1815-1975* (Chicago: St. James Press, 1987), had been planned to include labor union membership data, but this chapter was never completed.

Despite their social and economic importance, neither the United Nations nor the International Labour Organisation (ILO) accept the responsibility to regularly collect and publish global labor union statistics. This is a staggering omission from the global statistical record given that there were 166 million labor union members in the world in 2001. Membership data are gathered by the International Confederation of Free Trade Unions, but their efforts could hardly be described as readily available compared to those of the United Nations or the ILO; nor are they complete for a number of countries (for example, USA, Canada, Germany, Japan, and Switzerland) as they record only affiliates. Despite these defects, this is the only single international source available from 1949.

The record of the ILO is particularly strange in this field. Since 1927, it has been publishing world labor dispute statistics—information of often dubious accuracy and comparability between countries—but ignores the union membership data that are available for many member countries. The call made in the first edition of this work (1996) for the ILO to remedy this gaping statistical hole in a comprehensive, ongoing, systematic fashion is repeated here.

The need for an international impetus in this area has also been shown by the way in which certain countries have reduced their official statistical collections of labor union membership figures. Examples include Switzerland (which reduced its coverage greatly after 1987), New Zealand (which ceased its collection in 1980), and Australia (which ceased its annual census of labor unions in 1996 and reduced the amount of data it published on union members after 1999).

Organized Labor Statistics as a Source

There are two main categories of organized labor statistics: dispute statistics and union membership statistics. National collections of labor dispute statistics began earlier than for labor union members, largely because such disputes were seen by governments as a threat to the political and economic existing order. These data were easier to compile than for union membership because they could be obtained from employers, the press, and perhaps the labor unions.

In contrast, labor union membership statistics could only be supplied by the unions themselves, which may be unwilling to do so because of political suspicion, hostility, or lack of perceived gain. For instance, the legal recognition of labor unions in Australia in the late 19th century made provision for the registration of unions, but this did not result in the comprehensive registration of unions as there was little benefit to be gained from doing so. But when the system of compulsory arbitration and conciliation was introduced after 1900, unions had to be registered to participate in the benefits of the system. Similarly, India's voluntary system of union registration has meant that its published membership figures since 1932 have underestimated the true level of union membership.

There are two major problems with preparing historical statistics on the membership of labor unions. One is the nature of the membership data. Labor union membership is often very difficult to measure accurately, because of high labor turnover in some occupations, retirees who continue to be union members (this is an important feature of labor union membership in the United Kingdom and Germany), and the difficulty of keeping track of members who remain members but have ceased to pay their dues. Also, unions may exaggerate their membership to increase their bargaining power with employers or to gain greater representation at general conferences of unions.

The second major problem posed by union membership figures is linking them to the labor force of their particular countries. The concept of the labor force is a fairly recent one in statistical history, only being adopted widely since the 1930s. Before that, a variety of concepts and definitions were used, which severely hampers international comparisons over time.

The Labor Force

Understanding the structure of the labor force is essential to studying organized labor and how it fits into the broader society. The main components of the labor force are set out in the following diagrams. The first diagram shows how the principal groups that make up the labor force can be identified within the total population. For the purposes of studying organized labor, the main groups are employers and employees. It must be stressed that this is a comparatively modern way of looking at the labor force and that the relative importance of the relationships shown has changed over time. For example, the proportions of self-employed and those who worked in family enterprises were far higher before 1900 than after it.

Schema of the Labor Force

Total population			
Labor force (includes unemployed)			
Employed labor force			
Employer	Self-employed	**Employee**	
		Union member	Nonunion member

Within the employed labor force, it is important to grasp the distinction between an individual's industry and occupation to appreciate how the various divisions within the labor force have been a source of conflict within organized labor, particularly the century-old debate over whether unions should be organized by occupation or by industry.

The following diagram sets out some of the main features of the relationship between industry and occupation. It is based on how the United States classifies its labor force, but the broad principles are used by many other countries. Again, this is a modern way of examining the labor force, and the diagram makes no attempt to capture the large shifts in the industrial and occupational composition of the labor force that have occurred since 1900. Chief among these shifts have been the decline of the primary industrial sector and, since about 1950, the rise of the tertiary or service sector. As well, the occupational composition of the labor force has been greatly altered by technological change and the general maturing of Western economies. This has been most evident in the growth of white-collar jobs and the stagnation in the number of blue-collar jobs. Further consideration of these trends is outside the purpose of this appendix, but it is sufficient to draw the reader's attention to an analytical framework that is also useful as a tool for historical research.

Schema of the Relationship between Industry and Occupation

INDUSTRIES		
Primary	Secondary	Tertiary
Agriculture and mining	Manufacturing	Service (all other industries)
OCCUPATIONS		
White-collar:	White-collar:	White-collar:
Managerial and professionals	Managerial and professionals	Managerial and professionals
Technical, sales, and administrative support	Technical, sales, and administrative support	Technical, sales, and administrative support
Blue-collar:	Blue-collar:	Blue-collar:
Service occupations	Service Occupations	Service occupations
Precision production	Precision Production	Precision production
Operators, fabricators, and laborers	Operators, fabricators, and laborers	Operators, fabricators, and laborers
Farming, forestry, and fishing		

Only a few countries in the world are fortunate enough to possess labor force statistics covering the last hundred years. The main source for this information is the population census, which can be used to generate estimates of the number of employees at work not just for the whole economy but for particular industries and occupations. Union membership is linked to the labor force by *union density*—that is, the number of union members as a percentage of the total number of employees or of a particular subgroup of employees, for example, the percentage of employees in the manufacturing industry who are union members.

In 1940, the United States became the first country in the world to collect labor force statistics from a regular household survey, an example followed by other countries since 1945. As well as collecting standard labor force data, these surveys can also be used to monitor labor union membership. These data began to be available in 1973 for the United States (although the present survey began in 1983), in 1976 for Australia (with follow-up surveys held in 1982, 1986, and thereafter every two years to 1992, and then annually), in 1984 in Canada, in 1987 in Sweden, and annually in the United Kingdom since 1989. The European Commission has also included questions on labor union membership in its Eurobarometer Surveys in 1973, 1976, 1989, 1991, and 1993.

Comparisons of reported membership by unions and by those estimated from household surveys of trade union membership in Australia, the United Kingdom, and Canada in the 1980s suggest that unions tend to overestimate their memberships. Although subject to sampling error, household surveys are a far more reliable source and provide a wide range of sociodemographic information not available elsewhere, such as age, sex, birthplace, and income. Their only real drawback is their inability to provide information on the composition of individual unions.

Finally, mention should be made of the national workplace surveys that are available for the United Kingdom for 1980, 1984, 1990, and 1998, and for Australia for 1989-1990 and 1995. Using data collected from employers and unions, these surveys offer remarkable insights into labor relations. These works are set out in section D.3 of the bibliography.

Statistics need to be subjected to the same critical scrutiny as any other historical source. What is presented here is done in the spirit of capturing a general picture of changes in union membership over the past 130 years. For many countries, the information is approximate only. Blanks indicate not just lack of data but also times when free trade unionism has been suppressed. Because data for a number of countries are not always available for the year shown, the data for the closest year have been used.

For further information on the problems of labor unions statistics as a source, the discussions in George S. Bain and Robert Price, *Profiles of Union Growth: A Comparative Statistical Portrait of Eight Countries* (Oxford: Basil Blackwell, 1980), Jelle Visser, "Trends in Trade Union Membership," *OECD Employment Outlook*, July 1991, pp. 97-134, and Clara Chang and Constance Sorrento, "Union

Membership Statistics in 12 Countries," *Monthly Labor Review*, December 1991, pp. 46-53, are particularly important.

Regional Statistics on Labor Union Members

Most historical discussions of labor union membership statistics focus on the national level, but regional unions membership statistics—that is, statistics below the level of the nation—are an often overlooked topic and of great interest in themselves where available. The availability of these statistics varies greatly between countries, as the following table shows.

Country	Period available	Source
Australia	1912 to date	*Official Year Book of the Commonwealth of Australia*; *Year Book Australia*
India	1932-1933 to date	*Statistical Abstract for British India*; *Statistical Abstract, India*
Japan	1950 to date	*Year Book of Labour Statistics*
Philippines	1982 to date	*Yearbook of Labor Statistics*
Switzerland	1917-1932	*Statistisches Jahrbuch der Schweiz*, 1932 ed., p. 298
United Kingdom	1984, 1989 to date	*Employment Gazette*; *Labour Market Trends*
United States	1930 to date	*Directory of National Unions and Employee Associations*; *Statistical Abstract of the United States*

The smallest geographical unit generally available is by state (Australia, India, and United States) or prefecture (Japan), or region (Philippines and United Kingdom). For Australia, unpublished household survey data for below the state level are available from

1986. It should be noted too that regional statistics are particularly susceptible to boundary changes.

Structure of the Appendix

Part A contains tables that set out the growth of organized labor in the world since 1870. Part B presents statistics on international labor union organizations. Part C contains information on the proportion of union members among employees in selected countries. Part D considers the structure of labor unions, and part E sets out information on the current features of labor unions.

A. World Membership of Labor Unions

1. Growth of Organized Labor in the World, c. 1870-2001

2. Labor Union Membership in Selected Countries, c. 1870-1885/1886

3. Labor Union Membership in Selected Countries, c. 1890-1930

4. Labor Union Membership in Selected Countries, 1939/1940-1970

5. Labor Union Membership in Selected Countries, 1980-2001

B. Membership of International Labor Union Bodies

6. Membership of the International Federation of Trade Unions, 1901-1945

7. Membership of the International Confederation of Free Trade Unions, 1949-2001

8. International Confederation of Free Trade Unions: Membership by Region, 1949-2001

9. Largest Labor Unions in the World, 1900-2001

C. Proportion of Employees in Labor Unions

10. Labor Union Density in Selected Countries, c. 1890-1930

Appendix F

1. GROWTH OF ORGANIZED LABOR IN THE WORLD, 1870-2001

Year	Western Europe	Eastern Europe	Americas	Other	Total
	Membership in Thousands				
1870	486	4	300	0	790
1880	545	0	50	11	606
1886	828	0	1,010	53	1,891
1890	1,917	0	325	263	2,505
1900	4,193	235	869	133	5,430
1913	10,060	685	2,787	589	14,121
1920	27,692	8,501	6,367	1,221	43,781
1930	17,357	2,538	6,199	4,780	30,874
1939	11,493	100	9,111	2,920	23,624
1945	17,913	0	13,632	4,020	35,565
1950	31,194	0	20,523	12,063	63,779
1960	32,768	0	25,364	17,853	75,985
1970	39,591	0	34,005	24,687	98,282
1980	49,270	0	38,103	30,317	117,690
1990	45,484	5,000	30,328	33,207	114,019
1995	42,416	11,839	42,503	42,996	139,754
2001	39,615	37,526	36,890	52,268	166,299

2. LABOR UNION MEMBERSHIP IN SELECTED COUNTRIES, c. 1870-1885/1886

Country	c. 1870	c. 1880	c. 1886
Membership in Thousands			
UK	289	464	581
USA	300	50	1,010
France	120	60[a]	110
Germany	77	21	137
Austro-Hungarian Empire (Czech lands)	4	-	-
Australia	-	11	50
New Zealand	-	-	3
TOTAL	**795**	**606**	**1,891**

[a] Paris only.

Appendix F

3. LABOR UNION MEMBERSHIP IN SELECTED COUNTRIES, 1890-1930

Country	Early 1890s	Early 1900s	1913	1920	1930
Western Europe	Membership in Thousands				
Finland	-	-	28	59	15
Sweden	9	67	134	403	554
Iceland	-	-	-	1	4
Norway	20	20	64	143	140
Denmark	31	96	153	362	339
Luxembourg	-	-	-	-	18
Germany	357	850	2,974	10,517	6,925
Austria	47	119	263	1,004	817
Switzerland	-	90	122	313	320
Belgium	-	42	203	920	671
Netherlands	16	19	234	684	625
France	232	492	1,027	1,053	900
Ireland	50	67	70	189	102
UK	1,109	2,025	4,135	8,348	4,842
Spain	5	26	128	220	946
Portugal	-	-	90	100	-
Italy	41	280	435	3,410	-
Greece	-	-	-	-	83

3. CONTINUED

Country	Early 1890s	Early 1900s	1913	1920	1930
Eastern Europe	Membership in Thousands				
Russia	-	123	-	5,200	-
Bulgaria	-	3	30	36	19
Poland	-	15	160	947	979
Romania	-	4	40	300	80
Hungary	-	23	115	343	141
Estonia	-	-	-	-	13
Latvia	-	-	-	-	26
Lithuania	-	-	-	-	18
Bosnia	-	-	5	-	-
Croatia	-	-	7	-	-
Serbia	-	5	10	-	-
Yugoslavia	-	-	-	25	49
Czecho-slovakia	-	62	318	1,650	1,213

Appendix F

3. CONTINUED

Country	Early 1890s	Early 1900s	1913	1920	1930
Americas		Membership in Thousands			
USA	325	869	2,588	4,775	3,162
Canada		-	176	374	322
Argentina		-	23	68	280
Brazil		-	-	-	270
Cuba		-	-	-	71
Chile		-	-	150 [a]	204 [b]
Mexico		-	-	1,000	1,837
Peru		-	-	-	25
Uruguay		-	-	-	28

[a] 1923.
[b] 1927.

Country	Early 1890s	Early 1900s	1913	1920	1930
Other	Membership in Thousands				
Australia [a]	200	97	498	685	856
New Zealand	63	24	72	96	102
Japan	-	8	-	103	354
Korea	-	-	-	-	123
India	-	-	-	150	242
Ceylon	-	-	-	-	114
South Africa	-	4	12	135	118
Egypt	-	-	7	40	-
Palestine	-	-	-	4	20
Dutch East Indies	-	-	-	-	32
Philippines	-	-	-	-	67
China	-	-	-	-	2,800

[a] The Australian figure for 1890 was supplied by Michael Quinlan and Margaret Gardner of Griffith University from their database on Australian labor unions and labor disputes.

4. LABOR UNION MEMBERSHIP IN SELECTED COUNTRIES, 1939/1940-1970

Country	1939/1940	1950	1960	1970
Membership in Thousands				
Finland	66	269	468	950
Sweden	971	1,278	1,879	2,546
Norway	307	488	542	759
Denmark	543	714	987	1,143
Germany	-	5,513	7,687	8,251
Austria	-	1,291	1,501	1,520
Switzerland	385	627	728	843
Belgium	350	1,173	1,468	1,606
Netherlands	798	1,160	1,354	1,585
France	1,300	4,000	2,592	3,549
Italy	-	4,798	2,887	4,646
Ireland	163	285	319	381
UK	6,558	9,243	9,835	11,178
USA	7,877	13,430	17,049	21,248
Canada	362	1,006	1,459	2,173
Australia	956	1,605	1,912	2,331
New Zealand	248	267	332	379
India	511	2,371	3,077	4,887
Japan	9	5,774	7,662	11,605

5. LABOR UNION MEMBERSHIP IN SELECTED COUNTRIES, 1980, 1990, AND 2001

Country	1980	1990	2001
Membership in Thousands			
Finland	1,646	1,895	1,731
Sweden	3,486	3,855	3,278
Norway	1,049	1,291	817
Denmark	1,796	2,107	2,030
Germany	9,261	9,620	9,580
Austria	1,661	1,644	1,442
Switzerland	954	892	490
Belgium	2,310	2,291	1,229
Netherlands	1,741	1,426	1,226
France	3,374	1,970	1,909
Italy	7,750	6,930	3,998
UK	12,947	8,611	7,550
Ireland	381	490	759
USA	20,095	16,740	16,275
Canada	3,397	4,031	3,859
Australia	2,568	2,660	1,903
New Zealand	516	437	319
Japan	12,369	12,265	11,539
India	6,838	10,341	11,840

6. MEMBERSHIP OF THE INTERNATIONAL FEDERATION OF TRADE UNIONS, 1901-1945

Year	Number of Country Affiliates	Membership of Affiliates (Thousands)	Percentage of World Union Members
1901	8	1,168.0	21.5
1905	14	2,949.5	-
1910	18	6,118.7	-
1913	21	7,702.4	54.6
1920	21	22,701.1	51.9
1925	21	13,366.4	-
1930	26	13,578.8	49.1
1935	23	9,078.3	-
1939	26	14,638.0	62.0
1945	21	24,751.8	69.6

7. INTERNATIONAL CONFEDERATION OF FREE TRADE UNIONS: MEMBERSHIP, 1949-2001

Year	Number of Country Affiliates	Membership of Affiliates (Millions)	Percentage of World Union Members
1949	51	48.0	75.3
1953	63	47.3	
1955	75	54.3	
1959	97	56.0	73.7
1965	96	60.3	
1969	95	63.0	64.1
1975	88	51.8	
1979	87	67.0	52.7
1983	94	84.9	
1989	97	80.3	70.4
1995	135	124.9	89.4
2001	148	156.5	92.1

8. INTERNATIONAL CONFEDERATION OF FREE TRADE UNIONS: MEMBERSHIP BY REGION, 1949-2001

Region	1949	1959	1969	1979	1989	2001
Percentage of Total Membership						
Africa	a	2.3	0.9	0.5	0.8	8.2
Asia	13.7	17.6	10.8	18.4	21.7	16.9
Middle East	a	a	1.9	4.3	2.2	2.0
Western Europe	43.0	46.7	39.8	55.2	43.6	27.3
Eastern Europe	0	0	7.3	0	0	23.5
North America	30.5	26.3	22.4	2.5 [b]	17.6	9.6
Central and South America	12.3	6.5	14.6	15.8	11.5	11.1
Oceania	(a)	0.5	2.3	3.3	2.7	2.0
Total	**100.0**	**100.0**	**100.0**	**100.0**	**100.0**	00.0
Total (millions)	**48.0**	**56.0**	**63.0**	**67.0**	**80.3**	56.5

[a] Less than 0.5 percent.
[b] Fall caused by the withdrawal of the AFL-CIO between 1969 and 1981.

9. LARGEST LABOR UNIONS IN THE WORLD, 1900-2001

Year	Country	Name	Members (Millions)
1900	UK	Miners' Federation of Great Britain	0.4
1910	UK	Miners' Federation of Great Britain	0.6
1920	Germany	*Deutscher Metallarbeiter-Verband* (German Metal Workers' Union)	1.6
1933	UK	Miners' Federation of Great Britain	0.5
1937	UK	Transport and General Workers' Union	0.7
1950	Germany	*IG Metall* (Metal Workers' Industrial Union)	1.3
1960	Germany	*IG Metall* (Metal Workers' Industrial Union)	1.7
1970	Germany	*IG Metall* (Metal Workers' Industrial Union)	2.4
1980	Germany	*IG Metall* (Metal Workers' Industrial Union)	2.6
1990	Germany	*IG Metall* (Metal Workers' Industrial Union)	3.6
2001	Germany	*Ver.di* (United Services Union)	3.0

Appendix F

10. LABOR UNION DENSITY IN SELECTED COUNTRIES, c. 1890-1930

Country	Early 1890s	Early 1900s	1913	1920	1930
Percentage of Employees					
Finland	-	-	14	25	5
Sweden	1	5	8	28	36
Norway	-	3	8	20	19
Denmark	-	14	15	35	32
Germany	3	6	18	53	34
Austria	1	3	5	51	38
Switzerland	-	10	13	26	24
Belgium	-	3	10	45	28
Netherlands	2	2	17	36	30
France	3	7	13	12	9
Italy	-	6	6	39	-
Ireland	-	-	-	36	19
UK	10	13	16	48	26
USA	3	6	9	17	9
Canada	-	-	7	15	14
Australia	23	9	34	46	51
New Zealand	-	8	19	26	24
Japan	-	-	-	-	3

11. LABOR UNION DENSITY IN SELECTED COUNTRIES, 1950-2001

Country	1950	1960	1970	1980	2001
Percentage of Employees					
Finland	29	9	62	82	88
Sweden	68	73	73	88	90
Norway	50	63	51	57	57
Denmark	52	63	64	86	83
Germany	35	38	38	41	30
Austria	62	66	64	59	43
Switzerland	39	36	30	33	31
Belgium	49	58	57	46	40
Netherlands	42	39	37	32	19
France	38	21	22	17	9
Italy	41	26	32	44	27
Ireland	46	54	53	57	59
UK	44	44	47	51	29
USA	28	26	27	23	14
Canada	33	35	35	31	32
Australia	59	58	50	49	25
New Zealand	44	44	39	48	18
Japan	56	32	35	31	22

12. WOMEN IN LABOR UNIONS IN SELECTED COUNTRIES, 1900-2001

Year	UK	Germany	Australia	USA	Japan
Women as a Percentage of Total Members					
1900	8	3 [a]	-	-	-
1913	11	8	4	4 [b]	-
1920	16	-	11	8	-
1930	16	8 [c]	14	-	-
1940	17	-	16	9	-
1950	18	18	19	17 [d]	23
1960	20	18	20	18	26
1970	25	16	24	24	-
1980	29	21	32	24 [e]	-
1990	38	26	37	37	28 [f]
1994	44	32	40	40	[g]
2001	47	32 [h]	43	42	[g]

[a] 1902-1903.
[b] 1910.
[c] 1931
[d] 1954.
[e] 1978.
[f] 1991.
[g] Not published.
[h] 1997.

13. NUMBER OF LABOR UNIONS IN SELECTED COUNTRIES, 1900-2000

Year	Australia	New Zealand	UK	Japan
c. 1900	198	175	1,323	-
1913	432	372	1,269	-
1920	388	406	1,384	-
1930	362	416	1,121	-
1939/40	381	427	1,004	-
1950	360	370	732	29,144
1960	363	398	664	41,561
1970	354	353	538	30,058
1980	325	217	438	34,232
1990	295	114	287	33,270
1995	142	82	245	32,065
2000	n.a.	134	243	31,185

Appendix F

14. DISTRIBUTION OF LABOR UNION MEMBERS BY SELECTED INDUSTRY GROUPS BY PERCENTAGE, 1900-2001

Year	Australia	New Zealand	UK	USA
MINING				
1900	21.7[a]	20.7	28.1	15.1
1913	8.1	3.6	23.4	15.9
1920	6.1	4.3	15.1	8.7
1930	5.0	2.6	13.5	6.8
1940	5.2	1.6	11.7	8.7
1950	3.0	0.8	8.2	3.2[b]
1960	2.0	0.5	7.5	0.6
1970	1.5	0.2	3.3	1.0
1980	2.7[c]	0.1	3.3	1.0[d]
1990	2.2	0.9[e]	1.9	0.7
2001	1.2	0.2	0.3	0.4
MANUFACTURING				
1900	14.2[b]	37.7	43.7	34.2
1913	29.2	27.5	39.2	29.3
1920	32.5	36.6	42.2	37.9
1930	34.7	27.3	39.2	23.2
1940	39.5	31.5	38.0	38.3
1950	38.4	38.5	41.0	42.8[b]
1960	36.1	37.6	41.7	51.3
1970	35.4	38.6	45.0	41.9
1980	24.7[c]	34.6	29.4	29.9[d]
1990	19.6	22.3[e]	25.2	25.1
2001	16.3	22.4	14.9	16.3

14. CONTINUED

Year	Australia	New Zealand	UK	USA
TRANSPORTATION AND COMMUNICATIONS				
1900	22.5[a]	30.6	10.6	21.8
1913	25.2	30.4	8.8	20.5
1920	21.7	28.5	16.0	24.9
1930	19.1	28.7	19.4	26.0
1940	15.6	17.0	17.6	21.8
1950	15.2	14.8	16.0	26.6[b]
1960	12.1	15.2	14.5	13.2
1970	10.3	7.1	12.3	12.0
1980	12.0[c]	10.0	6.1	12.3[d]
1990	11.1	10.2[e]	7.8	11.6
2001	10.2	11.6	9.5	10.7
ALL OTHER INDUSTRIES				
1900	41.6[a]	11.0	17.6	28.9
1913	37.5	38.5	18.6	34.3
1920	39.7	30.6	26.6	28.5
1930	41.2	41.4	27.9	44.0
1940	39.7	49.9	32.7	31.2
1950	43.4	45.9	34.8	27.4[b]
1960	49.8	46.7	36.3	34.9
1970	52.8	54.1	39.4	30.3
1980	60.6[c]	55.3	61.2	6.8[d]
1990	67.1	66.6[e]	65.1	62.1
2001	72.3	65.8	75.3	72.6

[a] Data refer to New South Wales and Western Australia for 1902 and 1901 respectively.
[b] 1953.
[c] 1982.
[d] 1983.
[e] 1991.

Appendix F

15. MEDIAN WEEKLY EARNINGS OF UNION MEMBERS, AUSTRALIA AND USA, 1982/1983-2002

Year	AUSTRALIA		USA	
	Union Members ($)	Percentage Over Nonunion Members	Union Members ($)	Percentage Over Non-Union Members
	FULL-TIME EMPLOYEES-MALES			
1982/3	295	3.05	411	14.11
1986	391	4.86	482	18.26
1988	445	6.07	506	17.79
1990	506	4.15	542	15.68
1995	637	8.48	640	20.78
1997	675	7.56	683	21.08
1999	792	6.31	711	15.75
2002	912	7.46	780	16.41
	FULL-TIME EMPLOYEES-FEMALES			
1982/3	234	1.71	307	22.48
1986	319	5.02	368	25.54
1988	368	7.61	403	25.56
1990	426	7.51	448	27.23
1995	555	9.73	527	26.76
1997	604	10.43	577	28.77
1999	686	9.77	608	26.15
2002	778	8.87	667	23.54
	FULL-TIME EMPLOYEES-PERSONS			
1982/3	276	6.88	398	27.64
1986	372	7.80	444	26.80
1988	423	8.98	480	25.83
1990	484	8.06	509	23.38
1995	601	8.49	602	25.75
1997	655	8.55	640	25.31
1999	758	8.31	672	23.21
2002	866	10.05	740	20.68

16. LABOR UNION MEMBERS: MAIN LABOR FORCE CHARACTERISTICS—AUSTRALIA, UK, AND USA, 2001-2002

Characteristic	Australia	UK	USA
Number (thousands)	1,834	7,340	16,107
Percent Males	57	53 [a]	58
Percent Females	43	47 [a]	42
Percentage of Employees in Same Category			
Males	24	29	15
Females	22	29	12
Persons	23	29	13
Full-time	26	32	15
Part-time	17	21	7
Public sector	46	59 [a]	38
Private sector	18	19 [a]	9

[a] Data refer to 2001.

Appendix F

17. LABOR UNION MEMBERS BY OCCUPATIONAL GROUPS: AUSTRALIA, UK AND, USA, 2001-2002

Characteristics	Australia	UK [a]	USA
Number (thousands)	1,834	7,330	16,107
Percentage of Employees in Same Category			
Managers and administrators	11	17	6
Professional	28	48	19
Associated professional and technical	18	42	11
Clerical	17	24	13
Craft and related	30	30	21
Sales	20	13	4
Plant and machine operators	38	37	19
Laborers and related	25	22	17
All occupations	**23**	**29**	**13**

[a] All United Kingdom data shown refer to 2001.

18. LABOR UNIONS WITH ONE MILLION MEMBERS OR MORE, 2002

Labor union	Country	Members (Millions)
Ver.di (United Services Union)	Germany	3.0
IG Metall (Metal Workers' Union)	Germany	2.7 [2000]
National Education Association	USA	2.7
Service Employees' International Union	USA	1.4
United Food and Commercial Workers' International Union	USA	1.4
Teamsters	USA	1.4
American Federation of State, County and Municipal Employees	USA	1.3
UNISON	UK	1.3
Amicus	UK	1.1
American Federation of Teachers	USA	1.1

Appendix F

NOTES AND SOURCES FOR TABLES

1. GROWTH OF ORGANIZED LABOR IN THE WORLD, c. 1870-2001

SOURCES: Tables 2, 3, 4, 8. The membership of the International Confederation of Free Trade Unions (ICFTU) has been used as the basis of the world total of union membership from 1950. It should be noted that the figures compiled by the ICFTU are incomplete for a number of countries and periods and therefore require some upward adjustment. Other sources include H. A. Marquand et al., *Organized Labour in Four Continents* (London: Longmans, Green, 1939), p. 438 (for Mexico in 1940) and Elias T. Ramos, *Philippines Labor Movement in Transition* (Quezon City: New Day, 1976), pp. 8-9 (for the Philippines in 1940).

2. LABOR UNION MEMBERSHIP IN SELECTED COUNTRIES, c. 1870-1885/1886

SOURCES: **UK:** B. C. Roberts, *The Trade Union Congress, 1868-1921* (London: George Allen & Unwin, 1958), p. 379. Data are for 1871, 1881, and 1885. [Note: these data refer only to TUC affiliates and so underestimate total union membership, but this seems to be the only time series available for this period.] **USA:** Estimates in Lance E. Davis and others, *American Economic Growth: An Economist's History of the United States* (New York: Harper & Row, 1972), p. 220. Data are for 1870, 1880, and 1886. **France:** Val R. Lorwin, *The French Labor Movement* (Cambridge, Mass.: Harvard University Press, 1954), pp. 12, 18, 23; Edward Shorter and Charles Tilly, *Strikes in France, 1830-1968* (Cambridge: Cambridge University Press, 1974), p. 371. Data are for 1870, 1881, and 1886. **Germany:** Michael Schneider, *A Brief History of the German Trade Unions* (trans. Barrie Selman, Bonn: J. H. W. Dietz Nachf., 1991), p. 383. Data are for 1869, 1880, and 1885. **Austro-Hungarian Empire:** Marcel van der Linden and Jürgen Rojahn (eds.), *The Formation of Labour Movements* (Leiden: E. J. Brill, 1990), Vol. II, p. 334. Data refer to 1871. **Spain:** Dick Geary (ed.), *Labour and Socialist Movements in Europe before 1914* (Oxford: Berg Publishing, 1989), p. 245. Data are for 1881. **Australia:** J. T. Sutcliffe, *A History of Trade Unionism in Australia* (Melbourne: Macmillan, 1967), pp. 66-67. Data are for 1879 and 1885. **New Zealand:** H. Roth, *Trade Unions in New Zealand:*

Past and Present. (Wellington: A.H. and A.W. Reed, 1973), p. 167. Data are for 1885.

3. LABOR UNION MEMBERSHIP IN SELECTED COUNTRIES, c. 1890-1930

SOURCES: The primary sources were Arthur M. Ross and Paul T. Hartman, *Changing Patterns of Industrial Conflict* (New York and London: John Wiley & Sons, 1960), pp. 200-1; George S. Bain and Robert Price, *Profiles of Union Growth: A Comparative Statistical Portrait of Eight Countries* (Oxford: Basil Blackwell, 1980); Jelle Visser, *In Search of Inclusive Unionism,* Special Issue, *Bulletin of Comparative Industrial Relations,* No. 18. (Deventer, Netherlands and Boston: Kluwer Law and Taxation Publishers, 1990), p. 18; Marcel van der Linden and Jürgen Rojahn (eds.), *The Formation of Labour Movements* (Leiden: E.J. Brill, 2 vols., 1990), pp. 141, 143, 300, 334, 357, 385, 411, 517, 666; A. P. Coldrick and Philip Jones (eds.), *The International Directory of the Trade Union Movement* (London and Basingstoke: Macmillan, 1979), *passim;* W. Schevenels, *Forty-Five Years: International Federation of Trade Unions* (Brussels: Board of Trustees of the International Federation of Trade Unions, 1956), p. 63; Commonwealth of Australia, Bureau of Census and Statistics, *Labour Reports* (Melbourne/Canberra: Government Printer, 1922-1932).

Other data were drawn from Val R. Lorwin, *The French Labor Movement* (Cambridge, Mass.: Harvard University Press, 1954), p. 23; Edward Shorter and Charles Tilly, *Strikes in France, 1830-1968* (Cambridge: Cambridge University Press, 1974), pp. 371-72; Michael Schneider, *A Brief History of the German Trade Unions* (trans. Barrie Selman, Bonn: J. H. W. Dietz Nachf., 1991), pp. 383-86; Daniel L. Horowitz, *The Italian Labor Movement* (Cambridge, Mass.: Harvard University Press, 1963), pp. 44 n. 106 (1893 data), 59 n. 21, 75, 111, 125; John W. Boyle, *The Irish Labor Movement in the Nineteenth Century* (Washington, D.C.: Catholic University of America Press, 1988), pp. 125, 127; Charles McCarthy, *Trade Unions in Ireland, 1894-1960* (Dublin: Institute of Public Administration, 1977), pp. 622, 635; Leo Wolman, *The Growth of American Trade Unions, 1880-1923* (New York: National Bureau of Economic Research Inc., 1924), p. 124; Lance E. Davis and others, *American Economic Growth: An Economist's History of the United States* (New York: Harper & Row, 1972), p. 220; H. Roth, *Trade Unions in New Zealand: Past and Present* (Wellington: A. H. and A. W. Reed,

1973), pp. 167-70; New Zealand, *Official Year Books*; John P. Windmuller, *Labor Relations in the Netherlands* (Ithaca, N.Y.: Cornell University Press, 1969), p. 39; Dick Geary (ed.), *Labour and Socialist Movements in Europe before 1914* (Oxford: Berg Publishers Ltd., 1989), pp. 245, 254; Augustus D. Webb, *The New Dictionary of Statistics* (London: George Routledge and Sons Ltd., 1911), pp. 602, 606 (data for Austria for 1892 and 1901; and for 1906 for Hungary and Switzerland); Gary K. Busch *The Political Role of International Trade Unions* (London: Macmillan, 1983), pp. 110, 124; Walter Kendall, *The Labour Movement in Europe* (London: Allen Lane, 1975), Statistical Appendix; U.S. Bureau of Labor Statistics, *Monthly Labor Review*, December 1991, p. 48; Walter Galenson (ed.), *Labor in Developing Economies* (Berkeley and Los Angeles: University of California Press, 1963), pp. 216, 283; *Longman's Trade Unions of the World* (London: Longmans, 2nd ed., 1987), p. 205 for the Palestine figure for 1920.

Note: Irish data are also included in the UK figure up to 1920; the 1920 figure shown refers to 1922. They are included here separately for their intrinsic interest.

4. LABOR UNION MEMBERSHIP IN SELECTED COUNTRIES, 1939/1940-1970

SOURCES: Same as for table 3; Japan Institute of Labour, *Japanese Working Life Profile: Labour Statistics, 1992-93* (Tokyo: Japan Institute of Labour, 1992), p. 48; *Indian Labour Book*, 1973 ed., p. 55, 1990 ed., p. 73. [Official Indian figures are known to underestimate the true level of union membership.]

Note: The data for Italy have been adjusted to exclude retirees.

5. LABOR UNION MEMBERSHIP IN SELECTED COUNTRIES, 1980, 1990, AND 2001

SOURCES: Same as for table 4; U.S. Department of Labor, Bureau of Labor Statistics, *Monthly Labor Review*, December 1991, p. 48. 2001 data have largely been drawn from the International Confederation of Free Trade Unions; John Harper Publishing, *Trade Unions of the World* (London: John Harper Publishing, 2001); and Internet websites shown in appendix B.

Note: The data for Italy have been adjusted to exclude retirees and the 1980 figure for Australia refers to 1982.

6. MEMBERSHIP OF THE INTERNATIONAL FEDERATION OF TRADE UNIONS, 1901-1945

SOURCES: W. Schevenels, *Forty-Five Years: International Federation of Trade Unions* (Brussels: Board of Trustees of the International Federation of Trade Unions, 1956), pp. 23, 62, 423-5; tables 1 and 2.

7. INTERNATIONAL CONFEDERATION OF FREE TRADE UNIONS: MEMBERSHIP, 1949-2001

SOURCES: John P. Windmuller, *The International Trade Union Movement* (Deventer: Kluwer, 1980), p. 62; data after 1979 were supplied by the International Confederation of Free Trade Unions.

8. INTERNATIONAL CONFEDERATION OF FREE TRADE UNIONS: MEMBERSHIP BY REGION, 1949-2001

SOURCES: Same as for table 7.

9. LARGEST LABOUR UNIONS IN THE WORLD, 1900-2001

SOURCES: H. A Clegg, *A History of British Trade Unions since 1889*, Vol. II (Oxford: Clarendon Press, 1985), p. 570; *Statistiches Jahrbuch für does Bundesrepublik Deutschland*; John Harper Publishing, *Trade Unions of the World* (London: John Harper Publishing, 2001); Internet websites for the organizations shown in appendix B.

10. LABOR UNION DENSITY IN SELECTED COUNTRIES, c. 1890-1930

SOURCES: Same as for table 3; Australian data for 1890 and 1900 calculated by the author; Peter Flora and others, *State, Economy, and Society in Western Europe, 1815-1975* (Chicago: St. James Press, 1987), Vol. II, pp. 689-753 contains a valuable nonagricultural employees series that was used to calculate union density for some countries.

Note: (1) density refers to the number of labor union members as percentage of employees; (2) boundary changes affect the statistics (e.g., for Austria). Some of the data refer to nonagricultural employees only.

11. LABOR UNION DENSITY IN SELECTED COUNTRIES, 1950-2001

SOURCES: Same as for table 3; Jelle Visser, "Trends in Trade Union Membership," *OECD Employment Outlook*, July 1991, p. 140; and "In Search of Inclusive Unionism," *Bulletin of Comparative Labour Relations*, No. 18, 1990, pp. 18, 35.

Note: Density refers to the number of labor union members as percentage of employees. The data for Italy have been adjusted to exclude retirees.

12. WOMEN IN LABOR UNIONS IN SELECTED COUNTRIES, 1900-2001

SOURCES: George S. Bain and Robert Price, *Profiles of Union Growth: A Comparative Statistical Portrait of Eight Countries* (Oxford: Basil Blackwell, 1980), pp. 37-8, 102, 115, 123-24; United Kingdom Employment Department, *Employment Gazette*, January 1983, p. 26, January 1992, p. 188, May 1995, p. 192; Michael Schneider, *A Brief History of the German Trade Unions* (Bonn: J. H. W. Dietz Nachf., 1991), pp. 82, 184, 384-85, 387; *Statistiches Jahrbuch 1995 für die Bundesrepublik Deutschland*, p. 741; Australian Bureau of Statistics, *Trade Union Statistics, Australia* (Catalogue No. 6323.0) [1980 data]; Australian Bureau of Statistics, *Trade Union Members, Australia* (Catalogue No. 6325.0) [1990 data], *Trade Union Members, Australia* (Product No. 6325.0.40.001), p. 19 [1994 data], *Employee Earnings, Benefits and Trade Union Membership* (Catalogue No. 6310.0); Leo Wolman, *The Growth of American Trade Unions, 1880-1923* (New York: National Bureau of Economic Research, 1924), pp. 98-99; James J. Kenneally, *Women and American Trade Unions* (St. Albans, Vt.: Eden Press Women's Publications Inc., 1978), p. 218; *Statistical Abstract of the United States* [data for 1954-78]; U.S. Bureau of Labor Statistics, *Employment and Earnings*, January 1991, p. 229, January 1996, p. 210; *Japan Statistical Yearbook*, 1961, p. 351; Ministry of Labour, Japan, *Year Book of Labour Statistics*, 1991, p. 320.

13. NUMBER OF LABOR UNIONS IN SELECTED COUNTRIES, 1900-2000

SOURCES: **Australia**: Commonwealth Bureau of Census and Statistics, Labour Report No. 2 (1912), p. 13; W. Vamplew, Australians: Historical Statistics (Sydney: Fairfax, Syme & Weldon Associates, 1987), pp.162-63; Australian Bureau of Statistics, *Trade Union Statistics, Australia* (Catalogue Number 6323.0); Australian Bureau of Statistics, *Year Book Australia*, 1998, p. 215 (no data were published after 1996). **New Zealand:** Herbert Roth, *Trade Unions in New Zealand: Past and Present* (Wellington: Reed Education, 1973), pp. 169-70; New Zealand, *Official Year-Books*; data for 1989, 1995, and 2000 from *New Zealand Journal of Industrial Relations*, October 2001, Vol. 26, No. 3, p. 319. **UK:** Henry Pelling, *A History of British Trade Unionism* (Harmondsworth: Penguin Books, 3rd ed., 1976), pp. 293-96; *Employment Gazette*, June 1994, p. 191; *Labour Market Trends*, July 1998, p. 354; *Annual Report of the Certification Officer*, 2001-2002, p. 21. **Japan:** *Japan Statistical Year Book.*

14. DISTRIBUTION OF LABOR UNION MEMBERS BY SELECTED INDUSTRY GROUPS BY PERCENTAGE, 1901-2001

SOURCES: **Australia**: *New South Wales Statistical Register*, 1903, pp. 805-6 [1902 data]; *Western Australia Printed Papers, Reports Etc. of the Parliament, 1904*, Vol. I, Report of Proceedings under the Industrial Conciliation and Arbitration Act, 1902, pp. 10-14 [1901 data]; Commonwealth Bureau of Census and Statistics, *Labour and Industrial Branch Report* (Melbourne: Government Printer), 1912-1922; Commonwealth Bureau of Census and Statistics/Australian Bureau of Statistics, *Labour Report* (Melbourne/Canberra: Government Printer), 1923-1973; Australian Bureau of Statistics, *Trade Union Members, Australia* (Catalogue No. 6325.0), 1982, 1990; *Employee Earnings, Benefits and Trade Union Membership* (Catalogue No. 6310.0). **New Zealand**: Appendix to the Journals of the House of Representatives H.11 [for pre-1924 data]; *New Zealand Official Year-Book* [for data up to 1980]; Raymond Harbridge and Kevin Hince, "Unions and Union Membership in New Zealand," *New Zealand Journal of Industrial Relations*, Vol. 18, No. 3, December 1993, p. 358. **United Kingdom**: George S. Bain and Robert Price, *Profiles of Union Growth: A Comparative Statistical Portrait of Eight*

Countries (Oxford: Basil Blackwell, 1980), pp. 43-78; Department of Labour, *Employment Gazette*, January 1983, p. 27, April 1992, p. 189. **USA:** U.S. Department of Commerce, *Historical Statistics of the United States* (Washington, D.C.: U.S. Government Printing Office, 1975), Part 1, p. 178; George S. Bain and Robert Price, *Profiles of Union Growth: A Comparative Statistical Portrait of Eight Countries* (Oxford: Basil Blackwell, 1980), pp. 94-95; Department of Labor, Bureau of Labor Statistics, *Handbook of Labor Statistics 1975— Reference Edition* (Washington D.C.: U.S. Government Printing Office, 1975), pp. 383, 385; Department of Labor, Bureau of Labor Statistics, *Employment and Earnings*, January issues from 1985 onwards.

Note: The data used to construct this table were drawn from two different types of sources: data provided by unions for the period up to 1970 for Australia and the United States, up to 1980 for New Zealand, and up to 1990 for the United Kingdom; and data from household surveys for the remaining years. Consequently, the comparability within the table might be affected to some degree.

15. MEDIAN WEEKLY EARNINGS OF UNION MEMBERS, AUSTRALIA AND USA, 1982/1983-2002

SOURCES: Australian Bureau of Statistics, *Trade Union Members, Australia* (Catalogue No. 6325.0), 1982-1990. The data for 1982 were unpublished and were taken from table 6 of microfiche from the survey and refer to March to May 1982. The 1995 data are the author's calculations from grouped income data from Australian Bureau of Statistics, *Weekly Earnings of Employees (Distribution) Australia, August 1995* (Product No. 6310.0.40.001) and *Employee Earnings, Benefits and Trade Union Membership* (Catalogue No. 6310.0); U.S. Department of Labor, Bureau of Labor Statistics, *Employment and Earnings* (January issue from 1985 onwards).

16. LABOR UNION MEMBERS: MAIN LABOR FORCE CHARACTIERSTICS—AUSTRALIA, UK, AND USA, 2001-2002

SOURCES: Australian Bureau of Statistics, *Employee Earnings, Benefits and Trade Union Membership* (Catalogue No. 6310.0); U.K. Labour Department, *Labour Market Trends*, issues for July 2002 and 2003. U.S. Department of Labor, Bureau of Labor Statistics, *Employment and Earnings*, January 2003.

17. LABOR UNION MEMBERS BY OCCUPATIONAL GROUPS: AUSTRALIA, UK, AND USA, 2001-2002

SOURCES: Same as for table 16.

18. LABOR UNIONS WITH A MILLION MEMBERS OR MORE, 2002

SOURCES: John Harper Publishing, *Trade Unions of the World* (London: John Harper Publishing, 2001); Internet websites for the organizations shown in appendix B.

ABOUT THE AUTHOR

JAMES C. DOCHERTY was born in Gosford, New South Wales, in 1949 and is a graduate of the University of Newcastle (B.A.) and the Australian National University (M.A., Ph.D.). He is a second-generation Australian. Both of his parents were born in Scotland, his father in St. Andrews and his mother in Milngavie, near Glasgow. Before joining the Australian Bureau of Statistics in 1978, he worked as a research assistant with the Australian Dictionary of Biography at the Australian National University. Since 1984, he has been employed by the federal Department of Industrial Relations and by the federal Department of Immigration, Multicultural, and Indigenous Affairs (since October 1996). He was an Honorary Research Associate with the National Centre for Australian Studies at Monash University from 1990 to 1996. He has been a labor union member since 1978.

His publications include *Selected Social Statistics of New South Wales, 1861-1976* (1982); *Newcastle: The Making of an Australian City* (1983); and, "English Settlement in Newcastle and the Hunter Valley" in James Jupp (ed.), *The Australian People: An Encyclopedia of the Nation, Its People and Their Origins* (1988). He was an editorial consultant and contributor to *Australians: Historical Statistics* (1987), contributed the entries on Australian history, politics, industrial relations, and institutions in David Crystal (ed.), *The Cambridge Encyclopedia* (1990), and was an editor and contributor to *Workplace Bargaining in the International Context* (1993). He is the author of three historical dictionaries: *Historical Dictionary of Australia* (1992, 1999), *Historical Dictionary of Socialism* (1997), and *Historical Dictionary of Organized Labor.*